FROM HIGH SCHOOL TO COLLEGE

FROM HIGH SCHOOL TO COLLEGE

*Improving Opportunities for Success
in Postsecondary Education*

Michael W. Kirst

Andrea Venezia

Editors

JOSSEY-BASS
A Wiley Imprint
www.josseybass.com

Published by Jossey-Bass
A Wiley Imprint
989 Market Street, San Francisco, CA 94103-1741   www.josseybass.com

Jossey-Bass books and products are available through most bookstores. To contact Jossey-Bass directly call our Customer Care Department within the U.S. at 800-956-7739, outside the U.S. at 317-572-3986, or fax 317-572-4002.

Jossey-Bass also publishes its books in a variety of electronic formats. Some content that appears in print may not be available in electronic books.

Readers should be aware that Internet Web sites listed in this work may have changed or disappeared between when this work was written and when it is read.

Library of Congress Cataloging-in-Publication Data
From high school to college : improving opportunities for success in postsecondary education / Michael W. Kirst, Andrea Venezia, editors.—1st ed.
   p.   cm. — (The Jossey-Bass education series)
Includes bibliographical references and index.
   ISBN 0-7879-7062-X (alk. paper)
  1. Education and state—United States—Case studies. 2. College preparation programs—Government policy—United States—Case studies.
3. Postsecondary education—United States—Case studies. 4. School improvement programs—United States—Case studies. I. Kirst, Michael W. II. Venezia, Andrea, date. III. Series.
   LC89.F76 2004
   379.73—dc22   2003023724

Printed in the United States of America
FIRST EDITION
HB Printing   10 9 8 7 6 5 4 3 2 1

THE JOSSEY-BASS EDUCATION SERIES

CONTENTS

ACKNOWLEDGMENTS

THIS WAS TRULY a team effort. The work of many people is reflected throughout this book—from brainstorming with us at the very beginning, to collecting data in the six project states, to entering data, conducting analyses, and writing. Since 1997, more than seventy people have been involved in this work.

Some people played multiple roles, and we thank them more than once. We hope we have overlooked no one. A multiyear national project such as this is dependent on the talents, expertise, and time of scores of people. We owe many people a deep debt of gratitude; everyone worked hard to ensure that the findings, based on sound research, would be usable for people in the field and would contribute to a more equitable environment for high school students.

First, we must thank our funders: Jim England, Michele Seidl, and Ellen Wert at the Pew Charitable Trusts, and Gregory Henschel at the U.S. Department of Education. Many people helped conceptualize this project in its early stages. They include all of our steering committee members: Carl Cohn, Jim England, Sylvia Hurtado, Pat McDonough, Claire Pelton, Michele Seidl, Jan Somerville, Pat Callan, Dave Conley, Jerry Hayward, Bruce Johnstone, Yolanda Moses, Cynthia Schmeiser, and Lauri Steel. In addition, Patti Gumport, Kati Haycock, Chris Mazzeo, and Frederick Wright attended many of those meetings and contributed many wise thoughts. Andrea Venezia's dissertation committee members, Ken Tolo, Jorge Chapa, Michael Kirst, Ray Marshall, Pat Wong, and Deborah Kazal-Thresher, were instrumental in the development of the project's research design.

We thank all of the people we interviewed and surveyed in K–12 schools and districts, state agencies, universities, and related committees. Given the resource constraints all of those groups are under, we were overwhelmed by the interest shown and generosity given by thousands of people. We hope this research will be helpful for your day-to-day work and lives.

To the core Stanford team—Andrea Conklin Bueschel, Samuel H. Bersola, Frances Contreras, and Julie Slama: you all went above and beyond the call of duty and worked on every aspect of this project. We cannot thank our editor, David Ruenzel, enough; he edited all of our work over the years, including this book, and helped us conceptualize and highlight our most important findings. Thad Nodine, our media consultant, helped us articulate our major themes. Thanks to Vi Nhuan-Le, an associate behavioral research scientist with RAND, who conducted the research reported in Appendix B.

Thank you to our administrative associates, Terry Alter, Patricia McGriff, Ann McMillan, Shannon Shankle, and Jared Haun, who did a great job with all the behind-the-scenes work that kept us afloat over the years.

We wish to thank the lead researchers in each state. We were extremely saddened by the loss of Toby Milton, a practitioner and researcher in Maryland, and a dear colleague, midway through the project. We wish to thank Anthony Lising Antonio and Samuel H. Bersola (California); Caroline S. Turner and James C. Hearn (Georgia); Betty Merchant and Michael Kirst (Illinois); Rick Mintrop, Toby H. Milton, Frank A. Schmidtlein, and Ann MacLellan (Maryland); Andrea Conklin Bueschel and Andrea Venezia (Oregon); and Andrea Venezia (Texas). Special thanks to Amy M. Hightower for working on the initial protocols and California research. Also thanks to those who conducted the community college research: KC Boatsman (California), Ann MacLellan (Maryland), and Andrea Conklin Bueschel and Andrea Venezia (Oregon), and to Andrea Conklin Bueschel for examining issues across all the community college sites. Thank you all for your insights during the development of the project, your diligence in following the protocols (despite many logistical setbacks), and your quick turnaround time with your technical reports.

Additional state-level research, analyses, and writing were conducted by Frances Contreras, Leonard Goldfine, Julian Vasquez Heilig, Amy M. Hightower, Jennifer Hirman, Lisa M. Jones, Laura Lopez-Sanders, Colleen Medley, Sylvia Peregrino, Paul Pitre, Jon Rousseau, and Dawn Spivey.

Hernán Díaz, Vivian Haun, Felicia Hiley, Joe Kim, William Loríe, Victor Kuo, Sonia Samagh, Jennifer Test, and Beth Whitney were involved in additional research, writing, and data entry. Thank you.

Several people were involved in balancing our financial books and making sure we stayed within our budget; thank you to Autumn Zindel, Cheryl Nakashima, and Chris Roe. And thank you to Patti Gumport for housing us in Stanford's Institute for Higher Education Research.

Finally, thank you to Sumathi Raghavan, who provided early editorial assistance, and to Janet Vanides, Hernán Díaz, and Janet Rutherford for transcribing all of our audiotapes.

FROM HIGH SCHOOL TO COLLEGE

BRIDGING THE GREAT DIVIDE

HOW THE K–12 AND POSTSECONDARY SPLIT HURTS STUDENTS, AND WHAT CAN BE DONE ABOUT IT

Michael W. Kirst
Kathy Reeves Bracco

THERE ARE APPROXIMATELY 2.5 million public high school graduates in the United States each year, a number that continues to grow as enrollments increase. Over 70 percent of these graduates go on to postsecondary education within two years of graduating from high school, and over half of those students aspire to obtain a bachelor's degree. However, over 50 percent of students entering all postsecondary education institutions will take remedial courses, many in several subject areas. A large percentage of students do not continue on for a second year of college, and 41 percent who earn more than ten credits at a two- or four-year school never complete a two- or four-year degree.[1] The Education Testing Service (ETS) in a 2002 study concluded that "the proportion of young adults (age 25–29) getting a bachelor's degree—after rising throughout U.S. history—stabilized at 21 percent to 25 percent beginning 25 years ago, and only began to slightly rise again in 1996" (Barton, 2002, pp. 10–11). Student preparation and completion are particularly problematic at the institutions that are the focus of our research: the less selective two- and four-year institutions that enroll 80 percent of first-year students. Why is it that so many students are entering college unprepared for college-level work and often unable to complete a degree? We think the causes of remediation, noncompletion, and inadequate secondary preparation lie in part in the historical split between levels of our educational system and the subsequent lack of communication and connection between them. Public education in the United States essentially comprises two distinct levels: elementary and secondary (K–12) and postsecondary, or higher, education.[2] Most educational structures reflect this distinction, including educational committees in the state and federal governments that focus solely on one of the two systems. Increasingly, however, more and more people are calling for what is often called a K–16, or P–16, perspective on education, a recognition that this is ideally all one system (Hodgkinson, 1999; Timpane, 1998).[3]

Where once a high school diploma was all that was necessary for an individual to obtain a job that could guarantee entrance into the middle class, today at least a coherent program of postsecondary training, if not a college degree, is typically necessary to achieve the same economic status.[4] The high aspirations of our youth indicate that they understand the need for college: over 90 percent of high school seniors say they will go to college (Schneider and Stevenson, 1999). College-going rates reflect those numbers. Currently, over 70 percent of high school graduates pursue some form of postsecondary education (Education Trust, 2002). Data from the U.S. Census illustrate the significant economic returns of more education: in the year 2000, median annual earnings for workers aged twenty-five and over with a high school diploma was $24,267, compared with $26,693 for workers with an associate's degree (27 percent higher) and $40,314 for those with a bachelor's degree (66 percent higher) (U.S. Bureau of the Census, 2001). Grubb (1999) found that there are also economic benefits to completing community college certificates, although the amount of benefit varies by field of study.

In sum, the high aspirations of secondary school students are not being realized as evidenced by intensive remediation and low completion rates. This is especially true for low-income and minority students. According to the Census Bureau, about 85 percent of the growth in the age group eighteen to twenty-four years will come from minority and immigrant families over the next decade. Over 40 percent will come from low-income families (*Business Week*, 2002).

Now over 70 percent of the students who enroll at community colleges expect to obtain a bachelor's degree (compared to 50 percent in 1982), but only 23 percent receive the degree (American Council on Education, 2002).

We are concerned primarily in this book with broad-access institutions. For example, community colleges enroll 45 percent of all first-year postsecondary students, and 80 percent of first-year students attend minimally selective and nonselective two- and four-year institutions.[5] Broad-access institutions comprise 85 percent of all postsecondary schools. Our research reveals that these institutions have the greatest problems with student preparation and completion. Most media and public attention, however, focuses on the 20 percent of students who attend selective four-year schools that have the best-prepared students and use the ACT or Scholastic Aptitude Test to help sort out applicants who exceed available student places in the first-year class (Adelman, 2001). Only 3 percent of freshmen at the 146 most selective institutions come from the bottom quarter of Americans ranked by income; only 10 percent come from the bottom half of income (Savage, 2003). This book analyzes what is happening when students prepare for community colleges and four-year institutions that accept virtually all applicants who meet their academic requirements.

While the reality for students is that their education will likely continue past the secondary years, state and institutional policies continue to reflect a significant separation between K–12 and postsecondary education. The current organization of secondary schools and postsecondary institutions is such that communication and information dissemination between levels are often difficult. For instance, students—especially those who are economically disadvantaged or whose parents did not attend college—often do not know what colleges expect of them in terms of meeting their admission requirements. Many believe that nonselective four-year institutions and community colleges do not have academic standards. This is not the case, as is evidenced by the widespread use of placement tests for access to credit-level courses. Also, policies across the segments, particularly those concerning the transition from high school graduation to college admission, are fragmented and confusing. The research in this book addresses an array of policies in the context of how successfully students make the transition from high school to college, including what happens once they enroll in postsecondary education.

Our research demonstrates that in order to increase opportunities for all students to prepare for, attend, and graduate from postsecondary institutions, reform initiatives at various levels within the entire K–16 education system should be better integrated or created in tandem. In this way, information could flow more freely back and forth, providing students, teachers, parents, and counselors with better (and earlier) information about the academic expectations for students entering college. Furthermore, a better-integrated K–16 system would allow for greater dialogue between K–12 reformers and postsecondary faculty and administrators, reducing the chance that reform efforts in one sector might be at odds with (or on different tracks from) efforts in another.

The Bridge Project

This book is the result of research conducted by Stanford University's Bridge Project: Strengthening K–16 Transition Policies, which encompassed six years of field research, literature and document review, and data analysis. The Bridge Project was a national policy research study that focused on the policies, perceptions, and practices related to the transition between high school and college. An overarching purpose was to support the development of policies that improve opportunities for all students to enter and succeed in postsecondary education through the development of more consistent and equitable policymaking across the sectors. The Bridge Project examined policies related to student transitions between K–12 and postsecondary education.

The research that we report on focused on three understudied but essential components of the K–12 and postsecondary systems: admissions policies, first-year college placement or advising policies in two- and four-year institutions, and state-level policies affecting K–12 and postsecondary education (for example, on curricula and assessments in the K–12 system). We used case study research from regions in six states (California, Georgia, Illinois, Maryland, Oregon, and Texas) to understand better the dynamics of the transitions between systems within individual states and to offer a comparative framework among the regions and states. The criteria for selecting these states and the research methodology are discussed in Appendix A.

This research and related policy recommendations focused on the nearly 70 percent of students who go on to postsecondary education within two years of graduating from high school, and particularly the 85 percent who go on to nonselective or less selective institutions, both two- and four-year, public and private.[6] We were also concerned with whether the 30 percent of high school graduates who do not go on to college would do so if they received earlier and better information about preparation for college.

The conceptual framework that guided this research relied on several different concepts and theories that are integrated into a flow model (described in greater detail at the end of this chapter). We start with the view that policy signals and incentives are crucial drivers of students' college knowledge and actions regarding preparation for postsecondary academic success. Moreover, clear, consistent, and appropriate signals and incentives improve student learning and affect students' motivation positively (Bishop, 1990; Costrell, 1994; Powell, 1996). Even if motivation is high, many students do not complete their desired postsecondary programs, including vocational education certificates. The postsecondary completion problem is less a result of insufficient ambitions to go on to college and more one of a lack of articulated standards and clear signals concerning adequate academic preparation, and limited knowledge of what it takes to enroll and finish (Schneider, 2003).

We acknowledge that there are many reasons that students do not enter or complete college. Certainly, affordability is a significant issue for students in terms of their likelihood to persist and complete their postsecondary education (National Center for Public Policy and Higher Education, 2002; Choy, 1998). Family and work obligations such as taking care of children or parents or tending to a full-time job are also often cited as obstacles for some students (Adelman, 1999; Tinto, 1993). Lack of support from parents and friends, particularly for those who would be first in their family to attend college, keeps many from enrolling or persisting for long. In addition, many students have had inadequate opportunities to prepare for college (due to curricular tracking in their high schools), have lacked adequate counseling, or lack the motivation to continue their education any further. Although we acknowledge the significant role that these issues and others play, we do not address them fully in this book.[7] We focus rather on the hypothesis that the lack of consistent and well-communicated signals about what is required to enter and succeed in credit-bearing courses at the postsecondary level has a significant impact on student success. We believe that there is a role for better state and regional policy alignment that will create a more equitable policy environment, enabling more students to prepare well for postsecondary education.

Context: Twenty Years of Reform Efforts

Since the publication of *A Nation at Risk* (National Commission on Excellence in Education, 1983), education reform has remained at the top of most state agendas. A number of new policies have been implemented: forty-nine states have created K–12 content standards in most academic subjects, and most of these states have developed statewide K–12 student assessments. Several states, including California and Nevada, have experimented with lowering the maximum class size in the lowest grades (McRobbie, Finn, and Harman, 1998). Accountability systems have been developed and tied to incentives pushing educators and schools to improve teaching and learning, and many states are focusing on improving their data systems in order to monitor changes resulting from these reforms.

These changes are taking place as the student population across the country is growing larger and more diverse. Over 47 million students were enrolled in public elementary and secondary schools in 2001, a number that is projected to increase through 2005. In 1999, 38 percent of public school students were students of color, an increase of 16 percentage points from 1972 (U.S. Department of Education, 2001a).

Although postsecondary education has traditionally been much less affected by state education reform legislation than K–12 education, some significant policy changes in the past two decades have had a noteworthy impact. Beginning in the 1980s, many states began to adopt statewide admissions policies, particularly through the establishment of required high school course work units for college admission (Rodriguez, 1998). State legislatures and courts have more recently become active in post-secondary education admissions policies, something that was virtually unheard of twenty years ago. A decision by the Fifth Circuit Court of Appeals in Texas (*Hopwood*) and a statewide ballot proposition in California (Proposition 209) changed the way many of the more selective public institutions in those states could conduct their admissions process by eliminating the use of affirmative action.[8] Similar changes are under way in other states. As a result, new policies in some states have been put in place to reach the traditionally underrepresented populations.[9] State legislatures and state higher education agencies have also become more involved in addressing remediation issues at the state level, an issue traditionally handled at the institutional level (Rodriguez, 1998). Concerns about the number of students who need to take remedial-level courses in colleges and universities across the country (and about the costs associated with those courses) led many postsecondary education institutions and systems to adopt new policies to try to eliminate or significantly reduce the provision of remedial courses on their four-year campuses.[10]

Powell (1996) and Bishop (1990) note that traditionally what has been valued in American education is participation in the system for as long as possible. Getting the high school diploma has typically been more important than what was learned, particularly for movement from high school to work. Schools traditionally receive some streams of funding based on student seat time. Education systems therefore focused more on keeping students in high school and on providing opportunities for them to graduate than on what they should know and be able to do to succeed in postsecondary education. A current wave of reforms tries to address this issue (and focus more on knowledge and skills attained), but it comes at it from many different angles.

Although these academic standards reforms deal with many of the same fundamental issues and have been occurring simultaneously, there has, with some exceptions, been very little coordination of reforms across educational levels (Kirst, 1998; Maeroff, Callan, and Usdan, 2001). There are few incentives for postsecondary institutions and systems to collaborate with K–12 districts and schools. Although local K–16 partnerships focused on precollege outreach do exist, there are few state levers in place (such as K–16 accountability systems or funding mechanisms that cross both sectors) to encourage postsecondary education to change its practices (Kirst and Venezia, 2001). While college and university reforms seem to have often ignored K–12 reform efforts, K–12 reformers have also failed to look at changes in postsecondary education (Kirst, 1998). The problem lies in part in the reach of accountability: most state accountability systems stop at the tenth grade, and K–12 relationships are almost never a part of the accountability measures for postsecondary education. K–16 offices at postsecondary education institutions are generally staffed with people who have little influence on major policies and practices at the operating level, and there are few stakes or mandates regarding K–16 reform. No significant employee- or institution-based interest group lobbies federal and state policymakers for better K–16 linkages.

The Problem: Inadequate Readiness and Preparation for College

Some postsecondary education is now essential for success and flexibility in most labor markets, where a high school education was once sufficient. Students understand this, as evidenced by changes in student aspirations and ambitions about education beyond high school. A recent study sponsored by the Sloan Foundation reports that 90 percent of current high school seniors expect to attend college, compared with only 55 percent in the 1950s (Schneider and Stevenson, 1999). The U.S. Department of Education (2001a) reports that the percentage of high school seniors who report definite plans to complete a bachelor's degree increased from 36 to 55 percent between 1983 and 1998. Seventy percent of students who begin their postsecondary careers at a two-year institution expect to earn a bachelor's degree compared to less than 50 percent twenty years ago (Schneider, 2003).

Data show that it is not only aspirations that have changed but behavior as well. Information on course-taking patterns, percentages of students graduating from high school, and percentages of graduates going on to postsecondary education following high school illustrate these changes in behavior:

- Between 1982 and 1998, the average number of credits earned by high school graduates increased from twenty-two to twenty-five; the percentage of students taking a rigorous math curriculum rose from 6 percent to 12 percent (U.S. Department of Education, 2001a).

- In 1971, 78 percent of those twenty-five to twenty-nine years old had completed high school; in the year 2000, this number had increased to 88 percent (U.S. Department of Education, 2001a).

- A larger percentage of adults are obtaining at least some college education. In 1982, 33 percent of adults had some college compared to 51 percent in 2000; among those aged twenty-five to thirty-four, the percentage of those with some college grew from 45 percent in 1991 to 58 percent in 2000 (*Newsweek*, 2002).

- In 1999, 63 percent of graduates were enrolled in a two- or four-year college immediately after high school, compared to 49 percent in 1972 (U.S. Department of Education, 2001a).

If an increased number of students is taking more rigorous high school courses, graduating from high school, and going on to postsecondary education (all seemingly positive trends), what is the problem? While there are still significant challenges in terms of access to postsecondary education for many student populations, the problem facing most students is best illustrated by what happens once the students enroll in postsecondary education. Many are not ready for college-level work, cannot enroll in or complete the program of their choice, and do not graduate from college. These problems disproportionately affect first-generation students and economically disadvantaged students. The Sloan Study (Schneider and Stevenson, 1999) concluded that most high school students have high ambitions but no clear life plans for reaching them—what the authors call "misaligned ambitions" (p. 7). The data on student high school preparation, college persistence (the extent to which students continue to enroll in college), and college completion rates give us some insight into this paradox.

High School Course-Taking Patterns

Adelman (1999) finds that the intensity and quality of the secondary school curriculum is the best predictor of whether a student will go on to complete a bachelor's degree.[11] While the percentage of students taking more rigorous classes has increased since 1982, the overall percentage taking the highest levels of math and science courses is still small. While 72 percent of students went on to college (within two years of graduating from high school) in 1992, only 47 percent of them had enrolled in a college preparatory curriculum as preparation (U.S. Department of Education, 1997). Although it is not necessarily a full measure of academic intensity and quality, the college preparatory track is one indicator that students are taking the array of high school courses recommended for college admissions. Many community colleges do not articulate specific admission standards (and therefore students are not required to complete a college preparatory program in high school to be admitted to the community college), but they do require certain placement standards for entry into credit-level work. Without a strong high school curriculum, a student may be admitted to a college but not be placed into credit-level courses.

A report from the Education Trust shows that socioeconomic status and race/ethnicity do make a difference in terms of the likelihood of a student's enrolling in such a curriculum. Low-income students are less likely to be enrolled in a college preparatory track (28.3 percent enrolled) than medium- or high-income students (48.8 percent and 65.1 percent, respectively); African American and Latino students are less likely to be enrolled in a college preparatory track (25.7 percent and 22.6 percent) than either Asian (42.1 percent) or white (34.1 percent) students (Education Trust, 1999).

Algebra II is a crucial course for college for college persistence and avoiding remediation. Algebra II enrollments for African American, Latino, and Native American high school students doubled between 1982 and 1998. But only 41 percent of Latino students took algebra II in 1998, compared to nearly two-thirds of their white and Asian peers (Education Trust, 2003).

The level of high school math a student completes is a significant indicator of the chance a student has to complete a bachelor's degree (Adelman, 1999). Again, the data show that African American, Latino, and Native American students lag behind their white and Asian counterparts in terms of the percentage who complete higher-level mathematics courses, defined as precalculus or above (Education Trust, 2002).

While many students are enrolling in college after graduating from high school, the quality and rigor of their high school curriculum may well determine whether they are prepared for college-level work. As the data on remediation indicate, many are not prepared, and extensive remediation lowers their chances of postsecondary completion (U.S. Department of Education, 2001a). Even if students have weak academic preparation, they are more likely to receive a bachelor's degree if they enter a four-year rather than a two-year institution after high school graduation (Cabrera, Burkum, and LaNasa, 2003).

A Confusing Array of Exams

Between high school and college, college-bound students face a confusing set of exams. In high school, many students take state-mandated assessments and a number of other tests, including Advanced Placement (AP), International Baccalaureate (IB), the Scholastic Assessment Tests (SAT I and SAT II), and the ACT Assessment. Once they are admitted to a college or university, they typically have to take one or more placement exams to determine whether they are ready for college-level work. Although colleges use the same tests for admission, each may have its own placement test or series of tests, and there is little uniformity among these tests. In many colleges and universities, departmental faculty develop the placement exams. In the southeastern United States in 1998, for example, there were nearly 125 combinations of 75 different placement tests, all devised by university departments without regard to secondary school standards (Abraham, 1992). Texas has a required statewide postsecondary placement test, but many Texas universities also use their own additional placement exams. The different assessments (K–12 exit, college entrance, and college placement) often use different formats and emphasize different content (Kirst, 1999; Le and Robyn, 2001). Entering first-year students know little about the content of the placement exams, and ultimately, many score poorly and are placed in remedial courses.

High Remediation Rates

Currently, one of the most high-profile postsecondary education issues is that of remediation. Many students who are able to get into college often enter unprepared for college-level work and are placed in non-credit-bearing remedial courses. Forty-six percent of students who enter postsecondary education of any type (and 60 percent of those entering community colleges) are required to take remedial courses in one or more subjects (U.S. Department of Education, 2001a).

In some colleges, the remediation rates are staggering. For example, 95 percent of first-time students enrolled in the Baltimore City Community College (BCCC) in the fall of 2000 required remediation in math, and 65 percent of entering students needed remediation in math, English, and reading. At BCCC, nearly half of all entering students were assigned to the lowest level of remedial math in the year 2000. This placement would require a student to take as many as nine courses (27 credits) before he or she can begin credit-level work in math (Abell Foundation, 2002). This is significant not only because it means more time for students to get to the point of actually taking college-level courses (increasing the cost of their education and creating a somewhat demoralizing atmosphere for the student), but because the data show that students requiring extensive remediation graduate at lower rates (Adelman, 2001). Thirty-four percent of 1982 high school graduates who took any remedial reading course work in college had completed a bachelor's or associate degree by ages twenty-nine to thirty-four compared with 56 percent of those with no remedial reading courses (U.S. Department of Education, 2001a). Between 1980 and 1993, only 34 percent of students who had to take even one remedial reading course completed a two- or four-year degree, compared with 56 percent of students who had taken no remedial courses at all (U.S. Department of Education 2001a).

Insufficient Persistence from First to Second Year

Although students are going to college in record numbers, many do not continue on to their second year. Approximately one in four of the students who enter four-year colleges and almost half of those who enter two-year colleges do not return for their second year (Education Trust, 2003). Many factors can affect a student's decision not to return for a second year, including academic difficulties, poor institutional fit, financial concerns, and familial obligations (Choy, 1998; Adelman, 1999). Some students stop out for a time and then continue their education later. Others may have transferred from one institution to another, and thus appear to have dropped out when in fact they have just changed institutions. Mortenson (1998) reports that for most students, the key to graduating is returning after their freshman year, to continue their studies at the college in which they first enrolled. Students who do not continue on to the second year, whatever the reason, will have a more difficult time completing a degree.

U.S. Department of Education data (2001a) provide a look at persistence (defined as continuation toward a stated degree goal) three years after entering college; they show that outcomes varied with the students' initial goals, the type of institution in which they enrolled, and whether they transferred from one institution to the next. Over 3.3 million students enrolled for the first time in postsecondary education in 1995–1996, and the U.S. Department of Education studied what happened to these students three years later, in 1998. The data provide some indication of student persistence:

○ Of those seeking a certificate, 52 percent had attained one within three years, and 37 percent had left postsecondary education.

○ For those whose initial goal was an associate's degree, 15 percent had attained that degree by 1998, 6 percent had received certificates, and 39 percent were still enrolled as students (7 percent at a four-year institution). Forty-one percent of students who entered with the goal of receiving an associate's degree had left postsecondary education.

○ Those who entered seeking a bachelor's degree but started at a two-year institution were more likely to have left postsecondary education (33 percent) than those who started at a four-year institution: 13 percent for those at private institutions and 16 percent at public institutions. (U.S. Department of Education, 2001a).

While it is difficult to measure student intent (the default answer for many students when they enroll is that they eventually hope to obtain a degree), it is useful to see how students have moved through (or out) of the system in the first few years.

LOW DEGREE OR CERTIFICATE COMPLETION RATES. More students are going on to postsecondary education and aspiring to a bachelor's degree, but the percentage actually obtaining the degree has not increased proportionately. Over 50 percent of those enrolled in four-year institutions take more than five years to complete a degree. We look therefore at the U.S. Department of Education data on degree attainment by age twenty-nine. Fifty-five percent of high school seniors reported plans to complete a bachelor's degree in 1998, compared with 36 percent in 1983. Thirty-three percent of high school completers (age twenty-five to twenty-nine) had obtained at least a bachelor's degree in 1998, compared to 26 percent in 1983. Sixty-five percent of those who enroll in a four-year college or university obtain a bachelor's degree by age twenty-nine. This figure has not changed since the early 1970s, even though enrollment in the four-year system has increased by 30 percent over that time period.

While overall completion rates have improved, the gap between white students and African American and Latino students persists, as indicated in Table 1.1.

ACHIEVEMENT GAP. The disconnect between the aspirations of students and the preparation for and attainment of college degrees is particularly apparent when we look at low-income students, first-generation college students, and underrepresented students of color (Rosenbaum, 2001). The Education Trust (2001) reports that students from low-income families attend four-year institutions at much lower rates than those from high-income families, regardless of high school achievement level. Families in the top income quartile are almost seven times as likely to earn a bachelor's degree as students from families in the bottom income quartile.

Underrepresented students of color do not obtain higher education anywhere close to the levels of white students. African Americans are only about one-half as likely and Latino's one-third as likely to earn a bachelor's degree by age twenty-nine as white students (Table 1.2).

Not only are African American and Latino students not obtaining education at the same rates as their white counterparts, they are not graduating

---

Table 1.1. Percentage of High School Completers Ages Twenty-Five to Twenty-Nine with a Bachelor's Degree or Higher.

Year	Total	White	African American	Latino
1983	26.2	27.4	16.2	17.8
2000	33.0	36.2	20.6	15.4

Source: *U.S. Department of Education (2001a).*

Table 1.2. Number of Every 100 Kindergartners Achieving Different Educational Levels.

	Graduate from High School	Complete at Least Some College	Obtain at Least a Bachelor's Degree
White	93	62	29
African American	86	48	15
Latino	61	31	10
Native American	58		7

Source: *Education Trust (2001).*

from high school with the same level of academic skills: African American and Latino twelfth graders read and do math at the same levels as white eighth graders (Education Trust, 2002). This is particularly problematic given the data on remediation and the extent to which the necessity of one or more remedial courses (particularly in math or reading) negatively influences the chances that a student will obtain a bachelor's degree.

Schools often sort students into curricular tracks and ability groups that offer varying levels of academic preparation for college. Such sorting has been found to be inequitable in terms of race, ethnicity, and socioeconomic status, and it has implications regarding whether and where students choose to attend college (Oakes, 1992). Our research explores whether students in different curricular tracks have access to college preparation materials and whether they have similar understandings of college policies and practices.

The achievement gap may be exacerbated by the challenges facing today's high school counselors. There is an increasingly limited number of counselors per student at the high school level, and few counselors are able to spend a majority of their time on postsecondary issues. The counselors who are there focus on a host of other issues (such as disciplinary problems, emotional needs of students, and course scheduling) and do not have the time to work with traditionally underrepresented students (McDonough, Korn, and Yamaski, 1997).[12] Although counselors are usually the only source of information about college preparation–related course work and policies for all students, several studies have found that some counselors might not be giving students the information they need to make educated decisions about their college choices (see, for example, Orfield and Paul, 1994; Rosenbaum, 2001). Rosenbaum (2001) found that counselors do not believe that they have enough authority to give students bad news about the students' college prospects. He hypothesized that this unwillingness might prevent students from receiving the information that they need in order to make the best decisions regarding their future college careers. In addition, he found that counselors' avoidance techniques hurt economically disadvantaged students the most.

The Missing Link

Why is it that students are enrolling in postsecondary education in record numbers but are entering unprepared for college-level work and often leaving before completing a certificate or two- or four-year degree? We suggest that the disconnect between secondary and postsecondary education in this country is a major (though not the sole) factor and note several areas in which the disconnect is most apparent:

○ The content between high school exit exams and college admissions and placement tests differs, leading to understandable confusion about what students really need to know in order to succeed in college. There is a lack of preparation if students are being taught to the high school exit exam standards, which differ from admission and placement test standards.

○ While the research clearly indicates the importance of a rigorous high-quality high school curriculum for college success, students often believe that what they do in high school does not matter, that the existence of "second-chance" institutions will allow them to start over again after high school. The (misguided) message that the senior year in high school is not important is particularly troublesome.

○ General college knowledge of middle- and low-income students— about what is required in terms of grades and competencies and how to apply for college—is low (Rosenbaum, 2001).

○ There are very few policy mechanisms for addressing the connection between secondary and postsecondary education, and many existing policies simply perpetuate the separation. Many K–12 policies in this arena come out of the belief that not every student is going to go to college. Now that over 70 percent continue on to some form of postsecondary education, this belief is misguided and obsolete, and hurts many students.

Alignment of Graduation and Admission Requirements

Better articulation of K–16 policies and practices could help solve the problems outlined above. The disconnection between K–12 and postsecondary education is built into the structure of our educational systems. Postsecondary education institutions have traditionally been responsible for defining standards for college-level course work and remedial courses. At the same time, K–12 entities, whether at the local or state level, define the curricula for non-AP college prep courses in high schools (Kirst and Venezia, 2001). Hence, the high school curricula and postsecondary standards are not always consistent with one another. High school teachers and college professors often differ in their views of what students should know in order to go on to postsecondary education (ACT, 2000). It is not surprising, therefore, that students get many mixed signals about the relationship between high school course work and standards and college readiness. Many simply do not realize that fulfilling high school academic requirements does not entail college readiness.

The Education Trust (1999) reports that high school teachers and students often do not know the difference between what postsecondary education demands in terms of high school courses and test content and what is required by the state for a secondary diploma. State high school graduation exams are most often not aligned with the tests used for college admissions or for placement into college-level courses. By and large, high school tests are much easier, covering content often not exceeding the ninth- or tenth-grade level. Data from the National Association of System Heads (NASH, 2000) show that only ten states have high school graduation requirements in English aligned with college admission requirements, and only two states have the two requirements aligned in math. In most states, "students who know everything they need to know to pass the state K–12 tests can fall quite short on college examinations and end up spending valuable college time learning what they could, and should, have learned in high school" (Education Trust, 1999 p. 6).

One of our hypotheses at the outset of the research was that the lack of alignment between high school exit exams, college admission exams, and college placement exams (subject matter exams often specific to postsecondary academic departments) can be problematic for students. If students receive confusing or conflicting signals or no signals at all about what is required for college admission and placement, they are less likely to be prepared (however, this study did not address whether the policies caused students to be underprepared). To study the extent to which different assessments in the K–16 spectrum exists, we commissioned RAND to conduct content analyses of the high school exit and college entrance tests that exist in our case study states (Le and Robyn, 2001). The results demonstrate significant differences in content between assessments used in postsecondary compared to secondary school. These differences can send mixed signals to students about college standards and preparation. Interviews by Bridge Project staff with students and parents in six states confirm that they are frequently confused about the plethora of assessments.

Relating High School Effort to College Performance

Rosenbaum (2001) suggests that there is a systemic failure on the part of colleges, particularly community colleges, to convey clear information about the preparation that is necessary for high school students if they are expecting to complete a college degree. Rosenbaum contends that students' perceptions and understanding of college requirements are critical to their efforts in high school and ultimately to their success in college. He found that many students do not believe their high school education has relevance for their future success; furthermore, students believe there is little penalty for poor high school performance. A national survey conducted by ACT (2003) found that 20 percent of students headed to four-year institutions and 40 percent of those bound for two-year colleges were not planning to take all the courses that ACT had deemed necessary for college-level work. While it is true that students can obtain a second chance at open enrollment institutions like community colleges, Rosenbaum argues that students are rarely warned that they may have difficulty completing a degree if they do not take certain courses and achieve certain grades in high school. They are encouraged to go on to postsecondary education, but not necessarily informed of the obstacles they face if they are not well prepared.

Inaccurate or missing information about what is required for success in postsecondary education is not limited to students who go on to open enrollment institutions. Because most students apply to college during their senior year in high school, many colleges do not take grades and course work during the senior year into consideration for admission. Many students take their highest-level math courses during their junior year, often taking no math at all during the senior year (Kirst and Venezia, 2001). This can be particularly problematic when it comes time to take placement exams and students have not had any math for over a year.

A recent national survey of first-year college students (Cooperative Institutional Research Program, 2002) indicates some downward trends in student effort during the senior year in high school. Academic disengagement is at an all-time high, with 41 percent of students reporting boredom in their senior year compared with a low of 29 percent in 1985. Seniors report spending less time on studying and homework than ever before, with only 35 percent of students reporting spending six or more hours a week on homework in 2000, compared to a high of 47 percent in 1987. At the same time, senior-year high school grades continue to increase, with 44.1 percent of students reporting an A average, compared to a low of 17.6 percent with an A average in 1968.

Reflecting on these survey results, Alexander Astin, originator of the survey, notes that "the combination of academic disengagement and record grade inflation poses a real challenge for our postsecondary education system, since students are entering college with less inclination to study but with higher academic expectations than ever" (Cooperative Institutional Research Program, 2002).

Improving Student College Knowledge

Clearly, better knowledge about what is required for college success is needed, and not just by students. Parents, teachers, and counselors need better college knowledge to guide students to the right courses, skills, and competencies. This is particularly true for those working with low-income students and first-generation college students, all of whom do not traditionally have the same access to college knowledge as others.

This research explores how students from different backgrounds (for example, different income levels, race/ethnicity, type of school, and academic tracks) differ in terms of the types of college-related information they receive. It also looks at the understandings (and misunderstandings) that students, their parents, their teachers, and their counselors have of postsecondary policies and practices. Some of the results are analyzed within and across schools and districts to explore whether the understandings are consistent across the districts and schools or are different in each school. This issue—the dissemination and interpretation of college admissions–related policies and practices across and within different groups—has not been adequately addressed in the literature.

Although this study cannot determine causation, it explores educator attitudes and beliefs about their role as college information providers for students and student and parent perceptions regarding opportunities students have to receive such information.

Improving Policy Mechanisms

There are few adequate K–16 policymaking mechanisms at the state level to address these issues of transition from secondary to postsecondary education. Although there are local partnerships focused on outreach issues in different sites around the country, few levers are in place to develop systemic reform strategies between postsecondary education institutions and K–12 districts and schools. In California, for example, K–16 policymaking is divided among a dozen groups, creating a rather fragmented approach (Kirst, 2001). This is an American phenomenon: there is a much greater disjuncture between secondary and postsecondary education here than in most other nations (Kirst, 2001; Timpane, 1998). Tafel and Eberhart (1998) note that many state and local politicians in recent years have provided resources for school-college collaborative efforts, but argue that this is only a first step; sufficiently ensuring the successful student transition requires a reconception of current structures and practices and the development of new systemic approaches to link the two education sectors. Georgia,

Florida, and Maryland are examples of states that have created a K–16 statewide organization with limited responsibility for oversight of K–16 policymaking; we examine their efforts in the state chapters that follow.

Signals as a Theoretical Framework

With the above context and problem statement as background, we now turn to the development of a partial theory that shaped our research study. Within our research agenda, we view admissions and placement standards and institutional arrangements as policies that communicate signals, meaning, and expected behavior to students and secondary schools. By defining admissions and placement policies as policies that send signals to students, it is our intention to examine both existing policy structures and proposed reforms within the same analytical framework—specifically, the interaction that occurs within a state and region. In each state, our concern is with how admissions and placement-related standards and policies promulgated by states and postsecondary education institutions are understood, acted on, and interpreted by parents, students, and secondary school personnel. An underlying assumption of this research is that clear, consistent, and reinforced signals will enhance the college knowledge of prospective students in secondary schools. If the signals are embedded within incentives that provide extrinsic motivation to students, they will be more effective.[13] We focus on incentives that will help students be admitted to universities, meet placement exams standards, and complete their desired degrees (or community college competencies). We are also very concerned that the current flow of signals about necessary college knowledge is unequal between high- and low-socioeconomic students. Our work reformulates the access issue to focus more on access to preparation and success rather than the more traditional issue of access to a slot in postsecondary education.

Examples of incentives could be admission policies that reward students for completing numerous college preparation courses or teacher professional development that helps increase the probability of students meeting placement test standards. Both extrinsic and intrinsic motivations are important components of motivating prospective college student behavior.[14] We will return to motivation after discussing academic signals that can increase or decrease student motivation to prepare for postsecondary education.

Signaling theory suggests that streamlined and aligned high-quality and appropriate content messages have a positive impact on students' learning and achievement and that mixed signals—the current state of affairs—have the opposite effect (Fuhrman and O'Day, 1996). Crucial aspects of appropriate signals and incentives are simplicity, clarity, and consistency (Henry and Rubenstein, 2002). Consistency is enhanced when signals, incentives, and institutional policies are aligned—for example, the alignment of format and content of state and local student assessments with SAT I. We posit that if incoherent and vague signals and incentives are sent by postsecondary education institutions and state agencies to students, then there will be less adequate student preparation for postsecondary education. We build on related work by education scholars such as Costrell (1994), McDonough (1997), and Rosenbaum (2001). We should note that our use of the term *signaling* is slightly different from that of John Bishop (1990; Bishop and others, 2003) and other economists who have explored this topic.[15] As Bishop uses the term, *signaling* refers to the attributes—achievement, education level, and ability—that students consciously attempt to transmit to employees and colleges. Our use of the term focuses on the signals that policies send to students and schools (Mow and Nettles, 1990). School site educators, including but not limited to counselors, can be purveyors of information (for example, signals) about what students need to know and be able to do in order to succeed at postsecondary education. We found that many teachers play a large role in providing signals, especially for high-achieving students.

We believe that given high student and parent aspirations for postsecondary education entrance and completion, clear signals about necessary preparation and standards for postsecondary education will have a positive impact on motivation and are one mechanism for trying to equalize the playing field. Since many postsecondary institutions are minimally selective or nonselective, students need to be motivated to meet a preparation standard rather than beat the competition. This enhances motivation because success is attainable, and effort will have a payoff in postsecondary attainment (Deci, Koestner, and Tyan, 2001). This is particularly important because economically disadvantaged students and students of color are often placed in low-level academic high school courses and tracks that can decrease both motivation and preparation (Oakes, 1992).

Since it is easy to enter so many four-year and two-year schools, there are scant incentives to work hard in high school (Bishop and others, 2003). High school graduation standards and minimum competency tests are not sufficient preparation for postsecondary success, though many students think they are. Once students enroll, they face challenging placement exams, faculty expectations, and general education and graduation requirements that they often do not know about. They end up taking remedial noncredit courses that better signals may have prevented.

Our conceptual framework (see Figure 1.1) guides our research questions and provides an analytical lens. We concentrate on whether K–12

Figure 1.1. Conceptual Framework of the Bridge Project.

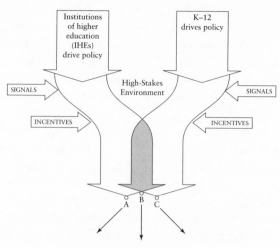

+ positive influence
− negative influence

	A Policy driven by IHEs in isolation from K–12	*B* Policy driven by combined efforts between IHEs and K–12	*C* Policy driven by K–12 in isolation from IHEs
K–12 stakeholders' understandings of K–16 policies and college knowledge	+ For elite pool of students − For more students − For postsecondary education since it has less information on K–12 students	+ For more students + For mutual reinforcement of understandings and expectations	− For more students enrolling in postsecondary − For K–12 since less information on postsecondary education policies
K–12 stakeholders' aspirations and actions	− Sends confusing signals that might have a negative impact on students' aspirations	+ For mutually reinforced signals that could have a positive impact on students' postsecondary aspirations	− Sends confusing signals that might have a negative impact on high school students' aspirations
Student mastery of college preparatory content and skills	+ For elite pool of students, who do not rely on high school information	+ For more students completing postsecondary education	− For more students not aspiring and completing postsecondary education

College Preparation and Qualification	+ For elite pool of students	+ For all students	− For most students
Postsecondary Success • Freshman placement and remediation • Dropout rate • Graduation rate	− Those not in elite pool face increased remediation and dropout rates and decreased graduation rates	+ Decreased remediation and dropout rate and increased graduation rate for more students	− Increased postsecondary remediation and dropout rate and decreased graduation rate for more students

exit-level and postsecondary entrance-level signals and incentives for students are delivered in isolation from one another or through interaction and reinforcement. We identify three possible scenarios for signal delivery: postsecondary education drives policy (column A), K–12 drives policy (column C), or policy is driven by the combined efforts of K–12 and postsecondary education. The preferred delivery is column B; columns A and C have serious shortcomings.

Signals and incentives sent along either through a separate postsecondary education or K–12 system result in less student preparation, college knowledge, and postsecondary outcomes. Combined efforts between K–12 and postsecondary especially help disadvantaged students, while honors students can succeed with less K–16 cooperation. Signals are related to outcomes such as less remediation and completion of a student's desired postsecondary program (Henry and Rubenstein, 2002).

Joint efforts between postsecondary and K–12 education (column B in Figure 1.1) are crucial in creating positive outcomes for more students, particularly those from economically disadvantaged families, families in which a parent did not attend college, and those students who face stigmatization and racism as they proceed through school. If there is no K–16 interaction and reinforcement of signals, we posit that the more advantaged students will receive ample signals and incentives to prepare for postsecondary education (see column A). But the more educationally disadvantaged high school graduates will enroll at lower rates, require remediation, and experience lower postsecondary completion rates (column C).

As path B in the framework indicates, combined efforts by postsecondary education and K–12 could improve college knowledge that is essential for student aspiration and preparation. College knowledge is acquired and possessed unequally among students and families of different social classes and racial/ethnic backgrounds. College knowledge by secondary school students and parents includes knowledge of tuition, curricular requirements, placement tests, and admission procedures and selection criteria. A high school's collegiate preparation culture cannot be fully measured by simple, visible, or discrete indexes such as standardized test scores, honors and AP courses, and postsecondary placement. Collegiate culture also encompasses the less tangible, more elusive qualities that can best be described through narratives that reveal the sustaining values or ethos of a high school.

One possible route to delivery of path B in the framework is under way in Oklahoma, where eighth graders take ACT's Explore and tenth graders take ACT's PLAN assessment that tests English, math, reading, and science reasoning (Carstensen, 2002). Since this policy was implemented, Oklahoma reports more students taking college preparation courses, increased enrollment in postsecondary education, and lower remediation rates. In a second example, the California State University System in 2002 approved dropping its internal math and English placement tests and instead will be using the high school California Standards Test for placement. This will provide secondary students with early indicators of their probable placement before they reach a California state university. Finally, the Georgia HOPE Scholarship Program, although initially problematic because of equity issues, is a simple but powerful signal that is reaching most secondary pupils who now know that a B high school average will result in a guaranteed state scholarship (Henry, 2002). For example, by middle school (grades 6–8), 51 percent of Georgia students and 59 percent of the parents knew the specific requirements for obtaining a Georgia state HOPE scholarship. This knowledge was present in 1997, only four years after HOPE scholarships started. Georgia students knew that only college preparation courses were computed as part of the B average required for a HOPE scholarship (Henry, 2002).

If K–12 schools are left to carry the brunt of college knowledge and preparation signals, then more students might receive vague signals and lesser incentives for adequate preparation. For example, a Metropolitan Life Survey in 2000 found that 71 percent of the students expected to go on to a four-year college, but teachers expected only 32 percent of their students to attend a four-year school.[16] A survey of twenty-six thousand high school teachers in twelve southern states found that only 38 percent believed that it was "very important" to "help all high school students master the essential content taught in college preparatory language arts, mathematics, and science courses." The Southern Regional Education Board determined that in its thirteen southeastern states, the percentage of high school students finishing a college prep curriculum ranged from 21 to 42 percent.[17]

Students who are in advanced, honors, or other accelerated tracks in high school usually receive clear and explicit signals about college preparation from the challenging content of their courses, university recruitment, their parents, other students, and some teachers who are knowledgeable about freshman-level standards (see column A in framework). But many students in middle and lower high school courses are not reached by postsecondary outreach programs or by their high schools. Frequently, counseling is inadequate, and parents lack experience concerning necessary college preparation. This is particularly true for students proceeding directly from high school to community college; because community colleges are open enrollment, they are viewed by some students as not having standards.

We have acknowledged that many factors contribute to the current problems with preparation for college, and better-aligned policy signals are not a panacea. However, if the signals and incentives to students concerning needed postsecondary education preparation are optimal, we believe that several positive outcomes will follow. These include substantial increases in higher student and parent aspirations and actions to prepare and enter postsecondary education, increased student mastery of college preparatory content and skills, and better outcomes, such as reduced need for postsecondary remediation, increased college and university persistence, and improved time to degree rates for postsecondary students.

Introduction to the Chapters

Because these problems vary by state and local context, we use this conceptual framework to examine the relationship between high school graduation, college admission, and college placement requirements at the state level. We conducted research in six states: California, Georgia, Illinois, Maryland, Oregon, and Texas. When we started this research, Georgia, Maryland, and Oregon were viewed as leaders in addressing these issues. We are particularly interested in the signals that are sent to students by institutional and state policies. Our case studies examine the college knowledge of students—the extent to which they understand college admission and placement requirements. We also examine relationships between what they do in high school, what they know about college, and their post–high school aspirations. We look to state and institutional policies to determine what signals are being sent to students about postsecondary education and look at the extent to which those signals come from a coordinated K–16 effort or several disjointed secondary and postsecondary approaches.

More information about the project's methodology can be found in Appendix A. The case studies begin with Chapter Two and continue through Chapter Seven. Chapter Eight presents findings from our work with several community colleges. Chapter Nine details the key findings of our research across all Bridge Project states and includes recommendations.

NOTES

1. For completion rates, see Adelman (1994). For other statistics on completion and remediation, see U.S. Department of Education (2001a, 2001b, 2001c) and American Council on Education (2002). All of these statistics are discussed later in this chapter.

2. U.S Department of Education (2001c). According to definitions provided by the U.S. Department of Education, *higher education* is the "study beyond secondary school at an institution that offers programs terminating in an associate, baccalaureate, or higher degree," and *postsecondary education* is "provision of formal instructional programs with a curriculum designed primarily for students who have completed the requirements for a high school diploma or equivalent. This includes programs of an academic, vocational, and continuing professional education purpose, and excludes vocational and adult basic education programs." We use the term *postsecondary education* in this study, as it is broader in the scope of institutions that it includes.

3. K–16 refers to kindergarten through grade 16, or the end of a four-year undergraduate program. Some states call their efforts P–16, or preschool through grade 16 reforms.

4. An associate's degree is awarded for completion of a sub-baccalaureate program of study and usually requires at least two years of college-level study. A certificate is typically awarded for completion of a program in a defined area of employment, usually requiring less than two years of study and limited general education (U.S. Department of Education, 2001c).

5. Using the 2001 Carnegie classifications, the 80 percent of students whom we focus on primarily go to Baccalaureate Colleges—General, Baccalaureate/Associates Colleges, Masters Colleges and Universities I and II. Some broad access schools are included in Doctoral/Research Universities, Intensive and Baccalaureate Colleges, Liberal Arts. See Carnegie Foundation for the Advancement of Teaching (2001). Researchers checked the Carnegie classifications with College Board data concerning the percentage of applications accepted.

6. See Carnegie Foundation for Advancement of Teaching (2001). Institutions are elaborated in note 5.

7. There is a growing debate whether limited financial aid, lack of preparation, or college knowledge is the major cause prohibiting low-income students from attending college. Pell Grants fell from 84 percent of public four-year college costs in 1974 to 40 percent in 2001. But skeptics contend that throwing financial aid at unprepared students will increase only entrance, but not completion, numbers. These critics favor expanding GEAR UP and other federal outreach programs as a higher priority than increasing Pell Grants. Both strategies seem needed to us, and financial issues may be more important at four-year schools.

   We are not taking a position on this debate, but our research focuses on college knowledge and academic preparation. See Burd (2002). See also National Center for Public Policy and Higher Education (2002).

8. In 1996, the Fifth Circuit Court of Appeals ruled that the University of Texas Law School had illegally used racial preferences in admissions; in 1996, California voters approved Proposition 209, which eliminated the use of affirmative action in public employment, education, and contracting decisions.

9. In several states, new admissions policies have been put in place to automatically accept students ranked at the top of their high school graduating class. Public universities in Texas admit the top 10 percent, Florida's universities admit the top 20 percent, and the University of California admits the top 4 percent of each high school graduating class (Kirst, 2000).

10. For example, the trustees of the City University of New York voted in 1998 on a policy to begin excluding students from its bachelor's degree programs who were not deemed ready for college-level math or English, ultimately moving most remedial education to its community college campuses. The California State University Board of Trustees voted in 1996 to set a goal of reducing to 10 percent (from 50 percent) the number of first-year students needing remedial education. See Marcus (2000) and California State University (2002).

11. See also Horn, Kojaku, and Carroll (2001).

12. Of 1,054 Latino parents surveyed by telephone in Chicago, New York, and Los Angeles, 65.7 percent missed at least half of "the rather straightforward information items." The survey included such questions as, "From what you know, does a community college offer the same bachelor's degree that a university offers?" (The possible responses were yes, no, and don't know.) The report also drew on data collected through case studies of forty-one parents. See "Study Cites Inability Among Many Latino Parents to Advise Children About College" (2002).

13. For the powerful impact of extrinsic motivation for high school students, see Steinberg (1996).

14. For intrinsic versus extrinsic incentives, see Deci, Koestner, and Tyan (2001). Especially useful for our framework is the rejoinder to the article in the same issue by Cameron (2001).

15. For a similar definition of signaling to ours, see Fuhrman and O'Day (1996).

16. Metropolitan Life Survey of the American Teacher (2000).

17. Abraham (1992).

REFERENCES

Abell Foundation. *Baltimore City Community College at the Crossroads.* Baltimore, Md.: Abell Foundation, 2002.

Abraham, A. *College Remedial Studies.* Atlanta: Southern Regional Education Board, 1992.

Adelman, C. *Lessons of a Generation.* San Francisco: Jossey-Bass, 1994.

Adelman, C. *Answers in the Tool Box: Academic Intensity, Attendance Patterns and Bachelor's Degree Attainment.* Washington, D.C.: U.S. Department of Education, Office of Educational Research and Improvement, 1999.

Adelman, C. "Putting on the Glitz: How Tales from a Few Elite Institutions Form America's Impressions About Higher Education." *Connection: New England's Journal of Higher Education and Economic Development,* 2001, *15*(3), 24–30.

ACT. "What Math Skills Should College Bound Students Have? High School and College Teachers Disagree." May 9, 2000. [http://www.act.org/news/releases/2000/05-09-00.html].

ACT. "Eighth Grade Students Underestimate College Preparation Needs." July 2, 2003. [www.act.org/news/releases/2003/7-02-03.html].

American Council on Education. *Access and Persistence.* Washington, D.C.: American Council on Education, 2002.

Barton, P. *The Closing of the Education Frontier.* Princeton, N.J.: Educational Teaching Service, 2002.

Bishop, J. H. "Incentives for Learning: Why American High School Students Compare So Poorly to Their Counterparts Overseas." *Research in Labor Economics,* 1990, *11,* 17–51.

Bishop, J. H., and others. "Nerds and Freaks: A Theory of Student Culture and Norms." In D. Ravitch (ed.), *Brookings Papers on Education Policy.* Washington, D.C.: Brookings, 2003.

Burd, S. "Rift Grows over What Keeps Low Income Students out of College." *Chronicle of Higher Education,* Jan. 25, 2002, pp. 18–19.

Business Week. May 30, 2002, p. 130.

Cabrera, A. F., Burkum, K., and LaNasa, S. "Pathways to a Four-Year Degree." Paper presented at the Annual Meeting of the Association for the Study of Higher Education, Portland, Ore., Nov. 2003.

California State University. "CSU Charts Remedial Education Progress." *CSU Leader,* Jan. 31, 2002. [www.calstate.edu/csuleader/020131.htm].

Cameron, J. "Negative Effects of Reward on Intrinsic Motivation: A Limited Phenomenon." *Review of Educational Research,* 2001, *71*(1), 29–42.

Carnegie Foundation for Advancement of Teaching. *The Carnegie Classifications.* Menlo Park, Calif.: Carnegie Foundation for Advancement of Teaching, 2001.

Carstensen, Don (2002). "Using Tests to Break Down Barriers to Education Success." *Basic Education,* 2002, *46*(6), 5–8.

Choy, S. P "College Access and Affordability." In *The Condition of Education 1998*. Washington, D.C.: U.S. Department of Education, 1998.

Cooperative Institutional Research Program, 2002. "The American Freshman: National Norms for Fall 2001." Los Angeles: UCLA, 2002. [http://www.gseis.ucla.edu/heri/norms_pr_01.html].

Costrell, R. M. "A Simple Model of Education Standards." *American Economic Review,* 1994, 956–971.

Deci, E. L., Koestner, R., and Tyan, R. "Extrinsic Rewards and Intrinsic Motivation in Education: Reconsidered Once Again." *Review of Educational Research,* 2001, *71*(1), 1–27.

Education Trust. "Ticket to Nowhere: The Gap Between Leaving High School and Entering College and High Performance Jobs." *Thinking K–16*. Washington, D.C.: Education Trust, 1999.

Education Trust. *Youth at the Crossroads.* Washington, D.C.: Education Trust, 2001.

Education Trust. "Add It Up, Mathematics Education in the U.S. Does Not Compute." *Thinking K–16,* Summer 2002, *16*(1), 14.

Education Trust. *Thinking K–16: A New Core Curriculum for All.* Washington D.C.: Education Trust, 2003.

Fuhrman, S. H., and O'Day, J. Rewards and Reform: Creating Education Incentives That Work. San Francisco: Jossey-Bass, 1996.

Grubb, W. N. *Learning and Earning in the Middle: The Economic Benefits of Sub-Baccalaureate Education.* New York: Community College Research Center, 1999. [www.tc.columbia.edu/ccrc].

Henry, G. T., and Rubenstein, R. "Paying for Grades." *Journal of Policy Management and Analysis,* 2002, *21*, 96.

Hodgkinson, H. *All One System: A Second Look.* San Jose, Calif.: National Center for Public Policy and Higher Education, 1999.

Horn, L., Kojaku, L., and Carroll, C. D. *High School Academic Curriculum and the Persistence Path Through College.* Washington, D.C.: U.S. Department of Education, 2001.

Kirst, M. *Improving and Aligning K–16 Standards, Admissions, and Freshman Placement Policies.* Stanford, Calif.: National Center for Postsecondary Improvement, 1998.

Kirst, M. "A Babel of Standards." *National Crosstalk,* 1999, *7*(4). [http://www.highereducation.org/crosstalk/ct1099/voices1099-kirst.shtml].

Kirst, M. "A New Admissions Game. Class Rankings Replace Affirmative Action." *National Crosstalk,* 2000, *8*(2). [http://www.highereducation.org/crosstalk/ct0500/voices0500-kirst.shtml].

Kirst, M. *Overcoming the High School Senior Slump: New Education Policies.* San Jose, Calif.: National Center for Public Policy and Higher Education, 2001.

Kirst, M., and Venezia, A. "Bridging the Great Divide Between Secondary Schools and Postsecondary Education." *Phi Delta Kappan,* Sept. 2001, 92–97.

Le, Vi-Nhuan and Robyn, Abby (2001). Alignment Among Secondary and Postsecondary Assessments. Santa Monica, CA: Rand Corporation.

Maeroff, G. I., Callan, P. M., and Usdan, M. D. *The Learning Connection. New Partnerships Between Schools and Colleges.* New York: Teachers College Press, 2001.

Marcus, J. "Revamping Remedial Education." *Crosstalk,* 2000, 8(1). [http://www.highereducation.org/crosstalk/ct0100/front.shtml].

McDonough, P. M. *Choosing Colleges.* Albany, N.Y.: SUNY Press, 1997.

McDonough, P., Korn, J., and Yamaski, E. "Access, Equity and the Privatization of College Counseling." *Review of Higher Education.* 1997, 20(3), 297–317.

McRobbie, J., Finn, J., and Harman, P. *Class Size Reduction: Lessons Learned from Experience.* San Francisco: WestEd, 1998.

Metropolitan Life Survey of the American Teacher. *Are We Preparing Students for the 21st Century?* New York: Metropolitan Life, Sept. 2000.

Mortenson, T. "Freshman-to-Sophomore Persistence Rates by Institutional Control, Academic Selectivity and Degree Level, 1983 to 1998." In *Postsecondary Education Opportunity.*

Mow, S. L., and Nettles, M. T. "Minority Student Access to, and Persistence and Performance in, College." In J. Smart (ed.), *Higher Education: Handbook of Theory and Research.* New York: Agathon, 1990.

National Association of System Heads. *Alignment Survey.* 2000. Washington, D.C.: Education Trust, 2000.

National Center for Public Policy and Higher Education. *Losing Ground: A National Status Report on the Affordability of American Higher Education.* San Jose, Calif.: National Center, 2002.

National Commission on Excellence in Education. *A Nation at Risk: The Imperative for Educational Reform.* Washington, D.C.: National Commission on Excellence in Education, 1983.

Newsweek, Apr. 1, 2002, p. 53.

Oakes, J. "Can Tracking Research Inform Practice? Technical, Normative and Political Considerations." *Educational Researcher,* May 1992, pp. 12–21.

Orfield, G., and Paul, F. G. *High Hopes, Long Odds: A Major Report on Hoosier Teens and the American Dream.* Indianapolis, Ind.: Youth Institute, 1994.

Powell, A. G. "Motivating Students to Learn: An American Dilemma." In S. H. Fuhrman and J. A. O'Day (eds.), *Rewards and Reform: Creating Educational Incentives That Work.* San Francisco: Jossey-Bass, 1996.

Rodriguez, E. "Overview of Study of State Strategies That Support Successful Transitions of Students from Secondary to Postsecondary Education."

Paper presented to the American Educational Research Association Annual Meeting, San Diego, Calif., Apr. 16, 1998.

Rosenbaum, J. *College for All*. New York: Russell Sage Foundation, 2001.

Savage, D. "Missing on Top Campuses: The Poor." *Los Angeles Times,* Mar. 7, 2003, p. 1.

Schneider, B. "Strategies for Success: High School and Beyond." In D. Ravitch (ed.), *Brookings Papers on Education Policy*. Washington, D.C.: Brookings, 2003.

Schneider B., and Stevenson, D. *The Ambitious Generation. America's Teenagers, Motivated But Directionless*. New Haven, Conn.: Yale University Press, 1999.

Steinberg, L. *Beyond the Classroom*. New York: Simon & Schuster, 1996.

"Study Cites Inability Among Many Latino Parents to Advise Children About College." *Chronicle of Higher Education,* July 15, 2002.

Tafel, J., and Eberhart, N. *Statewide School-College (K–16) Partnerships to Improve Student Performance*. Denver: State Higher Education Executive Officers, 1998.

Timpane, P. M. *Higher Education and the Schools*. Denver: State Higher Education Executive Officers, 1998.

Tinto, V. *Leaving College: Rethinking the Causes and Cures of Student Attrition*. Chicago: University of Chicago Press, 1993.

U.S. Bureau of the Census. *CPS Annual Demographic Survey, March Supplement*. Washington, D.C.: U.S Government Printing Office, Mar. 2001. [http://ferret.bls.census.gov/macro/032001/perinc/new03_001.htm].

U.S. Department of Education. *The Condition of Education*. Washington, D.C.: National Center for Education Statistics, 1997.

U.S. Department of Education. *Conditions of Education*. Washington, D.C.: National Center for Education Statistics, 2001a. National Center for Education Statistics.

U.S. Department of Education. *Projections of Education Statistics to 2011*. Washington, D.C.: National Center for Education Statistics, 2001b.

U.S. Department of Education. *Digest of Education Statistics: 2000*. Washington, D.C.: National Center for Education Statistics, 2001c.

2

WORKING TOWARD
K–16 COHERENCE IN
CALIFORNIA

Anthony Lising Antonio
Samuel H. Bersola

THREE ASPECTS OF K–16 education in California make the state a particularly interesting case study. First, California has an explicitly tiered and coordinated state college and university system that structures access to higher education (California Postsecondary Education Commission, 1993). The state also has at least one body attempting to address educational reform across sectors, the Intersegmental Coordinating Council of the California Education Round Table. Second, public higher education, particularly the University of California, has had to respond to the passage of Proposition 209 in 1996. The statute prohibits the use of race-based affirmative action in university admissions, compelling the nine campuses of the University of California to alter their admission policies to remain in compliance. Finally, K–12 education continues to experience waves of accountability-oriented reform, resulting in a barrage of assessments administered to students.

While the K–12 and postsecondary education systems still too often work at cross purposes, efforts are under way to align the two systems better and to ensure that students who have met standards for high school graduation will be prepared to do postsecondary work without having to undergo substantial remediation, as is too often the case. In this chapter, we provide an overview of the state's postsecondary education system and the policy initiatives launched in recent years. We look both at the ways these policies strive to create a more coherent system and at what short-comings still need to be addressed. We then focus on how students at six California high schools understand—and misunderstand—college admissions, costs, placements, and other policies.

An Overview of Public Postsecondary Education in California

In this section, we provide an overview of the public postsecondary education systems in California. First, we present the California Master Plan, intersegmental bodies and collaborative efforts, and recent policies and legal action affecting higher education. Second, we discuss the K–12 standards and frameworks and the K–16 assessments. Third, we present the admissions and placement policies of the University of California and California State University. Finally, we discuss the need for improved linkages between high school and postsecondary education and present some growing developments in alignment and coordination between the two sectors.

The Master Plan

California's Master Plan, legislated in 1960, regulated the selectivity and mission of the state's three-tired higher education system. The University of California (UC), currently serving roughly 130,000 undergraduates and 40,000 graduates at nine campuses, was charged to restrict admission to the upper 12.5 percent of high school graduates. The California State University (CSU), serving roughly 350,000 students at twenty-three campuses, was to restrict admission to the upper 33.3 percent. The Master Plan also limited lower-division enrollment to 40 percent of the CSU undergraduate enrollment, thus diverting substantial numbers of lower-division students to the community colleges, currently serving approximately 1.6 million students at 109 colleges (California Postsecondary Education Commission, 2003). The California Community Colleges (CCC), which cost the state the least amount of tuition per student among the state-supported segments, were to maintain open enrollment.

The governance structures for each segment are similarly distinct. Community colleges are characterized by a larger degree of local control relative to the CSU and UC. In addition to a board of governors that sets policy and provides some guidance, there are seventy-two community college districts statewide, each under the authority of a locally elected board of trustees. The CSU is governed by its board of trustees, which establishes systemwide minimum criteria for admission, procedures for course placement, and various other policies. Because the state legislature sets and approves the CSU budget, the state colleges have been subject to some direct control by several state agencies. In contrast, the University of California has had substantial autonomy from direct state controls. The UC regents have ultimate authority over all policies within the university, including admission policies and procedures.

Intersegmental Bodies and Collaborative Efforts

Although the three segments maintain separate missions and governance structures, several bodies attempt to coordinate the functioning of the three institutions and influence policymaking toward that end. The most influential of these is the Intersegmental Coordinating Committee (ICC), the programmatic arm of the California Education Round Table. Composed of staff, faculty, and student representatives from all segments of education, the ICC oversees working subcommittees and task groups that carry out Round Table priorities.

In December 1996, the ICC's Committee on K–18 Curricular Issues issued a report containing a set of policy recommendations aiming to provide the starting point for discussions about the issues surrounding the high school senior year. How, for instance, could better senior year preparation for college reduce the need for later remediation? The report concludes by stating that continuous intersegmental efforts are critical and that a focus on the senior year of high school should be a key lever for reform.

The ICC has also produced a set of articulation documents, *Standards for California High School Graduates in Mathematics and English*. In developing both math and English standards for California, the ICC attempted to clarify the relationship between graduation standards and expected competencies for entering college freshmen. The math portion of the ICC document is intended to convey mathematics expectations for all students who intend to graduate from high school. The ICC-developed English standards are intended to align directly with the recommendations of postsecondary institutions for entrance into freshmen English programs (ICC, 1997). In October 1997, the California Education Round Table published its *Standards for California High School Graduates*.

Recent Policies and Legal Action Affecting Higher Education

In 1996, Californians approved Proposition 209, a voter initiative that prohibits discrimination or the granting of preferences in education, employment, or contracting based on race/ethnicity, gender, or national origin. This followed on the heels of the UC Regents' passage of Standing Policy-1 (SP-1), which eliminated the consideration of race, religion, sex, color, ethnicity, or national origin in admission decisions to the university. SP-1, however, does not affect outreach efforts to individuals. The adoption of SP-1 has caused a wave of activity at the UC regarding both changes in selection criteria and increased focus on targeted outreach to underrepresented students. On February 2, 1999, African American, Latino, Filipino American students, and related organizations filed a class action lawsuit in the U.S. District Court in San Francisco, charging that UC Berkeley's undergraduate admissions process violates federal civil rights laws. The suit, *Castaneda et al.* v. *Regents of the University of California,* alleges that UC Berkeley's new admissions, now without provisions for race-based affirmative action, have a negative, disparate impact on African American, Latino, and Filipino American applicants. More specifically, the plaintiffs allege that the UC Berkeley admissions policy places too much weight on SAT scores and grades in Advanced Placement (AP) courses. SAT scores, the plaintiffs claim, represent a poor measure of an applicant's promise, and many schools with high concentrations of African Americans, Latinos, and Filipino Americans do not offer any AP courses (American Civil Liberties Union, 1999).

The availability of college preparatory courses and the enrollment patterns of students in those courses have been of central concern in recent years as the CSU and UC have decided to impose new course requirements for admissions. The outcome of the *Castaneda* case will have important policy implications for the UC, as the university continues to search for ways to maintain current levels of access for underrepresented racial minorities.

K–12 Standards and Frameworks

The State Board of Education has the primary authority to make K–12 policy. A major obstacle to achieving the goal of aligning standards, curriculum frameworks, and assessments, however, is California's fragmented, convoluted, and poorly defined system of governance in the K–12 sector. There is no master plan or road map that can guide policy toward a systemic end (California Legislative Analyst's Office, 1999). Nevertheless, California's K–12 system has made great strides in recent years.

California's reform efforts began with the development of content standards, then frameworks, and finally the Standardized Testing and Reporting (STAR) assessment program. Assembly Bill 265, signed into law in

October 1995, provided for the development of new statewide content and performance standards in the core curricular areas of language arts, mathematics, history and social science, and science. By 1997, the State Board of Education had developed and approved content standards for all grade levels in English, math, science, and social studies, and in 1999, it published frameworks for implementation. Performance standards, however, have yet to be implemented, which underscores some of the challenges the state faces in articulating what it considers to be adequate.

Although California does strive to align standards with assessments within the K–12 policy arena, there has been only a small effort toward improving compatibility and coherence between K–12 and postsecondary education. The lack of compatibility between K–12 and higher education policies and practices in California is evident in two ways: (1) policy-making bodies in the two education sectors have minimal interaction and opportunity for collaboration and coherence, and (2) education assessments are not aligned. The latter is discussed in the next section.

K–16 Assessments in California

The lack of coherence among the different assessments in California has created a challenge in terms of achieving alignment between K–12 and higher education. Some have suggested that unless the curriculum, standards, and assessments are carefully aligned, there will be serious ramifications for the effectiveness of the proposed system (Ed Source, 1998). The following presents the secondary and postsecondary assessments that California administers or plans to administer, followed by an analysis of the challenges California faces in aligning these assessments. (Assessment information is applicable to the 1997–1998 school year, the time at which the study was conducted.)

SECONDARY SCHOOL ASSESSMENTS. California has two existing assessment programs for its secondary schools: the Golden State Examination (GSE) and the Standardized Testing and Reporting (STAR) Program. In addition, the California High School Exit Examination has recently been legislated.

Golden State Exam. The California State Department of Education administers the GSE to students in grades 7 through 12. The voluntary examinations assess students' knowledge of key subjects and their ability to apply that knowledge. All of the examinations, except written composition, include a balance of multiple-choice items and questions or problems that require written responses. The science examinations include laboratory tasks. The GSE recognizes students for demonstrating outstanding levels of achievement on each examination. Success on six of the examinations can qualify students for the Golden State Seal Merit Diploma. This achievement is recorded on their high school transcripts and recognized by a special insignia on their diplomas.

California's Standardized Testing and Reporting Program. The STAR program was authorized by Senate Bill 376 in October 1997. As required by statute, the California State Board of Education designated a statewide assessment test, the Stanford 9, in November 1997. First administered statewide in spring 1998, the Stanford 9 is a multiple-choice test that allows comparisons to be made to a national sample of students. School districts in California are required to test all students in grades 2 through 11. High school–level testing includes reading, writing, mathematics, science, and history and social science.

In 1999, two sets of items were administered to supplement the Stanford 9 in order to address California's State Board of Education content standards in language arts and mathematics. These included thirty-five language arts items and thirty-five math items that were designed to assess progress toward the standards. Hence, a combination of selected items from the original Stanford 9 math and language arts exams and the thirty-five augmented questions was used to comprise the California Standards Test. In addition to the STAR augmentation, the Spanish Assessment of Basic Education, second edition (SABE/2), was added for Spanish-speaking and limited-English-proficient students.

High School Exit Exams. The legislation for this exam, enacted in 1999 as Senate Bill 2, appropriated $2 million to the State Department of Education for development of the exam and also required the State Board of Education to adopt state performance standards based on the exam by July 2000. The first administration of the exam was in spring semester 2001. Students will be required to pass this exam, which will be aligned to state standards, in order to earn a high school diploma beginning in the 2003–2004 school year. Students will be tested throughout grades 10 to 12 in language arts and mathematics.

HIGHER EDUCATION ASSESSMENTS. The high-stakes entrance exams for higher education present another maze for California students to navigate. We outline below four major exams that college applicants and newly matriculated college students in California take.

SAT I. The SAT I is a norm-referenced, multiple-choice test of verbal and math reasoning. California's state standards and assessments are not aligned with the SAT I; SAT I results are not indicators of students' overall academic performance in school. The UC requires all applicants to submit SAT I scores, and the CSU requires SAT I scores only for students with a high school grade point average (GPA) below 3.0. SAT I covers algebra and geometry, but also includes ratios and data interpretation that are not stressed on CSU placement tests.

SAT II. The SAT II tests (formerly called Achievement Tests) are norm-referenced, multiple-choice, and open-ended tests. The UC requires three SAT II subject tests: writing, mathematics, and a subject in an area appropriate to the chosen discipline of college study. Studies have shown that the SAT II predicts freshman grades as successfully as SAT I, and some UC departments, such as the College of Engineering at UCLA, believe that the SAT II is a better predictor of success in their program (Siporin, 1999). In fact, beginning with first-year applicants for fall 2001, the UC redefined its eligibility index to give each of the three SAT II tests required for admission twice the weight of the math and verbal portions of the SAT I test. In February 2001, former UC President Richard Atkinson recommended dropping the SAT I completely from admissions requirements ("UC President," 2001).

Advanced Placement (AP). Advanced Placement is a program sponsored by the College Board that provides secondary teachers with curriculum guides for thirty-two college-level courses in nineteen subjects. College and secondary school educators oversee the courses, develop and grade the annual exams, and lead workshops every year. AP exams are graded on a scale from 1 to 5 (the top score). Scores of 3, 4, or 5 can qualify students for academic credit for or placement into, or both, advanced courses at virtually all of the nation's colleges and universities. In addition to earning college credit, high scores on the English and math AP exams also exempt matriculated students from placement exams at the UC and CSU. Furthermore, the University of California allows extra weighting of grades earned in AP courses completed in the sophomore and junior year.

College Placement Exams. The CSU and UC systems administer criterion-referenced, multiple-choice, and open-ended English and mathematics entry-level placement exams for new students that are designed to determine college readiness and course placement. The CSU and UC administer different placement exams. The CSU administers two placement exams for admitted and entering first-year students: the Entry Level Mathematics examination (ELM) and the English Placement Test (EPT). At CSU Long Beach, the director of testing prepared a document that simulates the use of the SAT I (and ACT) on predicting EPT and ELM scores. These data suggest that the SAT I can be used to predict performance on the EPT accurately and, less closely, the ELM. An SAT I score above 550, however, exempts CSU entrants from taking the CSU placement tests.

The UC system administers the Subject A English Examination, and all UC campuses use the Mathematics Diagnostic Testing Program (MDTP) on a departmental basis. These placement exams are not fully aligned with the K–12 content standards because they were developed prior to the establishment of these standards.

ALIGNMENT AND COORDINATION OF ASSESSMENTS. The array of K–16 assessments in California covers a variety of purposes, such as assessing preparation for college, placing entering college students in appropriate levels of course work, predicting university performance, determining trends in statewide K–12 standards, and comparing state test results to national norms. Researchers (for example, Kirst, 1999) have argued that these varied purposes have contributed to poor alignment of standardized assessments in California.

As Kirst (1999) notes, the placement tests given by the UC and CSU appear to assess different skills for ostensibly the same purpose, determining readiness for college-level work. To determine freshmen English placement, the UC uses a student writing component that involves interpretation and analysis. In contrast, the freshman English placement exam at the CSU in writing emphasizes grammar and sentence structure. Misalignment between sectors is also evident. For mathematics, the entry-level mathematics test given by the CSU covers algebra, geometry, and algebra II. This test, which is devised by a committee of CSU professors, is a mismatch with the State Board of Education math standards that focus on math problem solving. Furthermore, the SAT II does follow course sequences, but CSU does not require this exam for its applicants. Consequently, clear linkage for high school teachers between the K–12 content and performance standards and the various university entrance and placement exams does not exist. The UC and CSU placement tests are not designed to diagnose student weaknesses, and teachers are not advised of their students' results. Using the language of signaling, Kirst (1999) asserts that universities send so many different signals to secondary schools that it is difficult for teachers to effectively coordinate course content with the universities' curricular expectations. Furthermore, the level of knowledge that students and parents have about the differing content among the different assessments is unknown.

Admissions and Placement Policies at UC and UC, Davis

In order to understand how institutions of higher education are responding to K–16 initiatives in terms of their admissions and placement policies, we focused on two public universities, the University of California, Davis (UCD) and California State University, Sacramento (CSUS). We first turn to the more selective UCD, which has approximately 25,500 undergraduate and graduate students. The mean GPA for new freshmen in 1998 was 3.72 and the mean SAT I scores were 556 Verbal and 593 Math. Forty-three percent of the undergraduates identified as white.

MEETING THE SYSTEMWIDE SUBJECT REQUIREMENTS AND GPA MINIMUM. When this research was conducted, applicants to all UC campuses, including UCD, needed to meet the fifteen-unit "a to f" subject requirement in order to be eligible for admission. (This is now "a to g" because the eligibility requirements merged with those for CSU and UC added an extra requirement.) These include, as minimums: (a) two years of history/social science; (b) four years of English; (c) three years of mathematics; (d) two years of laboratory science; (e) two years of a language other than English; and, (f) two years of college prep electives. According to the UC publication, "Quick Reference for Counselors," in calculating the GPA, extra weight is assigned to honors classes "to encourage students to undertake more challenging work at the advanced secondary level" (University of California, 1995).

Students with a GPA of 3.3 or higher in the a to f subjects fulfill minimum requirements for admission to the university. However, students with GPAs as low as 2.82 can still meet the requirements if they achieve a specified SAT I score. Students must also take three SAT II tests, which individual campuses use at their discretion.

ADMISSIONS POLICIES SPECIFIC TO UCD. The above requirements establish eligibility to the UC system, but each campus is responsible for determining specific admission criteria. Following are some of the specific criteria UCD used for selecting students for the 1997–98 academic year:

> Test scores: Each SAT II portion and each SAT I portion count the same weight in calculating the Academic Index at UCD (each section has a maximum possible score of 800). However, because

there are three required SAT II portions and only two SAT I portions, the SAT II factors more heavily for campuses like UCD that choose to use all three SAT II exams in calculating their academic index.

Senior year grades: While the GPA is calculated on grades earned in years 10 to 12, the senior year, as UCD director of admissions Gary Tudor explained, "is a validating year. We'll look at courses in progress for the 35 percent admitted. But there's no way, the way we do business, that we can even use the senior year." But he also noted that in 1997, UCD rescinded offers to two hundred admitted students largely because of D grades they received in AP courses or in a required a to f course.

Personal statements and recommendation letters: An applicant's personal statement appears to play a minimal role in admissions at UCD. Tudor told us that "for 99 percent of the cases, it doesn't matter." Furthermore, letters of recommendation are seldom used in the selection process at UCD.

SELECTION PROCEDURES AT UCD. The first 60 percent of admitted students come from those applicants with the highest indexes. The academic index is based on a point system, with the maximum number of points being 10,000 (see Table 2.1).

However, UCD uses supplemental criteria, in addition to academic criteria, to choose the remaining 40 percent of its freshmen class. These criteria mark the greatest change in UCD policies since Proposition 209 and SP-1. They are aimed at helping the university remain in compliance with 209 and SP-1 while still being able to admit nontraditional students.

The UC publication *Introducing the University* (1999), which accompanies the application for admission, describes to prospective students

Table 2.1. UC Davis's Academic Index for Regular Admission.

Criteria	Maximum Point Value
Calculated GPA[a]	6,000
Total SAT I or ACT[b]	1,600
Total SAT II[c]	2,400
Total points:	10,000

[a]*Including extra credit for up to eight honors courses, capped at 4.0.*
[b]*ACT composite score is converted to an SAT I score equivalent.*
[c]*Three tests at 800 points each.*

how UCD uses supplemental criteria. We include this direct quotation to demonstrate what UCD communicates to prospective students:

> The remaining percentage of freshmen will be selected on the bases of academic and personal achievement and experience, as assessed through a comprehensive review of all information provided on the application, including academic performance as described plus the following: demonstrated leadership, special talents, residency, presence of and responses to life challenges, honors, and awards, marked improvement in a challenging academic program, and participation in pre-collegiate programs that develop academic abilities [p. 39].

UNDERGRADUATE PLACEMENT POLICIES AT UC AND UCD. All UC campuses use the MDTP, but there is no official UC policy concerning math placement. (Each campus has a different cut-off score, which can vary by department and program. In addition, some campuses allow students to submit SAT math scores in lieu of taking these tests. Therefore, mathematics placement policies are beyond the scope of this study.) Systemwide, the UC has an official policy regarding only oral or written placement. Students are assessed for proficiency in these areas through the Subject A examination before they may enroll in the university. Students who have scored high marks on the SAT II or the AP English exam are exempt from taking the Subject A exam if the university has these scores on record by the April prior to enrollment. All other students must take the Subject A exam, which is given every May. Essentially, students must read a passage and then complete an essay that responds to set of questions posed at the end of the passage.

According to Cynthia Bates, who coordinates UC Davis's Subject A exam, of the approximately seventeen thousand students across all UC campuses who took the Subject A examination in 1996–1997, 47.5 percent passed it. This percentage has decreased slightly from years past, where passing rates were between 50 and 57 percent.

Students who pass the Subject A exam meet the Subject A requirement; those who do not pass can meet the requirement by completing, with a grade of C or better, a transferable college course in English composition. Or, once enrolled at the university, students can complete (with a C or better) an appropriate writing course; at UCD, this course is English 57. The final examination in this course is the Subject A exam, on which they must earn a passing score. Ms. Bates stated that about 75 to 80 percent of those who take this course are able to earn passing scores on the Subject A examination by course completion.

The level of remediation at UCD and the UC system as a whole is cause for public concern. The education policy question centers on the adequacy of high school preparation for university work: Why are so many students who are deemed admissible by UC eligibility and selection criteria unable to read and write at the college level? Moreover, who should pay for the necessary remediation? Nevertheless, it is important to note that despite the challenges raised by the Subject A requirement, UC Davis enjoys a high retention rate. Davis undergraduates persist at rates among the highest of all UC students. Among freshmen entering from 1991 to 1995, 91 percent returned for a fourth quarter, and 86 percent returned for a seventh quarter (University of California, Davis, 1999).

Admission and Placement Policies at CSU and CSU, Sacramento

All regularly admitted students to a CSU campus (including CSUS) must earn a minimum GPA of 2.0 in an academic core that varies somewhat from the a to f requirements at the UC. Students with a GPA under 3.0 must submit SAT I or ACT scores; however, students with GPAs above 3.0 qualify automatically for CSU eligibility. CSU campuses do not admit any student solely on the basis of SAT I or ACT scores. High school recommendations and personal statements are not considered strongly for admission. Because CSU eligibility is determined in November of the senior year, senior grades do not play a prominent role in most admission decisions. However, according to admissions policy, senior year grades are taken into account in determining eligibility, and admission offers can be withdrawn if a student fails to maintain a qualifying GPA upon graduation.

Sacramento State, which serves about twenty-four thousand students, follows the CSU systemwide admission policies. It has, however, supplemented them in some minor ways. For instance, the Admission and Enrollment Office at CSUS offers two special filing days in November on which eligible students may be admitted on the spot.

CONCERNS REGARDING REMEDIATION AT CSU. The increasing rates of remediation in the CSU system have been a source of growing concern over the past several years. The number of incoming freshmen who require remedial (also referred to as developmental) courses in math or English (or both) has risen to more than 50 percent of entering freshmen taking the placement tests.

The public has become increasingly concerned about the high number of students entering the CSU system from California public high schools who have not been adequately prepared, questioning the quality of education in the public schools and the standards developed by the California State Department of Education. The high level of remediation is expensive. The university must absorb the cost of providing classes and teachers for courses that are not offered for college credit. Parents and students bear additional expenses because remedial courses do not count toward graduation, and consequently, students are taking longer to finish college (Pesquiera and Hoff, 1995).

A committee formed by the CSU in 1995 initially proposed to eliminate remedial courses by 2001. Eventually, a modified policy was adopted with a series of phase-in target dates to reduce the need for remediation, extending the final target date to 2007 (Pesquiera and Hoff, 1995).

PLACEMENT POLICIES AT CSU AND CSU, SACRAMENTO. Official CSU policy states that nonexempt students must take placement tests by the end of their first semester or first quarter on campus. These tests—the EPT and the ELM—are intended to identify deficiencies in preparation necessary to perform adequately in typical English and mathematics freshmen-year courses. Beginning in 1998, nonexempt students have been required to take placement tests before they enroll in any classes their first semester or quarter. Those avoiding the tests will have a hold placed on their registration until the required tests are taken. At Sacramento State, for example, placement tests serve as gatekeepers to Math 1 and English 1A, which begin the typical course sequence in those subjects for freshmen. A student may qualify as exempt if he or she submits high enough SAT I, ACT, or AP test scores. Exempt students and those who make the cutoff scores on math and English placement tests may enroll in these courses upon entry into the university.

A Need for Improved Linkages Between High Schools and Higher Education

California has made great strides to align standards with assessments in K–12, as evidenced by the development and implementation of the STAR program. Unfortunately, efforts to improve compatibility and coherence between K–12 and higher education have lagged behind such efforts.

A theme that repeatedly surfaced in the interviews conducted for this case study was the nearly complete absence of communication between policymakers working with higher education and their policymaking counterparts in secondary education. Possible linkages between policy formulation in the two sectors cannot be recognized, yet alone formulated, without intersector communication and dialogue. Public institutions of higher education seem focused on their processes from the admissions point forward. And high schools, in addition to such pressing concerns as student safety, mental health concerns, and the professional development of teachers, must expend their energies on the many assessments required by the state. From a policy perspective, there are few incentives for either system to look outside its traditional boundaries and understand educational issues from a broader perspective.

As Kirst (1999) has noted, assessments used in California secondary education are primarily driven by state standards and accountability pressures, while the assessments in higher education are driven by a variety of purposes, from assessing general aptitude for success in college to placing entering college students in appropriate levels of course work. That these two sets of purposes are seen as competing and not complementary may serve as a barrier to successful student transitions from high school to college. For example, the math portion of the CSU math placement test is a mismatch with the STAR math test for high school juniors (Le, Hamilton, and Robyn, 2000), so preparation for state assessments may actually constitute somewhat limited preparation for placement tests in college.

Some Promising Developments in Alignment and Coordination

Despite the lack of collaboration within and between sectors, we found a few promising initiatives for greater alignment of educational policy and improving transitions from secondary to postsecondary education. For instance, articulation arrangements are being made through formal memorandums of understanding between Sacramento State and regional high schools and school districts. It is expected that these efforts will go far in increasing the number of freshmen who exceed minimal admission requirements and are prepared to begin the normal freshmen sequence of courses (that is, they are not in need of remediation). These outreach efforts are also expected to improve the number of freshmen admitted from underrepresented groups and will increase retention of all students at the university.

One of the most promising examples of policy coordination between the UC and the CSU is occurring in the context of admissions policy. The two systems recently developed a common fifteen-unit course requirement list that affects students applying for admission starting in fall 2003. This new policy greatly simplifies the policy communication and outreach efforts for schools, teachers, counselors, and the two universities themselves. It also signals hope that the two public systems in California are cognizant of the problems inherent in policy misalignment and are willing to collaborate on efforts to correct it.

What Do California Students and Parents Know About College?

This section explores the aspirations California students have for post-secondary education and their knowledge about college costs, placement exam policies, and admission policies. Such an examination is important because students whose aspirations align poorly with their college knowledge are likely to be less than well prepared for the challenges of college; they may not, for example, have taken sufficiently rigorous courses in high school.

We surveyed ninth and eleventh graders and their parents at two high-performing, two middle-performing, and two low-performing schools in the Greater Sacramento metropolitan area (we use pseudonyms for the schools). Half the students were enrolled in honors English classes and half were enrolled in college prep English. At these schools, honors courses are the most academically rigorous, with the college preparatory the next level of rigor. We also conducted focus group and individual interviews with students and faculty, respectively. Slightly more young women (63 percent) participated in our survey than young men. As teachers explained, honors courses are predominantly female; thus, our sample was skewed in this direction. In addition, more eleventh graders (53 percent) than ninth graders (47 percent) participated. In terms of socioeconomic status (SES), students tended to fall in our mid-SES and high-SES categories, with only 21 percent falling into the bottom third of our SES scale. SES was measured by a composite of two variables: maximum parental education and family income. Maximum parental education was scaled from 1 (less than high school) to 7 (graduate/ professional degree) and was taken as the higher level of attainment among the mother and father. Family income was scored 1 (below $15,000 a year) to 12 (over $100,000 a year). SES was computed as the sum of the two measures. For cross-tabular analyses, we divided these SES values into three major categories: low SES (2 to 7), middle SES (8 to 13), and high SES (14 to 19).

The sample was racially and ethnically diverse. Students of Asian descent composed almost 40 percent of our sample, yet student demographic information for the two counties in which our six schools reside indicates that only 17 percent of the high school population is of Asian descent. This oversampling of Asian American students is likely due to the fact that our sample included college preparatory and honors students only, and Asian American students tend to be overrepresented in these tracks. In contrast, African American and Latino students were under-sampled (11 percent African Americans in our sample versus roughly

15 percent overall within the two counties, and 10 percent Latinos in our sample versus roughly 16 percent within the two counties). Whites made up 27 percent of the sample.

After describing the case study high schools and presenting our student research, we briefly discuss parents' knowledge of college and the role teachers play in providing students with college counseling.

The Six Case Study High Schools

In this section, we describe the six California comprehensive public high schools in our case study. The names of these schools have been changed for anonymity.

THREE PALMS. Three Palms is a school with a strong collegiate culture. The school's Stanford 9 and SAT I averages are well above the district and state averages, and nearly 40 percent of all graduates matriculate directly into four-year institutions of higher education. Despite the fact that Bridgeport, the other case study school in District 2, also offers a wide array of AP courses (approximately a dozen AP courses each), Three Palms students earn AP credits at a rate twice that of Bridgeport and twice that of the state average.

According to the college counselor, standardized testing preparation is an important facet of his counseling program. This counselor quickly notified all faculty of UC Berkeley's new policy to weigh SAT IIs more heavily than the SAT Is. He urged teachers to advise their students to take the SAT II subject exams close to the end of a course of study so that they will have the best chance of retaining the subject matter. Teachers were instructed to teach their students how to "bubble in" the test form properly and how to narrow and eliminate choices on a multiple-choice exam. Even the honors students at Three Palms worried about the SATs; these students have high GPAs but feel that strong SATs will make a big difference in university admission. Teachers play an advocacy role at Three Palms through formal advising duties. Each teacher advises a group of students throughout the students' four years.

BELLVIEW. Bellview High, which is located in an upper-middle-class residential neighborhood, is known for its rigorous academic program and high academic achievement. Bellview has consistently earned the highest Stanford 9 scores in the district. Other indicators, such as the school's high UC matriculation rate, demonstrate that Bellview has strong college counseling. In fact, all of the students in the eleventh-grade honors English course who participated in a focus group indicated that they would apply to UC Davis.

Bellview administrators and teachers expressed great pride in the college prep school. Teachers explained that the school community is much more "academically conscious than the rest of the schools in the district." At the same time, some spoke with concern of the disproportionately high numbers of low-SES and minority students (with the exception of Asian Americans) in the lower-level courses. None of the students in our sample who were enrolled in both honors-level English and math courses were African American or Latino.

APPLEWOOD. Applewood (and Haverhill below) is a good representative of a middle-performing school. Academic performance indicators place it squarely in the middle of the state achievement levels. Administrators seem quite aware of their middling status. For example, the vice principal spoke of a specific goal set by the district's school board that by the year 2000, 50 percent of their students should be "CSU ready" and 35 percent should be "UC ready," with "ready" meaning that students will have completed all of the curriculum requirements for university admission. This administrator worried that the school had not established a working relationship with CSUS and UCD to achieve better UC and CSU matriculation rates. She mentioned that there was no connection between the AP teacher and the colleges and wished that colleges would give the school more information on what they look for in students.

Students at Applewood mentioned that some of their English teachers helped them inside and outside class to write their college essays. Overall, however, the students complained that the school's attention had not been on college preparation. These students felt that the push for adopting a year-round schedule and a disruptive teacher strike negatively affected students, "especially the ones who want to go to colleges," said one student. Another student spoke of the school's inability to fully prepare students for college: "I think they should prepare us better for the placement tests so that we don't get stuck in basic classes. I think we should have the opportunity to know, not necessarily what's on the test, but have a good idea of it so that we know what to expect."

HAVERHILL. Similar to Applewood, Haverhill is a school that struggles to provide more attention to its college-aspiring students. In focus group interviews, some students expressed that teachers do not care about preparing students for college, while others stated that some teachers encourage them to attend. One Haverhill teacher expressed that the school does not "wholly support" students' dreams. Several teachers worried that counseling did not start soon enough and that there were not enough counselors.

The vice principal, who had been at the school for several decades, chronicled the school's dwindling counseling resources: "At one time we had six counselors, and once, in the golden ages, we had eight. Now we have two really working with academics." One teacher spoke of how the sole counselor for seniors basically "catches" the 585 seniors. Haverhill's counselor of seniors justified the minimal attention given to students by arguing that the school encourages students to be "a little bit more industrious and self-sufficient" than other schools.

CENTER CITY. Among the six schools in our sample, Center City is the only one that can be easily described as a school with a non-college-going culture. Its teachers lamented the highly transient student population. The vice principal said that one-third of the students were failing algebra. The college counselor complained, "We call ourselves the college preparatory school, but we give less time to college and postsecondary counseling and paraprofessional than any other school in our district."

This counselor commented on her students' low college board scores, which she felt limited their chances of gaining admission to a highly selective university: "Do you know how many kids at our school [have scores of] 1100 or higher? Not even five." She cited poor attendance at college nights and financial aid assistance workshops. The eleventh-grade honors English teacher stated that only two students in twelfth-grade honors English had passed the college English placement exam that was sponsored by the local community college. In the focus groups, many students were quick to describe their school as "ghetto," meaning "run down, not smart kids, not bright, immature, bad teachers." When students were asked if they would go to a teacher for college advice, the students in the college preparatory class laughed, and the honors students said that they simply did not discuss college with their teachers.

BRIDGEPORT. Bridgeport High School is difficult to describe. On one hand, because it had the lowest Stanford 9 scores among the five comprehensive high schools in its district, it should merit a "low-performing" rating. On the other hand, Bridgeport had experienced a certain level of success in postsecondary placement that resembled middle-performing schools.

One Bridgeport teacher, who had studied the founding of Bridgeport and Three Palms for her doctoral dissertation, explained that while the racial diversity of the two schools was similar, the socioeconomic diversity

WORKING TOWARD K–16 COHERENCE IN CALIFORNIA   49

was very different. "Our kids are poorer . . . first generation," explained one of her Bridgeport teaching colleagues. Another teacher explained that a consequence of being first-generation college and poorer is that families are more reluctant to send their children away to college.

Bridgeport students complained about the lack of college counseling and guidance. Like the students at Applewood and Haverhill, the students at Bridgeport complained that the only time they had contact with a school counselor was when they needed to change their course schedule or to register for classes. The counseling, students recognized, was limited. As one student said, "A lot of times our counselors don't tell us the right things. They tell us what we should get for certain colleges but not necessarily the college we want."

Analysis of the Case Study Research

In our analysis we look at student aspiration for postsecondary education as well as student college knowledge (McDonough, 1994) in terms of students' understanding of tuition costs, curricular requirements, placement tests, and admissions selection criteria. Student aspiration and college knowledge are analyzed for differences by grade (ninth versus eleventh), race, SES, school performance, academic track, and use of key agents. We also present a brief analysis of parent college knowledge based on the data collected from parent surveys.

STUDENT ASPIRATIONS FOR POSTSECONDARY INSTITUTIONS. In our survey we asked students to state their interest in attending various postsecondary institutions. We allowed students to check as many as they wished of the ten types of institutions that we listed on our survey.

Aspirations by Grade. As Table 2.2 shows, the juniors in our sample expressed greater interest than the freshmen in attending three institutions:

Table 2.2. Postsecondary Aspirations by Grade.

Institution	Ninth Grade ($n = 214$)	Eleventh Grade ($n = 237$)	Total ($n = 451$)	t-Test p-Value
Local community college	19.6%	39.2%	29.9%	.000
UC Davis	51.4	45.1	48.1	.185
Other UC campus	42.5	52.3	47.7	.038
CSU Sacramento	27.6	36.2	26.8	.737
Other CSU campus	19.2	27.4	23.5	.039

Note: *Subgroup samples may differ from the total due to missing data.*

a local community college, UC campuses other than UC Davis, and CSU campuses other than CSU Sacramento. The largest difference by grade was associated with interest in community college. Eleventh graders were nearly twice as likely to include the two-year institution on their list of postsecondary options. One explanation for this difference in postsecondary aspiration is that juniors may have greater knowledge in terms of institutional variety (schools farther from home) and of their objective chances for admission across institutions, thereby including their local community college as a "safety school."

Aspirations by Race. Small cell sizes in the cross-tabulations make it difficult to render strong inferences with respect to racial differences. However, we feel it is instructive to note a few interesting trends. In Table 2.3, we find that white, Latino, and multiracial students were the most likely to include their local community college on their postsecondary options list. The students in all three Asian American subcategories, along with multiracial students, showed a greater interest in UC Davis than the other racial groups. Chinese American students by far showed the greatest interest in other UC campuses. Furthermore, Southeast Asians showed the most interest in CSU Sacramento. Finally, African American students were least interested in other CSU campuses, while white students were the most interested. In fact, the interest in other CSU campuses among African Americans was less than one-third that of white students.

Aspirations by SES. Aspiration trends with SES are shown in Table 2.4. One expected trend was confirmed: high-SES students showed greater interest in UC Davis (61 percent) than did low-SES (45 percent) and middle-SES students (48 percent). Similarly, and perhaps more telling, interest in other UC campuses increased with SES, with high-SES students aspiring to these schools at twice the rate of their low-SES counterparts. The opposite is true for interest in the less selective CSU Sacramento. Forty percent of low-SES students indicated interest compared to only 23 percent of high-SES students. Finally, mid-SES students indicated the greatest interest in their local community college (35 percent), which was significantly greater than the aspirations among students from high-SES families.

Aspirations by Grade Point Average. Figure 2.1 shows students' interest in UC, CSU, and local community colleges as a function of students' self-reported GPA. Interest in community colleges and GPA was inversely proportional; the stronger the student's GPA, the less interested he or she was

Table 2.3. Postsecondary Aspirations by Race.

Institution Aspired to	African American (n = 48)	White (n = 120)	Latino (n = 44)	Chinese American (n = 54)	Southeast Asian (n = 52)	Other Asian (n = 59)	Multiracial (n = 69)	Total (n = 450)
Local community college	25.0%	34.2%	34.1%	25.9%	21.2%	28.8%	36.2%	30.0%
UC Davis	33.3	40.8	45.5	57.4	53.8	57.6	53.6	48.0
Other UC campus	29.2	54.2	38.6	70.4	30.8	49.2	49.3	47.6
CSU Sacramento	27.1	22.5	27.3	22.2	36.5	32.2	23.2	26.4
Other CSU campus	10.4	35.0	22.7	16.7	17.3	16.9	30.4	23.6

Note: *Subgroup samples may differ from the total due to missing data.*

Table 2.4. Postsecondary Aspirations by SES.

Institution Aspired to	Low SES (n = 62)	Middle SES (n = 121)	High SES (n = 130)	t-Tests (p-Values) Low-Middle	Middle-High	Low-High
Local community college	32.3%	34.7%	21.5%	.728	.021	.124
UC Davis	45.2	47.9	60.8	.721	.042	.043
Other UC campus	32.3	49.6	66.2	.023	.007	.000
CSU Sacramento	40.3	28.9	23.1	.106	.305	.014
Other CSU campus	22.6	24.8	28.5	.740	.513	.379

Note: *Subgroup samples may differ from the total due to missing data.*

**Figure 2.1. Interest in UCD, CSUS, and CCC,
Ninth and Eleventh Graders.**

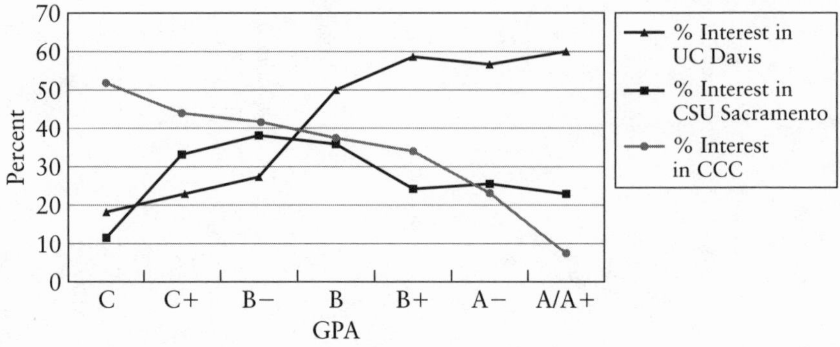

in attending a community college. Fifty-two percent of the C students were interested in the community colleges, while only about 7 percent of the A and A+ students were interested in these colleges.

In terms of four-year options, students in our focus groups consistently reported that applicants for admission needed a higher GPA to gain admission to UCD than to CSUS. On the surveys, interest in both campuses increased with GPA from C to B−. Within this grade range, interest in CSUS was generally greater than interest in UC. However, for students with a GPA of B or better, interest in UCD was consistently greater than interest in CSUS, and interest in CSUS decreased with GPA while interest in UCD increased. These trends may indicate students' awareness of UC's eligibility index, which sets the lower boundary for eligibility at a 2.8 grade point average (B−).

These trends are generally consistent even when comparing students' aspirations across school performance. Figure 2.2 shows interest in UCD by school performance and self-reported GPA. However, interest in UCD for students with C+ and B− averages was markedly lower in the high-performing schools, and the jump in interest at the B level is greatest in those schools as well. This difference suggests that the students in high-performing schools have better information of UCD requirements and are more realistic about their college aspirations.

Aspirations by School Performance, Academic Track, and Use of Key Agents. Interest in the UC campuses (Davis and other UC campuses) was significantly greater for students in high- and middle-performing schools than in low-performing schools. Only about 37 percent of students in

Figure 2.2. Interest in UC Davis by School Performance.

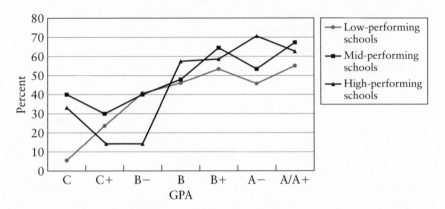

low-performing schools aspired to UC campuses other than Davis, compared to about 54 percent among students in higher-performing schools. In other words, students in the higher-performing schools appear to be more mobile in their aspirations for more selective institutions. Interestingly, while there was no significant difference in interest in CSU Sacramento by school performance, there were significant differences in interest in the other CSU campuses. In this case, the more mobile students are those at the middle-performing schools, who were twice as likely as were students at the low- or high-performing schools to indicate interest in other CSU campuses (37 percent versus about 18 percent).

We divided students into three academic categories or tracks, depending on the level of their current math and English courses: (1) nonhonors (neither math nor English honors), (2) single honors (either math or English honors), and (3) dual honors (both math and English honors). Analyses of aspirations by academic track confirmed some expected trends. Interest in local community colleges decreased with higher academic track; dual-honors students indicated a greater interest in the UC campuses than did nonhonors students; and single- and dual-honors students indicated a greater interest in other UC campuses than did nonhonors students. The contrasts are stark. Compared to nonhonors students, dual-honors students are 59 percent less likely to aspire to a community college (18 percent versus 44 percent), 51 percent more likely to aspire to UC Davis (59 percent versus 39 percent), and nearly one and a half times more likely to aspire to a UC campus other than UC Davis (64 percent versus 26 percent). Like those in high-performing schools, higher-track students appear to be more mobile and selective in their postsecondary aspirations.

Use of a key agent is defined as speaking at least once to a parent, teacher, counselor, or higher education outreach officer about college admission requirements. As shown in Table 2.5, a greater percentage of students spoke to their teachers than to their counselors. Juniors had significantly greater contact than freshmen with their teachers, counselors, and college representatives. The greatest difference between freshmen and juniors is that fewer than half of the freshmen had spoken to a counselor about college admission, whereas over three-fourths of the juniors had done so. Overall, parents remained as the primary information agent used by students.

Aspirations of students who reported use or nonuse of the four key agents varied somewhat. Students who had talked to a parent, teacher, or college representative at least once about college admission requirements were significantly more likely to show interest in the UC campuses. Teachers appear to be an important source of information to students; students who had spoken to a teacher were significantly more likely to indicate interest in attending a four-year institution. For example, among those who spoke to teachers about admissions, over 50 percent aspired to UC campuses other than Davis, compared to just 35 percent among students who did not consult a teacher. An even greater difference is evident for aspirations to CSU Sacramento, in which interest nearly doubled among students who spoke to teachers (30 percent versus 16 percent). Surprisingly, interest in each type of institution was not significantly different between those students who had and who had not spoken to a high school counselor.

Summary of Aspirations. To summarize briefly, in terms of postsecondary aspirations, students of Asian descent from higher-SES families,

Table 2.5. Use of Key Agents by Grade.

| Key Agent | Percentage Talking About Admissions at Least Once | | | |
	Ninth Grade ($n = 214$)	Eleventh Grade ($n = 237$)	Total ($n = 451$)	t-Test p-Value
Parents	91.6%	92.4%	92.0%	.740
A teacher	72.3	84.9	79.0	.001
A counselor	44.9	76.9	61.7	.000
A college representative	29.6	39.2	34.7	.032

Note: *Subgroup samples may differ from the total due to missing data.*

in higher academic tracks, from higher-performing schools, and with higher GPAs displayed greater aspiration for the most selective tier, the UC, and displayed greater geographical mobility in their aspirations as well.

STUDENT KNOWLEDGE OF COLLEGE TUITION. Our survey asked students to provide a dollar amount for their "best guess of the cost of tuition for one year" at UC Davis, CSU Sacramento, and their local community college, excluding "the cost of books, housing, [and] other expenses." For the 1998–1999 academic year, UC Davis charged an annual tuition of roughly $4,000, CSU Sacramento charged roughly $2,000, and the community colleges charged roughly $300. Across the board, students tended to overestimate these costs. On average, our sample of students estimated annual tuition costs of nearly $30,000 for UC Davis, nearly $27,000 for CSU Sacramento, and just over $10,000 for a local community college. When we informed students in the focus groups of the actual costs, they laughed in disbelief at what they perceived as great affordability. When asked why they had overestimated these costs, one student in our focus groups expressed, "Because people make such a big deal of it." The following analysis looks more closely at students' cost estimations.

Knowledge of Tuition by Grade. Table 2.6 displays the mean tuition estimates as well as the proportions of students estimating tuition within two times or over five times the actual cost.

Defining "gross overestimation" as guessing beyond five times the actual cost of tuition and "within target" as guessing within twice the actual cost, a greater percentage of students grossly overestimated the cost for community college than for the CSU and UC. Yet a greater percentage of students (40 percent) were within target for UC Davis than the other two sectors. One explanation for the latter result is that the ranges for all three institutions were so high that the students were more likely to guess within target for the highest-priced institution (UC Davis) and more likely to grossly overestimate the lowest-priced institution (community college).

That ninth graders possessed relatively less accurate information than their older peers concerning college access and entry is not surprising, and even somewhat expected, given that many are not even thinking about college yet. Therefore, in the subgroup analyses that follow for knowledge of tuition, admissions policy, and placement policy, we examine eleventh graders only.

Table 2.6. Knowledge of Tuition by Grade.

Institution	Ninth Grade ($n = 198$)	Eleventh Grade ($n = 223$)	Total ($n = 421$)	t-Test p-Value
UC Davis				
Mean estimate	$39,599	$21,429	$29,974	.016
% within twice the actual cost	41.1	39.7	40.4	.753
% more than five times the actual cost	22.9	16.5	19.5	.083
CSU Sacramento				
Mean estimate	$39,376	$15,170	$26,548	.001
% within twice the actual cost	32.7	31.6	32.2	.810
% more than five times the actual cost	37.9	26.6	31.9	.010
Local community college				
Mean estimate	$15,147	$5,744	$10,151	.010
% within twice the actual cost	27.1	34.2	30.9	.105
% more than five times the actual cost	56.5	42.6	49.2	.003

Note: *Subgroup samples may differ from the total due to missing data.*

Knowledge of Tuition by Race and SES. Among the seven racial/ethnic categories, Southeast Asian eleventh graders were the most likely to overestimate the three tuition costs. Although Latinos also overestimated the costs, they offered mean estimates that were closest to the actual values. Knowledge of tuition appeared to increase with SES (see Table 2.7). Low-SES students had mean estimates that were statistically greater than the mean estimates of high-SES students. As with the analyses of aspiration, the differences were stark. For low-SES students, the estimates for UC Davis and CSU Sacramento were roughly four times greater than the estimates for high-SES students. High-SES students were statistically more likely to guess within twice the actual costs of UC Davis and CSUS than their middle-SES eleventh-grade counterparts. For the local community college, the mean estimate for low-SES students was over six times greater than the mean estimates for high-SES students and four times greater than the mean estimates for middle-SES students.

Knowledge of Tuition by School Performance, Academic Track, and Use of Key Agents. In our analysis by school performance, an important and

Table 2.7. Knowledge of Tuition by SES, Eleventh Graders.

Institution	Low SES ($n = 36$)	Middle SES ($n = 59$)	High SES ($n = 62$)	Low-Middle	Middle-High	Low-High
				t-Test (*p*-Value)		
UC Davis						
Mean estimate	$47,391	$16,521	$12,095	.068	.751	.034
% within twice actual cost	38.9	25.9	50.8	.202	.005	.238
% more than five times cost	19.4	12.1	13.1	.358	.865	.431
CSU Sacramento						
Mean estimate	$31,561	$12,942	$8,430	.054	.573	.016
% within twice actual cost	27.8	20.7	41.0	.464	.016	.169
% more than five times cost	36.1	27.6	19.7	.363	.329	.078
Local community college						
Mean estimate	$17,162	$4,297	$2,675	.031	.742	.014
% within twice actual cost	25.0	32.8	37.7	.440	.202	.569
% more than five times cost	61.1	39.7	36.1	.044	.690	.018

Note: *Subgroup samples may differ from the total due to missing data.*

somewhat surprising finding is that students in the middle-performing schools generally provided tuition estimates that were closer to the actual values than those provided by students in high- and low-performing schools. The only significant difference in the means, however, was for community college tuition. The mean tuition estimate among students in low-performing schools ($9,021 per year) was over four times the mean for students in middle-performing schools ($1,939 per year). These students were also the most likely to overestimate grossly the cost of UC Davis and community colleges. Similarly, students in the high-performing schools were generally most likely to fall in the within-target range for tuition estimates. However, the only significant difference among our eleventh graders was found for tuition estimates to CSUS, where 44 percent of students in high-performing schools were within target compared to only 19 percent among those in middle-performing schools.

By academic track, nonhonors eleventh graders were more likely than their single- and dual-honors counterparts to overestimate tuition costs for the three institutions. For each postsecondary option, tuition estimates by nonhonors students were at least twice those offered by single- and dual-honors students. Statistically significant differences were found only among CSU Sacramento estimates, however.

Finally, our analysis by use of key agent suggests that key agents influence students' knowledge of college tuition. Students who spoke to their parents about college admissions were three times more likely to guess within twice the cost of CSU Sacramento and community college, compared to students who did not speak to their parents. Similarly, a majority (about 70 percent) of students who had not spoken to their parents about college admission requirements grossly overestimated the cost of community college compared to just 40 percent among students who had spoken to their parents. Speaking with high school counselors also appeared to improve students' knowledge of tuition, particularly with respect to CSU Sacramento. Overall, students who spoke to counselors were more likely to provide tuition estimates that were within target and not grossly overestimated for this institution. This pattern does not hold for estimates of UC Davis's costs, however. Students who spoke to their counselors were significantly more likely to grossly overestimate UC Davis's cost than students who did not speak to their counselors.

Summary of Knowledge of College Tuition. In sum, although the trend in responses may indicate that students understood the relative tuition costs among the three types of institutions, they greatly overestimated these costs. Knowledge of tuition appeared to increase with SES; the community college cost estimate for students in low-performing schools was over four times that of their counterparts in middle-performing schools. Nonhonors students were the most likely to overestimate tuition, and students who had spoken to their parents about college admissions were less likely to overestimate costs. Students in focus groups expressed the need to receive more information on college costs. As one student simply put it, "That's what we should talk about more, too, in school is how much it costs."

STUDENT KNOWLEDGE OF CURRICULAR REQUIREMENTS FOR COLLEGE ADMISSION. In our survey, we asked students to write down the number of years of study required for admission to UCD and CSUS in each of six subject areas: English, math, social science, laboratory science, foreign language, and visual and performing arts. For each university, we calculated the percentage of students who guessed the number of years correctly for each subject.

Generally, knowledge of the curricular requirements was extremely poor. Only 2.5 percent of all students in the sample knew the correct number of years for all subject areas required by UCD, and only a handful of students (less than 1 percent) knew the requirements for CSUS. Because of these extremely low levels of knowledge, we also constructed a more liberal measure: the percentage of students who provided the correct number of years required for at least half (three out of six) of the subject areas. In terms of the latter measure, students knew more about CSUS's subject requirements (about 50 percent got three or more correct) than UCD's requirements (only 29 percent got three or more correct). In focus groups, students consistently expressed that UC Davis was more difficult to gain admission to (it had more requirements) than CSU Sacramento.

Students in focus groups expressed some confusion as to what was required for high school graduation and what was required for admission to the CSU and UC. But college-bound students focused more on, and therefore displayed greater knowledge about, what it took to gain admission to college than what it took merely to graduate from high school. Overall, only a few students were familiar with the term "a through f" and its meaning, but most students mentioned having seen a list of university requirements that their high school provided them.

Many students spoke of a booklet given to them by their school counselors during class scheduling that listed the UC and CSU course requirements. Most understood that the universities expected a few more years of study than their high school in certain subject areas, but only a few could pinpoint these differences. Students expressed some confusion, however, as to what the universities required and what the universities recommended. Only a few students were able to articulate, for example, that their high school required only one year of foreign language, whereas the universities required two, and that their high school required two years of math, whereas the universities required three years of college preparatory math (beyond basic math and prealgebra).

Knowledge of Curricular Requirements by Grade. Table 2.8 shows the percentage of ninth and eleventh graders who gave the correct number of years among six subjects required for admission to UCD and CSUS. Overall, the two subject requirements that students knew best were for English and foreign language. The math requirement was the third most accurately reported requirement for UCD but behind visual and performing arts for CSUS. Juniors generally had better knowledge of the curricular requirements than freshmen.

Table 2.8. Knowledge of Curricular Requirements by Grade.

Course Requirement	Ninth Grade ($n = 214$)	Eleventh Grade ($n = 237$)	Total ($n = 451$)	t-Test p-Value
UC Davis				
% know English requirement (four years)	80.4	91.1	86.0	.001
% know foreign language requirement (two years)	47.2	53.6	50.6	.176
% know math requirement (three years)	31.3	50.6	41.5	.000
% know social science requirement (two years)	32.2	29.5	30.8	.536
% know lab science requirement (two years)	22.0	34.6	28.6	.003
% know visual/performing arts requirement (none)	2.8	2.5	2.7	.858
% know three or more of six requirements	36.9	56.1	47.0	.000
CSU Sacramento				
% know English requirement (four years)	69.6	80.2	75.2	.010
% know foreign language requirement (two years)	57.0	73.4	65.6	.000
% know visual/performing arts requirement (one year)	46.1	51.9	49.2	.233
% know math requirement (three years)	35.5	51.5	43.9	.001
% know lab science requirement (one year)	9.3	9.3	9.3	.982
% know social science requirement (one year)	11.2	7.2	9.1	.137
% know three or more of six	42.5	61.1	52.3	.000

Note: *Subgroup samples may differ from the total due to missing data.*

The data in Table 2.8 also show that knowledge of English requirements (over 75 percent correct) was much stronger than knowledge of mathematics requirements (under 50 percent correct). To explore how inaccurate students' estimates of the mathematics requirements were, we noted whether responses were underestimated or overestimated. Table 2.9 shows that students generally tended to overestimate rather than underestimate the three-year math requirement. Nearly half of the students

Table 2.9. Knowledge of Math Requirements by Grade.

Knowledge of Math Requirement	Ninth Grade ($n = 208$)	Eleventh Grade ($n = 236$)	Total ($n = 444$)	t-Test p-Value
UC Davis				
% underestimate (less than three years)	12.1	7.3	9.5	.088
% correct (three years math)	32.5	51.7	42.7	.000
% overestimate (more than three years)	55.3	41.0	47.7	.003
CSU Sacramento				
% underestimate (less than three years)	19.2	24.2	21.8	.194
% correct (three years math)	36.5	52.1	44.8	.001
% overestimate (more than three years)	44.2	23.7	33.3	.000

Note: *Subgroup samples may differ from the total due to missing data.*

overestimated the number of years for math for UC Davis, and one-third overestimated the number of years for math for CSU Sacramento. Moreover, freshmen were more likely than juniors to overestimate the number of years needed for both campuses. In other words, students tended to assume that the English and math requirements were identical.

Knowledge of Curricular Requirements by Race. Because juniors generally know the curricular requirements better than freshmen do, all remaining analyses include eleventh graders only. As shown in Table 2.10, African American students were among the least likely to report correctly the number of years of math and English required for each campus and for knowing at least three of the six subject requirements for CSU Sacramento. Chinese American students displayed the most accurate knowledge overall of UCD curricular requirements and were the most likely to know three of the six CSU requirements. Latino and Southeast Asian students appeared to have some specific but incomplete knowledge. For example, although 87 percent of Latinos knew the CSUS English requirement (the highest among all groups), only about 22 percent knew at least three of the subject requirements (the lowest among all groups). Similarly, although Southeast Asian students were among the most likely to know the UCD requirements (overall and particularly the math requirements),

Table 2.10. Knowledge of Curricular Requirements by Race, Eleventh Graders.

Course Requirement	African American (*n* = 19)	White (*n* = 67)	Latino (*n* = 23)	Chinese American (*n* = 29)	Southeast Asian (*n* = 29)	Other Asian (*n* = 29)	Multiracial (*n* = 37)	Total (*n* = 235)
UC Davis								
% know English (four years)	84.2	92.5	95.7	96.4	89.3	96.6	94.4	93.1
% know math (three years)	42.1	53.7	47.8	60.7	57.1	48.3	50.0	51.7
% know three or more of six	36.8	32.8	30.4	44.8	37.9	34.5	24.3	34.5
CSU Sacramento								
% know English (four years)	78.9	86.6	87.0	79.3	72.4	80.0	75.0	80.9
% know math (three years)	44.4	59.7	56.5	44.8	44.8	56.7	50.0	52.1
% know three or more of six	42.1	61.2	21.7	72.4	62.1	62.1	32.4	53.2

Note: Subgroup samples may differ from the total due to missing data.

these students were the least likely to provide the correct number of English courses required for CSUS.

Since only about half of the students knew the math requirements, whereas well over 80 percent of the students knew the English requirements, we ran further analysis on the responses for math alone. African Americans were the most likely to overestimate the requirements. In addition, Latinos and Southeast Asians were the most likely to underestimate the math requirements for UCD, while Chinese Americans and Southeast Asians were the most likely to underestimate the math requirements for CSUS.

Knowledge of Curricular Requirements by School Performance, Academic Track, and Use of Key Agent. No significant difference was found in knowledge among the three school performance levels with respect to the math and English requirements for UCD. For CSUS, students in high-performing schools were more likely than their counterparts in lower-performing schools to know that four years of high school English are required for admission (90 percent versus 79 percent). Patterns are slightly different when looking at knowledge of all the requirements. Students in the high-performing schools were again more likely to know at least three of the six curricular requirements for UCD (67 percent) than their counterparts in middle-performing (48 percent) and low-performing schools (54 percent), but for the CSUS requirements, the highest proportion of students who knew three or more of the course requirements were among those at low-performing schools (65 percent). Fewer than half of the students in high-performing schools could correctly name at least three of the six course requirements at CSUS.

Looking specifically at knowledge of the math requirements by school performance, we found that students in low-performing schools were more likely than students in middle-performing schools to underestimate the required number of years of math for UC Davis and CSU Sacramento. Furthermore, students in middle-performing schools were the least likely to underestimate these requirements, but these students were also the most likely to overestimate these requirements as well. These data suggest that students in middle-performing schools receive less information and therefore have less knowledge about the courses needed for admission to the four-year colleges.

Academic track and knowledge of curricular requirements were directly related: dual-honors students displayed the most knowledge, while non-honors students displayed the least. Over 60 percent of dual-honors students knew at least three of the course requirements for UCD, and over

70 percent knew them for CSUS. Fewer than half of the nonhonors students possessed this same level of knowledge. Interestingly, dual-honors students were more likely than nonhonors students to underestimate the math requirements for CSUS. This pattern may indicate that the higher-aspiring dual-honors students undervalue the entrance requirements to the less selective CSU campus.

Patterns of knowledge related to interaction with key agents produced mixed results. Students who spoke to teachers at least once about college admission requirements were more likely than those who did not talk to teachers to know the CSUS math requirement exactly and less likely to underestimate this requirement. Students who spoke to a high school counselor were twice as likely to underestimate the number of years of the CSUS math requirement, and those who had spoken to a college representative were three times more likely to underestimate the number of years of math required for UC Davis.

Summary of Knowledge of Curricular Requirements. In sum, students possessed more knowledge of the course requirements for CSUS than for UCD. Based on survey data as well as focus group responses, students in honors courses displayed more specific knowledge than students who were in college preparatory courses. Furthermore, students in the high-performing schools were the most knowledgeable about UC Davis's requirements, and students in the low-performing schools were the most knowledgeable of CSU Sacramento's requirements. Overall, students indicated the greatest understanding of the English requirements and much less understanding of the mathematics requirements.

STUDENT KNOWLEDGE OF UNIVERSITY PLACEMENT EXAMS. Our survey asked students to identify the subject areas in which CSUS and UCD test students for placement. The question read in the following way: "In what subjects does CSU Sacramento and UCD test new students to place them in college-level courses?" Students could mark any number of the following five subjects: English, mathematics, laboratory science, foreign language, and visual and performing arts. The correct answer is that both universities conduct placement tests in math and in English only. UCD administers the Subject A exam for English placement and the MDTP. CSUS administers the ELM test and the EPT.

Knowledge of Placement Exams by Grade. When counting the students who had indicated that each university required an English or math placement exam irrespective of their answers for the other third subjects, knowledge of the exams appears extremely high (see Table 2.11). The

Table 2.11. Knowledge of University Placement Exams by Grade.

Placement Exam	Ninth Grade (n = 214)	Eleventh Grade (n = 239)	Total (n = 453)	t-Test p-Value
UC Davis				
% know English placement	92.5	95.4	94.0	.206
% know math placement	93.0	94.9	94.0	.389
% know English and math (both and only)	10.3	23.6	17.3	.000
CSU Sacramento				
% know English placement	93.9	95.8	94.9	.376
% know math placement	93.0	93.7	93.3	.773
% know English and math (both and only)	16.8	39.7	28.8	.000

Note: *Subgroup samples may differ from the total due to missing data.*

greater than 90 percent figures, however, are most likely a result of students' assuming that colleges require placement tests in all subjects. The number of students who knew the policies accurately—that exams are required only for math and English—was actually quite low. Fewer than one in five (17 percent) students knew the UCD placement policy at that level, and less than a third knew the CSUS policy. Eleventh graders were more than twice as likely as ninth graders to know that math and English were the only two subjects tested at either state university.

Knowledge of Placement Exams by Race. Table 2.12 shows eleventh graders' knowledge of placement exams by race. In contrast to African Americans' relative lack of knowledge of curricular requirements mentioned earlier, African American students displayed the greatest knowledge of the two placement exam requirements for UCD and were equally knowledgeable to students of other races of the two exams required by CSUS. Chinese Americans were the least knowledgeable about UCD and Southeast Asians were the least knowledgeable about CSUS.

Knowledge of Placement Exams by School Performance, Academic Track, and Use of Key Agent. In general, knowledge of the English and math placement exams at the two universities was fairly low and not differentiated by type of school, track, or key agent. Similar to the previous analyses, knowledge of the two CSUS exams appears greater among students than of the two UCD exam requirements. Surprisingly, eleventh graders who did not talk to a high school counselor about admissions were more

Table 2.12. Knowledge of Required University Placement Exams (English and Math) by Race, Eleventh Graders.

English and Math Placement Exam	African American (*n* = 19)	White (*n* = 67)	Latino (*n* = 23)	Chinese American (*n* = 29)	Southeast Asian (*n* = 29)	Other Asian (*n* = 29)	Multiracial (*n* = 37)	Total (*n* = 235)
% know for UC Davis	22.9	20.0	15.9	11.1	17.3	15.3	15.9	17.3
% know for CSU Sacramento	29.2	29.2	27.3	31.5	21.2	33.9	30.4	29.1

Note: *Subgroup samples may differ from the total due to missing data.*

likely to know the placement policy for UCD (35 percent) than were students who did talk to a high school counselor (20 percent).

Although students displayed a low level of specific knowledge of university placement exams, they expressed the desire to know more about these tests and to be better prepared to take these tests. Teachers and administrators expressed their growing concern over issues of university placement and remediation. Students spoke of their schools' preparing them for the subject requirements and SATs needed for gaining admission to college, but not necessarily helping students to succeed once they are in college. As one English eleventh-grade honors student at Applewood said, "I think they should prepare us better for the placements tests so that we don't get stuck in basic classes. I think we should have the opportunity to know, not necessarily what's on the test, but have a good idea of it so that we know what to expect."

KNOWLEDGE OF COLLEGE ADMISSION SELECTION CRITERIA.   In focus groups, we asked students about the selection criteria for UC Davis and CSU Sacramento. Students generally stated that UCD was more difficult to get into, that students needed a high GPA, and that extracurricular activities mattered. In our survey, we gathered more specific data, asking students to rate the importance of fifteen possible criteria for admission to UC Davis and CSU Sacramento. Using a 5-point scale, students rated each criterion as "single most important," "very important," "moderately important," "minor importance," or "not considered/not important." In order to evaluate these responses, we compared them to rankings of the same criteria provided by the admission directors at the respective institutions.

We examined student knowledge of specific criteria rated by the UCD and CSUS admission offices at the two extremes—as important ("single most important" or "very important") or unimportant ("not considered/not important"). Seven of the fifteen criteria were rated as important by the UC Davis official, and four criteria were rated important by the CSU Sacramento official (see Table 2.13). Three criteria were deemed important by both universities: high school grades, SAT I, and high school courses. Two criteria were deemed unimportant for both universities: ability to pay and race.

Knowledge of Admission Criteria by Grade.   Knowledge of the criteria that might be termed traditional admissions criteria was quite high (see Table 2.13). Eighty to over 90 percent of students correctly marked grades, test scores, high school courses, and, in the case of UCD, the

Table 2.13. Knowledge of Admissions Criteria by Grade.

Admission Criteria	Ninth Grade ($n = 208$)	Eleventh Grade ($n = 237$)	Total ($n = 451$)	t-Test p-Value
% correct for UC Davis				
Important criteria				
High school grades	92.4	92.4	92.4	.994
SAT I or ACT	89.1	88.7	89.9	.882
SAT II	89.6	78.6	83.8	.001
Student's high school curriculum	85.8	82.6	84.1	.340
Application essay	80.2	87.0	83.8	.051
Exceptional talent	57.8	55.7	56.7	.651
Volunteer work	51.7	47.7	49.6	.400
Unimportant criteria				
High school's reputation	4.8	6.4	5.6	.463
Ability to pay	4.7	10.6	7.8	.021
Letters of recommendation	1.0	1.3	1.1	.753
Race	44.8	34.9	39.6	.032
% correct for CSU Sacramento				
Important criteria				
High school grades	87.2	80.7	83.7	.061
Senior year grades	73.5	42.8	57.0	.000
SAT I or ACT	90.0	81.5	85.5	.010
Student's high school curriculum	86.7	77.8	81.5	.007
Unimportant criteria				
Geographical background	27.8	24.7	26.1	.464
SAT II	1.0	2.9	2.0	.137
Rank in class	2.4	2.9	2.7	.707
Ability to pay	3.8	12.2	8.3	.001
Race	44.5	35.2	39.6	.043

Note: *Subgroup samples may differ from the total due to missing data.*

application essay as important selection criteria. Almost half the students failed to recognize senior year grades as an important criterion for CSUS, however. And similar proportions did not view volunteer work and exceptional talent in a specific area as important for UCD. Knowledge of unimportant criteria was extremely poor. Less than 10 percent of the total sample correctly identified three UCD criteria (high school reputation, ability to pay, and letters of recommendation) and three CSUS criteria (SAT II, class rank, and ability to pay) as unimportant. In other words, approximately nine of ten students overestimated the importance of these admission criteria; they placed importance on factors that are not considered in the admissions process. Given the public awareness of efforts to remove race from college admission policies in California, it is not surprising that a sizable proportion of students (about 40 percent) correctly marked it as unimportant. However, the conjugate result suggests that a majority of students still believe race to be a factor of some importance in admission policy at both public institutions.

Table 2.13 also shows that for both universities, juniors were more likely than freshmen to know that a student's ability to pay for college was not an important admission criterion. However, freshmen were more likely to know that race was unimportant. Two additional significant differences were found between freshmen and juniors. First, juniors were slightly more likely than freshmen to know that the application essay was a very important criterion for admission to UCD (87 percent versus 80 percent). Conversely, 90 percent of freshmen knew that the SAT II was an important criterion for admission to UC Davis compared to just 78 percent of the juniors.

Knowledge of Admission Criteria by Race. African Americans were the only group that placed greater importance on standardized test scores (SAT I, SAT II, and ACT) than on high school grades. Among the criteria deemed important by the UC and CSU admissions officers, the importance of volunteer work was underestimated, especially among white students. Although the ability to pay for college is not considered in UCD admission policy, all of the multiracial eleventh graders in our sample gave some importance to this factor, and even the group that displayed the most knowledge, Chinese Americans, erroneously cited ability to pay as an important factor at a rate of over 75 percent.

The majority of all racial groups continued to believe that race is considered in admission. The previous beneficiaries of affirmative action, however, were among the most likely to maintain that belief. For the UCD criteria, for example, about 75 percent of African American students and almost 80 percent of Latinos marked race as a factor in admissions. Similar patterns are evident in the data for CSUS. Two additional patterns in the data are unique to CSUS, however. First, although about 80 percent of all eleventh graders understood the importance of high school grades for admission to CSUS, almost one-third of Chinese American and multiracial students downplayed its importance. The knowledge base was worse for senior year grades. Almost 60 percent of the eleventh-grade sample underestimated their importance, including almost 80 percent of African Americans, the largest among all racial groups.

Knowledge of Admission Criteria by School Performance, Academic Track, and Use of Key Agent. We found significant differences in eleventh graders' knowledge of admissions criteria by school performance. Regarding UC Davis, students in the low-performing schools (82 percent) were less likely than students in the mid- and high-performing schools (91 and 94 percent, respectively) to correctly ascertain the importance of the SAT I and one's high school curriculum. These students were also more likely to underestimate the importance of having an exceptional talent compared to their peers in high-performing schools. Interestingly, students attending the middle-performing schools were the least likely to overestimate the importance of a high school's academic reputation.

Turning to CSUS criteria, only two groups showed significant differences by school performance. Almost 90 percent of the students in middle-performing schools correctly estimated the importance of high school curriculum for admission, a figure greater than that among students in high-performing schools (70 percent). Although the proportion is quite low (about 6 percent), students attending low-performing schools were the most accurate regarding the lack of importance of the SAT II for admission to CSUS.

Analysis by academic track indicates striking differences in knowledge of CSUS criteria among dual-honors and nonhonors students. In every "very important" criterion, students in the highest track undervalued the criterion much more than their nonhonors counterparts. The most striking difference was students' assessment of the importance of senior year grades. Only one-quarter of dual-honors students correctly believed senior grades to be important for admission, compared to about 60 percent among nonhonors students. Conversely, knowledge of UCD admission criteria was distinguished very little by academic track. It is apparent, then, that the significant undervaluing of CSUS admission criteria by dual-honors students is likely due to their low estimation of the university's academic competitiveness. Finally, in our analysis of admission selection criteria knowledge by use of key agent, we found some significant differences. Surprisingly, students who had not spoken to a parent were much more likely to understand that ability to pay did not matter for admission to both universities. Those who had not spoken to a parent about admissions were greater than three times more likely to understand this criterion for UCD (33 percent versus 9 percent) and more than twice as likely for the CSUS policy (29 percent versus 11 percent). A similar trend was apparent with regard to use of a counselor and the "ability-to-pay" criterion for UC Davis. "Negative" parent effects were also evident for knowledge of the CSUS policy regarding SAT I and class rank, where students were again more likely to understand the importance of the admission criterion if they did not speak to a parent about admissions. There were two expected trends or positive relationships with use of a key agent. Students who had spoken to a teacher or a college representative were more likely to correctly understand the importance of the application essay for UC Davis, and counselors appeared to have a positive impact on understanding one's class rank in the admission process for CSUS.

PARENT KNOWLEDGE OF POSTSECONDARY POLICIES. We looked specifically at parent knowledge of tuition costs and curricular requirements at UCD and CSUS. In general, we found no evidence of a relationship between student knowledge and parent knowledge. Parents' estimates of tuition were more accurate than students' estimates, although their knowledge of curricular requirements was less accurate.

Parent Knowledge of Tuition. In terms of mean estimates, parents were much closer to actual tuition costs than were students. Still, compared to actual annual tuition of approximately $4,000 (UCD), $2,000 (CSUS), and $300 (local community college), parents' estimates were still greatly overestimated at about $16,000, $11,000, and $5,000, respectively. Unlike the analysis of the student data, there were no significant differences in tuition estimates between parents of ninth graders and parents of eleventh graders. Across SES and school performance categories, we observed the expected patterns. Parents from higher SES backgrounds were much more on target with estimates of tuition compared to mid- and low-SES parents. Similarly, parents of children attending low-performing schools were also most likely to overestimate tuition costs at any of the three public institutions.

Parent Knowledge of Curricular Requirements. Parent knowledge of the curricular requirements for UCD and CSUS was no better, and perhaps a bit weaker, compared to the student responses. The number of parents who knew the requirements exactly (the required number of years for all six subjects) was exceedingly low. Only 4 of 433 parents knew all the requirements for UC Davis, and just 5 knew the requirements for CSU Sacramento. Similar to students, the English and foreign language requirements were the two that parents knew the best, but in lower proportions compared to students. For example, nearly 90 percent of the students in our sample correctly reported the four-year English requirement for UCD, compared to just two-thirds of the parents. Also, fewer parents appeared to know the math requirement. Although few parents knew all of the curricular requirements for either university, 40 percent knew at least three of the UCD requirements, and about 43 percent knew at least three of the CSUS requirements. These proportions were slightly higher among the student responses.

We already noted that students incorrectly reported math requirements because they tended to overestimate the number of years required for admission, particularly for UCD. Most parents also overestimated the math requirement for UCD but tended to underestimate the requirement for CSUS. Given that the math requirement for both universities is three years, parents may be erroneously assuming a higher requirement for the more selective UC campus, while many students assume the maximum number of math courses (four) is required for either school. Correlations between the number of requirements guessed correctly by parents and students were also somewhat weak.

Surprisingly, we found no significant differences by school performance and by SES for parent knowledge of three or more curricular requirements for either university. One additional distinguishing factor surfaced in our analysis, however. Parents who reported receiving course requirement information from their child's school were significantly more likely to know at least three of the CSUS requirements compared to those who said they had not received information (49 percent versus 34 percent, respectively). A similar but smaller difference regarding UCD requirements was also evident but not statistically significant.

Summary of Case Study Findings

If level of aspiration can be measured by the selectivity of the institutions in which students show interest, then students of Asian descent, from higher-SES families, in higher academic tracks, from higher-performing schools, and with higher GPAs displayed higher aspirations. These students accurately perceived that UC Davis was more difficult to gain admission to than CSU Sacramento and that CSU Sacramento was more difficult to gain admission to than their local community college. More specifically, students realized that they needed a higher GPA and stronger SAT scores to gain admission to UC Davis.

In terms of tuition knowledge, although students understood the relative costs of the three types of institutions, they greatly overestimated the costs. Students in low-performing schools were most likely to overestimate grossly the cost of UC Davis and community colleges, and students in the high-performing schools were most likely to fall within the target range.

As far as knowledge of curricular requirements is concerned, we found that students knew more about Sacramento State's requirements than UC Davis's. On our surveys and in our focus groups, students in honors courses displayed more specific knowledge than did students in college preparatory courses. Furthermore, students in the high-performing schools were the most knowledgeable about UC Davis's requirements, while students in the low-performing schools were the most knowledgeable about CSU Sacramento's requirements. Finally, students realized that four years of high school English were required but were less aware of the three-year mathematics requirement. In fact, one-third overestimated the math requirement for CSU, and nearly half overestimated the requirement for UC.

Students generally had a poor understanding of the English and math placement exams at the two universities. Less than 30 percent of students knew about Sacramento State's placement exams, and less than 20 percent of students knew about UC Davis's exams.

Students in the high- and mid-performing schools displayed a greater understanding of admission selection criteria than did students in the low-performing schools. Specifically, they realized that high school curriculum and SAT I scores were important factors for admission. Surprisingly, non-honors students were more likely than dual-honors students to understand the importance of high school curriculum and SAT I scores. We speculate that this disparity was caused by dual-honors students' dismissing the selectivity of the CSU system and having low aspirations for CSU, and therefore downplaying the importance of the admission requirement. This speculation is substantiated by the fact that honors students expressed in focus groups that it was relatively easy to gain admission to the CSU.

Overall, 60 percent of all students (including 66 percent of eleventh graders) gave importance to race as a criterion for admission to UC Davis and Sacramento State. Furthermore, 92 percent of all juniors believed incorrectly that ability to pay for college was a factor in UC Davis's and Sacramento State's admission selection process. Both institutions' information on financial aid provided detailed advice on how to apply for aid but made no mention of the fact that a student's ability to pay had no bearing on the university's decision to admit that student. In fact, neither institution's admission material stated explicitly that their admission selection procedures were need blind.

Finally, we compared student knowledge and parent knowledge and found no evidence of a relationship between the two. Parents' estimates of tuition were more accurate than student estimates, however, while their knowledge of curricular requirements was less accurate.

Policy Recommendations

The keys to better preparing students for college are disseminating college information and motivating students, developing students academically, and building collaborative administrative links.

First, increasing college knowledge requires informing students better of curricular requirements, college selection criteria (for example, that UC Berkeley weighs the SAT II more heavily than the SAT I), college placement tests, and college costs for all target colleges and universities among each high school's seniors. In doing so, all students should have access to disseminators of college information. Important sources of information include not only parents and counselors but, and perhaps more important, teachers. Second, developing students academically means increasing eligibility by ensuring that students successfully complete a college preparatory curriculum and are well prepared for standardized testing for admission and placement. Such efforts would also help to decrease remediation and increase graduation rates in college. Finally, building collaborative administrative links between K–12 and higher education requires that all sectors cooperate to align curricula and assessments that would promote higher levels of student success.

In working toward the establishing these components, we offer these policy recommendations:

- ○ Include among the duties and responsibilities of all teachers the dissemination of current college policies, procedures, and general facts.

- ○ Encourage colleges of education to require college knowledge and counseling course requirements for the completion of secondary teaching credentials.

- ○ Encourage school districts to implement professional development programs for principals and teachers that focus on college knowledge. This will help ensure that school personnel have up-to-date information on admissions and placement criteria for California's public postsecondary systems.

- ○ Create district-postsecondary partnerships to ensure a smoother academic trajectory from high school to college. Aligning K–12 and higher education will help reduce remediation.

REFERENCES

American Civil Liberties Union. "Minority Students Sue UC Berkeley for Discrimination Saying Admissions Process Violates Federal Civil Rights Laws." 1999. [http://www.aclu.org/news/1999/n020299b.html].

California Department of Education. *Standardized Testing and Reporting Program.* 1999. [http://star.cde.ca.gov/star99/index.html].

California Education Round Table. *Standards for California High School Graduates.* Sacramento: California Education Round Table, 1997.

California Legislative Analysts Office. *K–12 Master Plan: Starting the Process.* Sacramento: California Legislative Analysts Office, 1999.

California Postsecondary Education Commission. *The Master Plan, Then and Now: Policies of the 1960–1975 Master Plan for Higher Education in Light of 1993 Realities.* Sacramento: California Postsecondary Education Commission, 1993.

California Postsecondary Education Commission. "California Community College Information." 2003. [http://www.cpec.ca.gov/CollegeGuide/CCCSystemInformation.asp].

Castaneda et al. v. The Regents of the University of California, U.S. District Court for the Northern District of California, Civil Action No. C. 99-0525, 1999.

Ed Source. How California Compares: *Indicators and Implications for Our Public Schools.* Palo Alto, Calif.: Ed Source, Nov. 1998.

Intersegmental Coordinating Committee. *Committee Report on K–18 Curricular Issues.* Sacramento, Calif.: Intersegmental Coordinating Committee, Dec. 1996.

Intersegmental Coordinating Committee. Standards for California High School Graduates in Mathematics and English. Sacramento, Calif.: Intersegmental Coordinating Committee, 1997.

Kirst, M. W. "A Babel of Standards: Students Face a Confusing Array of Tests and Assessments." *Crosstalk,* 1999, 7(4), 11.

Le, V., Hamilton, L., and Robyn, A. "Alignment Among Secondary and Post-Secondary Assessments in California." In E. Burr, G. Hayward, B. Fuller, and M.W. Kirst (Eds.) *Crucial Issues in California Education 2000: Are the Reform Pieces Fitting Together?* Berkeley, Calif.: Policy Analysis for California Education, 2000.

McDonough, P. M. "Buying and Selling Higher Education: The Social Construction of the College Applicant." *Journal of Higher Education,* 1994, 65, 427–446.

Pesquiera, R., and Hoff, P. "CSU Committee on Educational Policy: Agenda Items 2 and 3." Long Beach: California State University Office of the Chancellor, July 18–19, 1995.

Siporin, R. L. Address to the University of California Counselors' Conference, Berkeley, Calif., Sept. 1999.

"UC President Calls for Ending SAT I Requirement." *Berkeleyan,* Feb. 21, 2001. [http://www.berkeley.edu/news/berkeleyan/2001/02/21_sat.html].

University of California. *Quick Reference for Counselors 1996–97.* Oakland: University of California Office of the President, 1995.

University of California. *Introducing the University.* Oakland: University of California Office of the President, 1999.

University of California, Davis. "UC Davis by the Numbers." 1999. [http://why.ucdavis.edu/facts_figures.cfm].

3

K–16 TURMOIL IN TEXAS

Andrea Venezia

In the ideal journey, the youth aspires to a certain career and . . .
chooses a course of study in high school, plans further education
or experiences beyond high school, and determines the amount
of training to pursue. . . . For many families—particularly those
whose adults have less education—the "choices" are not choices,
but unknown and missed opportunities. Real choice requires
knowledge that a choice exists, awareness of the alternatives,
and information to make a rational decision.

—Gary Orfield and Faith Paul (1994)

TEXAS PROVIDES UNIQUE legal, political, and educational challenges
related to student transitions from high school to college. It has a large
percentage of its students dropping out of high school (as compared to
other states), a relatively diverse K–12 student body, and many inequities
with regard to who graduates from high school, attends college, and graduates from college. Complicating all of this is a 1996 court ruling that
barred the use of affirmative action for higher education admissions.
These issues provide Texas with formidable challenges in terms of providing students access to college.

This chapter looks at those challenges and at the changes Texas has
made in its K–16 policy in an attempt to meet them. I begin, after briefly

describing the research, by providing some important context for this Texas study. I then describe the governance structures and policies of both the K–12 and higher education systems. In particular, I examine the admission and placement policies at two Texas public universities, the University of Texas at Austin and Southwest Texas State University. I then explore how much Texas high school students, parents, and educators know about the key policies of these two universities. I conclude by showing how misunderstandings can impair students' chances of college success.

Research Methodology

This chapter presents findings and analysis from the Central Texas pilot study for Stanford University's Bridge Project.[1] Research was conducted in 1997 and 1998 to document K–16 student transition policies (at the state and university levels) and analyze K–12 stakeholder understandings of those policies. I interviewed 33 educators, researchers, and administrators at the University of Texas at Austin (UT), Southwest Texas State University (SWT), and in state education agencies; 32 local school and district educators; and surveyed 110 high school, middle school, and junior high school students and 102 of their parents.[2] In addition, focus groups were conducted with all 110 students. The K–12 schools included in the study all feed directly into the two case study universities.

The Texas Context

The 1986 report entitled *A Generation of Failure: The Case for Testing and Remediation in Texas Higher Education,* published by the Texas Higher Education Coordinating Board (THECB), was Texas's equivalent of *A Nation at Risk* (National Commission on Excellence in Education, 1983). It sounded a warning call, stating that out of the approximately 110,000 freshmen who enter Texas's public institutions of higher education (IHE) annually, at least 30,000 could not communicate, read, or do the level of math required for postsecondary education. Like *A Nation at Risk,* it spurred the development of reform-focused committees, panels, reports, and assessment programs. In response to the report, the state developed and implemented the Texas Academic Skills Program (TASP), which includes a test that is currently administered before a college student can take courses at a state IHE.

Remediation and TASP

Remediation in Texas's public colleges and universities, as documented by the THECB, has increased in recent years. In 1996, it found that expenditures for remediation increased from $38.6 million in 1988–1989 to $153.4 million in 1996–1997. Approximately 53 percent of IHE remedial instruction was required for mathematics, 24 percent for writing, and 23 percent for reading. These increases in funding and course work for remediation could be due to increasing numbers of students who need remediation, or it could have occurred because the TASP legislation requires that every student be tested and that remedial courses and advising be offered—something that was not in place previously.

Historically, the majority of college-going students do not meet college-level standards (as defined by the TASP test); only 45 percent of the students who took the TASP in 1997 passed all three sections. Ron Swanson, the THECB's director of the TASP, has noted that Texas's high school students' performance on the SAT and ACT is below the national average.

Every two years since the inception of the program, the state legislature has made large changes to the TASP objectives, the number and kinds of exemptions, when students take the test, and the student populations tested. Thus, it is difficult to conclude much about the success of the TASP. To quote an official in the THECB, it is "virtually meaningless." Given the exemptions for high-achieving students, the results are skewed because only the middle- to low-achieving students are tested by the TASP.

The Challenge of Better Serving Underrepresented Students

The need to improve student preparation and access regarding gaining admission to and persisting in public IHEs is viewed as particularly pressing by many Texas policymakers, notes Don Brown, the former higher education commissioner. Statewide demographic projections show that student groups that have been traditionally underrepresented in higher education will grow faster than will traditionally well-represented student groups. Texas's population is expected to double between 1990 and 2030, with most of the change coming from large increases in the percentage and number of ethnic and racial minority residents. Historically, non-Asian students of color have dropped out of the K–12 education system at disproportionately higher rates—and have enrolled in institutions of higher education at lower rates—than have white, non-Latino students.

In 1995, Latinos, for example, constituted 29 percent of graduating high school students, 20 percent of college freshmen, and approximately 13 percent of freshman at UT, one of the most selective IHEs in the state. While approximately 12 percent of both the graduating classes of high school students and the entering college freshman classes across the state were African American students in 1998, only 3 percent of the University of Texas at Austin's undergraduate class in 1998 were African American. Since education is strongly correlated with income, if these patterns continue, Texas's population will be increasingly poor, with limited opportunities to participate in the state's economy (Murdock, 1998). In addition, the percentage of high school graduates in Texas who enroll in college is approximately 7 percent below the national average. Of those high school graduates who do enroll, about 48 percent graduate, ranking Texas forty-eighth in the nation in college graduation rates.

Hopwood *and the Top Ten Percent Rule*

Exacerbating this policy environment has been the legal environment created by the 1996 *Hopwood* decision and its after-effects. In *Hopwood* v. *Texas,* the plaintiffs claimed that UT Austin's Law School had a pattern of admitting less qualified minority applicants over more qualified white, non-Latino, applicants. The U.S. Fifth Circuit Court of Appeals ruled in favor of the plaintiffs, and the Texas attorney general wrote an opinion stating that all of Texas's public IHEs must abide by the *Hopwood* decree that eliminated the use of affirmative action in higher education admissions. As a result, public IHEs in Texas cannot recruit, admit, offer scholarships, or offer retention programs on the basis of race or ethnicity. IHEs can, however, recruit admitted students on the basis of race or ethnicity.

To try to reduce the effects of *Hopwood* with regard to student diversity, the 1997 Texas Legislature passed the Top Ten Percent Rule. It mandates that any student graduating from an accredited public high school in Texas in the top 10 percent of the graduating class must be admitted to any public IHE in Texas. To qualify, a student in the top 10 percent of his or her graduating high school class must complete the admissions requirements to the IHE of choice and fill out an application. In addition, it offers new admission criteria that will, if adopted by public IHEs, increase the number and proportion of underrepresented students in Texas's IHEs. These include the highest education level attained by the applicant's parents and family income.

Since the *Hopwood* ruling, admissions issues have been in the news throughout Texas. This might have brought about a higher-than-normal

awareness of admissions policies by parents, students, and other stakeholders. For example, almost every high school student interviewed for
this study had heard of the Top Ten Percent Rule,[3] and it went into effect
the same semester during which the field research was conducted.

Recent Policy Changes

Since this research was conducted, there have been several new state policies addressing student transitions, including the passage of a default high
school curriculum that is aligned with public university entrance requirements and the development of a higher-level statewide high school exit-
level exam. Recent changes are not, however, highlighted in this chapter.
The following sections outline policies that were in place when this
research was conducted.

K–12 Governance Structures and Policies

The commissioner of education and the fifteen elected members of the
State Board of Education (SBOE) oversee K–12 public education in Texas.
The commissioner is the head of the Texas Education Agency (TEA).
While the TEA serves many roles, it has few formalized activities that
connect its work with that of the higher education system in Texas. When
the field research was conducted, there was a joint TEA and Texas A&M
system official charged with work in this area. The goals were to reform
teacher education, improve public education through the strengthening of teacher education, and develop school and university partnerships between the Texas A&M University System and public schools
in Texas.

K–12 Assessments

From 1980 to 1990, Texas assessed minimum basic skills in reading,
mathematics, and writing—first with the Texas Assessment of Basic Skills,
and then with the Texas Educational Assessment of Minimum Skills. In
1990, the face of K–12 educational assessment changed with the implementation of the Texas Assessment of Academic Skills (TAAS; Texas Work
Group and others, 1995). According to the TEA, TAAS represents a shift
from testing basic skills to testing "higher order thinking skills and problem solving ability"; however, Ron Swanson, the THECB's director of the
TASP, asserts that the amount of analytical testing in the TAAS falls
between the TASP and the SAT but closer to the TASP. The grade levels

differ by subject area. Students must pass the exit-level TAAS in order to graduate (Brooks, 1998).

TAAS scores are highly publicized and schools are rated according to their students' aggregate scores; low-performing schools receive negative publicity and extra funds to rectify deficiencies.

The TAAS has had its share of controversy. The Mexican American Legal Defense and Education Fund (MALDEF) lost a lawsuit against the state's usage of the TAAS. MALDEF asserted that the TAAS is biased and discriminates against Mexican American and African American students, who fail the TAAS at greater rates than do white, non-Latino students. In addition, MALDEF found that more than half of the African American and Latino tenth graders who took the exit-level TAAS in 1996 failed at least one section. That compares with 29 percent of the white, non-Latino students. In addition, in spring 1998, seventy-nine hundred seniors failed to pass the retake of the exit-level test by graduation; 85 percent of those were Latino or African American students.

Scores from the National Assessment of Educational Progress (NAEP) have risen consistently over recent years. Texas and North Carolina posted the largest average state gains in student scores on the NAEP from 1990 to 1997. The NAEP results are mirrored by the continuing rise in the state's TAAS scores (Grissmer and Flanagan, 1998). In addition, grade point averages (GPAs) of SAT takers have risen nationally and in Texas over the past ten years, but SAT scores for Texas students have remained relatively flat over time, as they have nationally (College Board, 1998). ACT researchers found that fewer Texas students tend to take the most challenging courses; moreover, when compared to students nationally, Texas students report higher high school GPAs and achieve lower ACT scores (ACT, 1997).

State High School Graduation Requirements

When this research was conducted, there were three types of state-regulated high school programs: General, Recommended, and Distinguished. All students, regardless of the program they decide to follow, receive the same type of diploma. Overall, students must complete twenty-two credits, including the following:

- Four credits in English
- Three credits in mathematics, to include algebra I
- Two credits in science, to include one from biology, chemistry, or physics

○ Two and one-half credits of social studies that consist of world history studies or world geography studies, U.S. history since Reconstruction, and U.S. government

○ One academic credit that must be selected from world history studies, world geography studies, or any social studies course approved by the SBOE

○ One-half credit of economics, with an emphasis on the free enterprise system and its benefits

○ One and one-half credits of physical education

○ One-half credit of health education or health science technology

○ One-half credit of speech in communication applications, speech communication, public speaking, debate, or oral interpretations

○ One credit of technology applications

○ Five and one-half credits of electives that can include up to four credits of Reserve Officer Training Corps, courses off the SBOE's list of approved courses, or driver education

Students who follow just the minimum requirements listed above are in the General Program. The Recommended and Distinguished Programs require equal amounts of additional course work in the core areas, such as algebra I, algebra II, geometry, and precalculus; foreign language; and fine arts. In terms of curricular requirements, the Distinguished Program is the Recommended Program minus a technology requirement and plus an extra credit of a foreign language. In addition, students in the Distinguished Program must achieve the following measures: complete an original research project; score a 3 or above on an AP test, a 4 or above on an International Baccalaureate examination, or qualify for recognition through the Preliminary SAT (PSAT); and earn a 3.0 or higher on college courses that count for college credit, including tech-prep courses (Texas Education Agency, 1994). The General Program is not aligned with the entrance requirements for either IHE in the study.

Higher Education Governance Structure and Policies

Texas has thirty-five four-year public IHEs. Some of the IHEs are clustered into and governed by systems (the Texas A&M University System, the Texas State University System, the University of Texas System, and the University of Houston System). Other public IHEs within Texas are autonomous and are not affiliated with any system (among them are

Texas Southern University and the University of North Texas). The THECB is the state agency charged with oversight responsibilities for postsecondary education in Texas.

Public higher education institutions—including universities, community colleges, health-related institutions, technical colleges, and lower-division institutions—enrolled 836,527 students in 1997. Of that total, 396,265 were enrolled in public four-year universities. In 1997, private higher education institutions enrolled 100,814 students.

Eight institutions are not open enrollment and can therefore be considered selective. For political reasons, however, this is disputed by the campuses and is not stated openly by the THECB, IHE admissions brochures, or campus administrators. Those eight institutions are the University of Houston's downtown campus, Southwest Texas State University, Texas Tech University, the University of Texas at Austin, University of Texas at Dallas, University of North Texas, Texas A&M University-Corpus Christi, and Texas A&M University at College Station. The other four-year IHEs, despite having admissions criteria, are, in effect, open enrollment. This means that there are enough exemptions or no capacity problems at the other IHEs, and consequently every applicant gains admission. There are no published materials that rank these selective institutions relative to each other or rank the nonselective institutions relative to each other.

There are no general commonalities among institutions within a particular system. Unlike the University of California (UC) system, for example, there is no explicit tiering within or between systems in Texas. Admissions requirements vary by university, and most offer special programs that allow promising students to enroll even if those students do not meet the basic admissions requirements. The only requirements that are consistently in place in public university admissions policies across the state are a high school diploma or high school equivalency certificate; completion of the Texas Academic Skills Program (TASP) test; course work in English, math, and science; and, in most institutions, SAT or ACT scores).

TASP and the Transition from High School to College

The TASP is mandated by section 51.306 of the Texas Education Code, passed in 1987; it was developed jointly by the THECB and the TEA. It is a program that includes a test, remedial college-level courses, and undergraduate academic advising. The TASP test is a test of the reading, writing, and math skills needed to do college-level work.

The goals of the TASP have changed over the years, but the content of the test has not changed to meet the goals. Initially, students were required to take the TASP test in college in order to graduate. Then college students had to take it in their first semester of college. Starting in the fall of 1998, students had to take the test before beginning college work. Its current goals are twofold: to be a diagnostic tool for students and an exit-level high school exam in terms of what students should know and be able to do to enter college. Because the testing requirements have changed over the years, the test is currently unable to meet all of its original goals entirely.

The TASP is required for attending a public IHE (although there are many exemptions). A student cannot, however, be denied admission to an IHE based on TASP score. Students who do not pass one or more of the test's three sections are required to take remedial course work in college in the area in which they are academically deficient (Boylan, 1996). As part of the TASP, public IHEs in Texas are required to offer students support and advisory services related to the TASP test and to offer appropriate developmental education activities for students who do not pass one or more sections of the TASP.

Approximately three-quarters of the universities in Texas use their own tests in addition to the TASP (UT and SWT do not). The most common placement instruments are the ASSET, the Accuplacer/CPT, the College Board MAPS tests, the Nelson-Denny Reading Test, the Pre-TASP test, and institutionally developed mathematics tests (Boylan, 1996). These are not discussed in this chapter because they are not used extensively at the two institutions in the study. UT does not have a large student population that requires remediation, so it relies heavily on the TASP. It is the flagship institution and thus draws a more selective group of students who need less remediation than the incoming students at other IHEs in Texas. SWT, a less selective IHE, has a larger proportion of students with remediation needs, and because it gauges those needs to be in the area of basic skills, it uses the TASP test primarily as a complement to the College Board math placement exam.

Students are exempt from taking the TASP if they attain certain scores on the ACT (23 composite and 19 each on English and mathematics), SAT (1070 total with 500 on both verbal and mathematics), Texas Assessment of Academic Skills writing test, or the Texas Learning Index, or enroll in a certificate program of forty-two semester credit hours or less at a public community college or technical college. Also, students who fail one or more sections of the TASP can take a developmental course and then retake the TASP sections they failed. If they fail one or more sections again, they can take another developmental course. As long as they earn a B or better, they are then exempted from taking the TASP again.

University of Texas at Austin

The University of Texas at Austin has approximately 48,000 students, 2,700 full-time teaching staff, and 15,000 staff members. The university has fifteen colleges and schools and offers more than 270 degree programs. The largest undergraduate schools or colleges are Liberal Arts (10,571 undergraduates) and Natural Sciences (7,753 undergraduates). ("Student Profile," 1996–1997).

The median age of the undergraduates at UT is approximately twenty-one. Of the first-year students in 1996–1997, 48 percent were women and 52 percent were men. Approximately 65 percent were white, non-Latino; 0.4 percent were Native American; 4.1 percent were African American; 12.5 percent were Asian American; 14.6 percent were Latino; and 3.1 percent were international students. For the fall semester 1995, the average cumulative GPA for all undergraduates was 2.85 out of 4.0 (University of Texas at Austin, "Student Profile," 1997).

After the implementation of the attorney general's interpretation of *Hopwood* in 1996, the proportion of Latino and African American students gaining admission to UT fell in 1997–1998 and then rose only slightly in 1998–1999. The proportion of white, non-Latino and Asian American students rose slightly after *Hopwood*.

UNDERGRADUATE ADMISSION POLICIES. UT's deputy director of admissions stated that undergraduate admissions policies developed by UT are driven by the need to control enrollment, enroll high achievers, enroll a diverse class, and stay within legal parameters (interview, Apr. 1998).

Applicants must have four units of English, two of a foreign language (three recommended), three of mathematics at algebra I or higher (four recommended), two of laboratory science (three recommended), and three of social studies; one-half unit of fine arts is strongly recommended. However, due to House Bill 588, students are exempt from these requirements if they are in the top 10 percent of their respective high school graduating classes. The current admissions factors are listed in Table 3.1.

Non–Top Ten Percent students, who are not automatically admitted, are evaluated on the basis of their high school rank, high school course units, standardized test scores, essays, and personal achievement (for example, honors, awards, leadership, community service, work experience, and special circumstances). These factors are combined into

**Table 3.1. UT Admission, Scholarship, and Fellowship Factors
for Freshmen, 1997.**

Freshman Admissions		Scholarships/Fellowships
Top Ten Percent Rule	Criteria for Reviewed Applications	Nonacademic Factors That May Be Considered
The top 10 percent of each accredited high school class is automatically admitted to the university as a whole, although each college might have its own requirements.	Standardized test scores	Leadership and extracurricular activities
	Strength of applicant's academic background (including difficulty of high school courses and special accomplishments)	Status in national academic competitions
		Academic performance within a major or other performance criteria
	Parents' education level	
	First-generation college student	Financial need
		Socioeconomic background
	English not first language	
		Education level
	Geographical circumstances	First-generation college student
	Experience in surmounting obstacles to pursue higher education	English not first language

Note: *UT adopted these criteria from the list of options outlined in the 1997 Texas legislature's Bill 588.*

two indexes. The Academic Index (AI) is a weighted combination of high school rank, SAT or ACT score, and number of high school units. The Personal Characteristics Index (PCI) weights the personal essays and the personal achievement characteristics. A matrix is created with the AI on the horizontal axis and the PCI on the vertical axis. The matrix shows the probability of earning a certain GPA at UT by the end of the first year; students are sorted into the automatic admit, automatic denial, or borderline categories. In addition, four regression equations are used to generate predicted grades according to the following four colleges or groupings of colleges: Business, Engineering, Liberal Arts, Communication, Social Work, Fine Arts, and Education; Natural Science; Architecture; and Nursing. These indexes have given UT the opportunity to admit a more diverse class since they decrease the weight, or importance, of the SAT and ACT scores.

Although the university uses these indexes, the Texas legislature mandates that since UT is one of the two flagship IHEs in the state, it must admit any Texan who meets the minimum requirements. To meet this requirement, the university runs a provisional program during the summer for students who are on the borderline of being admitted. They must earn a 2.25 GPA or better in the summer program in order to be allowed to continue at the university. There is a general feeling in the Admissions Office that this requirement will keep the university from reaching the highest national selectivity ranking possible.

Each college or department can put limits on enrollment, but it does not set admissions policies and is not involved in the admissions process (unless auditions or other such requirements are relevant). The Admissions Office ensures that each class is diverse and well rounded within legal guidelines and the limit set by the college. The only undergraduate majors that are highly selective and receive more applications than available slots are engineering, business, architecture, and communication).

UNDERGRADUATE COURSE PLACEMENT AND REMEDIATION POLICIES. The staff interviewed at UT stipulated that it has no placement policies or procedures. Rather, the university calls its placement process *academic advising* because then it is seen as more of a student choice than a university mandate. The TASP places students who are not ready for college-level work into lower-level remedial courses. This form of advising is administered by the university's TASP Office.

Before students who have passed the TASP can register for freshman English or beginning math, they must take the College Board SAT II: Subject Tests in Writing and Mathematics Level I, IC, or IIC. The scores are then used to place students into the appropriate-level courses. The Measurement and Evaluation Center (MEC) at UT works with the Admissions Office to accelerate students, whether it is done by using scores on the AP exam or by conducting college- or department-specific placement exams. Almost all departments or schools have their own academic advising tests that are administered by the MEC. Also, all undergraduate colleges have academic advisers or student development specialists who assist students with their course work planning or other needs, but the programs and policies vary by college.

COMMUNICATION AND OUTREACH. During 1997 and 1998, UT's Undergraduate Admissions Office had thirteen outreach activities, including high school visits by the president of the university, sending representatives to regional college fairs, conducting workshops for high school counselors, mailings to students in the top 10 percent of their class and other high-achieving student groups, college preparatory nights in churches, and phoning prospective students. Several of these activities are new; many programs targeting economically disadvantaged students and top 10 percent students have begun in the wake of the *Hopwood* ruling. One of the problems inherent in any outreach program, and present in UT's, is that often the people targeted the most do not attend; the counselors who most need the information often do not attend workshops or programs, nor do many economically disadvantaged students and parents. Proportionally, private schools have the greatest show rate of counselors for UT's counselor sessions.

UT as a whole has sixty-seven outreach programs in the public schools in Texas. These range from rather small efforts, such as providing guest speakers and field trips, to the University Interscholastic League's sponsorship of organized academic, musical, and athletic competitions in Texas's public schools and to the Outreach Center. Some of the programs target teachers, while others provide services and programs for students. UT and its neighboring district have a collaborative partnership under way, almost exclusively devoted to teacher preparation, such as linking teacher training to current K–12 pedagogy.

Southwest Texas State University

Southwest Texas State University (SWT) is located in San Marcos, a city of 30,000 people between Austin and San Antonio. It is part of the state university system and enrolls approximately 57,000. UT is a more competitive institution than SWT as evidenced by the average GPA, class rank, SAT and ACT scores, and the remediation needs of the entering first-year students.

SWT began in 1903 as a teachers' college, as did all the other IHEs in the system, and it became a comprehensive university in 1969. It has eight undergraduate schools and forty master's degree programs, and it is one of the top ten largest public universities in the state. In the fall semester 1996, there were approximately 2,500 first-time freshmen at SWT and approximately 21,000 students in total. Most of the students who attend SWT are from the two nearby cities. In the fall of 1996, there were 17,572 undergraduates at the university. Its basic mission is still to train teachers, but it conducts more research outside of teaching than any other institution in the system. In addition, it produces more teacher candidates than any other IHE in the state.

ADMISSIONS INFORMATION. For the 1995–1996 school year, 7,269 persons applied; 4,520 of those were accepted. Sixty-two percent of those who applied were admitted, and 56 percent of those who were admitted attended. Of these, 1,884 were white, non-Latino; 16 were Native American/Alaskan; 127 were African American; 46 were Asian American; and 455 were Latino (Texas Higher Education Coordinating Board, 1995). For the 1996–1997 academic year, 68 percent of the applicants were accepted. In 1996, 15 percent of the freshmen were in the top 10 percent of their class, and 50 percent were in the top 25 percent. The mid-50 percent of enrolled freshmen had SAT I Verbal scores between 460 and 560 and Math scores between 460 and 560. ACT scores for those students ranged between 12 and 23 (College Board, 1998).

The high school that traditionally is in the top ten of high schools that sends the greatest number of students to SWT is the rural high school in this study. In 1997, it sent approximately sixty students, or about 3 percent of the total number of first-time freshmen. About 55 percent of the students who entered in the fall of 1997 were transfer students.

UNDERGRADUATE ADMISSIONS POLICIES. Table 3.2 displays the admissions requirements for SWT. In addition, prospective students are required to take four years of English, three years of mathematics, three years of natural sciences, three years of social sciences, and two years of a foreign language. In the fall of 1996, the freshman class had an average GPA of 2.55.

The main factors considered in admission are class rank and SAT or ACT scores. SWT does not seek a particular GPA. The lower the GPA, the more weight is given to the SAT or ACT scores. Recommendation letters and personal statements are not required, but they are encouraged.

Admissions standards between UT and SWT differ greatly. While UT focuses on recruiting students in the top 10 percent, SWT recruits students in the top 75 percent of their graduating classes. UT has adopted many new criteria in order to obtain a diverse student body, while SWT has not. In addition, at SWT, applicants who are in the top 75 percent of their high school class are eligible for an individual review during the admissions process.

Table 3.2. SWT Admissions Requirements, 1998.

High School Rank	SAT I	ACT
Top 10 percent	No minimum required	
Next 15 percent	920	20
Second quarter	1010	22
Third quarter	1180	26
Fourth quarter	1270	29

SWT's increasing level of selectivity seems to be related to UT's increasing level of selectivity. As UT has raised its admissions standards, SWT receives a more competitive student body. Many of the students who fall short of UT's requirements attend SWT and consequently raise the quality of SWT's student body.

UNDERGRADUATE COURSE PLACEMENT AND REMEDIATION POLICIES. SWT has more serious remediation issues than does UT. In the spring of 1998, 358 students did not pass one or more sections of the TASP. Since 1975, SWT has used its own math placement exam; it was started because about 70 percent of the students were failing the introductory-level math courses. Until the fall of 1998, students who did not meet the placement exam's standards took the required remedial course and then took the TASP. Beginning in fall 1998, all students must take the TASP before starting college course work. In addition, any student who earns below 480 on the math portion of the SAT or 21 on the ACT must take the math placement test and score 26 out of 35. The test is from the Descriptive Math Series from the College Board. Even with the test, the failure rate in college algebra at SWT is approximately 40 percent, although several staff interviewed stated that they believe that the test adequately identifies math remediation needs. The director of the Student Learning Assistance Center (SLAC) believes that math and related quantitative subjects are weak at SWT, and consequently the university does not draw students who excel in those subject areas. Overall, though, SWT has found that its remediation needs are decreasing over time; staff believes this is because the admissions process has become more selective.

POLICY EVOLUTION. In 1991, more than 40 percent of freshmen (those who earned below a 2.0 grade point average) were on academic probation. In 1992, SWT increased its admissions standards, and the next year the percentage of first-year students on academic probation dropped to 20. The university is trying to become an institution with a statewide draw rather than just a regional university. Consequently, it changes its admissions policies frequently to try to admit the desired student body. The most recent admissions policy changes are as follows:

> 1992: Reduced the automatic admission from students in the top 25 percent of their high school class to those in the top 10 percent. The result was an unanticipated 25 percent decrease in admitted students.

1994: Increased the requirements for students in the third and fourth quartiles of their high school class.

1995: Implemented an application fee for the first time.

1996: Recommended core courses became required core courses.

Many of these changes occurred primarily because students were dropping out at "alarming rates," according to SWT's director of admissions, and the university wanted to increase the quality of the students in order to decrease the dropout rate.

COMMUNICATION AND OUTREACH. Admissions staff visit hundreds of high schools every year, primarily those that historically are feeder schools for SWT and schools that have the potential to send many students but currently do not. They encourage prospective students to acquire their academic preparation at a community college prior to matriculating at the university.

The Admissions Office staff is not aware of high school standards, and they do not meet with K–12 officials in any regular fashion. The university will coordinate school visits if a high school initiates contact.

K–12 Stakeholder Knowledge of Key College Policies

This phase of the research sought to answer the following questions: How are UT's, SWT's, and the state's undergraduate admissions and placement policies, practices, and expectations communicated to parents, students, and school staff in the five schools sampled? What are the participants' understandings of the policies, practices, and expectations? Are all of the high schools and middle schools and their respective constituencies receiving the same information? Are students in different racial/ethnic groups receiving the same information and having similar understandings? Are students in different curricular tracks receiving the same information and having the same understandings?

In order to address these questions, I conducted research at two high schools, a middle school, and two junior high schools in two districts in Central Texas.[4] I surveyed students in the eighth and eleventh grades in honors and nonhonors classes;[5] surveyed their parents; conducted student focus groups; and interviewed those students' teachers, counselors, and administrators (110 students; 102 parents). Fifty-four were honors students and 56 were nonhonors students. Fifty-three percent of the students were from the urban district, and 47 percent were from the rural district. All students surveyed were also included in focus groups. The field research was conducted in fall 1998.[6]

The researcher with me chose English classes because they usually contain students from a single grade level, as opposed to subjects such as mathematics and science. Eleventh graders were chosen because they are close enough to the K–16 transition time to expect that they would have some knowledge of the relevant policies and practices. Eighth graders were chosen because by eighth grade, students have usually chosen or been placed in a particular curriculum track that affects their academic preparation for college. Most of the literature in this area suggests that students need to begin planning academically by eighth grade if they wish to attend a selective IHE.

The surveys asked participants about the college admissions and placement information students receive, courses were they taking, parental income and education, students' and parents' understanding of relevant policy mechanisms (for example, the SAT, tuition costs, and the TASP), students' and their parents' aspirations regarding the students' future college plans, their estimates regarding the total costs for one year of college at a public university in Texas,[7] and suggestions students and parents have for improving the college counseling program at the child's school. Analyses of these data were conducted to explore whether there were differences in terms of the information the students received; the students', parents', and local educators' understanding regarding higher education admissions- and placement-related policies; and the students' perceptions about the opportunity structure of their schooling experience and their own motivations and expectations regarding higher education.[8]

To select the specific schools to include in the pilot, the following criteria were examined to ensure as broad an array of schools as possible, given district constraints:[9]

- Percentage passing TAAS Grade 10 Reading (1997)
- Percentage passing TAAS Grade 10 Writing (1997)
- Percentage passing TAAS Grade 10 Math (1997)
- Percentage passing All TAAS Tests (1997)
- Percentage enrolled in advanced courses (1995)
- Percentage with SAT/ACT results at or above criterion (1996)
- Percentage tested—SAT or ACT (1996)
- Mean SAT I score (1996)
- Mean ACT score (1996)
- Racial and Ethnic diversity—percentage African American; Latino; white, non-Latino; Asian/Pacific Islander; Native American (1995)
- Percentage free and reduced price lunch (1996)

Student and Parent Demographics

Table 3.3 presents student and parent demographic information by district sample and for the sample as a whole. Students of color were underrepresented in honors classes (.001 level of significance). Thirty percent of the honors students and 70 percent of the nonhonors students were students of color. Latino and African American students were pooled together to increase the size in the expected frequency cells, and

Table 3.3. Student and Parent Demographics for District Samples and Total Sample, 1998–1999.

	Urban District Sample Percentage (Number)	Rural District Sample Percentage (Number)	Total Sample Percentage (Number)
African American	10.3% (6)	11.5% (6)	10.9% (12)
Latino	27.6 (16)	55.8 (29)	40. (45)
White, non-Latino	60.3 (35)	28.8 (15)	45.5 (50)
Other, non-Asian	1.7 (1)	3.8 (2)	2.7 (3)
Female students	50.0 (29)	57.7 (30)	53.6 (59)
Male students	50.0 (29)	42.3 (22)	46.4 (51)
Honors students	60.3 (35)	36.5 (19)	49.1 (54)
Nonhonors students	39.7 (23)	63.5 (33)	50.9 (56)
High school students	62.1 (36)	57.7 (30)	60.0 (66)
Middle school/junior high school students	37.9 (22)	42.3 (22)	40.0 (44)
Parent education: Less than high school	5.9 (3)	17.8 (8)	11.5 (11)
Parent education: High school degree or GED	15.7 (8)	28.9 (13)	21.9 (21)
Parent education: Some college	13.7 (7)	24.4 (11)	18.8 (18)
Parent education: College degree	39.2 (20)	24.4 (11)	32.3 (31)
Parent education: Postcollege	25.5 (13)	4.4 (2)	15.6 (15)
Parent income below $15,000	12.0 (6)	20.9 (9)	16.1 (15)
Parent income $15,000–30,000	20.0 (10)	30.2 (13)	24.7 (23)
Parent income $30,000–60,000	18.0 (9)	37.2 (16)	26.9 (25)
Parent income $60,000–100,000	30.0 (15)	11.6 (5)	21.5 (20)
Parent income above $100,000	20.0 (10)	0.0 (0)	10.8 (10)

Note: *Some totals might not equal 100 due to rounding.*

Percentages for parent education and parent income were calculated using the total number of parents who responded to the question rather than the total number of parents who returned the survey.

consequently, the category "students of color" was created. The proportion of honors students was not constant across the levels of family income (.001 level of significance). Honors students were disproportionately represented in the higher-income categories, and nonhonors students were overrepresented in the lower-income categories.

The proportions of white, non-Latino students and of honors students were not constant across all parental education categories (.001 level of significance for white, non-Latino, and parental education; .001 for honors and parental education); white, non-Latino students and honors students were overrepresented in the higher parental education levels (69 percent earned $60,000 a year or more). Latino students and nonhonors students were overrepresented in the lower parental education categories. The proportion of students from the rural district was not constant across all parental education level categories either (.004 level of significance). Families in the rural district sample were clustered around the lower education levels (47 percent in the first two categories), as compared to the urban district, in which 48 percent were in the highest two education categories. This same pattern occurred between parental income level and the two districts (.002 level of significance).

Placement Policies at the Case Study Schools

All three junior high schools in the study place students into courses according to their TAAS scores or scores on standardized tests. For example, in order for students in the urban middle school to be placed in an honors or pre-AP class, they need to score at least 85 percent on the subject-area TAAS tests. Parents can, however, sign a waiver for their children to be placed in honors and pre-AP level classes if the student scores below an 85. Placement into the tracks can start as early as kindergarten, but it usually starts in elementary school. At the urban high school, approximately 30 to 35 percent of the high school's students take all honors, pre-AP, or AP courses, and another 5 to 10 percent of students take one or more high-level courses. Students are placed on the basis of test scores and teacher recommendations, but parents can request that their students be placed into the high track even if they are not qualified by virtue of their test scores.

Profiles of the Case Study Schools

Below are descriptions of each of the studied schools. Their names have been changed to preserve their anonymity.

URBAN HIGH SCHOOL. Two major features that distinguish this school from other high schools in the district are the Arts Academy (a magnet program within the high school) and its stature as a relatively high-performing and diverse school. According to district staff, the Arts Academy does not draw students with particularly high or low GPAs or TAAS scores; therefore, the population of students drawn to the school for the academy is not skewed toward high or low performers. The white, non-Latino students mostly live in the surrounding areas of the central core of the city and are relatively affluent. The students of color are mostly bused in from outlying areas of the central city.

A fall in the school's TEA rating from Acceptable to Low Performing for the 1998–1999 academic year, in addition to assertions of TAAS data tampering during the 1998–1999 academic year, put the principal's job in jeopardy and the school into turmoil. The school was selected for this study prior to the ratings and data-tampering charges.

Forty-six percent of all seniors scored at least 1000 on the SAT or 24 on the ACT in 1995. Fifteen percent of African American seniors, 58 percent of white, non-Latino seniors, and 10 percent of Latino seniors all scored at least 1000 on the SAT or 24 on the ACT in 1995. Twenty-eight percent of African American students; 40 percent of Latino students; 77 percent of white, non-Latino students; and 28 percent of economically disadvantaged students passed all sections of the TAAS in 1995. The school's students tend, on average, to earn higher SAT scores than students in the district as a whole but lower TAAS scores.

URBAN MIDDLE SCHOOL. In terms of student achievement, 79 percent in 1998 passed the reading section of the TAAS, 77 percent passed writing, 75 percent passed mathematics, and 69 percent passed all of the sections. The student-to-counselor ratio is approximately 314:1. There is no precollege counseling. The main counselor responsibilities are scheduling, coordinating programs (such as those of Gifted and Talented and Special Education), offering counseling and guidance services, career counseling for eighth graders, and coordinating the testing program. The eighth-grade career planning session is a large unit in the counseling program. When the students plan their course-taking pattern for high school, it is aimed primarily toward career paths. In order for students to be placed in an honors or pre-AP class, they need to score at least 85 percent on the subject-area TAAS tests. Parents can, however, sign a waiver for their children to be placed in honors and pre-AP level classes if the student scores below 85.

RURAL HIGH SCHOOL. The rural high school was the only school in the study that had a counselor who devoted his or her time only to post–high school issues (specifically, scholarships and job placement), although this counselor spent most of his time on the latter. The high school counselors are divided by grade level, and the scholarship and job placement counselor works primarily with seniors. The student-to-counselor ratio is approximately 439:1, with the scholarship and job placement counselor serving as a floating counselor who is not assigned to particular students.

Approximately 30 to 35 percent of the high school's students take all honors, pre-AP, or AP courses, and another 5 to 10 percent take one or more high-level courses. Students are placed on the basis of test scores and teacher recommendations, but parents can request that their students be placed into the high track even if they are not qualified by virtue of their test scores.

In 1996, the passing rate for all subjects for rural high school students taking the exit-level TAAS was 15 percent for African American students; 41 percent for Latinos; 78 percent for white, non-Latinos; and 39 percent for economically disadvantaged students. Approximately 350 students at the high school took AP courses in the 1997–1998 academic year.

RURAL JUNIOR HIGH SCHOOLS. According to the rural district assistant superintendent for curriculum and instruction and the junior high school principals, the two junior high schools were very similar in terms of student demographics, number of teachers, types of courses offered, school policies, and other such attributes. This was done purposely by the district when both schools became seventh- and eighth-grade campuses (beginning in the 1998–1999 school year). A junior high school community group met for one academic year (May 1997–September 1998) to ensure that the campuses would be as similar as possible, including the information given to students about school policies and graduation requirements. In addition, the schools each draw students from across the city, so the student bodies are similar.

Compared to the urban middle school, the rural junior high schools each have a smaller proportion of African American students, almost twice as many Latino students, and a smaller proportion of white, non-Latino students.

Aspirations and Academic Preparation

The following section discusses the sampled students' post–high school aspirations and their perceptions of their level of college preparation.

POST–HIGH SCHOOL PLANS. Almost all of the students included in this study planned to attend college directly after high school. Eleven percent of the students sampled (twelve students) wrote that they planned to enter the workforce or the military directly after graduating from high school. All of the students who responded that they did not intend to attend college immediately after high school were students of color. Eighty percent of the parents stated that their child had shown an interest in college, while 84 percent of the parents who responded to the question wanted their child to attend college. The type of college the students most wanted to attend was a four-year out-of-state college or university (29 percent); it was almost an even split with the students who checked "four-year in-state college or university" (28 percent). Almost half of the parents wanted their child to attend a four-year in-state college or university (46 percent), and 35 percent had started saving for their child's college education.

Almost none of the students in the two district samples were confident that they would be prepared academically for college. Although almost all of those sampled voiced an interest in attending college immediately after high school, they viewed the preparation period for college slightly differently. Honors students, on average, believed that students need to start preparing academically no later than eighth grade. For example, most of the urban high school honors focus group stated that students in general should start preparing academically for college in junior high school, but most agreed that they started thinking about college in elementary school. The students in nonhonors classes, on average, believed that they should start preparing between eighth and eleventh grade, because they were concerned that they would forget the information or not be interested enough in eighth and ninth grades to take it seriously.

Although both honors and nonhonors students seemed to believe that they did not have enough information regarding how to prepare well for college, they planned their paths in different ways. On average, the honors students in the sample said they enrolled in the most difficult classes in the hopes that they would be able to gain admission to a selective institution. The nonhonors students stated that they assumed that although they were concerned that their courses were not rigorous enough, they could gain admission to some IHE if they graduated from high school.

The urban high school students were very concerned that their course-taking patterns were not compatible with college entrance requirements, but they believed that if they followed a sequence of honors, pre-AP, and AP courses, they would be relatively well prepared for college. They noticed the large differences between honors and nonhonors courses. Students stated that between the two tracks, "You're around almost a totally different environment, a totally different teacher, and totally different attitudes toward, like, school and, like, just everything"; and "[Nonhonors] classes are, like, read a book and answer questions"; and "I took nonhonors, like, World Geography. . . . and all I ever did was worksheets and, like, if I had taken Honors I would have done, like, projects. . . . It was a really really big difference [between the tracks]." They all agreed that not only does the honors track prepare students better academically, but that the teachers are more informative about college policies.

All of the rural honors high school students wanted to attend a college out of state; UT was their safety school. Unlike their honors peers in the urban high school, none of them planned to apply to an Ivy League school. They hoped to enter a flagship public university or a second-tier IHE out of the state. They were very concerned that the two IHEs in the study did not have good name recognition across the country, but they were not sure if their parents could afford to send them elsewhere. They were confused about whether selective institutions prefer students who earn A's in regular track courses or B's in advanced courses.

They said that in order to be prepared well for college, students should complete the most challenging core courses every year during high school. They thought that if they took all AP and honors courses every year, they should be able to gain admission "somewhere." They were not sure how their graduation plans related to college entrance requirements. One white, non-Latino male student stated, "Whatever you do here is not going to matter [in college]."

Many of the honors urban middle school students wanted the honors classes to be more difficult so they could be prepared better for high school and college. Although they thought that their classes were much more difficult than nonhonors courses, they believed that if their courses stayed at the same level of rigor when they were in high school, they would not be prepared for college. Several students stated that in order to get into college, it is important to exceed the required number of classes for high school graduation. Those students did not trust that the high school graduation plans were rigorous "enough to get us into a good college." One student stated that the high school requirements are "not even close because they're geared toward students who don't expect to, well, much less graduate from . . . high school, but maybe not even go to all their high school years. . . . That's not enough to get into a good college."

STUDENTS' PERCEPTIONS OF TEACHERS' EXPECTATIONS. Students frequently talked about their beliefs that educators did not have high aspirations for them. For example, one Latino male rural honors student related a story about feeling stereotyped as a noncollege-bound student at the school. He said that while some people at the school might think that he dressed like a gang member who would not take school seriously, he took only honors courses. He discussed trying to register for the PSAT: "'Cause, like, when I went to register they had forms right there and I guess 'cause of the way I was dressed the lady said, 'You're not going to take it [the PSAT] are you?' and talked to me about the military instead. So that was pretty sad for me 'cause like they don't expect things from me."

None of the rural nonhonors high school students thought that they would be prepared academically for college. They said they wished that teachers and others at the school site had higher expectations for them. Students said that the teachers, counselors, and administrators had "career expectations" for them and that "the teachers just want us to get out" and do not care if they attend college. They felt that the teachers thought they were "stupid" and that the teachers gave up on the nonhonors students. Educators and students at both high schools mentioned that college nights are often open only to seniors or honors students.

TEACHERS' ROLES IN HELPING STUDENTS PREPARE FOR COLLEGE. Between honors and nonhonors teachers, there were large differences regarding their role in helping students prepare for college. For example, at the rural high school, a nonhonors teacher believed that her students were regularly omitted from any conversation regarding college and that they did not receive any information or guidance regarding college policies or navigating the K–16 transition. She stated that most of the students had, however, expressed an interest in attending college, although many were seeking a "quick way to get rich" without focusing on the academic issues involved in the K–16 transition. She tried to talk with them about the importance of good grades and a solid curriculum, but she stated that she was not aware enough of college requirements and policies to give them accurate advice.

An honors teacher discussed college-related issues with the students consistently over the course of the year. She wanted them all to go to private liberal arts colleges for their undergraduate education and then attend one of the state's flagship universities for graduate school. The main goal of the course, in her mind, was to ensure that the students receive credit for college work. She stated that she received no information from the district, school, IHEs, or state agencies regarding the transition to college. She was unsure as to the admissions requirements for the IHEs in the study, but believed that students who followed the honors curriculum would gain admission to either IHE.

An urban high school nonhonors teacher said that although most of his students planned to attend college, he did not discuss students' future plans with them, nor did he receive any information about college-related policies. He believed that college-related discussions take place more in the honors, pre-AP, and AP courses. An urban high school honors teacher said that she discussed college preparation–related issues with her class, "because it's pre-AP." She discussed how to apply for financial aid, including finding out about obscure scholarships; the need for letters of recommendation and who should write the recommendation; and how to write good essays for college applications. She stated that she was confident that her students would meet the requirements if they followed the honors track. She received no information about college admissions–related policies, but did seek information on her own.

Role of Counselors

The urban high school provides a useful example of the varied responsibilities all of the counselors faced. At this high school, no counselor was able to devote all, or even most, of her or his time to college guidance and counseling. Each counselor had a caseload of over four hundred students. The counselors were responsible for scheduling; test administration; coordination of programs; consultation with parents, teachers, and social service agencies; referrals; guidance; school-to-college activities; school-to-career activities, including individual career planning procedures; and devising and implementing a guidance curriculum.

The counselors at the urban high school met with students one-on-one if a student made an appointment. Parents could ask counselors questions about college planning as well. The counselors believed that they did not have enough time to work with students on issues that are not mandated by the state. The high school used parent volunteers to talk with interested students about college or career preparation. The school had a small counseling library with brochures, catalogues, and videos that, according to the district's counselors, is of average-level quality for the district's high schools.

The urban high school's twelfth-grade counselor was not able to stay informed of policies at the state or university level. She said that she tried to attend conferences and visited a higher education institution to learn of policy changes; often, though, she was informed of policy revisions and reforms by her students. She did not stay abreast of IHE entrance requirements. In order to improve the college guidance program at the school, she believed that there needed to be more counselors and that they should be divided by function: scholarships, scheduling, guidance, college preparation, and outreach to parents. She believed that if counselors had authority over a particular area, they would not be distracted with the multitude of other tasks that they face.

All of the counselors interviewed stated that they did not have much time to spend on college preparation issues on account of their other responsibilities. Counselors at the two high schools said that they had time only to fulfill state mandates. Seventy-four percent of the students (81 students) stated that they had never talked with their counselors about college. Although the middle school counselors spent more one-on-one time with students than did the high school counselors, the middle school students had received very little information on college-related issues. The general belief among counselors and students was that only the most motivated students talked with their counselors about college and that the conversations were initiated by students.

The eighth-grade counselor at the urban middle school received no information from any IHE or state agency about admissions requirements or other K–16 transition policies. She was not aware of any mechanism that ensures that middle school counselors stay abreast of changes in state universities' policies. She believed this was a problem because students need to plan academically for college starting in middle school. She stated that if the counselors could not help them, then only the students with highly educated parents would know what classes to take.

K–12 and Postsecondary Connections

Although students and educators in both districts voiced their frustration regarding a lack of connection between K–12 and postsecondary education in their district and school, the networking function between SWT and the rural district was stronger than the networking function between UT and the urban district. Many of the teachers and counselors in the district's schools had attended SWT, and they often encouraged students to do the same. For example, at the end of one focus group, the teacher returned to the classroom and stated that although the group had just discussed many different college options, students needed to remember that SWT was the best place for them because she went there, it was affordable, and the students' parents probably went there.

The relationship between the urban district and its closest university, UT, was found to be relatively weak. The urban district–level counselors stated that they were "shocked" by the scant contact between the district and the university. They believed that UT had diminished its outreach into the community as it had become more selective. Recruiters had not visited the district's schools in five to eight years. There was a general belief that in order to receive any information from UT, students and school site staff need to be the initiators. Like the rural participants, urban district staff believed that SWT is very accessible to the urban district. SWT's Talent Search program includes students from the schools in this study and from other schools in the district. Admissions staff from SWT recruit in the urban district's high schools, including the high school in the study.

Both of the IHEs sent information back to the high schools in the study regarding the school's graduates' first-year performance; one of the high school principals had seen the reports, while the other had not. No other school staff in the sample had heard of the reports.

The high school and junior high school counselors stated that the line of communication between the schools and the state-level entities (IHEs and state agencies) starts at the top and then travels to the district level. Sometimes it filters down to the principal, but it rarely makes it to counselors, teachers, parents, or students. They stated they receive applications, brochures, and catalogues from SWT, but they did not think that any materials were sent from state agencies or UT. They receive information mostly because of their own initiative—by searching Web sites or attending meetings at SWT. None of them could state the current admissions requirements for either IHE, but they had catalogues available to use when students asked them specific questions. They did not receive information regarding recent changes in admissions or TASP policies. They stated that the Texas legislature changed K–12 graduation requirements and K–16 transition policies (mostly the TASP) every two years, and it was too difficult to stay current. They believed that they received information in a piecemeal fashion. Representatives from the military visited the campus every week and had a higher presence on the campus than did IHEs.

The TEA and THECB commissioners sent out joint packets of information to all high school test administrators and counselors regarding the recent changes in the TASP administration. None of the counselors, who were also the test administrators, reported receiving this information. The counselors knew that the TASP needed to be taken before college, but they stated they did not have the time to talk to students about the exam or to administer the test at the high school. Neither of the high schools in the study offered preparation for the TASP, and none of the counselors knew if their high school would become a TASP test site. The prevailing view was that the colleges would "quick TASP" students right before classes started (that is, students enter college and take the TASP before they enroll in courses), so secondary schools did not need to worry about informing their students about the TASP.

Very few students and parents had attended college-related programs, visited college campuses, or attended college fairs. Many students worked long hours and said they were unable to take challenging course work or be involved in extracurricular activities at the school because they had to help support their parents and siblings. In one focus group (nonhonors rural), seven of the eleven students worked on average thirty-five hours per week.

Sources of Student Information about College

I wanted to learn about the conversations students had with their parents and educators about college admissions–related issues. The sections that follow discuss the findings with regard to their parents and teachers.

CONVERSATIONS WITH PARENTS. Most of the students had talked with their parents about college-related issues. Eighty-seven percent of the students had talked with a parent about college-related issues, and 46 percent had talked with a parent about how to finance college. A greater proportion of honors students (96 percent) than nonhonors students (79 percent) had talked with their parents about college. Similarly, a greater proportion of white, non-Latino students had talked with their parents (96 percent) than had students of color (81 percent). The proportion of students who stated that they talked with their parents about college was greater in the urban district (95 percent) than in the rural district (79 percent). Approximately three-quarters of the parents wrote that they have talked with their child about their child's postsecondary plans (76 percent).

There seemed to be a difference in students' minds between whether they initiated conversations about college ("Have you talked with any of the following people?" was asked on the surveys) and whether people initiated conversations with them about college (as discussed in the focus groups with the question, "Who has talked with you about college-related issues?"). The students were not initiating conversations about college, but some students said that people were talking to them about college. For instance, honors teachers regularly talked to their classes about college, while most teachers of nonhonors courses did not.

CONVERSATIONS WITH TEACHERS. While the teachers were usually the most direct in-school conduits of information for students, they were usually one of the least likely groups to be involved in discussions regarding college admission and placement policies. Thirty percent of the students had talked with a teacher about college. The students who had talked to their teachers were clustered at the top of the parental income levels (54 percent were in the top two income levels), and the students who did not were overly representative of the lower-income levels (76 percent were in the bottom three categories). In the focus groups, it became apparent that the honors students received college-related information from nonschool sources, and their honors teachers were actively involved in sharing college information. Nonhonors students were not receiving college information from any consistent in-school source.

Teachers at one of the rural junior high schools stated that they did not talk with students about the students' future plans. The teachers said they often felt overwhelmed with the curriculum plan and did not stray from the required areas. In addition, they received no information about college admissions–related policies and practices, so they did not know what to tell the students. They would like additional information because students asked them how to prepare academically for college, but the teachers did not know the college entrance requirements for the local IHEs. The gifted and talented (GT) coordinator gives GT students information about taking the PSAT, but the other students are not informed of the test until high school. Both teachers believed that students need to start receiving information about college admissions requirements in elementary school, because by eighth grade, students are tracked, and they rarely switch tracks. Both felt that teachers and other school site staff would not alter their behavior (in terms of helping students prepare for college) unless they were mandated to change. Many of the teachers interviewed for this study stated that their main source for learning about changes in Texas's public university admissions requirements is the media, particularly the newspaper.

College Knowledge

I wanted to know what students knew about college admissions requirements, college costs, and college course placement, that is, their "college knowledge."

KNOWLEDGE OF COLLEGE ADMISSIONS REQUIREMENTS. Overall, students were unsure as to the relationship between the state's high school graduation plans (General, Recommended, and Distinguished) and the entrance requirements to any IHE, including the two IHEs in the study. The reaction to this confusion was markedly different between students in the two curricular tracks. On average, the honors students followed the more rigorous graduation plan in the hopes that it would be compatible with a selective IHE's admissions requirements. The non-honors students, on average, followed a less rigorous graduation plan, hoping that it would be compatible with any IHE's admissions require-ments. Almost all of the students in the focus groups, honors students and nonhonors students alike, were very concerned that they were not being challenged and that their courses would not meet admissions requirements at their IHE of choice.

The rural nonhonors high school students believed that the Distin-guished Graduation Plan is the most closely aligned to the admissions standards of an IHE such as UT. None of the students stated that they were following that plan. They thought that the only classes that would prepare students for college well are AP classes, but since they were not in the AP track, most planned to attend SWT or another local, less selec-tive, institution.

In terms of understandings of specific college admissions–related policy mechanisms, the majority of the nonhonors high school students could not explain or define the SAT, whereas almost all in the honors track could. Sixteen middle school students, the majority of them honors stu-dents, could explain the SAT. The urban high school honors students seemed to view test taking as a game. One student said, "If you really want to get a good SAT score, . . . you take SAT classes for two years and then you get a really good score." The other students agreed, and they all knew that the SAT can be taken repeatedly.

Few students had a clear understanding of the two IHEs' specific admis-sions requirements; four of the focus groups reached consensus that UT requires a 3.0 GPA but were not sure about other requirements. The high school students and the honors middle school students generally under-stood that UT's admissions standards were more selective than those of SWT. Although many high school students in nonhonors classes and some rural high school honors students seemed to view UT as a selective IHE, the majority of the urban high school honors students did not. For exam-ple, one student said, "I've kind of heard that UT is not that hard to get into—that you just can't be a total . . . ," and as he searched for the right word, a young man in the group said "idiot," while a young woman said "yeah, slacker" (all were urban high school honors students). Students in both urban high school honors focus groups believed this, and most stated that UT was their backup school. They believed that, as one of the stu-dents stated, "SWT is really easy to get into, but UT is not that hard, either." Most of the high school students had heard of the Top Ten Percent Rule, and some believed that other admissions requirements were now relatively immaterial, including course-taking patterns.

The nonhonors urban middle school students thought that successful applicants to UT need to have GPAs of 3.0 and above, but were unsure of any other specific requirements. None of the students had heard of SWT, so they could not compare admissions standards between the two IHEs. They did state that admissions standards differ between institutions. In comparison, all of the students in the honors sample believed SWT to be "a party school." The main difference between the two IHEs in the sample, they said, was that UT "might have more subjects" available to study. The students did not know the specific entrance requirements for the two IHEs in the sample, but they did think that UT's requirements would be more difficult. Many thought that volunteering is important, and most belonged to the Junior Honor Society because they believed that colleges look favorably on the association.

When asked how they would like to change the current process used to disseminate college admissions information at the high school, one white, non-Latino male honors student at the rural high school said angrily,

> I would like to know what the hell is going on—and not having to find it all out on my own. . . . Really, we don't get crap at this school. They don't give you anything. You either do it on your own with your parents, with your friends, with whoever you can coerce into helping you, or you bomb and you don't know jack and you end up with no scholarships. One teacher [the gifted and talented coordinator] helps you out. She's like the guidance counselor—one person on this campus. . . . And if you didn't have those singular people that were helping you, you'd be on your own.

KNOWLEDGE OF COLLEGE COSTS. On average, the students and parents in the urban sample overestimated the cost of attending a public university in Texas for a year more so than did students and parents in the rural sample. The student estimate, averaged across the sample, was $15,013; for parents, the number was $12,448. The actual cost in 1997–1998 was $10,481. One possible hypothesis to explain this difference is that the rural students' families earned significantly less than did the urban families, and consequently the relative view of costs is different between the two groups. In the focus groups, it was apparent that for a child from a less economically advantaged household, a guess of $5,000 signified a larger amount of money than for a more economically advantaged student. In the urban district, especially in the honors classes, the students guessed higher numbers, such as $20,000 per year, and did not seem put off by the cost. In one rural junior high focus group, for example, a student stated that her family would never be able to afford one year's worth of tuition because she guessed it would cost $1,000 and that was more than her parents could afford. Therefore, in many cases, the estimates seemed to be guesses in relation to family income.

KNOWLEDGE OF TASP. Few students could explain the TASP (eleven total).[10] A greater proportion of students in the rural high school than at the urban high school had heard of the TASP. The rural high school students attributed their knowledge of the TASP to one high school science teacher who wanted to make sure that every student was aware of the test. These findings are consistent with the main outside review of the TASP commissioned by the Texas Higher Education Coordinating Board (Boylan, 1996). The review found that "high school students are poorly informed about TASP policies, procedures, and requirements" and that "student confusion about the actual role of the TASP test contributes to problems in implementing TASP goals and objectives" (p. 2). Of the one hundred high school students interviewed for Boylan's review, approximately five knew what the TASP was, and those students tended to have parents who worked in a Texas IHE. Only one student had received information from a counselor. In addition, many students did not understand the difference between the TASP and the TAAS. Overall, students in every school voiced a concern that they are tested too often and that the frequency of testing is stressful and is distracting from their course work. This sentiment was echoed by educators interviewed for this study.

Conclusion: A Gap Between K–12 and Postsecondary Education

This project transpired at a crucial time during the history of K–12 and higher education relationships in the state of Texas. The connections between the two systems were in flux, and the project occurred in the infancy stages of major policy shifts brought about by the *Hopwood* ruling. The Top Ten Percent Rule had just gone into effect, as had new admissions requirements at the two IHEs in the study. TASP exemptions changed every two years, as did the requirement regarding at what time in a student's educational career the test must be taken. Adding to this confusion is the fact that IHEs did not employ broad outreach strategies to inform counselors or prospective students and their parents about the changes. In addition, the higher education systems in Texas are not well defined, leading to confusion about what it means to be in a particular system. Within the two IHEs studied, admissions staff were not aware of state-level K–12 standards and did not meet with K–12 representatives on a regular basis.

Most interviewees believed that K–16 reform needs to take center stage in Texas, but few were involved actively in activities that connect K–12 and postsecondary education. There have been gains in reforming the K–12 system, but these have happened in relative isolation from higher education. Many interviewees were concerned with disjunctures and changes in the systems. For example, several stated that prospective students could be confused by different expectations set forth by the TAAS, TEKS, and TASP; the specifications and objectives of the exit-level TEKS and the TAAS exit-level exam are not compatible with the TASP specifications. The exit-level TAAS is geared to the eighth grade but is taken in the twelfth grade. The TASP measures twelfth-grade work. Also, TASP exemptions change every two years, as does the requirement regarding at what time in their educational career students must take the test. This has had an impact on researchers' abilities to conduct longitudinal studies with TASP data and has led to confusion regarding when students need to take the exam.

When this research was conducted, the state's Recommended and Distinguished Graduation Programs were well aligned with admission requirements at UT and SWT. The General Graduation Program was not; it required less foreign language, math, and science than do the two institutions studied here. In addition, algebra was the highest required math class in the General Program; consequently, students who followed that path were most likely not prepared for the TASP, ACT, or SAT.

There is no process in place to ensure that the K–12 educators interviewed stay informed of changes in university or state-level admissions-related policies. Usually, the junior high and middle school administrators and other staff learn about changes in state or university admissions-related requirements several years after they occur—usually after the feeder high school changes its policies in response to the legislative or higher education changes. Then the junior high or middle school must alter its policies to reflect these changes.

Students and staff at the high schools reported that students are overwhelmed by the number of tests they need to take during their high school years, and they do not understand the purposes of each of them. When research reported here was conducted, students in the districts were tested on the TAAS and end-of-course exams in October, February, March, April, and May. Finals occur in December and June, and most classes have midterms as well. Therefore, students at different grade levels take high-stakes exams almost every month during the academic year. For students who do not pass the TAAS in the tenth grade, much of the instruction they receive is geared toward the TAAS until they pass all sections of the exam. Thus, many educators interviewed for this project believed that they did not have time to focus on issues that are not state mandates or are not directly related to pressing curricular needs or students' emotional or physical well-being. The majority of the counselors believed that they are responsible for implementing every new state directive and that they are unable to complete their required tasks.

Students in both district samples rarely talked to their counselors about college planning, but students in the honors sample received information from honors teachers. Counselors are traditionally the main source of college-related information in the schools, yet in the sampled schools, they are unable to fulfill that responsibility, and no other school site staff member is filling the void. The students often feel unable to make educated, rational decisions about college. The honors students in the sample received information in their college knowledge environment of parents, peers, and students. The nonhonors students in the sample on average received information in a relatively unstructured fashion, if at all. Most of the nonhonors students plan to attend college, yet most in the sample are not receiving information regarding college admissions, such as the type of graduation plan to follow, how to prepare for standardized tests, the appropriate courses to take, and how to seek financial aid. Many nonhonors high school students could not explain the SAT, while almost all in the honors track could. Almost no students in either track could explain the TASP. Almost no students had a clear understanding of UT's or SWT's admissions requirements other than that UT's are more rigorous than SWT's.

Students sampled from the nonhonors track in all of the schools had a clear understanding that they were being left out of the college policies information stream as compared to the honors students. They often felt stigmatized by the adults in the school. The honors students realized the differences too but believed that they did not receive enough information either. This finding is somewhat counter to findings in the literature. Dornbusch (1994), for example, writes that tracking students from disadvantaged minority groups is beneficial for schools and for teachers, and that parents and students do not notice problems when they are consistently left in the dark and the system is kept running smoothly.

This study presents an alternative view from a student perspective regarding the flow of college-related information. The nonhonors students and their parents sampled for this study realized, on average, that they received less information than did the honors students, but they felt powerless to change the status quo. Nonhonors students believed that they were second best at the school and that they were receiving educational experiences inferior to those received by the honors students.

Although both honors and nonhonors students seemed to feel as though they were stumbling blindly toward their respective goals, they planned their paths in different ways. On average, the honors students in the sample enrolled in the most difficult classes in the hopes that they would be able to gain admission to a selective institution. The nonhonors students assumed that if they graduated from high school, they could gain admission to some IHE, although they were concerned that their courses were not rigorous enough.

The findings of this study support the theory that honors track students rate factors such as the admissions process or graduation requirements as less important than do lower-track students, but pay more attention to the issue of academic pace and intensity (Galotti and Mark, 1994). For example, many of the honors students in the sample were concerned that the two IHEs in the sample were not prestigious enough. They were less concerned with the application process to the IHEs in the study than were the nonhonors students and were more concerned about the types of courses and status of the IHEs. The nonhonors students were more concerned with cost and process than were the honors students. In addition, nonhonors students on average were less willing to travel to attend college; many cited financial or family concerns about leaving the area. Most of the honors students stated that they were interested in applying to an out-of-state IHE. The findings also seem to indicate that tracking has a dual effect in terms of college aspirations: it limits exposure to the highest possible curriculum for some students, while limiting the amount of information students need to make choices about preparing for college.

NOTES

1. Texas was the pilot state for the Bridge Project. The research design used in Texas differed in several key ways from the design used in the other states: the pilot examined eighth and eleventh graders while the other states examined ninth and eleventh graders; it was more qualitative and exploratory in nature than the other states (and all students were included in focus groups as compared to twenty eleventh graders in the other states); and the pilot's surveys provided mostly demographic information (as compared to the surveys developed for use in the other states, which incorporated some of the pilot's focus group questions about college knowledge and preparation activities). In addition, the pilot had a smaller sample size. The general research questions remained the same.

2. Texas is the only one of the six states that included middle and junior high school students; the other state samples are entirely from high schools.

3. This law states that "each general academic teaching institution shall admit an applicant for admission to the institution as an undergraduate student if the applicant graduated in one of the two school years preceding the academic year for which the applicant is applying for admission from a public or private high school in this state accredited by a generally recognized accrediting organization with a grade point average in the top 10 percent of the student's high school graduating class. To qualify for admission under this section, an applicant must submit an application before the expiration of any application filing deadline established by the institution." This was implemented for the entering class in the fall of 1998. The legislation also recommends certain factors that can be used during the admissions process, such as family income, highest educational level attained by parents, and a student's SAT scores as compared with the average SAT scores from the student's high school.

4. The schools and districts requested that their names not be used.

5. One honors and one nonhonors English class were sampled per grade per school. For the purposes of this project, honors courses are AP, pre-AP, or honors classes; nonhonors courses are those that were classified by the school as not at an advanced, honors, or college preparation level. Each focus group contained fourteen or fewer students, and every student who obtained parental permission was included in a focus group and surveyed.

6. The focus groups were the primary source of information regarding the depth of students' understanding of particular policy mechanisms, including the TASP, IHE admission requirements, and standardized tests such as the SAT. The student and parent surveys provided background information (by race and ethnicity, family income, and the level of parental education) that made it possible to compare and contrast the knowledge bases and understandings of different student and family subgroups regarding IHE admissions–related policies and practices. In addition, they asked questions regarding student (and parent) aspirations for the post–high school years, the types of college–related information families receive, to whom students talk to learn about college preparation issues, and student and parent tuition estimates for Texas public universities.

7. This includes tuition, fees, room, board, books, and supplies.

8. Cross-tabulations were used to depict the relationship between dependent and independent variables of interest. When the sample sizes were large enough for the results to be valid, a significance test was conducted using the chi-squared value. The results are considered statistically valid if each

expected count cell totaled five, although a couple of exceptions are allowed if the table is greater than a 2 × 2 table (no expected count is less than one and no more than 20 percent of the expected counts are less than five). For this study, the test of significance was used to explore, for example, if there was a significant relationship between being an honors student and having an understanding of the TASP.

9. Project staff chose the urban high school because it was the most diverse school among the district's high-performing schools during the 1997–1998 academic year and the district staff would allow the project access to only one high-end-performing high school and one of its feeder middle schools. They were concerned that the project might take too much time away from counselors and that the information learned would add to the current negative perceptions of the district in general, and the counseling program in particular. Although the school's student body is diverse, it has two curricular, and consequently social, tracks in which white, non-Latino students are overrepresented in the higher track and students of color are overrepresented in the lower track. The urban middle school in the study is the primary feeder middle school for the urban high school in the study. The rural schools studied are the only junior highs and high school in the rural city.

10. Since the sample of students who did know about the TASP was so small, it was not possible to conduct any significance testing with other variables since the expected counts in several cells were always too small.

REFERENCES

American College Testing Program. *Some Observations About the Texas Graduating Class of 1997.* Austin, Tex.: American College Testing Program, 1997.

Boylan, H. R. *An Evaluation of the Texas Academic Skills Program.* Boone, N.C.: Texas Higher Education Coordinating Board, 1996.

Brooks, A. P. "TAAS Unfair to Minorities, Lawsuit Claims." *Austin American Statesman,* Sept. 16, 1998.

College Board. *Texas Highlights: The SAT I Program.* Austin, Tex.: College Board, 1998.

Dornbusch, S. M. "Off the Track." Address to the Society for Research on Adolescence, San Diego, Calif., Feb. 12, 1994.

Galotti, K. M., and Mark, M. C. 1994. "How Do High School Students Structure an Important Life Decision? A Short Term Longitudinal Study of the College Decision-Making Process?" *Research in Higher Education,* 1994, 35(5), 589–607.

Grissmer, D., and Flanagan, A. "Exploring Rapid Achievement Gains in North Carolina and Texas." Paper commissioned by the National Education Goals Panel, Washington, D.C., Nov. 1998.

Murdock, S. Presentation to the Texas Commission on a Representative Student Body, Austin, Tex., 1998.

National Commission on Excellence in Education. *A Nation at Risk: The Imperative for Reform: A Report to the Nation and the Secretary of Education.* Washington, D.C.: U.S. Department of Education 1983.

Orfield, G., and Paul, F. G. *High Hopes, Long Odds: A Major Report on Hoosier Teens and the American Dream.* Indianapolis: Indiana Youth Institute, 1994.

Texas Education Agency. *Texas Administrative Code, Title 19, Part II.* Austin: Texas Education Agency, 1994.

Texas Higher Education Coordinating Board. *A Generation of Failure: The Case for Testing and Remediation in Texas Higher Education.* Austin, Tex.: Texas Higher Education Coordinating Board, 1986.

Texas Higher Education Coordinating Board. *Applications, Acceptances, and Actual Enrollment.* Austin: Texas Higher Education Coordinating Board, 1995.

Texas Work Group and others, "Education Assessments in Texas," Austin, Tex.: Texas Higher Education Coordinating Board, 1995.

University of Texas at Austin. "Student Profile, 1996–1997." Austin, Tex.: Office of Admissions, 1997.

4

ROADBLOCKS TO EFFECTIVE K–16 REFORM IN ILLINOIS

Betty Merchant

IN 1997, ILLINOIS was typical of states in which there are few significant venues through which to integrate and coordinate higher and secondary school education policy. There was no policy mechanism or institutional structure to align K–16 standards and K–12 assessments, including admissions and placement exams. Moreover, Illinois K–16 policymaking was extremely fragmented because each public campus established its own admission and placement policies. This made it extremely difficult for students to know what colleges expected of them.

Attempting to address these roadblocks to developing a more coherent system, Illinois launched in 1998 a targeted campaign, Education for the 21st Century, focused on improving access to and quality of higher education. As a starting point, the Illinois Board of Higher Education (IBHE) stated its goals:

- Extend access to higher education.
- Ensure that college is affordable.
- Enhance access and success for members of underrepresented groups.
- Improve the quality of education.
- Enhance responsiveness to students, employers, communities, and the state.
- Strengthen school-college partnerships.
- Improve productivity.

A follow-up 1999 report, *The Illinois Commitment,* suggests focusing on improvement in partnerships, opportunities, and excellence (Illinois Board of Higher Education, 1999).

In 1997, the IBHE, in conjunction with the Intergenerational Initiative, launched the Illinois Partnership, which has changed the education policy arena in Illinois to promote a K–16 focus. For example, this initiative began a process to integrate policies and practice across all levels of Illinois education. The IBHE believes that the state must address the root causes of poor academic preparation and underperformance in order to eliminate the need for remediation in higher education. The IBHE explains, "Illinois colleges and universities share a joint responsibility with the state's elementary and secondary schools to improve the performance and success of students at all levels of education" (Illinois Board of Higher Education, 1999, p. 1). Although the universities often fail to discuss the existence of remediation, the IBHE acknowledges that it does exist and believes that through new K–16 partnerships, remediation can be eliminated.

Illinois public universities report low percentages of students enrolled in remedial courses. However, the degree to which universities acknowledge remedial course enrollment remains unclear. For example, Illinois State University (ISU) has algebra courses listed in its catalogue as well as other high-school-equivalent courses such as the introduction to trigonometry. In fact, what constitutes "remedial" remains largely up to the public institution of higher education. Moreover, many four-year universities transfer remedial students to community colleges, where remedial work is conducted and counted.

Recognizing that some of this could be alleviated by effective communication with community colleges, a collaborative was formed. The Illinois Articulation Initiative (IAI), a voluntary cooperative effort among more than one hundred Illinois colleges and universities, is designed to facilitate transfer of students from one college to another, increasing the number of students who complete their baccalaureate degree.

Although initiatives such as these have been valuable, this chapter demonstrates that there are still many roadblocks to developing a more coherent K–16 system in Illinois (Richardson, Bracco, Callan, and Finney, 1999). This chapter describes a number of institutional reforms that have been put into place, many of which have been diffuse and less than effective. It then turns to the two major public postsecondary institutions in the state, Illinois State and University of Illinois Urbana-Champaign (UIUC), discussing among other issues their admission and placement policies. Finally, it shows how students, parents, and educators at seven case study high schools perceive policies at these universities. The conclusion outlines the roadblocks to better alignment that must yet be cleared.

Institutional Process

Illinois policymakers started new K–16 institutional processes to overcome a history of disjointed K–12 and higher education policies in prior years. (Timpane and White, 1998).

K–12 Standards, Assessments, and Class Rankings

Before implementation of the Illinois Learning Standards in 1997, high school students participated in two assessments. The Illinois Goals Assessment Program (IGAP) was administered in the fourth, seventh, tenth, and eleventh grades, as well as in the fourth and seventh, and was based on 1995 Illinois Board of Education (IBE) standards. The Illinois Standards Achievement Test (ISAT), administered in grades 10 and 11, included specific grade standards for content knowledge developed in 1998. Neither test was used for university placement.

Illinois universities did not use the 1997 statewide K–12 IGAP assessment for admission or placement. According to university officials, this is because they were not involved in formulating IGAP and because the state changed the content of IGAP in 1997; hence, university officials have very little faith that it will be stable. IGAP was not a proven predictor of freshman grades, some university administrators said. Universities were confident that the SAT and ACT would make the necessary adjustments to account for new elementary and secondary academic policies. Bridge Project researchers did not find any admissions officer who knew much about the content, standards, or format of the IGAP.

In 1999, legislation eliminated the IGAP and ISAT at grade 11, establishing the Prairie State Achievement Exam (PSAE) as the only mandated statewide assessment beyond grade 8. Administered in the eleventh grade, the test measures progress toward the Illinois Learning Standards in reading, writing, mathematics, science, and social science. The test is not required for graduation and is not used for admission to higher education. But the Prairie State Exam was combined with the ACT in 2001 to provide better information about postsecondary standards to high school students. Some high school students scored high enough on the Prairie State/ACT exam but had not applied to any four-year colleges. Illinois state officials have contacted these high-scoring students and encouraged college applications.

Illinois universities rely heavily on class rank as an admission criterion and predictor of freshman success. Deemed to be more accurate than grade point average (GPA) due to grade inflation, use of class rank has created some confusion because there is no statewide standard. Local high schools weigh Advanced Placement (AP) and honors classes differently, and some exclude nonacademic classes from the GPA calculation.

For decades Illinois has been using high school class rank as one-half of an admissions index, with ACT scores for the other half. The state distributes a brochure showing typical class rank and ACT scores for universities ranging from UIUC to Northeastern Illinois University. But Illinois universities and the IBHE have never specified how high schools should compute class rank. Consequently, high schools use a variety of techniques and weighting systems. They include different courses in their calculations; for example, some schools count college prep courses for the most part, but others include electives and vocational classes. Some types of courses are more heavily weighted, but some schools compute class rank in several ways and then report the ranking that provides local students with the best chance of being admitted.

Confusion about class rank has created a group of special review schools, often private or public schools from suburban Chicago, claiming that their academic standards are so high that their class ranks should be adjusted upward compared to the rest of the state. Consequently, the University of Illinois has designated some schools with special review status. Generally, the University of Illinois will accept the highest class ranks for any student from the five or six methods a high school may use. The complexities of weighting grades add to the complexities of the admission process; for example, Illinois universities are perplexed about what admission criteria to use for the Illinois Math and Science Academy, a statewide competitive high school that refuses to rank students.

Governance of Higher Education

Until 1995 there were individual postsecondary systems that included four different public university governing boards with responsibility for twelve public universities. In 1995, this systems approach was abolished because of effective opposition from universities demanding independence (Richardson, Bracco, Callan, and Finney, 1999). Illinois has a historically strong local control political culture that resists centralized state control of education policy or procedures (Nardulli, 1989). Each university created a governing board and hired contract lobbyists to represent its interests in Springfield.

The higher education coordinating body, the IBHE, is criticized for a postsecondary policymaking style that is detached from K–12 policies (Richardson, Bracco, Callan, and Finney, 1999). The not-so-veiled resentment that characterized the reactions of many community college representatives to IBHE was mirrored in the comments researchers heard from K–12 respondents. For instance, researchers were told that the IBHE ignored the K–12 board in its discussion of admission requirements during the 1980s, despite the fact that K–12 was involved concurrently in looking at outcomes. IBHE's efforts to assess college affordability were described as another strain on the conversation because the board never considered the impact on elementary and secondary school costs. Rather, it sent the message to K–12 education that essentially said, "If you would do a better job of preparing students, our costs would go down." One respondent concluded, "No matter what happens, seems like the ball rolls downhill." IBHE representatives, however, reported that K–16 relationships are becoming better.

Efforts to Improve K-16 Connections

K–16 alignment in Illinois prior to 1997 was nonexistent. In 1997, as part of the Illinois Partnership, the IBHE committed to raising the standards and quality of Illinois public universities and strengthening the transition from secondary to higher education. The IBHE has begun the process of bringing together high school and higher education representatives from around the state to work on aligning high school exit standards with college entry standards. All three Illinois education agencies—the Illinois Board of Higher Education, the Illinois Community College Board, and the Illinois Board of Education—are working on the K–16 partnership to begin to address the inconsistencies.

The governor initiated a K–16 committee, the Illinois Joint Education Committee, but little happened regarding aligning assessment. The committee, which includes members of the K–12 State Board of Education and the IBHE, never met publicly, kept minutes, or had an impact on assessment or placement; consequently, it was ineffective.

In 1997, Illinois had a standardized university feedback report to high schools with data on the freshman achievement of specific high school graduates at the university. It included high school class rank; ACT scores; and performance in freshman English, math, and natural science. But high schools rarely made this university performance report public, and the universities have not been willing to advocate for its release into a more public forum.

The Illinois Education Research Council (IERC) was developed to support the Joint Education Committee in making informed policy decisions. The council established a research clearinghouse to assist in providing policymakers with analytical research. It also created a K–16 network to analyze and communicate effective K–16 practices and partnerships.

The Intergenerational Initiative is a collaboration among universities, community colleges, K–12 entities, and community organization. Funded by the IBHE, it is composed of a team of staff and policymakers working from all levels of Illinois education to better align policies. According to Jane Angelis, of the Southern Illinois University at Carbondale and Intergenerational Initiative member, "There is extraordinary potential to relate the curriculum of high school and college students to preschool needs and community action." One concrete achievement of this new K–16 perception is better test alignment.

In June 2000, the Illinois State Board of Education approved a contract with ACT to give each high school junior an ACT college entrance exam as part of a Prairie State Achievement Exam that also includes items based on K–12 content standards.

Illinois State University

Founded in 1857, Illinois State University (ISU) was the first public higher education institution in Illinois. It prides itself on a strong sense of community, labeling itself a residential university, with the majority of students coming directly from an Illinois high school. The board of trustees is the official governing body; however, the academic senate legislates university policies concerning faculty and students as well as academic programs and planning.

Admission Policies

ISU's admission policy has undergone significant changes in the past ten years. In the early 1990s, the university was overenrolled and underfunded. A plan to decrease enrollment by becoming more selective was implemented, but soon the university was left with an underenrollment problem—and fighting the perception that it did not want students. In three years, enrollment had dropped by five thousand. In order to increase enrollment, less qualified students were accepted, and it was not until 1999 that the university was able to reinstate a selective admissions policy.

As a result of that more selective policy, processes are changing. The application deadline for fall has moved from May 1 to April 1 and may change again as selectivity increases. Admissions requirements may change as well. Background statements from students became a requirement in 1999.

An applicant will be accepted if he or she meets minimum standards, regardless of other factors. These standards include completion of required high school course work, SAT or ACT scores, and class rank. According to the current undergraduate catalogue, 91 percent of ISU's freshman students admitted for the 2003–2004 academic year ranked in the top half of their graduating class, 49 percent ranked in the top quarter, and 19 percent ranked in the top 10 percent of their class. The average ACT score was 24. Some programs may have higher criteria.

ISU has five special admission programs:

○ The Talent Program, for outstanding talent in art, music, theater, or athletics

○ The Early Admit Program, for concurrent high school and college credit

○ The Veterans' Program

○ The Adult Learner Program

○ The Collegiate Opportunities Admission Program (COAP), designed to increase the number of underrepresented students by affording them special consideration, with determinations based on a background statement and proficiency on diagnostic exams

Placement and Remediation

Illinois State University hesitates to acknowledge the existence of remedial courses and believes that remediation is a task for the community colleges.

Entering freshman are assessed for mathematics placement using ACT's COMPASS test. Students take the exam on a computer, and the questions become progressively harder as the student answers them correctly. ISU switched from COMPASS to using ACT math admissions scores for some student placements. In a recent policy change, students are now required to complete a university-level math class to graduate; this may create a need for more developmental math courses.

The English/language arts placement exam consists of a writing sample from all students. The English department devises topic and grading criteria and grades all exams. There has been some pressure at the university to develop a new exam due to concern about the validity of data, including inconsistent grading and adjustment of grades based on number of available classroom seats.

University of Illinois, Urbana-Champaign

Following are descriptions of the admission- and placement-related policies of the University of Illinois, Urbana-Champaign (UIUC).

Admission Policies

Recognizing that a state school is designed to serve Illinois taxpayers, the university has had to defend its selectivity to the legislature as the pool of applicants grows. Several interviewees noted that any move to tighten standards would be at the political peril of the university, because strong candidates who are Illinois residents are already denied admission.

Unlike ISU's central application process, applicants to the UIUC must apply to a particular college, and often to a particular program. Minimum requirements for admission are the completion of fifteen units of college prep work and a high school diploma or general equivalency diploma. Admission decisions are based on high school course work and a combination of high school class rank and admission test scores. A selection index, based on high school class rank and ACT score, is used to predict students' first-year GPAs. Use of specific selection criteria are not made public; however, the criteria on which selection is based are publicized. Class rank as it is calculated by the high school is used for the admissions process. Background statements are also required. Letters of recommendation may be considered in borderline cases. According to the 2003 online UIUC Undergraduate Catalogue, "The median ACT composite score of entering freshmen is 27 and almost 80 percent of these students ranked in the top 20 percent of their high school classes."

Special admits make up about 10 percent of incoming classes. These are students who have met the minimum qualifications but just miss being competitive. These include General Assembly scholarship recipients and President's Award Program participants—students of color in the upper half of their class with an ACT score of 24 or above. Special admits are also accepted from the Educational Opportunities Program (EOP). Administered by the Office of Minority Student Affairs, EOP "is designed to provide opportunities for a college education to students who have historically been excluded from postsecondary education." Admission to the program is limited to Illinois residents. EOP applicants must satisfy the high school subject pattern requirements and the high school GPA and ACT combination.

The Liberal Arts and Sciences (LAS) school admits one hundred EOP students most at risk to special summer bridge and transition programs.

Some Illinois high schools are designated as EOP high schools, chosen because of the low socioeconomic status (SES) of their school population. Any student from an EOP school receives special consideration regardless of ethnicity. Typical EOP high schools include those in inner-city Chicago and East St. Louis. No explicit written guidelines for EOP high school students exist. Rather, the cases are referred to the dean of the appropriate college for consideration. Office of Admissions and Records (OAR) staff stated that the bottom-line EOP special review student must be in the upper half of his or her class, have English and math ACT scores of 18 or higher, have a selection index of 30 or higher (which predicts a C average on campus), and submit verification of ethnicity.

In addition, some high schools are designated as special review high schools to compensate for class ranks that may not demonstrate the caliber of student due to the abundance of high-achieving students at that school. Most of these high schools are in suburban Chicago. Most strong academic high schools have an ACT average of 22. The mean ACT score at special review high schools is over 26, often around 29 or 30. These schools typically have admission requirements rather than open enrollment, and large percentages of the high school graduates pursue postsecondary education. One OAR administrator expressed an opinion of the need to reevaluate these schools in the light of existing grade inflation. For example, in determining which schools qualify as special review, UIUC could ask what percentage of students have a B average or higher or what percentage of students are in the top half of the class. One special review high school had thirteen students tied for the highest class ranking.

Placement and Remediation

Placement tests at UIUC are administered after the student is admitted to the university. Tests are given in language, chemistry, math, and composition. The university cannot place students in math courses below college-level algebra. If students test lower than that, they may need to take a math course at a community college or may be able to participate in a transition program. Each college has its own placement tests and procedure. Interviews with LAS admissions personnel for the entire university revealed that LAS admissions officers are not knowledgeable about placement test content. Consequently, there is no information provided by central admissions to prospective applicants about placement content standards and very little provided about the placement process. In 1997, the largest undergraduate college, LAS, used written essays for placement and a math test designed by the college.

Outreach and Communication

The UIUC colleges maintain a strong commitment to their published admissions guidelines and competitive levels. The guidelines are based on admissions decisions from the previous year. As a result of publishing competitive levels, interviewees believe that students self-select and the university receives predominantly well-qualified applications. This benefits UIUC because it generates less work for admissions and college staff. It is helpful to students as well, who are not faced with as much guesswork as to their chances of admission. However, the value of advertising accurate cutoff scores carries makes for lower national rankings. Because of up-front competitive guidelines and resulting self-selection, UIUC has a higher ratio of admitted applicants to applicants than many other flagship state universities. Other universities seem more selective because they have lower yield percentages.

Student, Parent, and Educator Understandings— and Misunderstandings—of College

A crucial aspect of our research focused on how the admission standards and policies of state universities in Illinois are transmitted to and understood by students, parents (for the purposes of this chapter, "parent" is synonymous with "guardian"), and secondary school personnel. If they are understood well, students have a good idea of what they must do to prepare for college; if they are understood poorly, students become confused as to the college preparation path they should follow.

Research Methodology

Our research team selected five rural and two urban schools in central Illinois and administered surveys to ninth (or tenth) and eleventh (or twelfth) graders and their parents.[1] Students in ninth grade were targeted because they were just one year removed from the eighth-grade classes that likely influenced their course-taking trajectory in high school; eleventh graders were chosen because they were at or near the point where they were likely to be making postsecondary plans.

The student survey consisted of thirty items and was administered in English class. Parents were surveyed before their children on a similar nineteen-item questionnaire regarding their socioeconomic background, perceptions of their children's aspirations, and their knowledge of college admissions–related policies. At each grade level, the research team surveyed a minimum of one honors and one nonhonors English class, for a total of forty-eight classrooms. We collected 626 student surveys, 619 of which could be linked with surveys received from their respective parents. Although the response rate varied, thirty-one of the classes had a survey return rate of 60 percent or better.[2] Students were primarily of middle SES (53 percent), white (92 percent), and almost evenly divided as honors and nonhonors.

In addition to the surveys, the research team conducted focus group interviews with eleventh or twelfth graders from at least one honors and one nonhonors English class in each of the schools, for a total of twenty-three honors and twenty-five nonhonors focus groups.[3] The research team also conducted individual interviews with principals, teachers, and counselors.

The schools in the sample were chosen primarily because they were located in central Illinois and could provide useful information about students in rural communities as well as the few relatively large urban communities that are also located in this part of the state. Another factor in school selection was the schools' relative proximity to both ISU and UIUC, the two universities that are a key focus of this study.

The Case Study Schools and Communities

The communities within which the schools were located ranged in size as follows: 1,400 to 5,500 residents (three schools); 12,000 to 15,000 (two schools); and the two largest communities, one with a resident population of 34,000 and the other with a population of 82,000 (U.S. Census Bureau, 2000). The population figures from 1990 to 2000 indicate that the resident population of the villages and smaller communities in the sample remained relatively stable over this period of time, whereas the three largest communities experienced a decrease in population. The decline was related in part to the departure of employers that in previous years had contributed significantly to the economic vitality of these urban centers.

Student enrollment data for September 1999 indicate that the seven high schools clustered into three groups with respect to total student enrollment: 200 to 500 students (three schools), 800 to 1000 students (two schools), and 1100 to 1500 (two schools) (Illinois State Board of Education, 2000).[4] Students in the five smaller schools were predominantly white

(85.8 to 98.6 percent), whereas the students in the two large urban districts were more racially diverse (66.6 percent white and 26 percent African American at one school; 62.2 percent white and 36.4 percent African American at the other school). The two smallest schools in the sample had the lowest percentage of students from low-SES families (5.2 to 6.4 percent), whereas the two largest schools had the highest percentage of such students (30.6 percent and 60.9 percent, respectively). The three midsize schools reported between 12.7 and 14.4 percent of their students as low income (Illinois State Board of Education, 2000).[5]

The students in five of the schools tended to remain in the same schools as indicated by the mobility rates, which ranged from 5.2 percent to 16.7 percent, while approximately a third of the students moved in and out of the two urban schools (32.7 percent and 35.5 percent, respectively). There were very few English-language learners in the schools; one school reported 1.8 percent of its students as limited English proficient (LEP), and the other schools reported having less than 1 percent of these students or none at all. Spanish was the heritage language of almost all the students who were classified as LEP. The district instructional expenditure per pupil ranged from $3,130 to $4,453, generally increasing as the size of the district increased; a notable exception was the largest school, which reported a per pupil expenditure very close to that of the second smallest school in the sample ($3,143 compared to $3,240).

The high school graduation rates reported by the schools for the 1999–2000 academic year ranged from 79.6 to 93.0 percent, except for one of the urban schools, which reported a graduation rate of 66.2 percent. According to the 2000 *Illinois School Report Card* data (Illinois State Board of Education, 2000), the student dropout rate ranged from 0.9 to 5.6 percent in the four smaller schools to 12.0 and 12.4 percent in each of the two urban schools. The percentages of students taking the ACT exam ranged from 49.1 to 58.4 percent in five of the schools, whereas they were much higher in the two smallest schools (70.4 percent and 72.3 percent) (Illinois State Board of Education, 2000). The School ACT Composite Score for the class of 2000 ranged from 21.2 to 23.0 in the five smallest schools to 21.2 and 21.7 in the two largest schools.

Students' Plans After High School

Students communicated their postsecondary plans on the surveys and in the focus groups, parents stated their hopes for their children on the surveys, and teachers and counselors shared their aspirations for their students in their interviews with us. The postsecondary aspirations of students, their parents, and their teachers provide a useful point of reference for examining the degree of overlap among these aspirations and for exploring the extent to which students' course-taking patterns and school-related activities supported or contradicted their stated postsecondary plans.

A substantial number of students (90.6 percent) were planning to attend college either part time or full time. As indicated in Table 4.1, the percentage of students intending to pursue college full time increased as their families' SES increased, whereas the inverse was true for the percentage of students planning to attend college part time. A higher percentage of low-SES students than either middle- or high-SES students were planning to work full time after completing high school.

Although 87.4 percent of honors students reported that they were planning to attend college full time after high school, a considerable number of nonhonors students were also interested in attending college: 58.6 percent planned to attend full time, and 23.1 percent planned to attend part time. These college plans were out of synch with the actual course-taking patterns of students who were taking only non-college-bound classes.

The only striking differences between male and female students' post–high school plans were in two categories: joining the military (7.7 percent of males versus 2.9 of females) and working part time (19.5 percent of males compared to 33.0 percent of females).

EDUCATORS' BELIEFS ABOUT STUDENTS' POST–HIGH SCHOOL PLANS. Some teachers mentioned "native ability" and "brain power" as possible distinguishing factors separating the college bound from the non–college bound. Teachers most often cited parental influence and

Table 4.1. Plans After High School, by Student SES.

Post–High School Plans	Low SES	Middle SES	High SES
Work full time	11.7%	5.9%	2.2%
Attend college full time	54.1	73.1	91.2
Join military	7.2	4.6	3.6
Work part time	25.2	31.8	19.7
Attend college part time	27.9	17.9	5.1
Undecided	11.7	4.3	1.5
Other	2.7	2.5	2.2

Note: *Multiple responses permitted.*

affluence as the primary factors in determining whether a student was college bound. As one teacher remarked:

> I think the main reason why kids would or wouldn't want to go to college is because of family influence. In a smaller town like this, farm kids have a very strong inclination to follow their family. It's been ingrained in their minds that they don't need to go to college to be successful, and for many of them, they don't need to go to college to be successful. Then there are also a lot of farm kids whose parents never went to college who have very high aspirations and are good students.

Another teacher brought up socioeconomic factors:

> Parental push is a big part of it. If you looked at my honors and nonhonors Brit Lit classes, you'd see that socioeconomic background seems to be the biggest divider. Kids in the honors class are from very well-connected homes. They are children of college-educated, career-oriented parents who push them in that direction.

A teacher from another school expressed similar thoughts:

> I think that economic levels and value systems are so intertwined that it's very difficult to separate them. When I look at the kids who sign up for college prep and the kids who sign up for non–college prep, economic level is more a distinguishing factor than ability. The kids in the college prep group expect to go on. But the kids in the other group— it's just not part of their thinking. It wasn't part of their parents' thinking. And unless something happens to break that cycle, it won't be.

One of the teachers indicated that many students, "in the regular classes especially," perceive college as cost prohibitive. She stated that the guidance counselors meet with individual students and explain financial aid options and the relative affordability of community college enrollment: "But when the kids go home and the parents say, 'There's no way I can ever afford to send you to college,' that kid just gives up."

Few teachers reported details of college-related conversations in nonhonors classes. A teacher of nonhonors students said:

> They don't have the foresight that the other kids have; they cannot see that far into the future right now. The here and now is much more important to them. The reality of it is that most of these kids I am

teaching right now will not go to college. A handful of them will go to a community college, and even fewer will go to a four-year university. It seems to be their educational mind-set right from the beginning: they either know that they are college bound, or they know that they are not.

STUDENTS' POSTSECONDARY ASPIRATIONS. Students' aspirations to attend a four-year college within or outside Illinois were related to their families' SES: the percentage of students indicating an interest in each of the four-year postsecondary choices increased as their families' SES increased (see Table 4.2).

Students who wanted to attend a public university in Illinois expressed greater interest in attending UIUC or one of the other state universities than they did in attending ISU; this was especially true of students from high-SES families. In spite of UIUC's selectivity, only 49.4 percent of eleventh- and twelfth-grade honors students indicated they were considering applying. Interestingly, one-fifth of students in the C range (in terms of their GPAs) identified UIUC as an institution they were considering. Among A students, the percentage interested in UIUC (45 percent) was identical to the percentage interested in ISU.

Whereas over one-third of low- and middle-SES students were considering attending community college, only 18.2 percent of high-SES students were interested in pursuing this option. With rising tuition costs, community colleges offer a financially viable option for low-SES students who cannot afford to attend a four-year university as well as for middle-SES students who are seeking a relatively inexpensive method of acquiring their first two years of college.

Table 4.2. Students' Postsecondary Aspirations, by SES.

Postsecondary Aspirations	Low SES	Middle SES	High SES
Have not considered schools	15.3%	4.9%	2.9%
U.S. military academy	8.1	7.4	6.6
Two-year community or junior college	35.1	37.2	18.2
University of Illinois at Urbana-Champaign	26.1	39.1	54.0
Illinois State University, Bloomington	22.5	37.5	35.8
Another state university in Illinois	27.0	38.5	43.1
Private college or university in Illinois	16.2	22.2	31.4
Four-year college or university outside Illinois	23.4	28.6	52.6
Technical or trade school	9.0	8.6	8.0
Other	13.5	4.6	2.9

Note: *Multiple responses permitted.*

It is interesting to note that over one-fourth of low- and middle-SES students and slightly more than half of high-SES students expressed an interest in attending a college or university outside Illinois. In the focus groups, these students expressed their eagerness to get away from central Illinois and experience a different setting. The honors students in several schools, however, complained that parents, teachers, and counselors "pushed" local colleges or state universities that were less selective, less competitive, less expensive, and closer to home.

One frustrated student explained:

> I got a 28 on my ACT, and I'm in the top 11 percent of my class. My counselor said, "Well, you should think about ISU." I am really annoyed with that. I want to go to med school in California. Even by my parents, I'm not encouraged to do something above and beyond what most people do.

A similar story was shared by an honors student from another school who was interested in applying to Harvard and wanted admissions information from her counselor. The guidance counselor showed her a brief paragraph in a book that said, "This many students a year apply." The student said the teacher "couldn't give me any information because she didn't have any. She said she'd get it for me, but she never did."

Honors students were much more likely than nonhonors students to aspire to four-year colleges and universities. Higher percentages of non-honors than honors students reported being uncertain of their postsecondary aspirations, and these students were more likely than their peers in honors classes to express an interest in community colleges, technical schools, and the military.

Most students conceded that their parents play an important role in their college selection decision, as observed by two students: "My parents are paying for it, so . . ."; "Maybe your parents usually have the ultimate say."

PARENTS' POST–HIGH SCHOOL PLANS FOR THEIR CHILDREN. In examining whether parents' postsecondary choices for their children varied by their SES, the data in Table 4.3 indicate that a two-year community college was the first choice of both low- and middle-SES parents. Several factors may account for this, including the relatively low tuition of community colleges compared to four-year universities, the additional savings resulting from their children living at home while taking classes, and the flexible class schedules that allow for part-time employment while

Table 4.3. Parents' Postsecondary Choices, by SES.

Postsecondary Option (N = 610)	Parent Expectations for Child (%)			Parent Rank Order		
	Low SES	Middle SES	High SES	Low SES	Middle SES	High SES
Full-time work	3.7	.6	0	6	9	8
Military academy	3.7	1.9	2.9	6	8	6
Two-year community college	28.4	29.1	7.3	1	1	5
Technical or trade school	4.6	2.2	2.2	5	7	7
University of Illinois at Urbana-Champaign	11.0	13.3	16.1	2	3	2
Illinois State University, Bloomington	8.3	8.4	8.8	4	5	4
Four-year public in Illinois	10.1	15.5	16.1	3	2	2
Private four-year in Illinois	4.6	10.8	20.4	5	4	1
Four-year outside Illinois	2.8	5.3	10.9	7	6	3

taking classes. The second and third choices of low-SES parents were UIUC and a four-year public university in Illinois; middle-SES parents also selected these options but ranked them in reverse order. The three least favored options of low-SES parents were a four-year university outside Illinois, a military academy, and full-time work, whereas the three lowest-ranked choices of middle-SES parents were full-time work, a military academy, and a technical or trade school.

The top three choices of high-SES parents were a private four-year university in Illinois, followed by a four-year public university in Illinois, and a four-year public university out of state. High-SES parents were almost twice as likely as middle-SES parents and almost four times as likely as low-SES parents to select a private school for their children. This finding was consistent with most students' perceptions that their parents prefer that they attend an in-state college or university. The three lowest-ranked choices of high-SES parents were full-time work, a technical or trade school, and a military academy.

Parents of honors students were more likely to aspire to four-year colleges and universities for their children; parents of nonhonors students were more likely to select community college, the military, and technical schools as reasonable postsecondary options for their children. Parents of boys were more likely to select a college outside Illinois than were parents of girls; they were also less likely to choose another public university in Illinois (other than ISU and UIUC) than were parents of girls.

STUDENTS' PERCEPTIONS OF ISU AND UIUC. Asked to compare ISU and UIUC, students often said "big" in referring to UIUC. An honors student from one of the smaller schools said:

> The class size scares me. Here, you know your teachers, and they know you. When you go to UIUC, you'll be in a classroom with 300 or 400 people, where you're just a number. If you didn't show up, no one would even know or care. That's a big problem. It's not personal enough. It's just so different from here.

Students generally liked the fact that ISU was smaller, and many commented that it was less expensive than UIUC:

> A lot of people here talk about ISU. A lot of my friends say they plan on attending there because they got a good scholarship, and ISU has a good financial aid program. . . . All the schools would probably meet my needs; it's whichever one has the most financial aid and the best scholarship program so I can save money, because I have very little of that.

Although several honors students in different schools described ISU as "respectable," honors and nonhonors students in all schools perceived UIUC as "a better school" than ISU. Honors students recognized UIUC as the more esteemed of the two universities, based on its size, reputation, tougher admissions requirements, reputed level of difficulty, and number of celebrated graduates. Nonhonors students appeared less informed about colleges in general and tended to speak in more general terms about the qualities of the two schools, as indicated by the comments of three students: "They're pretty good schools. You get a good career education going there"; "I think it would be easier to get into ISU than UIUC."; "I really don't know [how ISU compares to UIUC]. I haven't heard much about schools recently." Students in nonhonors focus groups based their perceptions of UIUC as "better" and "harder" than ISU on their appraisal of the academic abilities of friends who attend those universities and on information they had received from peers:

> You can look at ISU, and then if you're really smart, you can go to the next level—UIUC. The requirements are higher, and a lot of smart people I know have gone there. It's not that if you're dumb you go to ISU; but smart, really smart, people go to UIUC.

Knowledge of Tuition Costs

The extent to which students and their parents think that the cost of college tuition is affordable undoubtedly affects their beliefs about whether a college degree is a reasonable avenue to pursue. At the time this study was conducted, the cost of community college tuition for residents in central Illinois was $880; resident tuition was $4,400 at ISU and $5,200 at UIUC. As indicated in Table 4.4, students and parents across all three SES categories were more accurate in their estimates of the cost of community college than in their estimates of the cost of tuition at the four-year institutions, although fewer than 25 percent of students and their parents were within range of the actual tuition for community college. High-SES parents were more accurate in their estimates of tuition at UIUC and ISU than were their middle- and low-SES counterparts, although the estimates of a substantial

Table 4.4. Students' and Parents' Estimates of Yearly Tuition Costs, by SES.

	Low SES		Middle SES		High SES	
Estimates by Institution	Students	Parents	Students	Parents	Students	Parents
Community college						
Within range (within $500 of actual cost)	21.0%	21.8%	15.0%	16.9%	18.8%	19.7%
Between two and five times actual cost	24.8	29.9	33.6	38.0	39.1	44.1
More than five times actual cost	47.6	43.7	45.9	34.2	31.6	22.8
University of Illinois at Urbana-Champaign						
Within range (within $500 of actual cost)	8.6	2.3	4.2	8.1	10.4	14.5
Between two and five times actual cost	42.9	46.5	44.8	45.1	36.6	31.3
More than five times actual cost	18.1	12.8	12.9	7.4	6.0	1.5
Illinois State University, Bloomington						
Within range (within $500 of actual cost)	1.0	3.6	5.5	10.1	14.2	13.2
Between two and five times actual cost	44.8	51.2	47.2	45.2	39.6	34.1
More than five times actual cost	23.8	19.0	14.2	7.3	6.0	2.3

percentage of high SES parents were still two to five times more than the actual cost of tuition. Students were more likely than their parents to over-estimate the cost of tuition by more than five times the actual amount.

Knowledge of Required Courses

The minimum number of years of high school courses required for admission in each of the following subjects at both institutions at the time of this study were English, four years; social studies, two years; math, three years; science, two years; and foreign language, two years (ISU permitted two years of one language or two years of fine arts).

By and large, both honors and nonhonors students in the focus groups had little knowledge of what might be expected of them academically once they entered college. Nonetheless, they believed that their academic preparation was far less adequate than that of their peers in larger districts or more exclusive schools—for example, "schools in the suburbs of Chicago," where students "actually go to college prep schools."

We also examined the extent to which students' and parents' knowledge of course requirements for admission to UIUC and ISU varied by students' track placement. Slightly higher percentages of honors students than nonhonors students were knowledgeable about course requirements for ISU and UIUC. Eighty-one percent of honors students listed four years of English as a requirement for ISU compared to 70.1 percent of nonhonors students. Similarly, 90 percent of honors students compared to 76.5 percent of nonhonors students listed four years of English as required for admission to UIUC. The percentage of students who knew the math requirements for ISU and UIUC was comparatively low among honors and nonhonors alike. Only 56.6 percent of honors and 48 percent of nonhonors students listed three years of mathematics as a requirement for ISU, and the percentage of students who listed three years of mathematics as a requirement for admission to UIUC was even lower (49.8 percent of honors and 43 percent of nonhonors).

Knowledge of the number of English courses required for admission to ISU was more accurate among parents of honors students than parents of nonhonors students (82.9 percent versus 73.6 percent); this was also true for UIUC (90.4 percent of honors parents compared to 77.7 percent of nonhonor parents knew these requirements). A relatively small percentage of the parents of honors and nonhonors students knew the math requirements for ISU (49.3 versus 42.4 percent) and UIUC (44.0 versus 39.6 percent). The differences between these two groups of parents tended to be far less pronounced with respect to the course requirements in the other content areas, however. In fact, the estimates of course requirements by parents of honors and nonhonors students for social science, laboratory science, and foreign language tended to be separated by only a few percentage points. Overall, students and their parents tended to overestimate the number of courses required for admission to UIUC and ISU.

Low-income students and their parents were more likely than were either their middle- or high-income peers to overestimate or underestimate the course requirements for admission to ISU.

When asked which courses best prepared students for UIUC or ISU, honors students identified AP courses and honors classes. Among nonhonors students, vague, general responses were common. Asked which curriculum track offered the best preparation for UIUC and for ISU, a student in the nonhonors focus group in one school replied, "I have no idea." A nonhonors student in another school answered, "Not the one [track] I'm on." He added, "I don't think any of us has a clue what we're going to get into in college."

The data reveal similar findings with respect to students' and parents' estimates of course requirements for UIUC, with the exception of English. Higher percentages of students across all income categories correctly estimated the number of years of English needed for admission to UIUC; the estimates of parents also improved, but this was true only for those in the middle- and high-income categories.

At all seven schools, from the smallest to the largest, students perceived themselves as at a disadvantage academically compared with students who attend "college prep schools," or schools that offered an array of AP and advanced college prep courses. In speaking of the academic disadvantages of attending small, rural schools, one student said, "People from here who go to UIUC say they were behind a lot of the other people there because we don't have the college prep classes." Similarly, students in another school noted the dearth of advanced courses at their high school. A student in the nonhonors focus group remarked, "My honest opinion is that this school does not have enough advanced classes to prepare us for UIUC in any way, shape, or form." A college prep student commented, "I don't think that we're prepared enough to go to UIUC. I think that if we did, we'd probably flunk out."

In all seven districts, students' initial exposure to college preparation information occurs during eighth grade. Typically, high school counselors go to eighth-grade classrooms prior to freshman registration as part of an orientation program, and they discuss college preparation with students at that time. Parents are briefed on college requirements at an evening orientation session.

Sources of Information about Admission Requirements

Rather than relying on information from school personnel, students talked more with parents and friends than with anyone else about college admission requirements (56.3 percent and 40.1 percent, respectively; see Table 4.5). The people whom students were next likely to talk with about college were brothers and sisters (18.7 percent) and relatives (16.5 percent). Only 14.0 percent of students reported talking "many times" with their counselors, and only 9.8 percent talked "many times" with their teachers. It is potentially problematic that students tend to seek information from individuals who may be less knowledgeable about college admissions policies and procedures than school counselors or college recruiters (72.8 percent of students never talked with a college recruiter).

The proportion of students who spoke "many times" with family and friends increased from one SES level to the next, with high-SES students having substantially more conversations about college admissions than either their middle- or low-SES peers (see Table 4.6). The percentages of students who discussed college with school personnel (counselors and teachers) were remarkably similar across SES, with comparatively low percentages of low-, middle-, and high-SES students accessing these individuals for information about college.

Although nonhonors students were less likely to engage in conversations about college than their peers in honors classes, many of these students were also interested in going to college (see Table 4.7), although their aspirations were not well aligned with their high school course-taking patterns.

Table 4.5. Frequency of Student Conversations with Others About Admission Requirements.

	Many Times	Once or Twice	Never
Parents	56.3%	33.8%	9.9%
Friends	40.1	42.0	17.9
Counselors	14.0	52.7	33.3
Teachers	9.8	52.9	37.3
College recruiters	4.5	22.7	72.8
Coaches	6.6	20.4	73.1
Private counselors	.3	4.8	94.9
Brothers or sisters	18.7	32.3	48.9
Clergy	3.0	11.4	85.6
Family friends	9.2	37.9	52.8
Relatives	16.5	42.2	41.3

Table 4.6. Students Discussed Admission Requirements "Many Times," by SES.

	Low SES	Middle SES	High SES
Parents	45.9%	52.2%	74.3%
Friends	27.9	39.8	50.0
Brothers or sister	10.0	19.6	26.9
Relatives	16.2	17.0	18.5
Counselors	13.5	13.4	16.2
Teachers	11.0	9.3	11.0

Table 4.7. Number of Discussions About Admission Requirements, by Honors Status.

	Many Times		Once or Twice		Never	
	Non-honors	Honors	Non-honors	Honors	Non-honors	Honors
Parents	50.3	61.9	35.9	31.8	13.7	6.3
Friends	33.7	46.2	44.4	39.6	21.9	14.2
Brothers or sisters	17.8	19.7	29.6	34.9	52.6	45.4
Relatives	15.1	17.9	40.7	43.7	44.3	38.4
Counselors	12.1	15.8	47.5	57.6	40.3	26.6
Teachers	8.6	11.0	43.2	62.1	48.2	26.8

Female students tended to talk more than their male counterparts with friends (45.5 percent versus 32.8 percent), brothers and sisters (21.0 percent versus 15.8 percent), and relatives (17.4 percent versus 15.4 percent). Male students were more likely than females to talk about college with clergy (4.1 percent versus 2.2 percent), college recruiters (6.7 percent versus 2.8 percent), and coaches (8.2 percent versus 5.3 percent).

Knowledge of University Selection Criteria

When honors students were quizzed on their knowledge of the admission requirements for UIUC, a few were well versed in what was required. Nonhonors students' answers were more varied than those of the honors students. A student responded that the main requirement is "money. It's expensive." One student from a small school said, "I don't know—I would think that colleges look at your attendance to see if you went to school regularly, that you missed no more than a couple of days. But if you're not at school a lot, then they're going to look at that. And I think they look at your letters of recommendation to see if you did your home-work." At one school, a student responded:

> Sometimes colleges look at you as a person, and they might accept you, even though you might not have the best grades. But they know you try, and you just need some help; and especially if you've talked to a recruiter face to face, they just look at you and can tell that you're a determined person.

In all of the schools, students in all the focus groups said that "there are always ways" of getting around admissions requirements. "Athletic ability" was mentioned most frequently; "money" came in a distant second.

When students were asked to rank the importance of specific items for admission to UIUC and ISU, their top three choices were as follows:

ISU

1. SAT I score
2. High school grades
3. SAT II score

UIUC

1. High school grades
2. SAT I or ACT score
3. SAT II score

According to the UIUC undergraduate catalogue, admissions decisions are informed by three types of information: courses taken in high school, a combination of high school rank in class and admission test scores, and subjective information submitted on students' personal statements. ISU relies on similar information in making admissions decisions: ACT or SAT score, high school transcript (grade trends and rigor of courses com-pleted), high school class rank and GPA, personal statement, and in some cases letters of recommendation.

Regrettably, the majority of the students in our study were unaware that their high school courses and their personal statements were signifi-cant factors in getting admitted to UIUC as well as ISU. Other factors that at least two-thirds of the students felt were important included senior year grades, application essay, class rank, and college preparation courses.

A somewhat surprising finding was the high percentage of students who selected the "ability to pay" option as an important factor for admission to both universities (49.4 percent for ISU and 50.3 percent for UIUC), though this is not a factor in admissions. More than half of the students in all income categories felt that race was not a factor in the college admissions process at ISU and UIUC. Students from high-SES families were more likely to believe that a variety of factors were taken into account in admissions decisions at ISU and UIUC than were students from middle- and low-SES families.

Knowledge of Placement Policies

Few students at any of the seven schools were versed in the specifics of placement policies and procedures. Students in the nonhonors focus groups were no more or less knowledgeable about placement practices and procedures than the honors students. Asked what content would likely be included on a math placement test at UIUC, one student skirted the question: "I know that the math test is really, really long, and hard." Another student responded, "Probably some stuff from, like, back in the day that we don't even remember how to do—like fractions, algebra, geometry." She added that students are placed in math classes at ISU "the same way. The tests are the same."

Exposure to Higher Education

We also explored the extent to which students participated in activities that prepared them for college. Both honors and nonhonors students participated in college-related activities to some extent across all categories listed on the survey, although a slightly higher percentage of honors than nonhonors students did so. The data in Table 4.8 reveal that just under half of the honors and nonhonors students had visited a college or university; the percentages for both groups were relatively similar (46.6 percent and 40.1 percent, respectively). This suggests that students did not possess a great deal of exposure to colleges or universities. Almost 60 percent of honors students participated in varsity athletics in comparison to 41.8 percent of the nonhonors students. A large percentage of students reported using a computer at home: 96.2 percent of honors students and 88.1 percent of nonhonors students. Almost 35 percent of honors students and 27 percent of nonhonors students had taken an SAT or ACT test preparation course. Only 22.4 percent of honors students and 19.1 percent of nonhonors students reported having attended a college night.

Table 4.8. Students' College Activities, by Grade Level and Track.

College Activities	Honors	Nonhonors	Ninth and Tenth Grades	Eleventh and Twelfth Grades
Visited a college or university	46.6%	40.1%	35.8%	51.7%
Participated in varsity athletics	59.1	41.8	39.5	62.7
Used a computer at home	96.2	88.1	94.0	90.5
Taken an SAT or ACT test preparation course	34.5	27.1	8.5	54.4
Attended a college night	22.4	19.1	7.4	35.2

Note: *Multiple responses permitted.*

Although eleventh- and twelfth-grade students reported higher levels of participation in college activities than did ninth- and tenth-grade students (except for using a computer at home), only about half of these students had visited a college or university or taken an SAT or ACT test preparation course, and just over one-third had ever attended a college night.

In examining the responses of students from low-, middle-, and high-SES families, the data in Table 4.9 indicate that participation in college activities increased from one SES level to the next, with the most dramatic differences occurring between high- and low-SES students. This notwithstanding, only 52.6 percent of the students from high-SES families had visited a college or university, 41.5 percent had taken an SAT or ACT test preparation course, and only one-third had attended a college night.

Parents' Responsibilities Pertaining to College

Parents held themselves primarily responsible for helping their children prepare their college applications and the schools responsible for informing their children about the course requirements for admissions to college.

In looking at whether low-, middle-, and high-income parents varied from one another with respect to holding schools and families responsible for students' college preparation, 85.2 percent of low-income parents held schools primarily responsible for college application preparation compared to 71.4 percent of middle- and 60.5 percent of high-income parents. High-income parents were more likely than either middle- or low-income parents to hold families primarily responsible for college application preparation.

Table 4.9. Students' College Activities, by SES.

College Activities	Low SES	Middle SES	High SES
Visited a college or university	37.6%	41.0%	52.6%
Participated in varsity athletics	27.4	48.7	68.6
Used a computer at home	77.6	93.8	99.3
Taken an SAT or ACT test preparation course	25.5	29.0	41.5
Attended a college night	16.3	18.3	33.6

Note: *Multiple responses permitted.*

Parents of honors as well as nonhonors students held families primarily responsible for students' college application preparation, whereas they held schools primarily responsible for informing their children about the course requirements for college.

Student Interaction with Guidance Counselors

Descriptions of the physical guidance facilities across the seven high schools were enough alike to be almost interchangeable: each school had a guidance center that was a separate area, complete with one to three computers with access to the Internet, where students could peruse the college and career materials and meet with college representatives and military recruiters. There was also a private office for each counselor, where they could meet with students individually. The number of full-time counselors employed at each high school ranged from one to six.

Although all seven schools reported that they had at least one full-time guidance counselor, few of the schools had the luxury of a full-time counselor whose time was devoted exclusively to college and career preparation. As one counselor remarked, "It seems like a lot of things fall under our umbrella." In addressing the reality of time constraints, another counselor explained:

> Each of us has a counseling load of 350-plus students, so we just don't get a chance to see kids as much as we want. I might be able to see a student for fifteen or twenty minutes once individually, unless they come to me. We have no study halls, so we have to call students out of classes. Teachers do not like that.

In general, students reported that their guidance counselors had been of little help in providing them with college admissions and placement information. One honors student said, "They just look at what you're required to take to graduate high school. The counselors don't look at what you have to have to get into college." When asked at what point counselors began meeting with students to talk about college, another honors student responded, "I don't know that they ever meet with you to talk about college. You have to hunt them down to talk to them on your own."

At the larger schools, a few students recognized the efforts and the limitations of the counseling staff. One student said, "We have 1,337 students in this school, and four counselors. They could work their absolute hardest, and there's no way they could get to all of us and spend the time they need to spend with us."

According to several students, materials provided by their guidance offices were sometimes outdated. A student from one school said that her counselor had recently given her an application for a state university that was dated 1993. Students also complained that their counselors have given them erroneous or misleading information that might prevent or delay their application to schools of choice or cause them to take courses at the university level that they could have taken in high school. Honors students at most schools stated that they received information about college prep courses "too late" and that ideally, they would have learned about college admissions requirements in their freshman year. Both honors and nonhonors students reported that college preparation was first addressed by their counselors during freshman registration, when they were given sheets listing college-bound classes. In most cases, however, the subject of college preparation was not revisited by counselors until students were preparing to enter their final year of high school Students in the nonhonors focus groups appeared more satisfied with the status quo; most reported that junior year was early enough to begin discussion of college preparation information. At all of the schools, few students appeared to have given the subject of college selection serious thought before their junior or senior year. Generally, honors students reported that junior and senior year was too late to begin the college preparation process but the right time to start the application process.

All of the counselors interviewed indicated that their primary source of college admissions and placement information was the State Articulation Conference, sponsored by the State University System in conjunction with the Illinois College Counselors Association. The articulation conferences are one-day meetings held each fall at various campuses throughout the state to which all high school guidance counselors are invited. The main purpose of the conferences is to update counselors on changes in university admissions and placement policies and procedures. Feedback from counselors about the conferences was unequivocally positive.

Student Interaction with Teachers

Honors and nonhonors students alike reported that for the most part, college-related issues were seldom discussed in any depth in their classrooms; rarely was specific college admissions information shared in the classrooms, outside of discussions surrounding ACT preparation. One group of students said that their AP English teacher was "our source for everything: what kinds of things you need to do to get prepared academically, different credits that you might need, different study skills you might use." Honors and college prep students were more likely to initiate and engage in classroom discussions of college-related topics; non–college prep students "rarely ask." A teacher said that honor students' college-related questions often refer to course content in college.

Most of the veteran teachers interviewed said that they knew little about college admissions and placement policies other than the fact that their "college-bound students need four years of high school English." For the most part, those who considered themselves "somewhat knowledgeable" obtained their information through their own initiative. Veteran teachers who professed to having "some degree of awareness" of admissions procedures reported that they learned what they know through "memories, now distant," of their own undergraduate experiences, through helping their own children with the college application process, or through their own participation in on-campus continuing-education classes and programs. These teachers reported that they, rather than their students, initiated classroom discussions of college-related issues.

Younger teachers who are recent college graduates reported that honors students frequently asked them about their personal college experiences. A teacher who graduated from UIUC four years before the interview said that students asked specifically about her social and academic experiences at UIUC. She said they asked about "everything, from what classes to take to what ones to avoid," the content of placement exams, housing options, "the Greek system," and the benefits of concurrent enrollment in UIUC and the local community college.

None of the teachers interviewed recalled receiving college preparation information from their school districts. Without exception, the teachers who were provided admissions and placement information received it from the guidance department or from building-level administrators. Teachers whose schools offered AP classes seemed more confident in their knowledge of college placement exams. An AP teacher said, "We have an AP class structure at this school, and so we have lots of samples, lots of the exams to look at for the different areas, and we get lots of ideas from that." She reported, however, scant familiarity with college admissions information: "I think a lot of that is just restricted to the counselors. I, on the whole, don't know, so when students ask, I just say, 'You're going to have to speak to your counselor. I don't know.'" Most teachers complained about being left out of the information loop.

At many schools, teachers reported that most of the information that filters down from the guidance office is in the form of announcements or postings notifying students about visiting campus representatives, ACT testing, due dates for college applications, and scholarship application deadlines. Several teachers remarked that they learned what they know about college requirements at the same time and in the same manner that their students did: when guidance counselors came in and spoke to their class about course registration and scheduling. Most of the teachers interviewed were aware that college representatives visited their schools, but none of the teachers reported meeting with the representatives.

Information from Parents

A substantial percentage of parents reported talking with their children "many times" about their plans after high school (84.3 percent) and whether they were specifically interested in attending college (83.8 percent). A smaller percentage of parents said that they discussed their children's course planning "many times" (56.3 percent), and even fewer indicated that they frequently discussed specific college requirements with their children (44.7 percent). Higher percentages of the parents of honors students than the parents of nonhonors students reported discussing college topics with their children. The differences are particularly apparent in the "many times" category.

In examining the responses of low-, middle-, and high-income parents with respect to discussing college topics with their children, the percentages of parents reporting that they engaged "many times" in discussing all of these topics varied according to income level, with low-SES parents much less likely than either middle- or high-SES parents to have engaged in these discussions. Conversely, a higher percentage of low-income parents than either middle- or high-income parents reported never having discussed these topics with their children. These differences were particularly striking with respect to discussing college requirements and course planning. Parents of honors students were more likely than were parents of nonhonors students to discuss college topics with their children.

Parents of honors students were much more likely than were parents of nonhonors students to engage in college-related activities on behalf of their children. Of these, the differences were greatest with respect to volunteering at school (19.2 versus 42.4 percent), reading a college brochure (39.4 versus 56.9 percent), reading a news magazine (16.0 versus 31.9 percent), and visiting a college campus (14.3 versus 30.6 percent).

The percentages of parents who reported being involved in college-related activities rose considerably from one income level to the next. Although the differences in parental participation between each of the income categories are notable, the most striking differences occur between the percentages of low- and high-income parents. The largest differences occur with respect to saving money for their children's education (18.3 versus 66.7 percent), looking at college and university Web sites (7.7 versus 48.1 percent), visiting a college campus (5.8 versus 43.7 percent), reading news magazines (7.7 versus 43 percent), and reading college brochures (27.9 versus 60 percent). Higher percentages of the parents of sons than the parents of daughters reported attending a college fair (21.7 versus 12.5 percent) and saving money for their child's education (45.3 versus 35.9 percent).

Other Sources of Information

At all seven schools, students reported that individual college representatives visited their high schools during the day; in many schools, counselors arranged for these individuals to talk with students in specific classes, such as senior English or some other advanced class. In other cases, students were invited to sign up for individual visits with the recruiter. According to some of the students, the representatives "actually know about the specific college, whereas the counselors just have a general idea." Several students mentioned that these visits are often not publicized. One honors student remarked, "You usually don't know about their visits unless you go into the counselor's office and look on their calendar. Last year, I remember, I missed three I wanted to go to because I didn't even know. It wasn't on the announcements or anything; it was just on their little calendar."

Students at all schools reported that most of the informational and promotional materials provided by the college representatives are too general and insubstantial to be of much help. One student said:

> Get rid of the nice, beautiful pictures and give us the actual details— what specific departments have to offer; the curriculum—what classes you'd be taking; what exactly you might be able to test out of, so that you'd know how heavy your class load would be; the job opportunities available after you graduate from college.

At several schools, students complained that the information they were given rarely addressed financial aid issues in terms that were sufficiently specific. A student in one school said, "Money is a big issue with me, and we don't have any discussion about that. There are scholarships you can apply for your sophomore year, but we didn't know about these."

Recommendations for Improving College Knowledge

Despite overall satisfaction with the state universities' methods of disseminating admissions and placement information to high school guidance departments, the educators interviewed expressed little awareness or understanding of specific university placement policies and performance expectations. The consensus among teachers was, in the words of one teacher, "We have no idea what their expectations are, and they have no idea what we're doing."

Several teachers, counselors, and administrators offered suggestions for improving communication between high schools and universities, most of which included improved communication and articulation of requirements. One teacher stated, "I don't know that I have ever received anything in written form that said, 'These are our expectations. This is the type of material that's going to be on a placement exam in your content area.' And I think that certainly would be helpful."

In commenting on the inconsistent and inaccurate information he receives from college admissions offices, one counselor urged, "We need consistency. When you call university admissions offices, people need to be all on the same track." In discussing a similar concern, a teacher from one of the larger schools said:

> It would be good just to know that there was someone whom you could call and say, "I've got six classes of seniors who really want to know what you want from them," and to know that Joe Smith, at whatever phone number, was the person who would answer my questions, and tell me to whom to direct my students.

In acknowledging teachers' lack of information about college course requirements, one counselor suggested, "Departmental meetings or discussions, or mailings from, for instance, the math department at UIUC to math teachers here, so that the teachers here would know and could relay this to students."

A principal suggested another approach to improving communication between K–12 and colleges and universities:

It would be nice if universities had a liaison officer assigned to a geographical area of responsibility, who would pay attention to meetings that are being held, to state edicts that are coming down to the schools, and have those representatives monitor those edicts, monitor the seminars that are going on at the high school level for administrators regarding reforms, and pick up clues that this is what the high school is doing.

One teacher summarized the feelings of many of her peers:

In an ideal world? Come and sit down with us when we plan our curriculum, and we'd plan a coherent K through 16 program that would have the outcomes that we want. I think what happens now is we have a K through 6 program that gets chopped off, and then a 7 through 8 program that gets chopped off, and then a 9 through 12 program that gets chopped off, and then a four-year institutional program, which are totally disconnected. And I don't know that we've ever stopped to say, "Are we preparing our students for a smooth transition from here to there?"

Conclusion: Many Roadblocks Remain

The students from central Illinois who participated in this study were not thinking broadly about college options, and the lack of advanced curricular opportunities in many of their schools put them at a serious competitive disadvantage with respect to the college admissions process, particularly with respect to nationally recognized, academically rigorous universities. Although some students with strong academic credentials expressed an interest in attending an out-of-state or highly selective college or university, for the most part, they received very little encouragement to do so. In fact, some of their counselors or teachers actively discouraged them from applying by emphasizing the strong academic competition they were likely to encounter. This tended to underscore the concerns that these students already had about the adequacy of their high school preparation.

As a group, the students were surprisingly naive with respect to the specifics of the college admissions process, although students from higher-income families knew more about this process than did students from low- or middle-income families. In particular, there was a dismaying lack of congruency between the college aspirations of the students in the non-honors track and the courses they were taking, most of which did not fulfill the admissions requirements of the colleges they were interested in attending.

Students tended to identify high school grades and scores on the SAT I and ACT exams as important considerations in getting accepted to college. There was a general lack of understanding about the importance of other factors, such as the specific courses they took and the rigor of those courses, and the content of their personal statements. For the most part, the students expressed a great deal of inadequacy with respect to the extent of their competitiveness with college applicants from larger and wealthier suburban and urban districts, and this contributed in part to their reluctance to apply to colleges and universities they associated with a more selective admissions process.

The ways in which students obtained information about the college admissions process tended to reinforce the distinctions between honors and nonhonors students and low-, middle-, and high-income students. That is, honors students were more likely than were nonhonors students to engage in discussions about college, and overall, the percentages of students participating in these discussions increased as their family's income level increased. Interestingly, students discussed college admissions requirements more frequently with their parents and friends than with school personnel. Guidance counselors were often described as too busy responding to the multiple demands of their jobs to take time to talk with the students about these issues. The informational materials distributed to students by college admissions offices were of little to no help in addressing their most important questions and concerns, particularly those related to financial aid.

Although the yearly articulation conferences sponsored by the state's university system and the Illinois College Counselors Association appear to be doing an excellent job of providing counselors with up-do-date information on the college admissions process, there is a noticeable gap in communication between the guidance counselors and the classroom teachers with respect to this information. This contributes to the teachers' inability to respond adequately to their students' questions; this is unfortunate, given the lack of interaction between many of the students and their guidance counselors. The knowledge that teachers do possess about college tends to be linked to their own college experiences, however dated, supplemented by information they obtain from their own college-going children or the student teachers who work in their classrooms.

The differential levels of outreach described for UIUC, ISU, and the various community colleges point to a hierarchy of accessibility, with community colleges the most active of the three in providing information to students and their parents, followed by ISU and then UIUC. The outreach efforts of UIUC, the most selective of the three institutions, are woefully inadequate as characterized by the majority of students and teachers in this study. The lack of visibility of UIUC recruiters in the majority of the schools in this study confirms a fairly widely held belief that the only students from these schools who are likely to be noticed by UIUC are athletes who have achieved statewide recognition for their talents.

The findings of this study make a strong case for the desirability—in fact, the necessity—of promoting stronger linkages between institutions of higher education and the K–12 educational system. At present, students' and parents' information about the college admissions process is mediated by students' track placement, parents' income level, teachers' knowledge, and counselors' outreach efforts. Counselors' information is mainly derived from attending the annual state articulation conferences and reviewing the brochures mailed to them by colleges and universities. Students' academic preparation for college is conditioned, to a large measure, by the number and kind of advanced courses that are part of the regular curriculum or negotiated in partnerships with local community colleges and universities or learning centers.

This chapter has outlined ideas for improving the linkages between colleges and universities and K–12 institutions in Illinois most notably the comments offered by students who participated in the focus groups and the suggestions made by teachers, counselors, and principals. Achieving these critical linkages will entail reexamining and removing the long-held distinctions between colleges and universities and K–12 institutions. The separated roles and blurred responsibilities of people within these institutions has hindered their ability to inform students about the college admissions process, undermining their chances of obtaining a postsecondary degree.

NOTES

1. For this research, 268 ninth- and eleventh-grade students from three schools were surveyed and interviewed in May 2000 at the end of the academic year. To increase the size of our sample, 358 tenth- and twelfth-grade students from four additional schools were added in September 2000, less than a month into the following school year.

2. Specific return rates were as follows (n = the number of classrooms in each category): 10 percent (n = 1), 20–39 percent (n = 5), 40–59 percent (n = 11), 60–79 percent (n = 19), 80–99 percent (n = 10), and 100 percent (n = 2).

3. Honors classes included English classes labeled honors, accelerated, and advanced, and in the absence of these labels, the courses described as such by classroom teachers and counselors. Nonhonors classes included regular track English courses that were neither college preparation nor remedial.

4. The school pseudonyms and student enrollment were as follows: Field View-211, Horizon-330, CityVille-479, Plum Springs-811, Harvest Town-998, River City-1,069, and City View-1,472.

5. "Low income" is defined in the *Illinois School Report Card* (Illinois State Board of Education, 2000) as follows: "Students may come from families receiving public aid, may live in institutions for neglected or delinquent children, may be supported in foster homes with public funds, or may be eligible to receive free or reduced-price lunches" (p. 2).

REFERENCES

Illinois Board of Higher Education. *The Illinois Commitment*. Springfield: Illinois Board of Higher Education, 1999.

Illinois State Board of Education. *Illinois School Report Card 2000*. Springfield: Illinois State Board of Education, 2000.

Nardulli, P. F. (ed.). *Diversity, Conflict, and State Politics*. Urbana: University of Illinois Press, 1989.

Richardson, R. C., Bracco, K., Callan, P., and Finney, J. *Designing State Higher Education Systems for a New Century*. Phoenix, Ariz.: American Council on Education and Oryx Press, 1999.

Timpane, P. M., and White, L. S. (eds.). *Higher Education and School Reform*. San Francisco: Jossey-Bass, 1998.

U.S. Census Bureau. "Population, Housing Units, Area, and Density: 2000. Census 2000 Summary File 1 (SF 1) 100-Percent Data: Illinois-Place." 2000. [http://factfinder.census.gov/servlet/GCTTable?ds_name= DEC_2000_SF1_U&geo_id=04000US17&_box_head_nbr=GCT-PH1&format=ST-7].

5

OREGON'S K–16 REFORMS

A BLUEPRINT FOR CHANGE?

Andrea Conklin Bueschel
Andrea Venezia

OREGON'S LEGACY OF progressive reform has led its education systems to launch a number of connected and ambitious initiatives over the past decade. The K–12 system has introduced several major reforms, as has the Oregon University System. At the heart of these K–12 reforms were assessments tied to real proficiencies—what students know and can actually do—as opposed to standardized tests. Over time, these assessments have become more traditional and are now mostly multiple-choice tests. The state's higher education–focused reform, however, has retained its original proficiency-based model. At the time this research was conducted, many of the reforms of the K–12 and higher education systems had been neither fully implemented nor aligned, often creating confusion for teachers and students. And many parents and students, as the second part of this chapter demonstrates, expressed confusion about what it takes to get into college. In sum, there remains a disjuncture between K–12 and postsecondary education in terms of the effectiveness of their reform efforts and the mixed signals students are getting regarding postsecondary admission and placement.

This chapter begins with a look at reforms that have taken place across the K–16 spectrum and their ramifications for Oregon's public universities. We then shift to a discussion regarding the perceptions that students, parents, and teachers at four high schools have about the reforms and what it takes to get into college. We conclude by contrasting these perceptions with the reality, demonstrating a significant gap. We also discuss both the promise and possible pitfalls of the Oregon reforms, including concerns we have about their long-term sustainability unless more coherent K–16 connections are established. The research[1] was conducted in 1999 and 2000; research in the universities and state agencies occurred in 1999, and research in high schools was in 2000.

The Blueprint: The Oregon Educational Act for the Twenty-First Century

The 1983 publication of *A Nation at Risk* raised concern about student performance nationally and called for higher standards and greater accountability. Oregon responded by rethinking its educational system and developing in 1984 the Oregon Plan for Excellence. This plan contained the seeds for the 1991 Oregon Educational Act for the Twenty-First Century, which mandated the development of the current standards, assessments, and certificates. These standards, as well as the assessments tied to them, were to be performance based, emphasizing what students could actually do as opposed to what they had crammed for a test.

Concurrently, the Commission on the Skills of the American Workforce published a report supporting the use of certificates of mastery that would be awarded in high school. The commission wrote, "Once a student has acquired the Certificate of Initial Mastery, he or she could choose a college preparatory program, go right into the workforce, or enter a program designed to culminate in a Technical or Professional Certificate. These certificate programs would combine formal education and on-the-job training in a unified curriculum" (Marshall and Tucker, 1992, p. 153). Influenced by such research, Oregon's legislature authorized the development of Certificates of Initial and Advanced Mastery.

The Oregon Educational Act for the Twenty-First Century, and the subsequent amendment to that act, Bill 2991 in 1995, marked the beginning of a new era of education policymaking in Oregon. Important legislation from that act includes the authorization of benchmarks for all students, assessed in grades 3, 5, 8, 10, and 12; the CIM (Certificate of Initial Mastery, issued after grade 10); and the CAM (Certificate of Advanced Mastery, issued after grade 12).[1] Although each of the grade-level assessments is considered important, the most focus has been on the CIM and CAM. But were reforms such as CIM and CAM really needed?

Oregon students were consistently performing near the top in national and international tests of student performance; consequently, some wonder if there was an effort to fix something that was not really broken. But the central premises of the CIM and CAM were built on the notion of proficiency, something that cannot always be measured by standardized tests. As a Portland State University administrator explained, "Our educational system is built on the notion of grades, seat time, credits, that is, in credentialing people. . . . The sudden change to proficiency-based is going to take a long time."

In reaction to the 1991 legislation, the Oregon University System (OUS) developed the Proficiency-Based Admission Standards System (PASS) to reform the admission process for Oregon's public universities and to ensure that students met a high standard of academic preparation prior to matriculation into an OUS institution. Although the CIM, CAM, and PASS have different histories, philosophies, and overall goals, they are often viewed as part of the same education reform package. They are, however, two distinctly separate, but interrelated, sets of reforms. As Christine Tell, the former director of PASS Implementation and current director of PASS, explained, "It's appearing to me that what it is, it's more like constructing a web, but purposefully, than we're held together by a common vision. But we have to keep restringing the web over and over again, making it larger, smaller, making new connections."

Certificate of Initial Mastery

The most visible components of the new statewide standards and assessment system were the CIM and CAM, which are the responsibility of the Oregon Department of Education (ODE). The certificates were designed to be capstones to student mastery of the standards during high school, though neither has been required for high school graduation or college entrance in Oregon or is intended to denote college readiness. Furthermore, both continue to evolve in terms of their design and use, though their legislative mandate stands.

To earn a CIM, students must demonstrate the knowledge and skills necessary to learn, read, problem-solve, think critically, apply concepts learned in science and math across the disciplines, communicate, use technology, and work effectively alone and as the member of a team (Oregon Department of Education, 1995).

The CIM assessment includes a series of performance-based assessments (a combination of selected response, performance tasks, and student work samples) benchmarked to mastery levels at approximately grades 3, 5, 8, and 10. Individual assessment is designed to be ongoing to provide students continuous feedback regarding their progress toward meeting the standards at the benchmark and CIM levels.

The CIM, which was designed to lead to the CAM, is seen as a rigorous set of standards (Oregon Department of Education, 1995). Students begin working on the CIM in kindergarten and complete requirements in high school. Districts were first able to award CIMs to students in June 1997. Some students earn a CIM prior to age sixteen, while others take longer.

The early years of implementation were marked by changes in timelines and requirements. A big area of concern for most schools and teachers has been in social studies. The social studies standards have undergone continual modification, and there is still confusion about what students are expected to know and be able to do. Because of these and other concerns, the State Board of Education has made a number of postponements.

Certificate of Advanced Mastery

The CAM was not yet fully implemented, but the ODE had piloted it in approximately six high schools across the state. The CAM may include both college preparatory and professional training, and students will be able to earn one at the end of high school. The curriculum must include "focused opportunities for structured work experiences" or cooperative work-study programs in one or more broad occupational areas. Students are required to demonstrate the knowledge and skills necessary to meet high content and performance standards (Oregon Department of Education, 1995).

CAM standards are divided into Foundation Skills and Advanced Applications that require the same standards of performance of all students. The CAM program provides the content and context to prepare students for their individual goals beyond high school. Students, with the involvement of parents and school staff, develop individualized plans that will build on their aptitudes, interests, and goals. These plans provide a road map to prepare students to continue their education and to enter the workforce.

The CAM program differs from the CIM program in its fundamental purpose. Students continue to focus on the CIM as they prepare for the CAM, but in order to earn a CAM, they must demonstrate the skills in a context requiring a more sophisticated use of knowledge and performance. It takes approximately two years to earn a CAM.

Because there has been difficulty clarifying what the CAM is and how it fits into the overall reform, ODE delayed implementation in order to define it more explicitly. Many interviewees believed that the CAM is stalled and does not have a realistic implementation timeline.

The Oregon University System and the
Proficiency-Based Admission Standards System

Oregon's K–12 reforms, centered on CIM and CAM, spurred on the OUS, consisting of eight universities and about forty-eight thousand students, to launch a reform initiative of its own.

The Proficiency-Based Admission Standards System (PASS) was initiated by the OUS in 1993 to examine how higher education's needs fit in with the CIM and the CAM and to ensure that high standards were developed and maintained. According to David Conley, the former executive director of PASS, a major impetus for PASS was that the OUS did not want to lose control of admissions. The campuses wanted more and better students and were concerned that CIM would be mostly focused on remediation, while the CAM would be more career and vocationally based. There was little in the two reforms that was seen as focused on college preparation. PASS was part of a movement to support the development of higher standards to increase students' preparation for college-level work, improve the school-to-work process for students, and decrease the amount of time it takes for students to graduate from college.

A goal of PASS was to move the focus of the admission process from the courses taken to the knowledge and skills mastered. When PASS is fully implemented, students will have to demonstrate that their knowledge and skills meet or exceed the required PASS standards in order to gain admission to a public university in Oregon.

The proficiency areas are broken down into six academic content areas: English, math, science, visual and performing arts, second languages, and social science. Proficiency in these areas is demonstrated though activities in class and through test taking. Students receive a summary judgment score for each of the PASS standards in a content area. There are five possible scores: Exemplary (E), High-Level Mastery of the Proficiency (H), Meets the Proficiency (M), Working Toward the Proficiency (W), and Not Meeting the Proficiency (N). Students who score E and H may be eligible for scholarships, special programs, advanced class placement, and university credit possibilities.

Results from CIM tests and CIM work samples can contribute to determining proficiencies. Higher scores can result in the awarding of college credit. Teacher scoring guides will be coordinated with the CIM and CAM guides so that student work will not have to be scored more than once.

Other recognized standards-based assessments, such as the SAT II Subject Tests, Advanced Placement (AP) tests, International Baccalaureate (IB), American College Test (ACT), and various language proficiency tests will be acceptable to show proficiencies in the designated subject areas. Students who do not meet the proficiencies can be reviewed for admission on a case-by-case basis during the standards implementation process.

Proficiency standards were adopted in 1994, and since then, the OUS has worked to develop more detailed descriptions of the knowledge and skills required to prepare for college. Teams of faculty members from high schools, community colleges, and all the four-year campuses have been involved in developing and refining the proficiencies. The training of teachers and other educators to score student work is the responsibility of schools, districts, and Education Service Districts (offshoots of the Oregon Department of Education that are located throughout the state). During the 1998–1999 academic year, PASS staff worked with English and mathematics teachers at the sixty PASS schools to train them how to generate collections of student work and how to assess student proficiency.

PASS Alignment with CIM and CAM

PASS staff worked with ODE staff to align the content standards for grades 3, 5, 8, 10, and 12 with the PASS proficiencies. The OUS stated in a memo in 1996–1997, "This alignment will create a continuous set of performance expectations for students so that they will know clearly what they need to do at each benchmark level, and, ultimately, what they must do to be acceptable for university admission." The other major area of key coordination with the ODE focuses on the development of the assessment system that will provide data for CIM and CAM determinations and university admission.

PASS documents state that "the Certificate of Initial Mastery (CIM) serves as the foundation for PASS. As students earn their CIM in a content area, such as math, they may already have demonstrated proficiency in one or more of the PASS standards" (Confederation of Oregon School Administrators and PASS, 2000, p. 11). Two types of assessment can be used to determine students' level of proficiency, teacher judgment or state and national tests, but only one method is necessary for each PASS standard. Students may use CAM collections to demonstrate PASS proficiencies if the CAM collections meet proficiency and sufficiency criteria. The director of PASS Implementation stated, "Because the standards are aligned, it would be very hard to actually earn your proficiencies in PASS and not meet CIM standards."

The complete implementation of the PASS is to begin with students in the 2005–2006 academic year, two years after the full implementation of the CIM. The CAM might be implemented by then. This strategy was developed to ensure that the PASS, CIM, and CAM can be aligned and that teacher training and assessments can be developed in a coordinated fashion (Oregon University System, 1998).

K–16 Reform and the University of Oregon

The hope is that these reforms will encourage educators at all levels to think about teaching and learning in a new way. But this will not be easy. As David McDonald, the director of enrollment services and high school relations in the OUS, stated, "There are some individuals who are resistant in general, who believe that the CIM and the CAM have already cost so much in terms of effort, hours, energy, and inertia that now we're adding something on top of that—how dare [we]."

At the University of Oregon (UO) in Eugene, the flagship campus with over seventeen thousand undergraduate and graduate students, there is both hope and uncertainty regarding the K–16 reforms. Martha Pitts, the director of admissions for UO was unsure as to whether teaching styles at the UO would evolve in the same direction as are K–12 teaching styles:

> Our faculty have been really involved in a two-year-long process for change, evaluation, looking at an emphasis on undergraduate education, on graduate education, on recruitment and retention, looking at our advising processes, really doing some in-depth evaluation, and looking for ways to be more student centered and more learning centered. How fast and how far that can go in an institution of this size and academic caliber is a real question, I think.

One of the major tenets behind PASS is that it will improve access for more students to enter, and succeed in, public higher education. The feeling is that students will no longer be screened out, as they once were, by such traditional measures as the SAT. But not everyone is convinced. One OU official, for instance, believed that "the potential is there [for PASS to create a more equitable system], but the potential is also there for even greater numbers of students to be overlooked in the process. I worry that the PASS effort is all at the end, and so that system, rather than being a record of achievement over four years, may be a glimpse . . . [of] cobbled-together work and achievement that may not help us identify students who really do have the potential to succeed once they get here."

K–16 Reform and Portland State University

Within the OUS, Portland State University (PSU), with over sixteen thousand undergraduate and graduate students, has the highest number of transfers from community colleges. PSU's commitment to access, its diverse community (one-third of its students are nonwhite), and its urban campus make it an interesting contrast to the University of Oregon in terms of its responses to K–16 reforms.

Because the K–12 reforms affect to some degree how admission officers evaluate applicants, it will be necessary for admission offices such as that at PSU to disseminate those changes. Agnes Hoffman, the former director of admissions, speculated, "[We have] to engage parents and high schools students to help them understand CIM and CAM, how is that translated in terms of PASS, and what they need to know to become admitted. Because it is very clear now what they need to know: a GPA is a well-understood concept and so is an SAT or ACT [score]."

The reforms may affect not only admissions but the entire culture of higher education. The vice provost for enrollment, Janine Allen, stated:

> Once the school reform efforts are fully implemented, we are going to have students coming to higher education who have been educated and . . . evaluated under a system much different from what higher education currently delivers. So I think that we may have a situation where K–12 may actually be influencing higher education because the students are going into a system that involved seat time and credits and grades, and you know they are going to present portfolios and the faculty members are going to go, "What is this portfolio?"

It will likely be necessary for universities such as PSU to alter how they communicate with schools and students once the reforms are fully implemented. This will not be easy because of the traditional suspicions and divisions between higher education and K–12. Allen explained:

> When we in higher education identify a prescribed high school curriculum we want students to come with, it felt like we were prescribing the high school curriculum for the high schools. . . . And I think there was resistance on the part of the K–12 people to say, whoa, wait a minute, we are not going to adopt your proficiencies, we need to develop our own. And on the other hand, there was the haughtiness of higher education that always seems to get in our way.

In essence, the K–12 and higher education systems constitute two very different cultures that will need to be bridged.

What Do Oregon Parents, High School Students, and Educators Know About College and K–16 Reforms?

As a major component of our research, we examined how the standards and policies implemented by Oregon's education agencies and postsecondary education institutions are understood, interpreted, and acted on by parents, students, and secondary school personnel. Project staff surveyed and conducted focus groups with students, surveyed their parents or guardians, and interviewed district- and school-level administrators, counselors, and teachers.

Four high schools in the greater Portland metropolitan area were examined. In each of the schools, researchers surveyed classes of ninth graders and eleventh graders, including one honors and one nonhonors class for each grade.[2] Bridge staff also conducted two focus groups per school with eleventh graders: one with students from an honors class and another with students from a regular-track class. Researchers chose ninth graders because they could speak retrospectively about their eighth-grade experiences (generally considered a gateway year in terms of whether students take college preparation courses); eleventh graders were included because they are generally at a stage in which they are thinking about their postsecondary options.

The schools were chosen on a variety of factors, including their level of student diversity, percentage free or reduced-price lunch, scores on K–12 student achievement tests, college-going rates, scores on the SAT or ACT, proximity to an urban area, and involvement in K–16 reform efforts. Researchers sought as diverse a group as possible within the constraints of the project. Two of the high schools are categorized as more urban, and two are more suburban.

Researchers conducted field research prior to the annual statewide K–12 test administration in the spring of 2000.[3] Most of the quantitative data reported in this chapter are the result of a thirty-item survey administered to ninth and eleventh graders, most in their English classes. Researchers attempted to balance the honors and nonhonors course representation, though there were higher response rates in the honors classes. The classroom-level response rate from the four schools ranged from 41 percent to 97 percent. In some cases, supplemental surveying was conducted to ensure high enough response rates from all schools. The students' parents were surveyed prior to the student survey, with a similar survey of nineteen items to determine socioeconomic background and parental perceptions of their children's aspirations and of admissions-related policies. There were 334 student responses and 341 parent responses. A subset of 318 of the survey responses matched parent to child. That subset is used for certain of the analyses.

The Case Study High Schools

Following are descriptions of each of the high schools included in the Oregon study, and related findings. Each high school was given a pseudonym to protect its anonymity.

CENTRAL HIGH. Central is an urban school that has two teachers participating in PASS. It is among the higher-performing schools in its district and is racially, ethnically, and economically diverse, though not the most diverse in the area. About 26 percent of its 1,255 students are nonwhite,[4] and 48 percent take the SAT.

A teacher, echoing other staff, states that Central is "about 40 percent free and reduced-lunch program. . . . We have a large ESL [English as a Second Language] series of groups: Russians, Samoans, Hispanic, Asian—which makes it real exciting. It makes it real diverse, offers a lot of culture to the students and everyone else. We [also] have some folks . . . [from] more of an upper-middle-class-environment." In terms of average family income level, Central is about in the middle for the district, but, says an eleventh-grade teacher, "the middle class [around Central] is a little stronger than in other middle-class areas."

Between 85 and 90 percent of Central's students attend some form of postsecondary education after high school. Approximately 40 percent of its students go to four-year colleges, 40 percent attend community colleges, and another 5 to 10 percent go to technical schools. Central has a higher college-going rate than almost all the other high schools on its side of town.

EASTSIDE HIGH. Eastside is in the same district as Central and is among the lower-performing high schools in the district. About two-thirds of its students are white; 34 percent take the SAT. A couple of years ago, the staff was told that Eastside is the most diverse high school in the state. One teacher described Eastside by saying, "It's pretty blue collar. Low to middle [income]. [The students are] not necessarily expected to go to college."

The student body is fairly transitory. Some interviewees stated that a lot of Asian families move to the area for jobs and relocate often. The regular-track global studies teacher signs approximately forty to fifty course withdrawals a year. A large proportion of the students who withdraw from courses end up leaving the school.

The 1999–2000 academic year was the principal's first year at Eastside. She stated that "the mind-set for some students, which is probably a reflection of family, [is that] learning stops at twelfth grade." She and the lead counselor were disappointed by a recent low college night turnout.

In terms of student achievement, a handful of students reach calculus. Eastside students' SAT scores are "terrible," as one English teacher put it. According to a school survey, about 25 percent of seniors said they were going to a four-year college, and 35 percent or higher said they were attending a community college.

HILLTOP HIGH. Hilltop is mostly white but has a variety of white ethnic groups, particularly Eastern European and Russian. Interviewees often described it as serving a predominantly blue-collar population. Before the state reforms were fully implemented, Hilltop High designed and implemented its own version of the certificates of mastery. This school is in a different district from Central and Eastside. About 40 percent of Hilltop's students take the SAT.

Hilltop is viewed as stable and innovative. Its staff considers it a leader in state and national school reform efforts, such as the New American Schools network. The principal believes that it was chosen because it developed its own CIM and CAM before the advent of the state certificates. The staff enjoys being a research site and plans to become involved in widescale research and evaluation efforts with prominent national research firms so that it can learn more about itself.

VISTA HIGH. Vista is a largely white, high-performing school that is often viewed as preparing students well for college; 80 percent go on college. It is the largest school in the study, with almost twenty-three hundred students. The minority population of 22.9 percent is primarily Asian American. Seventy-three percent of Vista's students take the SAT. Vista also developed its own version of CIM.

Vista has a partnership with PSU in which faculty from PSU and Vista teach sixty to ninety seniors in good standing in a thematic, interdisciplinary course called Capstone.[5]

When asked what students at other high schools would say about Vista, students in both focus groups were fairly positive. One representative student said, "Vista is an environment where you can pretty much act on your own desires for your own education. It's all up to you. Every door is open."

Knowledge of K–16 Reforms at the Four High Schools

Oregon's dramatic reforms have caused K–12 stakeholders to experience many conflicting emotions, including frustration and excitement. This became evident as we researched participants' understandings of and attitudes toward the state's CIM, CAM, and PASS. Amid the policy turmoil caused by the development of three reforms almost simultaneously was a concern for resources and a feeling that the state is not supporting the existing infrastructure for either K–12 or higher education. One participant expressed resentment that the K–12 system is doing all the changing, while higher education watches from afar. Most interviewees expressed pessimistic opinions about the reforms, though a few supported the state's efforts. The sections below explore interviewees' knowledge and views regarding the CIM, CAM, and PASS reform efforts.

CERTIFICATE OF INITIAL MASTERY. Hilltop and Vista have their own CIM in addition to the state's CIM. At these schools, there was more buy-in and support for the school's CIM than for the state's CIM. Indeed, staff members at both schools were pleased with their CIMs. Nevertheless, across all four schools, there was a great deal of hostility about the state's CIM.

When asked about their view of the state's CIM, many interviewees responded initially with negative comments such as these:

> I can honestly say the only thing that the CIM stuff has done to my teaching is frustrate me because it takes so much time and I don't feel like it's valuable time.

> I've really negative feelings about it [the CIM]. I mean, I have, I believe in high standards, and I think that it's really neat and important for students and educators to have high standards and benchmarks. But the CIM is terrible. It has been top-down implemented from noneducators, pushed on to educators and to students. And it's been incredibly punitive, disorganized—and, in some ways, a destroyer of good curriculum and good teaching.

Students knew that many of their teachers do not support the CIM. One student stated, "I have talked to teachers here, and they say that if you have never done any CIM in my entire time at high school that it wouldn't affect anything. . . . From what I have seen from the teachers and the counselors, nobody knows what it means. They said that you have to try and do this, and nobody really figured out how."

More specifically, faculty and staff complained about the faulty logistics of the CIM and the extent to which it kept changing. For example, the schools were supposed to give the social studies CIM test two weeks from this project's field research dates, but staff found out the week before the researchers' arrival that the administration was cancelled. After the first administration of CIM tests, schools and teachers did not receive test scores in time to use them for course placement or to change their curriculum. One principal summed up his school's experiences by saying, "We've been through this so many times that the credibility is just really shot."

Many adult participants were disappointed that the tests had evolved from authentic assessments to a series of multiple-choice assessments. Another major issue for all interviewees is the lack of stakes; students must take the CIM tests, yet there are no consequences for students who do not meet the proficiencies. It is not required for graduation or promotion from grade to grade and is not tied to higher education admission or placement.

Although participants stated mostly negative views about the CIM, most appreciated one or more aspects of it. These included views that the math test is at an appropriate level, that the scoring guides are well constructed and useful, that it started as a good idea but is now "a sinking ship," and that it has raised standards in writing.

CERTIFICATE OF ADVANCED MASTERY. Everyone who was interviewed had an opinion about CIM; the CAM, however, was not as controversial a topic. This is probably because the CAM has not been fully developed or implemented across the state. In fact, although all participants had heard of the state's proposed CAM (and one of the participating high schools had its own CAM), no one believed it would be developed and implemented soon. One principal stated that it would happen after his retirement, "so I don't need to worry about it," and a student remarked, "It's like this thing that our little brother will get." There was concern that the ODE was trying to accomplish too much with the CAM—that a single reform could not effectively address preparation for college and for entering the workforce. Similarly, many were concerned that having CIM, CAM, and PASS would overload an educational system that was already functioning with an acute lack of resources.

Hilltop, along with having its own CIM, had its own CAM. To earn a Hilltop High CAM, students decide on their CAM path at the end of the sophomore year and then must take two years of CAM classes and earn a C or better in each of the classes. They also must complete twenty hours of community service. English teachers supervise all the CAM activities. Prior to that, students enter ninth grade in a preliminary CAM career path (one of seven offered at the school). They spend two years in career exploration classes. All ninth graders go on company tours, create resumés, and write cover letters; in tenth grade, they do some job shadowing.

Some students voiced frustration with Hilltop's CAM because they think it limits their course-taking choices. They want to take more electives and college preparation courses, and they want more specific information rather than the more general information they have learned in their CAM classes. They said it is hard to fit in all the college preparation courses, journalism, band, choir, and CAM classes. Some other students, though, said they were in smaller CAM courses and were really enjoying them and gaining information that would help them decide what to focus on in college.

PROFICIENCY-BASED ADMISSION STANDARDS SYSTEM. Although the CIM and CAM are legislated reforms run through the ODE, they are connected with PASS. ODE and PASS staff members have worked together to align standards in an effort to create a seamless system across K–12 and public higher education. Currently, PASS is in about sixty-five Oregon high schools, and in most cases it has been implemented in two to four classrooms in each of those schools.

Of the four schools in the study, one is designated as a PASS school: staff members have attended PASS training sessions, there is a PASS coordinator, and there are at least four PASS teachers—two each in English and mathematics. One is not a PASS school and has not been involved in PASS activities, and two had been PASS schools but had withdrawn from the reform effort.

Teachers, administrators, and counselors at Central, the PASS school, had mixed reactions to the implementation process. The PASS coordinator was the most positive, stating that, "I went [to the initial PASS meeting] and I got hooked." The PASS English teacher, in contrast, has been involved in PASS for six years at several schools and believes the effort might not succeed. He said, "PASS is getting hard to bring to the staffs of the schools I have been at. Standards are overwhelming people, and the CIM standards in the state are still enough to keep occupying people's minds." The PASS math teacher provided a relatively pragmatic view that fell between the others.

All three teachers were enthusiastic about PASS's content and expectations for students, stating that PASS reinforced their work, provided high standards for their students, and gave them the opportunity to collaborate with teachers from across the state. They all believed that PASS had not changed their fundamental teaching styles and were appreciative that PASS staff had aligned its standards with the CIM, IB, and AP. But they were concerned that CIM is overshadowing PASS; PASS is not required and consequently will not "catch on."

Unlike Hilltop, Vista has never participated in PASS. Its staff members were very aware of PASS and the content of its reforms but felt that Vista had little to gain from the effort. The majority of Vista's students attend college, and the staff is fairly confident that its students enter college well prepared. Hence, they do not view PASS as a useful reform.

Those concerns were echoed by teachers and counselors from Eastside and Hilltop, the high schools that had discontinued their involvement in PASS. These schools felt they had more than enough to do in meeting the state's CIM requirements, and the principal at Hilltop felt that the PASS standards were too high and unrealistic.

Most students and parents were unfamiliar with PASS; approximately three-fourths of those populations responded, "I don't know what PASS is." Given the limited implementation of PASS when we conducted this research, these results are not surprising.

Postsecondary Aspirations at the Four Schools

Students articulated their post–high school aspirations in focus group discussions and in response to a survey question, their parents expressed their aspirations for their children on the parent surveys, and the many educators interviewed discussed their hopes for their students, in addition to their perceptions of the students' hopes for themselves. Understanding their aspirations helps provide the context for such issues as students' involvement in college preparation activities and their knowledge of college policies. In a later section, we talk about how realistic student aspirations are in the light of their circumstances and opportunities.

STUDENT ASPIRATIONS. A vast majority of students in our sample aspired to matriculate into college after high school: 93.1 percent reported planning to attend college, 78.3 percent of them full time and 14.8 percent part time. In addition, 29.5 percent planned to work part time, most of them in conjunction with full-time college studies. A small percentage reported plans to enter the military or to work full time.

Students were considering a wide range of types of institutions for their postsecondary plans. Of the two universities discussed earlier in this chapter, students favored UO. PSU enrolls many more adult and returning students, which may partially explain why 22 percent of the students sampled indicated that they plan to apply to PSU, as opposed to 43 percent for the UO. Perceived differences in selectivity and prestige might also contribute to the discrepancy. Prestige issues might be a factor in the percentage of students reporting interest in colleges and universities outside Oregon. Table 5.1 lists the percentage of the total student sample that is "thinking about attending" each type of institution or option after high school.

Despite interest in the in-state colleges and universities, most students expressed a preference for four-year out-of-state institutions. That number may be large in part because the out-of-state option includes both public and private institutions and the in-state options were disaggregated. When aggregated, the total number identifying an in-state institution exceeded the out-of-state total. Higher-SES students were more likely to express aspirations to four-year and private schools, while slightly more low-SES students overall checked the two-year option. The most dramatic finding was the high number of students who expected to enroll in some postsecondary institution.

Table 5.1. Postsecondary Options Considered, by Student SES Group.

Postsecondary Options	Low SES	Middle SES	High SES	Total ($N = 316$)
Four-year college or university outside Oregon	13 (35.1)	86 (56.6)	64 (71.9)	163
University of Oregon	20 (54.1)	64 (42.1)	38 (42.7)	122
Another public university in Oregon	12 (32.4)	47 (30.9)	27 (30.3)	86
Four-year private college or university in Oregon	6 (16.2)	42 (27.6)	34 (38.2)	82
Portland State University	15 (40.5)	50 (32.9)	14 (15.7)	79
Two-year junior or community college	11 (29.7)	38 (25.0)	10 (11.2)	59
Technical or trade school (e.g., ITT Tech)	5 (13.5)	9 (5.9)	3 (3.4)	17
U.S. military academy	3 (8.1)	13 (8.6)	4 (4.5)	20
Other type of school (such as music, art)	1 (2.7)	4 (2.6)	3 (3.4)	8
Haven't considered any schools	5 (13.5)	6 (3.9)	4 (4.5)	15

Note: *Multiple responses were accepted. Some SES data are missing. Reported are numbers of students, with percentages in parentheses.*

In terms of specific schools, Vista emerged in this analysis as having the most distinct responses, specifically in the high rate of response for four-year colleges outside of Oregon. Vista has the highest percentage of high-SES students, who may be more comfortable aspiring to schools out of state that are likely to be more expensive. Eastside, with a much lower-SES profile, had the highest percentage of students aspiring to Portland State.

EDUCATOR PERSPECTIVES. Almost all the educators interviewed for the study stated that they hoped that all of their students would attend postsecondary education; however, many said that realistically, their honors students were more likely to go to four-year institutions and their non-honors students were more likely to attend community colleges. At Vista, one teacher was concerned that students' aspirations were so high that they were putting too much pressure on themselves. At Hilltop, a teacher said he tried to convince all of his students to go out of state for college, but his students did not want to be too far from home. He stated that, "It's weird. I just don't understand. I have had kids go to very prestigious schools, and they couldn't handle it, and they came back and go to the community college and it's like, 'I miss my friends and, like, the friends are gone pretty quickly.'"

PARENT ASPIRATIONS FOR THEIR CHILDREN. Analyses of parent responses regarding their expectations for their children after high school (they were asked where they "hoped" their children would go) suggest that no parents in this sample wanted their children to work full time or go to trade or technical school immediately after high school. The greatest number of parents (74 of 304) responded that they wanted their child to go to a four-year college or university outside Oregon. The institutions in Oregon, public and private, were also popular choices.

The most notable distinction by SES was the small percentage of high-SES parents (3.4 percent) who wanted their children to attend community college.

Fulfilling Aspirations: Opportunity to Learn

The issue of opportunity to learn arose repeatedly in our research. Students often talked about their perceptions of academic opportunities for both themselves and others. Teachers, counselors, and administrators often contrasted what they would like to see in their schools, and in the rest of society, with what they perceived as their school's reality.

ACCESS TO AP AND HONORS COURSE AT HILLTOP HIGH. Hilltop recently eliminated all of its AP course offerings except for AP Mathematics and AP English; teachers believed that AP classes were too demanding to teach. To place students into courses, the school relies on a forecasting process in which eighth-grade teachers send recommendations to Hilltop's counselors regarding their students' ninth-grade course options. One student's perception of the placement process, and a related issue of motivation, was, "It seems that the advanced classes are the ones that are more interested in academics because they are actually trying. Because it is not something that you just get in. You have to be asked in."

ACCESS TO AP AND HONORS COURSES AT EASTSIDE HIGH. Eastside has no AP classes. There are, however, honors courses in English, global studies, and U.S. history. While students can decide which courses they want to take because there is no formal placement process, a veteran English teacher said that the honors classes have a disproportionate number of white and Asian students. One student in the honors focus group stated, "Most of us have been together since freshman year."

ACCESS TO AP AND HONORS COURSES AT CENTRAL HIGH. Like Eastside, Central has no AP courses. Central has started an IB program, has several PASS classes in English and mathematics, and offers honors classes in core subject areas. Currently, in order to place into high-level courses, ninth graders need to get recommendations from their eighth-grade teachers and to have earned good grades in previous courses. Over the next two years, Central will be working to detrack its ninth-grade classes. One of the teachers interviewed stated that she tries to recruit "nonhonors students" into her honors courses. Of those efforts, she said, "I think, socially, it's more difficult . . . I've had a lot of students this year to whom I've said, 'I want you to be in the honors class next year,' and it freaks them out. They see that as a whole different world."

ACCESS TO AP AND HONORS COURSES AT VISTA HIGH. Vista offers general education, honors, and AP courses in core areas, in addition to the Capstone program. In order to place into honors courses, students need a teacher recommendation, they must have completed honors courses in the past, and they should be earning "A's and possibly B's in their courses." A student in the nonhonors focus group said, "You have to have a teacher's signature to get into those higher-level classes, and if they don't feel that you are ready to go into that class or that you would be able to manage that class, then they don't sign you up."

TEST-TAKING PATTERNS. Over two-thirds of eleventh graders who responded to our survey administered in the spring reported having taken the SAT, an important step for admission to many four-year institutions. The Preliminary SAT (PSAT) is also the National Merit Scholarship qualifying test, so those not reporting taking it may be missing scholarship opportunities.

A striking feature of the findings on test-taking patterns was the overall small number of low-SES students who reported having taken any college preparatory tests; only 25 percent, for instance, took the SAT. Despite the fact that some of these students aspired to two-year institutions that generally do not require standardized entrance exams, many low-SES students expressed an interest in four-year colleges, the majority of which require an entrance exam for admission.

College Knowledge

This section focuses on when survey participants believed students should start preparing for college, what students are doing to prepare, and how well they think their schools were helping them prepare for college.

ACCESS TO COLLEGE COUNSELING. Counseling was a major area of focus throughout the interview and focus group discussions. We interviewed one counselor per school—usually the lead counselor or, when there was one, the college counselor. Counselors discussed their frustrations at not being able to spend time on college issues, and students sometimes mirrored those frustrations. Teachers often took on a college counseling role, and some students went to teachers first to ask questions about which courses to take and how to study for college admission tests. This section explores these and related issues. The services and resources offered at the four schools span a relatively wide range, with Eastside at one end (relatively poor resources), Central and Hilltop in the middle, and Vista at the other end.

Eastside does not provide individual college counseling for its students. The lead counselor said that she tries to target juniors she believes are potentially college bound and gives them information about college preparation. The student-to-counselor ratio is 500 to 1; there are 3.6 counselors whose responsibilities include providing general academic counseling, going to middle schools to do course forecasting, scheduling, crisis management, and oversight of internships. The counselors divide the students up by English class and follow them for four years. The teachers interviewed were split about their roles; an honors teacher said she was actively involved in providing college counseling for students, while a non-honors teacher said he was not. Students interviewed said that although they had not received any information about course requirements or the SATs, they believed that the resources are there and that the counselors are accessible.

Like Eastside, Central does not provide individual college counseling for its students. There are four counselors, one of whom works primarily with "alternative students" (for example, students who are at risk of dropping out of high school or are dealing with other risk factors) and has a caseload of about 100 students. The other three have caseloads of about 375 each and focus mostly on academic counseling, scheduling, group counseling, running student elections, and planning homecoming. The counselors divide up the students by global studies class, and each visits a class once a month. Counselors begin talking to students about college during the junior year, although students have to fill out a four-year plan in ninth grade. All interviewees stated that there is not enough college counseling at Central, but several students said they knew they could make an appointment with a counselor to talk about college. They did not find the counselors as helpful as their parents and written materials when they wanted to learn about a specific college. Teachers often stepped in and offered college counseling, but the vice principal said, "The counselors actually get a little upset when the teachers step on their territory."

Hilltop has six counselors, each responsible for general counseling and guidance, CIM- and CAM-related work, scheduling, testing, creating college and scholarship materials, and college counseling. The counselors also staff the resource center that has college materials such as guidebooks, computers with college-related Web sites marked, meeting spaces, college recruiting opportunities, videotapes, and financial aid materials. The counselor interviewed believed that students use the information in the center but are overwhelmed by all the materials at their disposal. Each counselor has a caseload of about 300 students, and students are divided up alphabetically by grade level. Each year, the counselors meet with students individually to discuss course-taking plans, making sure that students who are college bound take the appropriate sequence of courses. When students are in tenth grade, counselors talk about loans and financial aid and help students make their CAM choices. In twelfth grade, they reassess the students' plans and make sure they can be met.

Vista's counseling staff, like those at the other schools, is responsible for a wide range of activities, including college counseling, scheduling, and general academic counseling. In addition to the counselors, every teacher and administrator at Vista is assigned an advisory group of about twenty-two students. They meet once every three to four weeks to talk about course planning for high school and college, logistical issues regarding college applications, and other similar issues. The vice principal said the groups are an attempt to help the large school feel smaller. Vista's advisories are set up so that the adviser and students are together for four years.

EXPOSURE TO "COLLEGE TALK" AND CULTURE. Our research explored to whom students speak about college-related issues, how frequently they talk, and the usefulness of those discussions. Teachers and counselors talked about when and whether they discussed issues such as college preparation, college options, admission, and placement with their students.

Several teachers voiced the opinion that students talk to them about college more often than they talk with their counselors. They cited talking to students about academic issues relating to college readiness, filling out applications, academic planning for college, higher education options, college "survival," their own experiences in college, the need for financial aid, college visits, SAT preparation, and goal setting. Two teachers mentioned that they embed college preparation activities, such as writing college essays or using SAT vocabulary words, into their curricula.

Although a couple of the teachers said they talked to all of their students equally about college, the majority said that the amount of time spent and the topics discussed differ, depending on whether they were talking to honors or nonhonors classes. The following are representative statements:

> Open conversation about college seems to happen a lot in advanced classes. . . . On my wall there is this whole thing on how you get ready for college, what to do when you are a freshman, sophomore, junior, senior year. It's posted and occasionally I will refer to it.

> Only honors. I never talk about it with the other kids. I tried it before, and a lot of kids will say, "No, I'm not going to college." And sometimes you'll, they'll be so adamant that it's like, "Okay, twelve years here is enough. I don't want a longer sentence."

In our sample of students, 53.6 percent and 47.3 percent reported talking "many times" with parents and friends, respectively. At the other extreme, 9.6 percent and 16.3 percent reported never talking to parents and friends about admission requirements. The overall response frequencies to that question are presented in the Table 5.2. It appears that most students have spoken to someone at least once or twice about what is required for college.

Additional analyses reveal that high-SES students are talking the most about college admissions in general. Table 5.3 identifies the people students were likely to talk with "many times."

Because high- and mid-SES students are more likely to have had parents and siblings who attended college, it is not surprising that more of them report talking with those people about college requirements. Also, high-SES students were not talking to counselors as much as others, but they were talking to teachers. This general pattern also holds for honors students, which is not surprising given that many are also high SES.

The parents in the sample were asked about whether they talked with their children about college. Table 5.4 reports the findings by SES.

Overall, parents reported a lot of discussions, but when the topic became more specific (concerning courses and requirements), there was more discussion among mid- and high-SES families. It may be that parents

Table 5.2. Conversations About Admissions Requirements.

	Many Times	Once or Twice	Never
Parents	53.6%	36.4%	9.6%
Friends	47.3	35.2	16.3
Counselors	18.1	48.5	32.8
Teachers	12.7	52.7	33.1
Coaches	6.3	20.2	73.2
Brother or sister	20.1	31.1	47.5
Family friends	14.8	33.0	51.3
Relatives	15.7	36.8	47.2

Table 5.3. Discussed Admissions Requirements "Many Times," by SES.

People	Low SES	Middle SES	High SES
Brother or sister	18.4%	15.8%	28.1%
Counselor	21.1	21.7	14.6
Friends	44.7	43.4	56.2
Parents	42.1	53.3	62.9
Relatives	10.5	17.8	15.7
Teachers	10.5	13.8	14.6

Note: *Multiple responses accepted.*

Table 5.4. Parents' Responses to College Topics Discussed with Their Children, by SES.

	Many Times			Once or Twice			Never		
	Low SES	Middle SES	High SES	Low SES	Middle SES	High SES	Low SES	Middle SES	High SES
Discussed plans after high school	73.7%	86.8%	89.9%	23.7%	11.2%	10.1%	2.6%	1.3%	0%
Discussed interest in attending college	60.5	77.0	85.4	18.4	11.2	7.9	0	2.0	0
Discussed specific college require-ments	15.8	37.5	57.3	60.5	44.7	31.5	21.1	15.8	10.1
Discussed child's course planning	28.9	54.6	69.7	44.7	28.9	19.1	15.8	10.5	10.1

with more education have a clearer understanding of the specifics of requirements and what is needed to meet them, that they know the general topic areas, or that they feel more comfortable discussing those topics. There also appeared to be more discussion with honors students, particularly as the topics got more specific.

We looked into the extent to which students were exposed to the culture of college through various activities occurring outside the classroom (Table 5.5). Particularly provocative is the finding that honors students reported having had much more exposure to these activities than did students in nonhonors courses.

Typical Understandings and Misunderstandings Regarding College

The student and parent surveys and the interviews and focus groups resulted in extensive information regarding participants' knowledge of UO's and PSU's admission and placement policies, tuition, and level

Table 5.5. Exposure to College Since Entering High School, by Grade and Honors Status.

Activities	Ninth Grade (*n* = 142)	Eleventh Grade (*n* = 173)	Nonhonors (*n* = 129)	Honors (*n* = 189)
Attended a college information workshop or college night	45 (31.7)	81 (46.8)	47 (36.4)	80 (42.3)
Visited a college or university	7 (4.9)	35 (20.2)	9 (7.0)	34 (18.0)
Took an SAT or ACT preparation course	7 (4.9)	72 (41.6)	19 (14.7)	62 (32.8)

Note: *Reported are number of students with yes responses. Percentages are in parentheses.*

of selectivity. This information casts light on the understandings and misunderstandings participants have regarding college.

PREPARATION FOR COLLEGE AND MEETING REQUIREMENTS FOR ADMISSION. Some teachers stated misconceptions about college preparation, such as students' needing to take two years of math to be prepared for an OUS institution. For the students, specific policy issues and related understandings discussed in the focus groups included the following topics:

- Admissions requirements. Students believed they need "four years of math, and, like, you need to take English and economics and stuff"; good SAT scores; approximately a 3.0 to 3.5 for UO and a 2.5 to 3.0 GPA for PSU; and athletic prowess, community service, and letters of recommendation. Several groups discussed how colleges want students to be well rounded and that they did not "expect you to be a genius when you get there."

- Placement. Many students seemed to understand the concept of placement exams, but were not clear about how to prepare for the tests or how to learn about them.

- Preparation. Several honors students voiced concern that if they took difficult classes, their GPAs would suffer. Several students were confused about the differences between honors classes and AP courses.

Overall, in most groups, while students said they would like to know more about college policies, they admitted to a bit of apathy in terms of seeking out information and were often confused about admissions and placement standards. This is illustrated in the following dialogue:

STUDENT: I have never heard a college say it, but they ask for, we are told that we have to take three math classes beyond algebra.

STUDENT: But . . . I mean, naturally, somebody is going to look more attractive to a college if they have taken AP Calculus and all these AP classes and everything than someone who has just done the minimum.

STUDENT: On the other hand, they also look at what you did outside of class.

STUDENT: Yes, it's the Harvard solution: take the people who are well-rounded, not just bookworms.

STUDENT: It's also how you did in the class because if you take AP Calculus and end up with a C, it doesn't look as good as if you take the next lower and get an A.

Our survey asked students about the importance of specific items for admission to UO and PSU. Out of seventeen items, the three factors cited by students as "most important" most often were, in order, the following for each institution:

UNIVERSITY OF OREGON

1. High school grades
2. SAT I
3. SAT II

PORTLAND STATE UNIVERSITY

1. SAT I
2. High school grades
3. SAT II

Because there were seventeen items listed in the question, it is interesting that the top three were the same for both institutions, although ordered slightly differently in terms of perceived level of importance. The admission policies for the UO and PSU (as specified by the admission officers who filled out the same survey items for comparison purposes) cite high school course-taking patterns as most important, as well as student performance in those courses. Only if a student does not meet the minimum GPA requirement for admission (3.0 for the UO and 2.5 for PSU) do the admissions offices look at SAT scores. Because these institutions do not seriously consider other factors, such as essays, recommendations, or extracurricular activities, the fact that students realized the relative importance of grades and test scores is significant. The Oregon University System (OUS) institutions have capacity to accept all qualified students, so admission requirements are a standard to be met rather than factors to use in selectivity. An important finding is that PSU may need to think about how to communicate to its prospective students that courses and grades are more important than SAT scores.

The survey also asked students to offer their best guess as to how many years of specific subjects were required for admission to the UO and PSU. Although the UO and PSU require the same number of courses, students tended to report that the UO required more years in each subject. Student responses and the actual requirements are in Table 5.6. Percentages reflect correct responses and overestimations.

Students were most likely to underestimate social science requirements and overestimate science requirements. And despite identical course requirements, students assumed that more years were required for admission to the UO.

Parents were also asked about their knowledge of course requirements for admission to the UO and PSU. In general, students and parents seemed to have the overall sense that UO is more difficult to get admitted to than PSU. They stated higher admission requirements in several categories.

Table 5.6. Student Knowledge of Course
Sequence for Admission.

	University of Oregon		Portland State University	
	Percentage Correct or Above	Actual Requirement	Percentage Correct or Above	Actual Requirement
English	88.0	4	83.0	4
Math	73.3	3	62.2	3
Social sciences	50.3	3	41.5	3
Science	94.4	2	92.1	2
Foreign language	95.3	2	90.9	2

On paper, the UO and PSU have somewhat similar admission policies. Both require the same course sequence (number of years in specific subjects) and use SAT scores only if students do not meet minimum GPA requirements. The UO does have a higher GPA requirement than PSU (3.0 versus 2.5). Both institutions admit a large majority of their applicant pool, suggesting that there may be self-selection occurring given the perceived difference in admission difficulty. PSU promotes itself as more of a commuter school focused on access, while UO promotes itself as a flagship institution. It appears that students are receiving those messages.

TUITION. Students were asked about tuition costs for the UO, PSU, and local community colleges.[6] Interpreting the data is difficult because there can be confusion about annual tuition versus overall costs (despite efforts to limit confusion); Bridge researchers focused on overall trends in the analysis of tuition responses rather than actual dollar amounts.

The actual annual tuition costs for the UO and PSU in the academic year 1999–2000, the year students were surveyed, were $3,771 per year for UO and $3,438 per year for PSU for in-state residents. Community colleges averaged around $1,200. With regard to estimating tuition costs, the largest percentage of students and parents overall believed that the postsecondary institutions are far more expensive than they truly are. For example, 43 percent of students thought that tuition for community colleges in Oregon is over $4,000 per year. Sixty percent of students and 44 percent of parents believed that the UO is over $8,000 per year. Fifty-three percent of students and 30 percent of parents thought that tuition at PSU is over $8,000. The most accurate responses were with regard to community college tuition. Thirty-one percent of students and 35 percent of parents were on target.

Overall, parents, not surprisingly, had a better understanding than students of what postsecondary education costs. There was also a clear understanding by all that community colleges are a less expensive alternative to the four-year institutions. Also, they believed that the UO is more expensive than PSU, yet their tuition costs are quite similar. It could be that the perceived and actual status and selectivity differences between the campuses (flagship versus urban commuter campus) are driving these responses. Table 5.7 provides the averages of the tuition responses for each category.

Student averages by SES do not reveal significant differences between groups; all responses were within approximately $1,000 of each other. However, the parent responses showed greater overestimation at the lowest SES levels (Table 5.8).

Table 5.7. Average Responses About Tuition from Students and Parents.

	Student Response	Parent Response
Community college	$7,218	$4,729
Portland State University	15,829	11,203
University of Oregon	17,592	12,728

Table 5.8. Average Parent Tuition Response, by SES.

	Low SES	Middle SES	High SES
Community college	$9,235	$4,033	$2,913
Portland State University	15,305	9,529	8,284
University of Oregon	20,029	11,126	9,162

Summary and Analysis

As a small state, Oregon has been able over the past ten years to develop and implement reforms that would be much more difficult to sustain in a larger state. From a school-site and student perspective, these reforms have caused confusion, anxiety, and uncertainty. This study analyzed the relationships between those reform efforts and college preparation, and students', teachers', counselors', and K–12 administrators' knowledge of those reforms.

It is difficult to predict the effects that Oregon's reform efforts will have on the structure of schools, teaching, and learning and on educators within the schools. This study occurred at a time of great policy flux with a transition of governance and policy from local control to a greater level of state oversight.

The legal mandates behind CIM and CAM suggest that they will affect more students than PASS, but it is not clear yet whether they will become embedded in school culture and will truly change teaching and learning. Since PASS implementation began in the 2000–2001 year, it is too early to gauge its statewide effects. Until 2000, the PASS focus had been on the mission, vision, and technical aspects rather than on implementation. When this research was conducted, PASS was in sixty-five schools in the state and affected approximately two to four classrooms in each of those schools. Consequently, the PASS proficiencies were not yet deeply embedded in school culture across the state. PASS cannot be considered high stakes because it is not yet fully implemented and the stakes have not been determined. At one point, a PASS transcript was going to be required of Oregon applicants, but now it is recommended. Those applying to the university system will encounter some PASS information, but because it is not required for admission, a non-PASS background will not prevent students from being admissible to Oregon public universities.

As far as K–12 is concerned, neither the CIM nor the CAM is required for graduation from any high school in Oregon.[7] Neither is required for entry into an OUS institution or a community college. Although the standards and assessments are legally required, the stakes for students are not high. Several high schools have, however, developed their own CIMs that are aligned with the state CIM. There are higher stakes for schools and districts. Their success, according to state-issued Report Cards, includes some measure of how students perform on the state-mandated assessments in grades 3, 5, 8, and 10 (CIM).

Although CIM, and the standards and assessments leading up to it, has survived for almost a decade, it is possible that the enduring legacy of the reform may be a single, regularly administered assessment. The ODE has already reduced the required number of work samples, and most of the interviewees focused more on the assessments than on any other aspect of the CIM. It is not clear what the ramifications would be for this kind of system. If the assessment is authentic and students are taught and learn in a different way, perhaps the reform has met the stated mission. Although no one is actively talking about a single certificate with different levels of achievement that would represent the full range of student achievement (from basic CIM skills to highest PASS proficiency), it is not unreasonable to consider that as a way to bring together the reforms.

As the implementation efforts gain momentum, Oregon will continue to be an important case study for other states proposing large-scale education reforms. Despite multiple efforts that sometimes seem at crossed purposes and despite concerns of overextended schools and staffs, Oregon education does look different than it did a generation ago.

Students and teachers were concerned that the current focus on the CIM will not help prepare students for college; this is an accurate perception, since the CIM was not developed as a mechanism to connect high school and college academic expectations. The CAM was developed to make that link, but when this research was conducted, it had not been fully implemented. Many respondents were concerned that the CAM would have a more vocational bent, and consequently, there would be no embedded, articulated connection between K–12 and postsecondary education standards. In addition, the timing of the CAM assessments in the twelfth grade would be too late for most four-year university admission cycles.

PASS is supposed to fill that gap, but its implementation plan called for thin and wide filtration in the schools. PASS's goals and objectives are laudable, but it remains to be seen whether it truly changes the way Oregon students prepare for college. When this research was conducted, PASS had trained approximately two teachers per school in about sixty-five schools throughout the state. Although those schools educate the majority of the state's students, the "teach the teacher" model of implementation was not spreading quickly. Also, many interviewees were concerned that PASS served only the college-bound students and that it added too much to already overburdened schools.

A major set of findings from this study focuses on inequalities with regard to the courses students take, the people with whom they talk about college, and even aspirations. Because Oregon is less diverse racially than other states, SES became the stratifying variable. Students from lower-SES backgrounds (lower parent education and family income) were:

○ Less likely to aspire to four-year institutions: 71.9 percent of high SES aspired to four-year institutions outside of Oregon; only 35.1 percent of low SES did.

○ Less likely to be in honors or advanced classes where college is more often discussed: 68.5 percent of high-SES students were in honors classes; only 36.8 percent of low-SES were.

○ Less likely to talk with parents, siblings, or teachers about college, though they were more likely to talk with counselors.

The good news is that there were not differences in PSAT-taking rates, a process that tends to be highly structured by schools, though some differences emerged in SAT I–taking patterns. Also, the majority of all students reported receiving course-taking advice in ninth grade or earlier. And there was little difference between student subgroups in terms of responses about OUS course requirements for admission.

Similar trends emerged in parent responses, especially in terms of aspiration for their children and their own behavior and activities for their child's college preparation, from talking with teachers to researching guidebooks or Web sites. High-SES parents were much more likely to be involved and have participated in precollege activities. Interestingly, while students had a fairly similar perception of tuition costs, there was a much larger difference in parents' responses by SES on average tuition guesses:

low-SES parents overestimated costs much more dramatically than high-SES parents.

Overall this study points to a set of potentially exciting reforms that have not yet reached their potential. Currently, there is concern, confusion, and anxiety about college preparation on the part of students, teachers, and counselors; vague student college knowledge; inequalities between student groups; and some promising local school-college connections. Oregon's reforms, and their impact, should be studied over the years to see if they reach their goals.

NOTES

1. Recent policy changes have shifted the focus from grade-level performance to overall benchmarks. Rather than grades 3, 5, and 8, the assessments refer to benchmarks 1, 2, and 3.

2. Honors classes encompassed courses called honors, college preparation, advanced, college, Advanced Placement classes, and courses that were the highest in the sequence for that subject and grade level. Nonhonors classes were regular-track courses that were not designated as college preparation courses, but were not the absolute "bottom"-level course in each school.

3. Students who were juniors during the field research (1999–2000 academic year) were the first class that could be awarded a Certificate of Initial Mastery (CIM).

4. Statewide, whites make up 85.6 percent of the population; in Portland, they are 78 percent.

5. The name of the program has been changed to protect the anonymity of participating schools.

6. In the classes where students were surveyed, researchers called students' attention to this question, explaining that tuition does not include room and board costs. Although this was not possible with parents, who completed the survey at home, this point was also made in writing on both student and parent surveys.

7. One high school did institute a CIM requirement for graduation, but the requirement was dropped a year later.

REFERENCES

Confederation of Oregon School Administrators and PASS. *An Introductory Guide to PASS for Secondary School Administrators.* Eugene, Ore.: Confederation of Oregon School Administrators and PASS, 2000.

Marshall, R., and Tucker, M. S. *Thinking for a Living: Education and the Wealth of nations.* New York: Basic Books, 1992.

National Commission on Excellence in Education. *A Nation at Risk: The Imperative for Educational Reform.* Washington, D.C.: U.S. Government Printing Office, 1983.

Oregon Department of Education. *Oregon Goals 2000: An Annotated State Plan.* Salem, Ore.: Oregon Department of Education, Jan. 30, 1995.

Oregon Department of Education. *1997–98 State Report Card.* Salem, Ore.: Oregon Department of Education, 1997.

Oregon University System. *The College Guidance Counselor's Handbook, 1998–1999.* Eugene, Ore.: Oregon University System, 1998.

6

GEORGIA'S P–16 REFORMS AND THE PROMISE OF A SEAMLESS SYSTEM

Caroline Sotello Viernes Turner
Lisa M. Jones
James C. Hearn

THE IMPORTANCE OF academic preparation for access to and success in the workplace as well as in postsecondary education has prompted a national discussion of efforts to align K–12 and postsecondary reforms. For these reasons, the development of multiple reform efforts in Georgia's P–16 public education systems, within the context of a dynamic political environment, a growing state population, demographic change, and a growing need for highly skilled workers in an expanding economy, is being closely watched by policymakers across the country.

In 1999, Governor Roy Barnes appointed the Education Reform Commission to examine the state's educational system and recommend targeted improvements, concentrating efforts on reforms in K–12 education. The commission consisted of legislators, business and industry leaders, and education representatives. One of its goals was to develop a seamless path from prekindergarten through postsecondary graduation.

Georgia's public educational system comprises four sectors that serve the multiple needs of state citizens: the Office of School Readiness administers Georgia's prekindergarten programs; the Georgia Department of Education administers K–12 education; the University System of Georgia oversees all public colleges and universities; and the Department of Technical and Adult Education oversees all technical colleges. Aligning these four sectors to serve stakeholders has been a challenge for Georgia policymakers. Statewide P–16 councils act as a communication vehicle across these groups.[1]

The underlying theme of Georgia P–16 reform rests on the state's desire to increase intellectual capital, which will then enhance economic development. The four major strands of reforms are the HOPE (Helping Outstanding Pupils Educationally) Scholarship program, expanded access to pre-K education, expanded K–12 testing programs, and more rigorous college admissions standards. The HOPE Scholarship is a merit-based student aid program implemented in 1993 by former Governor Zell Miller with oversight by the Georgia Student Finance Commission. This merit-based program, funded by lottery revenues, is available to Georgia students who graduate from high school with a B average. It pays for full tuition, essential fees, and books at a Georgia public college or university or provides a $3,000 scholarship to students attending one of the state's private postsecondary institutions. Because it benefits only students who remain in Georgia, it encourages academic performers who may otherwise attend college out of state to remain inside Georgia borders. It also aims to increase college attendance among students who may not otherwise participate in postsecondary options for financial reasons.

The second of Georgia's reform efforts is improved pre-K education. Third are aggressive norm- and criterion-referenced testing programs administered by the Georgia Department of Education. The fourth major reform involves implementing more academically challenging college admissions standards. The University System of Georgia (USG) has established a Freshman Index (FI) score dependent on students' performance in a college preparatory curriculum and has increased the SAT and ACT requirements for admission to Georgia colleges. The FI is a central element in the admissions standards for the different sectors in the USG. The index is calculated using the following formula: FI = SAT Verbal score + SAT Math score + high school GPA × 500. Minimum admission standards for traditional freshmen (those who graduated within the past five years) are as follows:

○ For research universities: 16 college preparatory curriculum (CPC) units plus four additional academic units and an FI of 2500

○ For regional universities: 16 CPC units plus two additional academic units and an FI of 2040

○ For state universities: 16 CPC units plus two additional academic units and an FI of 1940

○ For two-year colleges: 16 CPC units and a FI of 1830 (for "limited admission": 13 CPC units and an FI of 1640)

Each institution in the system is allowed some admissions not meeting the standards, but there are caps on the number of allowable special admissions.[2]

This chapter provides an overview of statewide policy development from the perspectives of state and institutional stakeholders. It begins with a description of the organizational context for Georgia's dramatic policy initiatives, followed by brief presentations of educational reforms affecting P–12 and postsecondary admissions and placement policies. Data collection relevant to this part of the study included interviews with researchers and faculty as well as with state agency personnel.[3] In addition, data on policy as interpreted by higher education institution staff were collected through two college case studies. Policy implementation and meaning as perceived by students, parents, teachers, counselors, and administrators are then explored. At the K–12 level, two high school districts participated in this study.[4] In order to gain an understanding of how policy information is disseminated and interpreted, students and their parents were surveyed. Some students also participated in focus group interviews. School counselors, teachers, and administrators participated in individual interviews.

The Organizational Context

Educational reforms toward a seamless system are set within the relational context of organizations that provide pre-K through postsecondary schooling. The discussion describes this organizational context in Georgia during the time period examined.

The Office of School Readiness and the pre-K Program

The Georgia Department of Education (DOE) regulates the public K–12 schools, although there is notable local autonomy within the school districts. The state superintendent is elected by popular vote, and the governor appoints the board of education. Georgia is currently home to 1,843 P–12 schools, over 1,150 of which are pre-K–elementary schools.

The Georgia public school system is more extensive than that in many other states, in that Georgia was the first state to offer a voluntary prekindergarten program, funded by state lottery proceeds, to all four-year-olds. In 1996, the Office of School Readiness (OSR), a separate state agency, was created as a one-stop children's preschool department authorized to administer Georgia's pre-K program. In 1998, by popular vote, the state constitution was amended to ensure that the lottery fund would always be spent on free prekindergarten as well as postsecondary student scholarships (HOPE Scholarships). By providing opportunities for academic development and achievement at an early age, the innovative pre-K program hopes to ensure future school success. In fact, a study by the Department of Early Childhood Education at Georgia State University has shown that at-risk children participating in the prekindergarten program achieved higher scores on several measures of general academic skills compared to others who did not participate. More studies to determine program effects are ongoing. This Georgia initiative, which has won several national awards, has been a model for a number of other states. While the Georgia prekindergarten program is acknowledged as providing the largest preschool initiative, per capita, in the nation, some policymakers think the development of mandatory pre-K attendance is necessary to promote school readiness further. As a state-level policymaker noted:

> If you look at pre-K, we need to expand it because . . . evidence shows the kids who need it the most don't go. We don't have a requirement that they have to go to a pre-K or a kindergarten, so theoretically the kids can show up in first grade never having set foot in a school.

Pre-K–12 Curriculum and Assessment Reforms

In general, Georgia has weak ratings in key indicators of educational quality.[5] Test scores tend to be in the bottom quartile of all states across all K–12 grades. Progress in the educational outcomes of students is coming only slowly. In order to address this issue, a set of core courses and a standardized testing program was developed in K–12 education. Senate Bill 11 (School Law Code 20–2–281) requires norm- and criterion-referenced testing at various grade levels to provide indicators of educational effectiveness. The administration of nationally norm-referenced assessments provides students, teachers, and parents with grade equivalencies and percentile ranks, and criterion-referenced tests yield results about learning and mastery of the Quality Core Curriculum (QCC), adopted by the State Board of Education in 1977, at the student, classroom, school, system, and state levels. These tests are designed to measure the impact of curricular changes on student performance. The measures are also used to identify successful schools.[6]

The Georgia Kindergarten Assessment is a performance-based assessment tool that measures first-grade readiness. It is also designed to identify individual students' academic deficiencies and assess needs for special instructional assistance. Later, students take norm-referenced tests, such as the Iowa Tests of Basic Skills, to provide ways of comparing Georgia students with students across the nation. Major content areas of reading, language, mathematics, social studies, science, maps, and diagrams at grades 3, 5, and 8 are assessed. This enables schools, as well as policymakers, to assess student standing and identify curricular strengths and weaknesses. Georgia educators also use the Preliminary SAT, or PSAT as a tool to inform students about their academic performance levels so they can select courses that better prepare them for college admissions and, ultimately, postsecondary success. PSAT practice exams are offered by the state at no charge to tenth graders who want to take the SAT. Use of the PSAT Summary of Answers provides invaluable information to students, teachers, and parents in relation to identifying strengths and weaknesses to improve SAT performance.

Georgia also administers a series of criterion-referenced competency tests to provide accountability tools for schools to show stakeholders and policymakers measures of cumulative knowledge and skills spanning grades 1 to 8. These tests also have the potential to provide diagnostic information about individual students and assess program strengths and weaknesses in relation to the QCC.

The DOE requires students to complete a high school graduation test. Recently revalidated, these graduation tests are designed to ensure curricular alignment. The Georgia High School Graduation Tests (GHSGT) cover English, mathematics, social studies, science, and writing. Writing assessments are used in early grades as a developmental tool to identify specific areas where individual students need improvement, but at graduation time the writing assessment is conducted on a pass-fail basis. A passing score on each of the sections is needed to receive a high school diploma; otherwise, if all other graduation requirements have been met, students may be eligible to receive a certificate of performance or a special education diploma. High school students planning to go to college must also take the SAT.

Postsecondary Options in Georgia

Two major administrative units oversee Georgia postsecondary education: the University System of Georgia (USG) and the Department of Technical and Adult Education (DTAE).

The USG is a unified system with constitutional autonomy. The Georgia Board of Regents, appointed by the governor, oversees thirty-four institutions comprising the four institutional divisions of the USG: four research universities, two regional universities, thirteen state universities, and fifteen two-year colleges. One study respondent notes, "We have thirty-four institutions in the system that are very different from each other."

In 1997, the board established a set of rigorous admissions policies to ensure student preparation for college success. College-bound students must complete an established college preparatory curriculum to be considered for admission to the system. The next step in the process uses the FI to allocate students to the four institutional divisions. This measure incorporates high school grade point average (GPA) and SAT scores to determine the college environment in which a student is most likely to achieve. An underlying intention of Georgia's admissions reform efforts was to eliminate open enrollment and institute minimal admissions criteria at USG public colleges and universities. This in turn affects P–12 standards. In addition, USG has set minimum standards for admission with an eye toward eliminating learning support (developmental studies) in all but the two-year institutions. Two-year colleges in USG provide the first two years of the baccalaureate curriculum along with some vocational programs.

While USG's higher standards are viewed as "raising the bar" and "closing the back doors" by some policymakers, others worry that the changes will narrow the path for access to higher education, especially for Georgia's minority students. For example, the phasing out of learning support in the four-year college may make transportation a problem for students who must take learning support courses in institutions farther from their home.

The following sections briefly describe the effects the reforms have had on two USG educational institutions that are the case studies for this chapter.

UNIVERSITY OF GEORGIA. Located in Athens, the flagship UGA educates thirty-one thousand students. As one of the state's two public research-extensive institutions with high admissions requirements, UGA has a competitive admissions policy and does not consider the FI in its admissions process. UGA staff use it only as an "advising tool" by which families can identify the colleges and universities in which the student has a reasonable chance of academic success. However, just because students may be admissible to the system does not mean they will be admitted to UGA. Some UGA respondents expressed frustration about the inadequate communication of the meaning of the FI to parents and prospective students, who sometimes think that meeting minimal standards for an institution guarantees admission to that institution.

Other study respondents describe UGA as "suddenly selective" and "a public Ivy League in the Sun Belt." Tightened admission standards have resulted in a tension in UGA offices as legacies—the children and grandchildren of alumni—have often been denied admission. This has challenged an alumni community steeped in historical tradition.

A related challenge for UGA administrators is the increased demand for entry into UGA because of the promise of the HOPE Scholarship. Before the launching of the HOPE program in 1993, many talented Georgia students chose to attend out-of-state institutions such as Duke, the University of North Carolina, Princeton, Vanderbilt, or the University of Virginia. Now, similarly qualified students may seriously consider UGA as a viable postsecondary alternative because of the availability of the HOPE Scholarship. This is desirable to UGA admissions officers, because they can be more selective and target higher-performing students, but it has reduced opportunities at UGA for other student applicants.

A third compelling pressure faced by UGA is the state's increasing population. Georgia is regularly reported as one of the five fastest-growing states in the nation. In 2001, the state was estimated to be home to 8.38 million people, ranking it tenth nationally (U.S. Bureau of the Census, 2003). The U.S. Census growth forecast for 1995 through 2025 indicated Georgia would grow by an estimated 2.67 percent annually (U.S. Bureau of the Census, 1998), but subsequent growth suggests that may be an underestimate. In addition, Georgia is growing in racial and ethnic diversity. For example, Georgia's Hispanic population grew from 109,000 in 1990 to 436,000 in 2000, and continued growth is predicted. As the state becomes increasingly cosmopolitan and its economy more global, Georgia is clearly facing a new era of educational challenges and opportunities (U.S. Bureau of the Census, 2003).

Despite the growing numbers of potential high school graduates, UGA leaders have not indicated any plans to increase the university's capacity past an enrollment cap of thirty-five thousand. According to the board of regents, UGA will not grow to an institution of fifty thousand students. This means that many students, unable to attend increasingly selective institutions like UGA, are turning to Georgia's other postsecondary institutions, including four-year schools, community colleges, and technical colleges.

STATE UNIVERSITY OF WEST GEORGIA (WGA) AND THE POST-SECONDARY READINESS AND ENRICHMENT PROGRAM. Located on Georgia's western border, WGA, one of thirteen state universities, is home to nine thousand students. Unlike UGA, the WGA admissions committee uses the FI to make admissions decisions. However, the FI has created a tension: WGA has clear enrollment targets to meet, but it must do so in the context of more rigorous admissions requirements that potentially limit enrollment. Prior to the system's admission changes, WGA provided open access to virtually all students and also provided extensive learning support programs for underprepared students. Now, new academic standards provide a context in which WGA must decrease learning support to incoming freshmen with CPC and GPA deficiencies, steering many of these students to two-year postsecondary institutions. One exception to these requirements is the nontraditional student, defined as students who have been out of high school for at least five years. If these students require learning support, they can still be admitted.

WGA served as a pilot institution for the Postsecondary Readiness and Enrichment Program (PREP), an effort targeted at middle-grade students deemed at risk. Respondents describe PREP as a "supplemental program," a "safety net for children," and the "direct service arm of educational policy in the state of Georgia." Students who participate in PREP are usually those who are otherwise unlikely to consider college or who may even drop out when they are in high school.

PREP relies on postsecondary institutions to inform students about what happens in colleges and universities. Students in seventh through ninth grades visit a college or university campus overnight for exposure to the higher education environment. Bobby Powell, PREP coordinator at WGA, constructed the STARR program (Science, Technology, Art, 'Ritin' and 'Rithmetic) to encourage students to attend college. Professors demonstrate how physics can be fun, and art teachers teach students how to tie-dye t-shirts. Such demonstrations are designed to show students that the classroom experience can be enjoyable. Overall, the goal is to help students gain insight into the value of learning.

PREP is largely praised as a successful initiative to promote college going for at-risk youth. However, some of the students who could benefit most from the program are unable to attend because they need to work or care for family members or they have no transportation. A PREP administrator told the story of one family whose children did not participate in PREP because it required an overnight stay, and they did not have any pajamas. When students do not participate in such programs, educators and policymakers can interpret this as a lack of commitment or motivation, which is usually not the case. Furthermore, although PREP provides resources for tutoring and participation in academic enrichment programs as well as counseling assistance, a college administrator remarks that it does not focus enough on academic development:

> PREP does not have a focused curriculum [to overcome CPC deficiencies and improve standardized test scores]. . . . People are bringing students to campus, giving them a tour, taking them on field trips, engaging them in mentoring relationships, and each year you have a different set of PREP kids. PREP has done a very effective job of reorienting a generation to the values of a college experience. . . . It is a great cultural and socialization experience, but I don't think that it is academically rigorous enough to prepare students for twenty-first-century education.

One partner institution representative in an active P-16 council was deeply involved with organizing a campus PREP program. This respondent viewed the P-16 and PREP programs as initiatives that "spread the news of the requirements, increase students' ability to do college work, and foster collaboration among middle schools, high schools, and colleges . . . [but PREP is] where direct interaction with parents and potential postsecondary students takes place."

Department of Technical and Adult Education

Another important postsecondary option for Georgia residents is DTAE, which is separate from the university system. DTAE oversees thirty-four technical colleges, which offer applied degrees, certificates, and adult education programs. They provide adult literacy training, continuing education, customized training for business and industry, and technical education to the associate degree level. Many Georgians believe that the technical colleges play a major role in helping students pursue technical careers and contribute to the state economy.

DTAE cooperates with local industry in three fundamental areas. First, the business community sets standards to determine the curriculum taught at the state's technical colleges. Second, the DTAE offers customized training processes for the business community. Finally, employers establish the competencies required of those who earn a DTAE certificate. The same curriculum crosses institutions throughout the state.

Recently, DTAE and the USG formed an alliance to facilitate an efficient transfer between technical and system institutions. The pact "addresses animosity and competition between the two- and four-year colleges and technical colleges by suggesting that students be able to move between systems, with USG concentrating on general education and DTAE focusing on job-entry occupational instruction" (Richardson, Bracco, Callan, and Finney, 1999, p. 121). One technical college representative participating in a P–16 council focus group described recent successes with such agreements as "a groundbreaking effort" that has helped students transfer credits from the vocational institution to the university.[7]

The admissions procedures of DTAE institutions are fairly straightforward, with one caveat: students enroll in programs rather than institutions. Specific programs have definite requirements related to math or verbal skills. Essentially, how well an individual reads, writes, and computes determines whether that student will gain admission into one of DTAE's many programs. Programmatic curricula are not based on high school preparation. Thus, if a student is deficient in reading, math, or verbal skills, DTAE provides developmental courses for students to increase their performance. The higher standards developed by the University System of Georgia have the potential to increase enrollment in DTAE institutions.

Barriers to a Seamless System

Several disjunctures exist in Georgia's current educational policy environment, posing barriers for student transition from high school to postsecondary education. Notably, the absence of a single CPC creates problems. One statewide P–16 Council participant described this situation in the following way:

> There are still some difficulties. One is that we had a committee look at CPC between the state department of education and the university system. . . . And we know there are different definitions [of what constitutes a college preparatory course] and that is a problem. We are still in negotiation. There is not one single college prep curriculum, and that will be an issue.

Another statewide P–16 Council participant explained the challenge created by the lack of a single college preparatory curriculum:

> Just because I take courses toward a college prep diploma (with a college prep seal) does not mean I will get into college. There are courses that count in K–12 schools for the college prep seal but are not acceptable for admissions to the university system. . . . Some students can take a program in a high school and take courses, and it sounds like it will satisfy courses and it really will not. There is a difference between college prep courses and college prep courses that will count for admission.

At a May 20, 1999, state-level P–16 subcommittee meeting, participants agreed that the current system was flawed and decided that parents must be informed of the existing differences and encouraged to work with their school counselor. Individuals attending the meeting were attempting to establish a list of courses that would be accepted for college admission. Discussion centered on what to include in a brochure to clarify expectations so counselors can understand them and relay the information to students and parents.

One issue is that Georgia lacks a standardized method to assess high school transcripts. One P–16 Council participant described confusion caused by different grading scales:

> The problem is we have eighteen different grading scales in use. Some systems do not have a D. Some have F's set at 50; some have F's set at 60. Some have a 0 to 100 scale. Some have a 60 to 100 scale. There are many different scales. A student with a 3.0 GPA can get HOPE. They have translated it so that a student with an 80 can get the HOPE Scholarship. And in some school systems, C students are eligible for HOPE.

While adopting different grading scales may raise the number of students eligible for the HOPE Scholarship, it presents a challenge in college admissions. Related to this is the potential for grade inflation by teachers who want to increase their students' participation in postsecondary options. However, such students may not truly be prepared to attend college. Another issue related to grading is "title inflation." Nonhonors courses may be given honors titles to elevate a student's GPA. Another P–16 Council respondent made the following observation: "There are some [nonhonors] courses in high school that are branded 'honors.' There is nothing to keep a school from doing that. There is no standardized definition of honors. There is no standard definition or control over grades assigned to honors classes." In addition to these transition challenges, some challenges are specific to institution types. For example, Georgia's two-year colleges and DTAE technical institutes will be greatly affected by USG reforms as they need to provide educational avenues for those denied admission to public four-year colleges and universities as well as meeting the needs of their present student population.

Historically black colleges and universities (HBCUs) are also profoundly affected by USG reform efforts to limit developmental education provided in four-year postsecondary institutions. The historical mission of HBCUs includes service to students who may need learning support to succeed in college. One educator expressed concern over the ability of the two-year college to take on this role for students currently attending public four-year historically black colleges and universities.[8]

P–16 Councils: Attempting to Overcome the Barriers

Georgia has adopted a number of communication strategies to rectify the misalignment between the K–12 and postsecondary sectors. Electronic Web sites and brochures, for example, are employed to communicate admissions information to schools, students, and parents.

To inform students and all other organizational actors further affected by rising admission and placement standards, the chancellor and the board of regents created and approved initiatives in the 1990s to improve communication between the OSR, DOE, USG, and DTAE. These are the P–16 Councils and PREP. Georgia's regional and state P–16 Initiative provides a viable avenue to address the state's complex admissions and placement issues by bringing representatives from public schools and postsecondary institutions to the same table. Such opportunities for interchange can lead to collaborative solutions.

The mission of the P–16 councils is to promote student success throughout the entire system. The state P–16 council, housed in the USG system office, serves as an oversight unit for the local councils and communicates and implements policy changes.

Exhibit 6.1 shows the long-term goals and measurable objectives of Georgia's P–16 Initiative. Three activity strands comprise the P–16 councils: alignment of preschool through college educational systems, including standards expected of students at each level; teacher quality (involving both teacher preparation and professional development); and with an elevation of educational standards, an alignment of expectations for students to move smoothly from prekindergarten through higher education completion.

While the P–16 Initiative is generally applauded for "bringing disparate entities to a common table to discuss common interests and try to improve educational opportunities for all students," said a P–16 council respondent, there are some criticisms. First, there is variation in the capacities of local councils to meet objectives as set by the state-level council. While some P–16 councils focus on P–16 transition issues, many place primary emphasis on teacher preparation issues. Some local councils are impeded by geographical distance among participants and lack of finances or leadership to address the issues. Another criticism of statewide K–16 systems in Georgia, according to Wallhaus (1997), is that the many "overlaps and discontinuities served by different programs are not conducive to effective communications and coordination and may disadvantage

Exhibit 6.1. Georgia P–16 Council Goals and Measurable Objectives.

Long Term Goals
1. To promote the achievement of Georgia's students at all levels of education, pre-school through post-secondary (P–16).
2. To help students move more smoothly from one educational sector to the next.
3. To ensure that all students who enter post-secondary institutions are prepared to succeed, and to increase the success rate of those who enter.
4. To close the gaps in access to post-secondary education between students from majority and minority groups and between students from high and low income groups.
5. To focus the co-reform of schools and teacher education on practices that bring P–12 students from diverse groups to high levels of achievement.
6. To help students become more responsible in their citizenship.
7. To have a qualified teacher in every classroom.

Introduction
P–16 is a collaborative of pre-kindergarten through high schools, technical institutes, colleges and universities, and the broader community. The collaborative serves as a catalyst at both the state and local levels for achieving the goals of the Georgia P–16 Initiative. P–16 councils refer all recommendations to appropriate governing authorities. While each partner in the P–16 Initiative sets individual goals and objectives, the objectives that follow represent cooperative efforts across two or more partners in the Georgia P–16 Council.

Measurable Objectives
1. To improve student performance in reading by end of third grade
2. To increase the number of high school students successfully completing the gateway courses of algebra and geometry by the end of the tenth grade
3. To increase graduation rates in high school, technical institutes, and college
4. To close the gaps between the expectations set for students to graduate from high school and those set to enter technical institute, college, and work
5. To have a qualified teacher in every classroom by the year 2003
6. To enhance learning environments in schools in ways that support the success of students from diverse ethnic, cultural, socio-economic, and international groups

Source: *Georgia P–16 Initiative Work Plan 1998–2003, approved by the Georgia P–16 Council, December 16, 1998.*

Georgia's efforts to sustain well-conceptualized policy linkages and effective communications in the long run" (p. 18). Some confusion is reflected in the following comment by a local P–16 Council member: "Was that P–16 or was this P–16? We have had so many collaborative efforts with the College of Education that I am not sure where one starts and the other ends."

According to some study respondents, turf issues continue to challenge the process of collaboration. One state-level respondent captured the essence of this critique by stating, "P–16 is not really an issue for [us]. It is a university system baby." Another policymaker said, "I wonder how much influence higher education can have on K–12 in policymaking. They are a totally separate governing body. . . . I am not really sure how to better coordinate them." One P–12 school administrator who is a P–16 Council participant made the following remark:

> We've been a little bit disappointed in the P–16 to be honest. We got together . . . and wrote the objectives. They were published and distributed those to the teachers and that's been it. . . . I understand there's been a change of the leadership at the top. We basically have taken those initiatives and done them district-wide on our own but not in an official P–16 capacity because we really haven't heard from P–16.

Nonetheless, successful transition programs have resulted from the efforts of some P–16 councils, and there remains optimism, as this P–16 Council participant conveyed: "P–16 has really helped in this area to focus on [academic] standards for both university and school district. This is a chapter that is not yet complete."

Information on Policy Reforms: Dissemination and Interpretation

The section examines how well information about higher education—the standards and policies developed and implemented by Georgia institutions—is understood, interpreted, and acted on by parents, ninth- and eleventh-grade students, as well as secondary school and district personnel.

High Schools in the Study

Two high schools agreed to participate in this part of the study, Eastside High School (EHS) and Westside High School (WHS). Both names are pseudonyms. The majority of students attending these schools are white and come from lower-socioeconomic status (SES) backgrounds. Their experiences may reflect challenges other low-income students across the state and the rest of the nation face. Compared to Georgia's college-going rate (over 60 percent), lower percentages of EHS and WHS students enter postsecondary education.

EASTSIDE HIGH SCHOOL. Eastside High School is a small school of approximately eight hundred students in a rural community that is becoming suburban as more urban dwellers move into the area. About one-third of the EHS student body participates in the reduced-price or free lunch program, with approximately 30 percent attending Georgia public colleges and almost half eligible for the HOPE Scholarship. Sixty-eight percent of the students receive a diploma with the college preparatory endorsement, the same as the state average. Approximately two-thirds of the students are white, mirroring the racial population in the county.

A school official made the following comments regarding demographic changes:

> We are seeing some of Atlanta's larger city attitudes move into our little community. We're seeing our community become more white as, where we used to be about 45 percent African American, 55 percent white. It's now more like 65/35 already. We're seeing more people come in who are professional people, moving in or moving out of what used to be the suburbs, now they're moving even farther out.

WESTSIDE HIGH SCHOOL. Westside High School is in a county of about forty-two thousand students, over twice as large as that of Eastside High School. The percentage of diplomas awarded with the college prepara-tory endorsement at WHS is below the state average of 68 percent. This is significant because the college preparatory endorsement reflects the number of CPC units completed successfully by the students in the schools. The lack of the college preparatory endorsement on a high school graduate's diploma limits the student's access to various postsecondary institutions.

About one-third of WHS's twelve hundred students participate in the reduced-price or free lunch program, with approximately 30 percent attending Georgia public colleges and over half eligible for the HOPE Scholarship.

Approximately 90 percent of the students are white. The WHS county is experiencing dramatic growth with a number of new schools being built.

The HOPE Scholarship: Knowledge of Requirements, Benefits, and Effects

Students' knowledge of HOPE program characteristics was assessed using a survey. One hundred sixty students responded from WHS, with eighty-three responding from EHS. Students were presented with eight items and asked to select which were HOPE requirements. Only two of the eight items offered to students were actual requirements: Georgia residency and a B average. Of the respondents to this question, 90 percent of EHS students knew about both requirements compared to 35 percent of WHS respondents, even though more WHS students qualify for HOPE. This finding suggests that EHS students may be presented with more information about the HOPE requirements, possibly to help them improve their grades and eligibility for the scholarship. Of the parent respondents, only 32 percent of EHS parents and 25 percent of WHS parents knew about both HOPE requirements. This suggests that better communication with families about the HOPE requirements is needed.

A further analysis examined knowledge of the HOPE requirements among EHS and WHS students of different SES. We found that there were no statistically significant differences between lower-, middle-, and high-SES groups. This finding suggests that lower-SES students are equally informed about HOPE as other groups. This result was replicated when questioning parents about HOPE.

The survey revealed different levels of understanding of the benefits of the HOPE Scholarship. HOPE provides full tuition and fees to a Georgia public college, university, or technical school, or $3,000 toward the cost of attending a Georgia private school. The majority of students understood that they can receive full tuition to a Georgia public college or university (59.8 percent), but less than a third (30.3 percent) understood the provision for partial tuition for private Georgia institutions. Two students discussed their interpretations of the HOPE benefits for public and private universities:

> It gives you a lot more money if you go to a public school. I mean, if you decide you want to go to a private college it helps some, but like she said, any money's better than not getting it at all.

> If you get HOPE, a lot of people can take the HOPE and get, like, a state college almost completely paid for. But if you go to a private school, they give you like $1,000 a year.

Less than one-third (26.4 percent) of the students recognized that HOPE also covers full tuition and fees to Georgia technical colleges. These data suggest that students associate the HOPE Scholarship with two-year and four-year colleges that are part of the USG rather than, for example, the two-year technical colleges that are part of the DTAE. Regardless of a student's interest in a particular postsecondary institution type, a B average is required for students to earn and retain the HOPE Scholarship.

Of the students surveyed, 18.9 percent incorrectly believed that the HOPE Scholarship guarantees admission to public Georgia institutions, and 7.9 percent believed it guarantees admission to private Georgia colleges and universities. But as one USG official states with regard to the FI, "admissibility is not admission"; having a HOPE Scholarship is not a guarantee of admission to any Georgia college or university.

STUDENT PERCEPTIONS OF HOPE. A critical component of the HOPE Scholarship is its perceived effect on student academic performance. Students were asked if the availability of the HOPE Scholarship motivated them to enhance their performance in high school. Ninety-one percent of 243 students sampled reported that they agree or strongly agree with the statement "The HOPE Scholarship motivates me to do better in school." This suggests that the promise of funding for a college education encourages students to engage academically.

The lack of significant differences in the perceived effect of the HOPE Scholarship on student performance across SES levels could indicate that individuals from lower-SES backgrounds interpret the HOPE as an opportunity for them to afford college. Therefore, they become more motivated to perform academically because of the promise of college.[9] However, it is important to note that over 11 percent of low-SES students suggested that the HOPE does not contribute to their motivation to perform academically, compared to 8 percent and 4 percent for middle- and high-SES students.

TEACHER PERCEPTIONS OF HOPE. The research design used to compare student responses with those of the teachers who work with them has provided important insights. Narrative data gathered from teachers regarding the perceived effects of the HOPE Scholarship on student academic performance are presented here.

Across the two high schools, teacher perceptions of the HOPE Scholarship are mixed. One teacher voiced strong support for HOPE and its obvious effects on students: "I think you see that they are beginning to work a lot harder because they have that option out there. It's no longer that they know by sixth grade that mom and dad can't afford college, so 'I can't go.' They realize, 'Gee, there is a way that I can go if I work really hard.'"

Another believed that the HOPE Scholarship motivates students to perform at their highest ability levels: "I've just seen an increased number of them thinking of college and being able to afford it and perhaps going on to [a four-year] university where they might have gone somewhere else first [like a two-year institution]."

Not all teachers acknowledged the HOPE program's effectiveness in raising academic aspirations and performance. For example, this teacher described effects of the HOPE Scholarship program in this way: "It's filled our colleges full of kids that are not adequately prepared for college. . . . They're exploiting those children. . . . They're taking their money. They're putting them in remedial classes, and then when they don't have any more money, they say, 'Oh, sorry, see ya.'"

Concern was expressed during data collection that the HOPE Scholarship encourages teachers to inflate student grades. Some state-level actors suggested that well-meaning teachers, pressured by the desire to encourage student success, would actually give students higher grades to help them qualify for the scholarship. However, when teachers were asked about pressure on their grading practices associated with the HOPE Scholarship, they consistently responded that there was no pressure to grade differently. The following teacher comment was representative: "I've not had any pressure from a parent. I've had some in the past with athletes . . . but I haven't had any experience with the HOPE."

SCHOOL COUNSELOR PERCEPTIONS OF HOPE. School counselors' perceptions of the HOPE Scholarship's effects on students were consistently positive across the two sites. A counselor at one of the schools commented on the financial rewards associated with the HOPE Scholarship:

> The impact of that HOPE Scholarship has truly been remarkable. Kids are thinking more about college than they ever had because that myth about "I can't afford college" has been taken away a little bit. . . . It's changed from not even a percentage [going to college] to 30 to 40 percent of the kids who go on. And that still means 60 to 70 percent right into the world of work, but it's made a dramatic difference. Kids do have a change, a very, very much ingrained idea that you graduate from high school, you go to work, or you go to the army. Not so anymore. Now it's tech school, two-year school, college. Big change.

Another counselor focused on student intentions to remain in Georgia: "I think we have a lot more in-state people, students not looking at out-of-state universities because of the HOPE Scholarship. . . . I see a lot of students looking in-state, saying, 'I'm going to UGA or I'm going to Georgia College or State University.'" The same counselor said that students who decide to remain in Georgia because of HOPE availability are better-performing students. In general, school counselors' remarks about the HOPE Scholarship are more positive than those made by teachers. One plausible explanation for these differences lies in the types of relationships students share with school counselors and teachers. Unless students have personal concerns or disciplinary problems, they may rarely see the school counselor. This experience contrasts sharply with teachers, who typically encounter students daily. Teachers are also more likely to encounter a broad range of academic performers. These differences suggest that teachers and counselors need to confer more frequently with one another on the broader range of student performers. This could maximize the potentially positive effects of the HOPE Scholarship on student motivation and ultimately student performance.

SCHOOL ADMINISTRATOR PERCEPTIONS OF HOPE. Different perspectives also emerge from administrators. While several praise the HOPE program for making it possible for more students to attend postsecondary education, some discuss the distributional issues related to the HOPE Scholarship (for example, providing assistance primarily to middle-income families). One administrator asserted that students from lower-income families need more funding than the HOPE Scholarship provides: HOPE "is something, but it's not enough [for poor kids]. It pays tuition but it doesn't pay meals, it doesn't pay for dorm rooms or housing."

When the HOPE Scholarship was introduced in 1993, it was restricted to students whose annual family income was less than $100,000, but the income eligibility cap was abolished in 1995. Some respondents described HOPE as a middle-class benefit. Since its inception, the HOPE program had been criticized by many observers because it did not allow financially needy students to add their HOPE Scholarship funds to the funds they were already eligible for under the federal need-based Pell Grant program (see Mortenson, 1999). Instead, the program required that students and families subtract their Pell funds from their potential HOPE funds, such that Pell funding was a substitute for HOPE funding. Academically talented lower-income students therefore received appreciably less marginal benefit from HOPE funding than other students.

In 2000, the program was revised to allow students to receive the full benefits of both the HOPE Scholarship and the Pell Grant. Hence, a controversial and regressive feature of the program was removed, making talented students from lower-income backgrounds eligible for substantially more generous student aid packages. A study by Henry and Rubenstein (2000) concludes that merit-based aid has improved the quality of K–12 education in Georgia and reduced racial performance disparities by motivating students and their families to commit greater effort to school-ing. Nonetheless, controversy continues nationally regarding the benefits of merit-based scholarships for low-income students (see Schmidt, 2000, and Heller and Marin, 2002).

PLANS TO APPLY FOR THE HOPE SCHOLARSHIP. One of the goals of the HOPE Scholarship is to encourage top academic performers to remain in Georgia. When comparing honors students to nonhonors students regard-ing intent to apply for the HOPE Scholarship, no statistically significant differences emerged. However, 29 percent of 91 honors students remained unsure of their intention to apply for the HOPE Scholarship. This is higher than that of nonhonors students (17 percent of 146) and all eleventh graders (18 percent of 127) in the sample. Four percent of hon-ors students indicate that they do not plan to apply for HOPE. Taken together, these results might indicate that honors students, aware of their competitive standing as academic performers, may wait to see what other educational opportunities emerge (such as a full scholarship to an Ivy League college) before they commit to a HOPE Scholarship application. However, the results are not alarming because the data indicate that two-thirds of honors students do intend to apply for the scholarship.

The relationship between HOPE availability and student decisions to remain in Georgia is an important component for policymakers, as they need to prepare for either increases or decreases in postsecondary atten-dance as a result of HOPE availability. Student comments generated from focus groups indicate that the HOPE Scholarship's effect on students attending Georgia institutions is mixed. An eleventh grader remarked, "If you get the HOPE Scholarship, then you basically, you don't have to but you're basically going to have to go to a college in Georgia because it doesn't pay for anywhere else, and if you want to go somewhere else, you either have to get a scholarship or you have to pay for it yourself." Some viewed the HOPE Scholarship as a viable alternative if they do not gain acceptance to an out-of-state institution. An eleventh grader told the researchers, "If you're not accepted to a college out of state that you wanted to go to, then you . . . have it to fall back on." When asked about intentions to remain in Georgia if they received HOPE, responses by SES level (low, middle, high) did not yield statistically significant differences (see Figure 6.1), a potentially important policy finding. High percentages of students at all socioeconomic levels agree or strongly agree that they would stay in Georgia if they received a HOPE Scholarship. When asked about intent to remain in Georgia, minority study participants also reported high percentages (above 80 percent).[10] When these figures are associated with

Figure 6.1. Student Intentions to Remain in Georgia If They Receive a HOPE Scholarship, by SES.

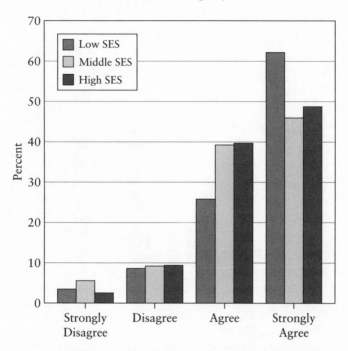

"I Will Stay in Georgia If I Receive a HOPE Scholarship"

the motivation percentages discussed earlier, the findings suggest that the HOPE Scholarship's influence on student performance may contribute to individuals' decisions to apply for and attend college in Georgia.

No statistically significant differences emerged between the two participating high school sites when students were asked if they would remain in Georgia if they received a HOPE Scholarship. Students were provided choices on a four-point Likert scale (strongly disagree, disagree, agree, strongly agree). Half of the surveyed students (50.2 percent) strongly agreed with the statement, "I will stay in Georgia if I receive a HOPE Scholarship," and 36.9 percent agreed with the statement. Thus, of the total sample, 87.1 percent of students said they would stay in Georgia if they received a HOPE Scholarship. Figure 6.2 compares nonhonors and honors students who agree that they will state in Georgia if they receive a HOPE Scholarship.

An important caveat about the HOPE Scholarship concerns the perceived benefits afforded by HOPE. For example, as discussed earlier,

Figure 6.2. Student Intentions to Remain in Georgia If They Receive a HOPE Scholarship, by Honors versus Nonhonors Students.

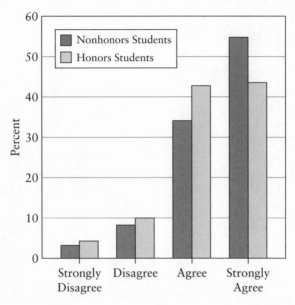

"I Will Stay in Georgia If I Receive a HOPE Scholarship"

lower-SES students might believe that the HOPE Scholarship guarantees admission to a Georgia public or private institution. This misconception could create tensions between parents who want a Georgia college education for their children and policymakers who may not have successfully communicated the actual benefits of the HOPE award to their constituents. However, the percentages presented earlier indicate that many students and families do not understand the requirements associated with the scholarship award. It would be crucial in future analyses of additional sites to examine the relationships between knowledge of the HOPE requirements and benefits and student desire to remain in Georgia for postsecondary education.

The survey did not measure student interest levels in attending out-of-state colleges. Thus, we do not have precise information on the extent to which the HOPE Scholarship encourages students to remain in Georgia for college who would normally leave the state. However, an underlying assumption about the HOPE Scholarship was that it would motivate the top-performing students (those who often attend college out of state) to remain in Georgia. The current findings are promising because a significant majority of honors students intend to remain in Georgia.

SUMMARY OF HOPE SCHOLARSHIP FINDINGS. The following items provide a summary of the main findings about the HOPE Scholarship reported in this section:

○ A majority of students and parents did not understand the academic requirements for a HOPE Scholarship. However, a greater percentage of students at EHS were aware of the requirements.

○ No statistically significant differences between SES groups or between racial/ethnic groups emerged in terms of knowledge about the HOPE benefits.

○ There were mixed results in students' knowledge about HOPE Scholarship benefits, especially as they related to private universities and technical colleges.

○ Less than one-fifth of the students sampled believed that the HOPE Scholarship guarantees admission to a Georgia public university.

○ The effects of the HOPE Scholarship on student motivation differed within and between groups. Students and counselors are generally positive about the HOPE Scholarship, while both teachers and administrators expressed mixed views.

○ The majority of students surveyed strongly agreed or agreed that they would remain in Georgia to pursue their postsecondary education if they were offered the HOPE Scholarship. Some statistically insignificant differences were observed among different ethnic groups and between honors and nonhonors students.

School-Level Understandings of USG Admission Reforms and Tuition

In addition to school-level knowledge of the Georgia HOPE initiative, knowledge of and response to USG admission policy reforms and tuition was studied at both high school sites.[11] SAT scores, high school GPA, and college preparatory curriculum courses are critical in the calculation of the FI.

ADMISSIONS POLICY. The study survey examined students' perceptions of what is important in admissions considerations. Students were presented with a list of items and asked to rate the importance (on a scale of 1 to 4, with 0 meaning "not considered/not important," and 4 meaning "single most important factor") of each item in gaining admission to each institution. The results in Table 6.1 indicate that slightly over half of

Table 6.1. Percentages of Student Perceptions of the Relative
Importance of Specific Criteria for Admissions.

	State University of West Georgia	University of Georgia
SAT scores	50.4%	52.0%
High school GPA	55.8	52.0
College preparatory curriculum units	51.8	53.1

the students realized that SAT scores, high school GPA, and college preparatory curriculum courses are important in gaining entry into WGA or UGA.

When the data were compared across the two high schools surveyed, one interesting difference emerged: students at EHS were more likely to believe that GPA is a very important factor in admissions. For WGA admissions, 63 percent of EHS students rated it as very important compared to 52.4 percent of WHS students. Similar results were obtained for UGA admissions, with 65.4 percent of EHS students rating GPA as very important compared to 45.5 percent of WHS students. These findings suggest that EHS students may encounter more teachers, counselors, or other sources of information to impress on them the importance of academic performance to gain college entry. No differences emerged between school sites for the importance of SAT scores and college preparatory curriculum units.

However, changes in college admissions requirements may have created some confusion for students, parents, and teachers. One teacher commented on this situation: "And one of the things, if I'm not mistaken about, is there's a freshmen index that will be used in 2001. . . . Different universities and colleges will be having different expectations. . . . I'm not sure that I necessarily understand that fully and I know the students, and their parents don't." One school counselor, echoing others, expressed some frustration with the college admission processes: "I guess I would like to see the colleges actually send me a bottom line. And I know that's hard to do with admission requirements because you take a lot of different things into consideration, but that would be nice for me to have it to tell the students."

TUITION ESTIMATES. Students were asked to provide their best estimates of tuition for one year at UGA and WGA. The respondents were instructed not to consider the cost of books, housing, food, or any additional expenses and to limit their estimates to the actual tuition cost.

Students wrote in a specific amount of money. Tuition costs were overestimated for both UGA and WGA. Table 6.2 illustrates differences reported across SES levels and honors versus nonhonors students. Although no statistical differences emerged between socioeconomic groups and honors or nonhonors students, it is important to note that two-thirds of the students surveyed overestimated tuition costs. Furthermore, nearly half of the lower-SES students estimated tuition costs in excess of five times the actual cost of tuition for both institutions. This perception of higher tuition costs suggests that lower-SES students believe that they need to apply for every financial aid program available (including the HOPE Scholarship) should they decide to participate in postsecondary education. More needs to be done by policymakers to inform Georgia students and their families about actual tuition costs.

ADDRESSING MISPERCEPTIONS ABOUT ADMISSIONS INFORMATION. Data presented thus far suggest that college information sources play a central role in student understanding of college academic requirements. This study also examined other sources eleventh graders ($N = 127$) use to gather important information. Students were asked how frequently they talk with parents, counselors, and teachers about college admission requirements (see Table 6.3). These three sources were chosen because of their proximity to the student on a daily basis.

From these responses, it appears that students communicate more with parents and teachers than they do with school counselors. Whereas students were more likely to talk frequently with their parents about college admission requirements, they tend to talk to teachers and counselors only once or twice. However, the content of these reported conversations remains unknown. We do not know, for example, if lower-SES students conversed with their parents about college costs while higher-SES students talked to their parents about academic requirements.

Student survey responses to questions about communication between students and parents, teachers, and counselors indicate no statistically significant differences across SES groups in their frequency of discussions with individuals about college admissions requirements. When students responded that they talk many times with their parents about college admissions, the data suggest that across low- and middle-SES groups, students engaged less frequently with their parents (68.8 percent, 62.2 percent, respectively) than did high-SES students (82.4 percent). However, neither group "never" discussed admissions with their parents. The SES groups are fairly evenly matched regarding discussions with teachers and counselors.

Table 6.2. Student Estimates of Tuition, by SES
and Honors versus Nonhonors.

	Socioeconomic Status			
	Low SES (*n* = 55)	Middle SES (*n* = 66)	High SES (*n* = 41)	Total (*n* = 162)
University of Georgia (actual cost of tuition $2,414)				
% within two times the actual cost (less than $4,828)	20	36.4	26.8	28.4
% between two and five times the actual cost	32.7	34.8	31.7	33.3
% more than five times the actual cost (more than $12,070)	47.3	28.8	41.5	38.3
State University of West Georgia (actual cost of tuition $1,808)				
% within two times the actual cost (less than $3,616)	16.7	29.2	25	23.9
% between two and five times the actual cost	29.6	32.3	30	30.8
% more than five times the actual cost (more than $9,040)	53.7	38.5	45	45.3

	Honors Versus Nonhonors		
	Nonhonors (*n* = 133)	Honors (*n* = 88)	Total (*n* = 221)
University of Georgia (actual cost of tuition $2,414)			
% within two times the actual cost (less than $4,828)	31.6	23.9	28.5
% between two and five times the actual cost	28.6	35.2	31.2
% more than five times the actual cost (more than $12,070)	39.8	40.9	40.3
State University of West Georgia (actual cost of tuition $1,808)			
% within two times the actual cost (less than $3,616)	24.2	22.1	23.4
% between two and five times the actual cost	29.5	27.9	28.9
% more than five times the actual cost (more than $9,040)	46.2	50.0	47.7

Table 6.3. Frequency That Eleventh-Grade Students Talk with Others About College Admissions.

	Parents	Teachers	Counselors
Never	7.9%	26%	37%
One to two times	30.7	57.5	49.6
Many times	61.4	16.5	13.4

When we compared honors and nonhonors students' interactions with parents, counselors, and teachers, honors students reported more frequent interactions with teachers than did nonhonors students. This is the only statistically significant difference found between these groups. Clearly, honors students are more likely to talk with their teachers at least once or twice, if not many times, about what they need to get admitted to college. This is not surprising since honors students are more likely to have greater contact with their high school teachers, overall.

A further analysis examined differences among racial/ethnic groups in the frequency of discussions about college admissions requirements with parents, counselors, and teachers. The only statistically significant difference involved students' interactions with counselors. In particular, the data indicate that African American students were more likely to talk to counselors about admissions criteria at least once or twice compared to others in the group. However, the small sample (responses from only eleven African American students in these mostly white schools) makes it difficult to draw conclusions.

While counselors are important sources of information for students examining their postsecondary options, teachers are also taking on more of a role in this area. Often the school counseling office receives current information about college admissions requirements that they then pass on to the teachers. For example, WHS teachers, who are divided among groups of fifteen to twenty-five advisees, advise students on their courses and college aspirations. The same teacher will advise these groups from tenth through twelfth grades. A counselor stated that "our advisement system is a teacher advisement system." As one teacher described it:

> When we advise, we have a little sheet telling us the requirements for the college bound [students], what the requirements are for the technical school or vocational. . . . Then we advise according to that sheet. We look at it and try to see where a student is going, and then we meet individually with each of our students that we advise, and their parents are invited to that so they can come too.

Once a year, each teacher runs a college information group in the library. Counselors attend the sessions to answer questions about college admissions requirements. Each student is allocated twenty minutes to discuss issues that pertain to college. The overall purpose of these special advising programs is to help college-bound high school students select appropriate classes for the upcoming school year. One eleventh grader described the process:

> We go over a list of all the classes that I've taken and compare that to the requirements of getting into college, like you have to have so many years of this class or so many years of this subject or something, and they make sure you're on track for the next year. And then signing you up for the classes you'll need to take in order to get those requirements.

One teacher described this experience as terrifying:

> I wish the counselors did it instead of us. It terrifies me, and I think most teachers feel the same way, that we just do not know enough to be doing all this advising with our little hour or hour and a half session and our notebooks and the way they [college requirements] change. I had seniors this year; I'm always really worried I'll miss something.

The student-to-counselor ratio at WHS is 400 to 1. Since students are not assigned to counselors as they are for teachers, they can meet with any counselor of their choosing. A counselor suggested, "You'd have to say that all three counselors have a caseload of twelve hundred students." Counselors advise students on many issues (teen pregnancy, conflict resolution, abuse cases, attendance cases, discipline matters) in addition to educational and career planning. Even more problematic is that students must seek out counselors on their own rather than rely on regularly scheduled meetings as with teacher advisers. This creates additional pressure for college-bound students committed to their academic responsibilities. A student told us:

> I think it would help if the counselors set aside time for college prep students to come into the office and talk to them about college and answer questions instead of us having to come to them and having to make time for them because they—I don't know if they know that we just don't have time right now. You know, because in my [advanced math class] if I was to miss a day . . . it's over from there, you know?

The situation at EHS is similar to WHS with the same student-to-counselor ratio: 400 to 1. One EHS administrator believed that new state-level policies would provide relief for overwhelmed students and counselors: "The governor is going to require that the guidance counselors spend five-sixths of their time in guidance and counseling next year. So the assistant principals are making arrangements to take over scheduling and that's not a bad thing. . . . The services weren't getting to the students." A counselor responded positively to this new policy: "Since we are no longer doing the testing . . . [and] doing the scheduling, we are looking forward next year to doing some classroom guidance."

As the EHS administrator pointed out, the burden for testing and scheduling shifts from the counselor to other building administrators, such as the assistant principal. However, teachers still play a critical advising role for students—one that includes many tasks a counselor could perform. For example, EHS students were paired with teachers to get to know them better. Teachers then worked with students in career planning and resumé development. One of the students interviewed described the process:

> They take all the kids and they divide them up into groups of . . . fifteen to twenty [students]. . . . They just give each group to any random teacher, and then the teacher's job is to discuss the topic for that particular month. It's just once a month for, like, thirty minutes out of one day, and some teachers care, some teachers participate in activities, and some don't, like mine.

Unlike the school counselors, who advise the students who seek them out for academic advising (or those referred for other issues), teachers must work with their assigned student groups. Often a wide range of student skills and aspirations is represented in these groups. A teacher, frustrated with this design, described the advising process:

> In my particular advisement group I have probably fourteen children, only three of whom are college bound. . . . I'm lucky to even have them come to school on a regular basis. . . . It's not very productive encouraging them to do this or do that or get involved with this essay contest or apply for this scholarship because most of the time, I'm trying to keep order between the kids. . . . The three or four who might look into the future are almost overlooked in order to maintain and get accomplished something with the other ten or eleven.

However, a counselor pointed out that these groups are not primarily for college advisement: "[Advisement groups are] more of a relationship builder for the students and an additional person that they could connect with on campus."

Recommendations for Improving College Knowledge

Student and parent access to accurate and current college information remains problematic for the high schools represented in this study. However, the focus group and interview data yielded a series of recommendations that can perhaps result in better communication.

CREATE OPPORTUNITIES FOR STUDENT INTERACTION WITH POST-SECONDARY FACULTY. EHS and WHS host advisement fairs, to which several colleges send representatives to campus to talk with students. Although students said these are helpful, some indicate that this activity does not provide enough time to address their individual concerns. These students believed that more prolonged visits from university representatives could eliminate some of the misconceptions about college requirements:

> I would love to just take a day for UGA and have, like, maybe a guidance counselor person . . . show me and explain a lot about the campus and not just the basic qualifications, application form, but so I could get a feel. . . . I feel like it's pretty important for me.

> I've heard a lot of things about UGA. . . . They're raising their qualifications and their SAT scores and the ratios and just odds and ends, basically. . . . Maybe I should just get a little bit more informed.

Teachers also suggested that high school students should have more opportunities to interact closely with the postsecondary community. A teacher briefly discussed an idea:

> One of the things I would like to see happen in our county is for senior level, they get to go . . . out and visit some of the colleges and that kind of thing and get a shadowing type experience. . . . I feel like they need to see that earlier on so that they can make some decisions, some good decisions early on and due to the fact that a lot of kids in our county don't pursue college. I think that if they kind of saw the atmosphere and found out a little bit more about what it's like, . . . they might be

turned on to it a little more. And I think if we did that early on, that would help tremendously. . . . It's beneficial to them [the seniors] but I think more so to the freshmen.

CREATE OPPORTUNITIES FOR TEACHER INTERACTIONS WITH POST-SECONDARY INSTITUTIONS. When students need clarification about college academic requirements and expectations, they often seek information from teachers. This situation raises problems because teachers complain that postsecondary institutions do not provide sufficient information. Also, many of the teachers interviewed for this study graduated from college many years earlier. The distance between their firsthand college history and current student academic experiences is substantial. One teacher suggested, "I think one thing that would be helpful, even at the middle school level, is some shadowing experiences where they [teachers] could go see what a college classroom is like."

Summary of College Admissions Findings

This section of the case study report examined what students and parents know about college and where students and parents get their information. Two types of issues arose: those that affect pragmatic decisions (admissions, costs, and HOPE Scholarship requirements and benefits) and those that affect academic experiences (what students should know about the academic expectations of college professors). Despite efforts to improve communication between educators at all levels, study results reveal a disconnection between postsecondary expectations and student preparation in high school. Following is a summary of our findings:

○ Students have a basic understanding of college admissions requirements. However, they do not fully comprehend the role college preparatory curriculum units play in their postsecondary education options.

○ Students consistently overestimated the cost of tuition at UGA and WGA.

○ Counselors carry large student loads and devise creative ways to address the varied needs of students. They anticipate having more time for college advisement as their responsibilities for testing and scheduling are lessened by a new state policy.

○ Teachers increasingly play a disseminator role in helping students navigate the admissions process. Teachers, uncomfortable with this role, seek alternative information sources to inform students fully.

○ Teachers are assigned advising roles that require them to guide students through career and academic preparation programs.

○ High schools maintain multiple sources of college information in a variety of platforms (print, audio, and video) that students, teachers, and parents can access. They also host advisement fairs.

○ Students get college information through both formal (counselors and teachers) and informal (friends, siblings, parents) networks.

Conclusion: On the Road to a Better and More Seamless System

Educational reform efforts in Georgia, as with many other policy arenas, are characterized by complexity. There is a divide between policymaking and policy implementation. While policymakers and those directly associated with putting policy into practice generally express excitement and enthusiasm with the educational reforms examined in this study, tensions and frustrations are also expressed. Divergent interpretations of the meaning and potential benefit of state- or institutional-level initiatives emerge. These are exemplified in mixed respondent reviews of the changing USG admissions requirements, the Georgia HOPE scholarship, and the outcomes precipitated by the P–16 Councils. In addition, Georgia's movement away from subsidizing remedial offerings in four-year colleges, coupled with a potential for redistribution of enrollments, presents differing pressures across institutional types, such as the two-year college, the research university, the state university, and the HBCU. Researchers and educational policymakers need to undertake a close examination of these situations, particularly as they affect low-income and minority populations in Georgia.

One respondent referred to such a changing policy landscape as a "moving target." While students and others are pressed to make sense of state- and institutional-level policies, state and institutional policymakers also need to gain further understanding of particular challenges confronting all Georgia citizens.

A major goal of this research was to explore the links between K–12 and postsecondary education. Policymakers underscore efforts to strengthen these links, such as P–16 and PREP, as both accomplishing a great deal and not accomplishing enough. Interview comments regarding pre-K and PREP initiatives expressed concern that those who need them the most are not participating in these programs. Most state-level education respondents agreed that there is a long way to go to improve the communication and collaboration leading to policy alignment across education sectors. At the same time, many feel that the initiatives are making a difference, as expressed by this state-level system representative: "There has been excitement in the air when you think about it related to Georgia. We have been listed in some places forty-eighth among education and going on to college. . . . Then we were launched into this major change—the whole PREP program, the P–16 initiative, and others. We are making a difference."

P–16 councils provide an opportunity for educators at all levels to share their ideas and devise ways to ease students through their educational transitions. As a result, some cooperative relationships have been negotiated. However, turf issues between and among institutional sectors provide challenges to these attempts at creating a seamless education environment. Nonetheless, regardless of whether the P–16 initiative is successful in addressing all misalignments across educational sectors, continued efforts to align high school and college systems will benefit Georgia students. In this regard, the P–16 model itself provides a road map to success.

Our research suggests that communication of college admissions requirements, tuition costs, and financial aid information to potential students and parents needs improvement. Many teachers and students reported a need for more specific information, not only on institutional-level admissions requirements but also specific program admission requirements, and more direct and prolonged contact with school counselors and college faculty. Student surveys suggest that they may need clarification regarding specific admissions criteria such as the relationship between the CPC requirements and calculation of GPA. Furthermore, in order to meet current requirements for USG admissions and HOPE, respondents underscored the need to provide such information long before students reach the eleventh grade.

One central recommendation emerging from this research is that students, teachers, and counselors need to know more about what college professors expect of entering students. It is not enough to rely on college admissions offices to relay this information to teachers, counselors, and prospective students. Teachers, who increasingly advise students, often lack confidence in their knowledge of higher education requirements.

One idea is for college faculty to meet formally and informally with high school teachers so they can communicate to teachers what entering students should know within specific disciplines. In addition, students, teachers, and counselors need specific information about what exactly students will be expected to know and do in college. College faculty complain that students enter their classrooms unprepared, while educators at the K–12 level want a better understanding of what students need to master for college.

These issues are especially salient in Georgia because of the availability of the HOPE Scholarship. In 2002, the HOPE Scholarship program awarded $1.5 billion to over 600,000 students. The benefits realized from a more educated population can contribute to the overall economic, social, and cultural health of the state for years to come. As noted in the interviews, teachers, counselors, and administrators generally believe that the HOPE Scholarship serves two important functions: it encourages academically talented students to pursue higher education in the state of Georgia, and it provides the necessary support to allow many students to attend college who considered higher education an unreachable goal. Some state- and school-level policymakers express concern that HOPE may influence teachers to inflate grades so students can qualify for the scholarship, resulting in inadequately prepared students attending colleges or universities. At the school level, teachers in this study did not feel pressured to increase student grades so that their students would qualify for the HOPE Scholarship. Also, students and parents reported a lack of understanding of HOPE requirements and benefits. This suggests that the Georgia State Finance Commission and both secondary and postsecondary schools must more aggressively explain the requirements of HOPE eligibility and benefits to students and parents, particularly in schools with high numbers of low-SES students.

While many of our study respondents praised HOPE scholarships, others raised concerns. Their concerns are echoed by studies conducted by higher education researchers. For example, Heller and Marin (2002) argue that state merit scholarships, including HOPE, are awarded disproportionately to populations of students who have the highest college participation rates and provide little financial assistance to the students who need it most. Heller and Marin propose four principles to remedy this situation, two of which have already been addressed by the HOPE initiative: (1) allow qualified low-income students to receive both need-based and merit-based aid and (2) simplify and standardize the scholarship application process for all who apply. To promote further educational opportunity for poor and minority students, Georgia policymakers might consider their other suggestions: (1) expand definitions of "merit" so that financial decisions are based not only on measures such as SAT scores, other standardized tests, or grades,[12] and (2) apply an income cap so that funds are directed to students who truly need them to be able to afford college.

Our findings point to a need for future evaluation and research that explores issues portrayed here in greater breadth and depth. Nevertheless, while most study participants expressed doubts or misunderstanding about some reforms, they also felt that progress has been made toward creating a better and more seamless education system. Ultimately, it appears that the student and the state can greatly benefit from educational reform toward the articulation of policies and practices that bridge student transitions from pre-K through postsecondary education.

NOTES

1. On May 24, 2001, the Georgia P–16 Council was reconstituted as the Education Coordinating Council.

2. For further details, see http://www.usg.edu/news/1997/2001admiss.html.

3. In 1999, data were collected through document reviews, published studies and reports, Web sites, and interviews with forty-five administrators and institutional researchers directly involved with educational initiatives, including admissions and placement policies and processes.

4. In 2000, data were collected in two high schools through 249 parent surveys, 243 student surveys (ninth and eleventh grade), 59 students participating in focus groups, eight interviews with teachers, three interviews with counselors, and four interviews with school- and district-level administrators. An analysis of student, teacher, and parent knowledge of higher education policies and practices related to admissions and placement is also of great importance and is discussed here.

5. The sources for data reported are documents available at the State of Georgia's Web site (http://www.state.ga.us), the Web site of the state's Department of Education (http://www.doe.k12.ga.us), and the Web site of the state's Office of School Readiness (http://www.osr.state.ga.us).

6. The full breadth of Georgia's testing programs includes norm-referenced testing at grades 3, 5, and 8; performance-based writing assessments at grades 3, 5, 8, and 11; the revised Georgia Kindergarten Assessment Program; the Georgia High School Graduation Tests at grades 11 and 12; criterion-referenced competency tests in grades 4, 6, and 8; and the National Assessment of Educational Progress, a mandated assessment program, at grades 4 and 8. Incentives and provisions are also provided through state funding for the Preliminary Scholastic Assessment Test and Advanced Placement exams.

7. Although DTAE is a member of the state P–16 Council, it maintains other collaborative programs with high schools across the state. For example,

the Middle Georgia Aerospace Apprentice Program includes McDonnell-Douglas, Boeing, Robbins Air Force Base, Macon Tech, Bib City, and the public school system. Juniors and seniors compete for entry into the program, which instructs them in aircraft structural techniques. Students participate in an internship program, and by the end of the senior year, they are ready for industry and qualified for the program.

8. While researchers recognize the importance of a closer examination of educational policy reforms and their effects on Georgia's two-year colleges and technical colleges as well as HBCUs, time and financial constraints precluded these efforts.

9. In July 1996, the high school grade requirements were tightened, such that entering freshmen high school students (beginning with the Class of 2000) were required to earn a B average in the core curriculum courses of English, math, social studies, foreign language, and science to receive the HOPE Scholarship upon graduation. Previously, a wider array of courses was included in the calculation of the high school GPA. This refinement more directly targeted HOPE funds on academically meritorious students. In 1998, the National Association of State Student Grant and Aid Programs ranked Georgia first among the fifty states in academically based student financial aid because of the HOPE Scholarship. That same year, Georgia voters endorsed a constitutional amendment protecting the HOPE program from legislative and political tampering. In 2002, total awards surpassed $1.5 billion, and students served passed 600,000.

10. Responses were from nineteen minority student study participants.

11. These changes were introduced earlier in the chapter. The new requirements include higher SAT scores, an increased number of college preparatory curriculum units, and higher high school GPA. Criteria are defined according to the institutional type for which students wish to apply. Overall, admissions decisions are made based on a calculated FI. This index equals the sum of the SAT verbal score plus the sum of the SAT mathematics score plus (high school GPA × 500). High school GPA is computed using only college preparatory curriculum units; therefore, the number of college preparatory classes that students complete critically affects their GPA for college admissions. The University of Georgia requires a minimum FI of 2500, and the State University of West Georgia has a baseline level of 1940. However, just meeting the FI requirement does not guarantee admission to either of these universities.

12. Based on the FI, this suggestion would also apply to postsecondary admissions decisions.

REFERENCES

Bugler, D. T., and Henry, G. T. *An Evaluation of Georgia's HOPE Scholarship Program: Impact on College Attendance and Performance.* Atlanta: Georgia State University Applied Research Center, June 1998.

Heller, D. E., and Marin, P. (eds.) *Who Should We Help? The Negative Social Consequences of Merit Scholarships.* Cambridge, Mass.: Harvard Civil Rights Project, 2002.

Henry, G. T., and Rubenstein, R. "Paying for Grades: Impacts of Merit-Based Financial Aid on Educational Quality." Paper presented at the Association for Public Policy Analysis and Management Research Conference, Seattle, Wash., Nov. 2000.

Mortenson, T. "Refocusing Student Financial Aid: From Grants to Loans, from Need to Merit, from Poor to Affluent." *Postsecondary Education Opportunity,* Apr. 1999, pp. 1–4.

Richardson, R. C. Jr., Bracco, K. R., Callan, P. M., and Finney, J. E. *Designing State Higher Education Systems for a New Century.* Westport, Conn.: Greenwood Press, 1999.

Schmidt, P. "Report Criticizes Upper- and Middle-Class Focus of Merit-Based State Scholarships." *Chronicle of Higher Education,* Jan. 27, 2000.

Selingo, J. "Hope Wanes for Georgia's Merit-Based Scholarships." *Chronicle of Higher Education,* Nov. 17, 2003.

U.S. Bureau of the Census. *Population Profile of the United States: 1997.* Washington, D.C.: U.S. Government Printing Office, 1998.

U.S. Bureau of the Census. "Population Estimates." [www.census.gov/popest/estimates.php].

Wallhaus, R. A. (1997). *Statewide: K-16 Systems: Helping Underprepared Students Succeed in Postsecondary Education Programs.* Denver: State Higher Education Executive Officers, 1997.

7

K–16 REFORM IN MARYLAND

THE FIRST STEPS

Heinrich Mintrop
Toby H. Milton
Frank A. Schmidtlein
Ann Merck MacLellan

MARYLAND WAS WELL known in the early 1990s as a pioneer in implementing systemic reforms in its K–12 system. Less well known are the steps the state has taken to coordinate its K–12 and postsecondary education systems better. This chapter examines those steps and the extent to which they have attempted to bring two very separate systems into closer cooperation. It also examines the sizable challenges the state yet faces.

We begin with an examination of the admissions policies, practices, and collaborative efforts of higher education institutions in Maryland. Subsequently, we examine how these policies and the state's K–16 efforts have affected key stakeholders at the secondary school level. For instance, what knowledge do high school students and their parents have about college? Are their aspirations commensurate with the opportunities the system affords? Do students and parents know about various institutions'

The research and writing of the phase I report on the Maryland case study was primarily the work of Toby Milton, who passed away shortly after its completion. Her husband, Frank Schmidtlein, and the other coauthors dedicate this chapter to her outstanding career in higher education research.

course-taking requirements, tests, and grades? Are they informed about the role of social criteria (such as racial/ethnic background, first-generation college student) for admission? And do they have a realistic idea about the cost of various college options? These are some of the questions we seek to answer. We also explore how teachers, counselors, and administrators see their role in constructing the link between high school and college and what kind of formal services and informal knowledge they provide to students in order to help them make well-informed decisions regarding college.

The Maryland Educational System

This introduction to Maryland's education system provides the context for the state's efforts to link its elementary and secondary systems more closely to its higher education system.

The Maryland Postsecondary System

Maryland's fifty-three higher education institutions encompass thirteen four-year public universities and colleges, sixteen community colleges, and twenty-four private colleges and universities. Eleven of the thirteen public four-year colleges and universities are part of the University System of Maryland (USM), which include the University of Maryland, College Park, and Towson University, the two universities our research focused on. These institutions are both governed by the USM Board of Regents. Maryland's two other public four-year institutions, Morgan State University and St. Mary's College, remain outside the USM and have their own governing boards. Fifteen of the state's sixteen community colleges are county based and governed by local boards of trustees appointed by the governor. The Maryland Association of Community Colleges represents community college interests to state government and undertakes cooperative activities among the colleges. Eighteen of the independent higher education institutions are represented at the state level by the Maryland Independent Colleges and Universities Association. Maryland also has approximately 128 proprietary and other postsecondary institutions, many of them represented by the Maryland Association of Private Career Schools. All of these segments of postsecondary education are coordinated and regulated by the Maryland Higher Education Commission (Berdahl and Schmidtlein, 1996).

Maryland's higher education institutions enrolled over 267,653 students in fall 1999, including 218,305 undergraduates (Maryland Higher

Education Commission, December, 1999a). Almost half of all undergraduates in state institutions were enrolled in community colleges, nearly 40 percent attended four-year public institutions, and approximately 11 percent enrolled in independent colleges and universities. In addition, more than 20,000 students attended private career schools. More than three-fourths of the undergraduates in the state's public institutions, as well as over half of those enrolled in the private colleges and universities, were Maryland residents. However, almost 30 percent of Maryland's high school graduates who enroll in college went to out-of-state institutions in comparison to approximately 16 percent nationally (Maryland Higher Education Commission, 1999a).

The Maryland Higher Education Commission (MHEC) is Maryland's higher education regulatory and coordinating agency. It is not a governing board and therefore does not play a direct role in the administration of the institutions. However, certain general policies and regulations adopted by the Commission establish parameters limiting institutional discretion in setting policies and procedures. MHEC has specific responsibilities in a number of areas related to student access and success in higher education, including admissions, remedial education, student transfer, student outcomes reporting, and student financial aid (Maryland Higher Education Commission, 1999a). Its regulations concerning admissions policies are contained in the Code of Maryland Regulations (Maryland Higher Education Commission, 1999b) and apply to all degree-granting institutions in the state.

MHEC prepares a Student Outcome and Achievement Report (SOAR) "to improve information to high schools and local school systems concerning the performance of their graduates at the college level"(Maryland Higher Education Commission, 1999c, p. 1). SOAR provides annual compilations and reports about SAT and American College Test (ACT) scores; students' need for remedial work in math, English, and reading; students' grades in their first mathematics and English courses; students' cumulative grade point averages (GPAs) after their first year; and students' fall-to-spring persistence in their first year after high school graduation. All of Maryland's public two- and four-year colleges and universities that typically admit students directly from high school and the twelve participating private higher education institutions annually submit individual student records to MHEC containing this information.

In 1999, legislation (State of Maryland, 1999) mandated that MHEC establish a "college preparation and intervention program" in cooperation with the state's public and nonpublic institutions of postsecondary education ". . . to raise the level of academic preparedness of economically and environmentally disadvantaged students to enable them to attend and succeed in college" (p. 429).

The K–12 System

Maryland's twenty-four local school districts are contiguous with its twenty-three counties and Baltimore City. This countywide organization of its school districts has resulted in some of the nation's largest school systems (Maryland Electronic Capitol, June 2000). An earlier case study of K–12 education in Maryland suggested that the large size of its school systems "has created economies of scale in district operations, along with a tradition of local independence with respect to curriculum and instruction." The study's authors went on to write that "this localist tradition, however, is beginning to give way as the high-stakes, politically secure assessment regime increases state authority" (Timar, Krop, and Kirst, 1997, p. 186).

The State Board of Education sets education policies and standards for prekindergarten through high school. It also certifies teachers, monitors school performance, and provides some funding for school construction. The board can pass regulations that have the force of law, enact school policy without the consent of the state assembly, and "interpret the true meaning and intent of the law" (Maryland State Department of Education, 2000a). In addition, the board approves the annual budget of the Department of Education, the state aid to local education budgets, and the state-aided institutions' budgets prior to their submission to the governor and general assembly for review and approval.

The Maryland State Department of Education implements state laws and carries out the policies of the MDSE. The department is involved in a wide variety of projects, including developing curriculum frameworks, content standards, learning outcomes, and core learning goals. Maryland's most recent school reform program began in 1989 after the Governor's Commission on School Performance reviewed the state's public education system and made recommendations for improvement. A major focus of these recommendations was on establishing comprehensive statewide accountability, assessment, and reporting systems. As a result, the Maryland State Board for Education adopted a reform initiative entitled Schools for Success, one of the first state reform movements to "hold schools accountable for a high quality education and measurable results for all students" (Maryland State Department of Education, 1997, p. 1).

Maryland's school reform efforts in the early and mid-1990s largely focused on increasing expectations and raising standards at the elementary

and middle school levels. At the high school level, graduation requirements for students entering ninth grade in 1993 or later were somewhat
strengthened by increasing course and credit requirements in some areas.
However, there were no substantial increases in academic expectations
and standards for high school students. Although high schools were
included in the reports, their performance was measured largely by indicators such as high school program completion, attendance and dropout
rates, and passing rates on the Maryland Functional Tests.

Currently, Maryland's high school graduation requirements are twenty-
one academic course credits, among them four credits in English and three
credits each in math, science, and social studies. Students can choose
between a foreign language or career or technology option (Maryland
State Department of Education, 2000b). In addition, students must pass
the Maryland Functional Tests in mathematics, reading, and writing and
take an approved government course (or pass a citizenship test if such a
course is not offered by the local school system). At the time of this
research, the state had created high school assessments, but their use was
highly contested and their legitimacy questionable.

Toward the Development of a K–16 System

The Education Coordinating Committee (ECC) was established by law in
1976 to facilitate collaborative activities between the State Board for
Higher Education (now MHEC) and MSDE. This committee is composed
of three MHEC commissioners, three members of the board of education,
the secretary for higher education, and the superintendent of schools. Each
agency appointed a senior staff member to direct the work of the
committee.

In 1996, a newly established Maryland Partnership for Teaching and
Learning K–16 began to fulfill the functions of the ECC, although the
ECC continues to be a legislatively mandated entity. The partnership is a
voluntary alliance created to foster connections throughout all levels of
education and the workplace. The secretary of higher education, the chancellor of USM, and the superintendent of schools are the three principal
leaders of this intersegmental cooperative venture. Its work is supported
by a twenty-seven-member K–16 Leadership Council that includes cor-
porate, civic, and public and private education leaders. The K–16 Workgroup was created by the K–16 Leadership Council to provide advice and
support for its work. The work group has nearly sixty members, repre-
senting constituencies similar to those represented on the Leadership
Council. It meets at least six times a year.

The USM Board of Regents has overall responsibility for establishing and reviewing admissions policies for all system institutions. Its undergraduate admissions policy addresses freshman admissions, transfer student admissions, and admission of second baccalaureate and nondegree students. For entering freshmen, the USM policy establishes relatively general minimum high school course and GPA qualifications for regular admissions. Furthermore, it stipulates that no more than 15 percent of freshmen can be admitted who do not meet minimum system requirements. The USM policy also delineates principles for developing procedures for early admission of high school students, home-schooled students, and students from nonaccredited, non-U.S., or other nontraditional secondary schools environments (University System of Maryland Board of Regents, 1990).

The USM undergraduate admissions policy grants substantial autonomy to each system institution to "publish its own decision criteria, which may be more rigorous than the systemwide minima" (University System of Maryland Board of Regents, 1990, p. III-4.00–1) and to "publish other criteria for admission that may include (a) strength of the high school curriculum, (b) trends in performance, (c) citizenship and leadership, (d) special talents, and (e) personal circumstance" (p. III-4.00–2). The extent of campus flexibility in determining admissions standards is clearly demonstrated by the lack of any minimum SAT or ACT scores, the minimal GPA criteria of only a C or better (with no discussions of how this GPA is to be calculated), and the absence of any clear definitions regarding the content of the required courses. In 1991, USM's Office of Academic Affairs prepared a document describing acceptable course content to provide some guidance to high schools regarding the system's expectations on course content. Approximately twenty-five thousand copies of this document were distributed to school superintendents, principals, and others throughout the state.

The Focal Institutions: University of Maryland at College Park and Towson University

The University of Maryland at College Park (UMCP) and Towson University were selected as our case study institutions for a number of reasons. First, both are part of the USM. Second, they have very different missions: UMCP is Maryland's major public graduate and research institution, while Towson is a comprehensive university historically focusing on undergraduate and master's education. Third, both enroll relatively large numbers of first-time freshmen (in fall 1999, 3,906 at UMCP and

2,115 at Towson). Together, they served 48 percent of USM's fall 1999 total undergraduate population of 38,698 students (Maryland Higher Education Commission, 1999a). Fourth, the institutions are located in Maryland's two major population centers around Washington, D.C., and Baltimore.

UMCP's formal admissions requirements closely parallel USM policies, but UMCP admissions staff uses these requirements as minimums. UMCP, like highly selective private institutions, uses a qualitative as well as a quantitative approach in determining admissions. The number of minimally qualified applicants substantially exceeds the number of available spaces, so selecting entering freshmen has become increasingly subject to complex judgments, with fewer made on the basis of traditional quantitative criteria. More than forty-five variables are employed to select a diverse, highly talented student body. Prospective students are informed in a variety of publications about UMCP's minimum requirements, its selectivity, and its approach to making admission decisions. Almost all students are required to take UMCP's Mathematics Placement test, the only placement test employed by the university. In fall 1998, 18 percent of all new first-year students were placed into remedial math based on results of their scores on UMCP's in-house placement test.

Individual UMCP schools and colleges have a long history of collaborative programs with K–12 schools and the community. Some of these partnerships stem from the 1960s and 1970s, or earlier. Campuswide efforts to work with schools were initiated in the late 1970s with the establishment of the Office of School/University Programs. More recently, the campus has become a participant in statewide K–16 initiatives and instituted its own K–16 Council. The major focus of these efforts was aligning high school and college curricula and standards, teacher education reform, and the application of research knowledge to classroom practices.

Towson, like UMCP, has the autonomy to develop and implement admissions policies and practices that are consistent with its own mission and goals. Towson essentially has adopted USM's admission policies but has established some specific minimums, such as grade point averages lower than 2.50 and less than a 920 combined SAT I. Among other things, the catalogue also indicates that freshmen are expected to have two years of a foreign language. It does require one more lab science unit than do the USM requirements.

An SAT-GPA grid is used in making most enrollment decisions at Towson. A complex quantitative procedure is used to develop annual enrollment targets and adjust the SAT-GPA grid to meet these targets. A substantial percentage of Towson's entering freshmen require remediation in one or more of the basic skills areas, with the highest percentage requiring remediation in math (Maryland Higher Education Commission, 1999c). Towson currently uses the Nelson-Denny for placement testing in reading and the ACT Asset test for English placement. It offers two developmental reading courses (basic and intermediate-level college reading skills) and one developmental writing course that provides a review of grammar, usage, and writing effective sentences. None of these courses counts as graduation credits, and all are graded on a satisfactory-unsatisfactory basis. Placement in mathematics is based on a test selected and adapted by the mathematics department that is a modified version of the Mathematics Association of America test and similar to the test used at UMCP.

Towson faculty and staff have been involved in a broad array of collaborative activities with K–12 education, in the Baltimore metropolitan region and statewide. Many of these activities were initiated at the campus level and were designed to improve instruction in elementary and secondary schools and help alleviate Maryland's teacher shortage. Faculty and administrators from Towson's College of Education have been involved in preparing K–16 Workgroup reports and recommendations on teacher education. Other administrators and faculty have played an active role in several discipline-based statewide K–16 initiatives.

Issues Confronting Maryland K–16 Efforts

Accessibility to postsecondary institutions, alignment of K–12 tests with college admissions requirements, placement, and remediation are the key issues discussed in this section.

Accessibility

Maryland high school students generally have access to its four-year public institutions. Four-year campuses are relatively close to the majority of the homes of prospective undergraduates. Students in areas most distant from existing four-year colleges and universities are served by distance education programs and partnerships in which institutions collaborate to establish higher education centers. Access for students with differing educational aspirations and abilities is facilitated by the diverse missions of Maryland's four-year public colleges and their variety of admissions standards and criteria. USM's broad admissions requirements, as well as the relatively flexible admissions polices of UMCP and Towson, do not automatically exclude minority or disadvantaged students who are judged to have the potential for success but may not fulfill stringent GPAs or test score requirements.

The four-year institutions' very different admission policies pose complex problems for high schools seeking to align their graduation requirements with college and university admission requirements. This problem is compounded because a large proportion of high school graduates attend community colleges or some other type of postsecondary institution, or do not seek postsecondary education at all. A "one size fits all" high school graduation requirement is not feasible if the high schools are to equip students with the differing competencies required for a variety of postsecondary academic and career opportunities.

Alignment

Maryland's public institutions have a great deal of discretion in setting their admissions requirements. Mandating that they adopt specific course requirements or use benchmark scores on specific tests would be contrary to long-standing principles. The admissions process at UMCP perhaps could use the results of high school assessment tests as one of the many criteria employed to make admissions decisions. Towson would have to incorporate the test scores in the current quantitative approach it employs or devise a different approach for making admissions decisions.

However, the migration of Maryland high school graduates to institutions in other states and out-of-state high school graduates' migration to Maryland institutions pose problems for a Maryland high school assessment test. Forty percent of college-bound Maryland high school seniors attended out-of-state institutions in 1996 (National Center for Education Statistics, 1999). At the same time, Maryland institutions attracted 28 percent of their freshmen from other states. Maryland students seeking admission to an out-of-state institution could have a problem if their high school curricula are too closely aligned with unique Maryland requirements. Similarly, out-of-state students seeking to enroll in Maryland's colleges or universities could be handicapped if their admission is linked too closely to a specific Maryland test. Also, if Maryland tests are not aligned with the content of national examinations such as the SAT and ACT, which are used across states for making admissions decisions, they might have a negative effect on students' possibilities for admission to institutions using these tests as a key criterion for admission. Thus, in the case of Maryland, alignment of high school assessment tests with college admission needs careful examination and may not be particularly effective.

Placement and Remediation

Available data from MHEC's SOAR system and institutional studies, despite their limitations, strongly suggest that considerable numbers of students enrolling in the state's four-year institutions are not fully prepared for college-level work. Even UMCP, which has eliminated placement testing in English and reading because of the strong credentials of its admitted students, has a substantial number of new students who are not prepared for college-level mathematics or, even if they attain minimum levels, are not prepared for the mathematics course work required by their intended programs of study.

SOAR seeks to link information about students' high school experiences and their performance in college, but concerns about the system continue to be raised. Maryland's four-year institutions and, until recently, its two-year institutions have not had standard testing practices, cutoff scores, or other common criteria for determining who needs remediation. Thus, remediation rates are not comparable across higher education institutions. Moreover, because the system does not include data on students who attend out-of-state schools, the results can sometimes be paradoxical, with high schools in more affluent areas that send larger numbers of their highest-achieving students to out-of-state institutions showing lower college-going rates and less success among their graduates than schools who send most of their students to in-state institutions.

Programs that focus on maintaining students' academic progress in the early grades seem likely to hold the greatest promise for avoiding the social and economic costs of remedial programs. Recognizing this imperative, the State Board of Education recommended delaying implementing its high school assessment program until sufficient state resources were made available to schools to address lack of adequate preparation in the lower grades. The board did not want to confront the prospect that an unacceptable number of high school students, many of them undoubtedly minorities, would be denied their high school diplomas.

Maryland's K–16 Partnership for Teaching and Learning

Most of those interviewed at the two case study institutions were aware of the Maryland Partnership for Teaching and Learning K–16 and believed that it had increased awareness and communications about the issues across both the K–12 and higher education sectors. But many were unclear about its agenda and specific accomplishments. Some administrators believed the partnership's activities were too divorced from campus realities and were, in part, responses to political agendas. Others indicated that the purposes and the work of the partnership's work groups were not well known on many campuses in the state; they observed that state-level initiatives often spread their efforts too broadly and consequently had not particularly helped campus efforts. They suggested that more opportunities were needed for midlevel administrators and faculty to become involved in state-level efforts to bring about meaningful changes.

Several said the partnership's status as a voluntary alliance with no reporting authority except through the participating parties was both a strength and a weakness. They noted that the voluntary nature of the alliance limits bureaucracy and unnecessary formality and that the arrangement allows participants to work together as peers. However, some also noted that the partnership had no direct authority to ensure that its initiatives and programs were implemented and suggested that the strength and directions of the partnership were heavily dependent on the specific individuals now serving as CEOs of the collaborating agencies. Another concern was the partnership's lack of funding for both its own activities and the institutional programs required to carry out its recommendations.

In summary, linking the K–12 system with higher education institutions faces some formidable challenges in Maryland:

○ With the exception of very basic college preparatory requirements spelled out by the University System of Maryland, requirements for admissions were set autonomously by institutions of higher learning. As a result, an array of placement tests that are not consistent across institutions was in use.

○ As of the year 2000, K–16 efforts were voluntary and took place at a very high level of state leadership. Bridges between high school and college were established through outreach activities between postsecondary institutions and individual schools.

○ The fate of high-stakes accountability testing for high school graduation was uncertain, diminishing the level of concern for school service providers and clients.

○ Many Maryland students attended college out of state, and many students enrolled at Maryland institutions of higher learning were from out of state, making intrastate alignment between in-state institutions highly problematic.

Student and Parent Understanding of Critical College Issues

After analyzing state and institutional policies, we explored what students and parents understood—and misunderstood—about the connection between high school and college. Did they realize, for instance, the grades and curricula they needed to gain admission into UMCP? Did they understand the importance of placement exams? Did they have a realistic idea about the cost of various college options? We further asked how teachers, counselors, and administrators viewed their role in forging the link between high school and college and what kind of formal services and informal knowledge they provided to students. As focal points for our research, we selected four high schools, all of them primary feeder schools for Towson University and the University of Maryland, College Park (see Tables 7.1 and 7.2). The schools were chosen in two jurisdictions representative of the state's racial and geographical diversity. One of the schools had a predominantly African American student body. Two of the schools were predominantly white, and the fourth school was more evenly proportioned in terms of ethnic diversity.

Table 7.1. Student Demographics and Other Characteristics, Case Study High Schools (N = 232).

Student Demographics and School Data

Race/ethnicity
African American	73 (32%)
White	115 (50%)
Latino	10 (5%)
Other	33 (13%)

Gender
Female	140 (60%)
Male	91 (40%)

Grade level
Ninth grade	127 (55%)
Eleventh grade	103 (44%)

English class
Nonhonors	99 (43%)
Honors	133 (57%)

High school grade point average
A	76 (33%)
B	106 (46%)
C	40 (17%)
D or below	3 (4%)

Table 7.2. Characteristics of the Four High Schools.

	School A	School B	School C	School D
District Code	1	1	2	2
Total student population	1,537	1,750	1,696	1,457
Number in ninth grade	383	482	436	477
Number in eleventh grade	386	423	419	323
Total minority population	56%	30%	19%	97%
Attend four-year college	72%	66%	76%	54%
Completed University of Maryland system course requirements	73%	73%	77%	27%

The schools were similar in student population and size. With regard to minority student enrollment, School D stands out. School D had the largest minority population, 97 percent, almost all of whom are African American. Attrition rates were higher here than at the other schools, and fewer School D graduates attended four-year and two-year colleges. They also completed fewer minimum Maryland system course requirements than graduates from the other three schools. While the selection of prime feeder schools for universities skews our sample toward the college bound, within these bounds, our four schools represent school profiles that are quite typical for the state of Maryland.

The students completed the Maryland Bridge Student Survey in their honors and nonhonors English classes during the spring 2000 semester. The student survey response rates for the four schools were between 56 percent and 72 percent. The same percentages apply to surveyed parents. Interviews with the principals, guidance counselors, and four teachers who teach ninth- and eleventh-grade honors or nonhonors English at each school helped us understand schools' activities with respect to college. In addition, focus groups were conducted with honors and nonhonors eleventh-grade students who had completed the student survey.

Student College Aspirations and the Maryland System

A number of factors cause students to aspire to admission to a particular postsecondary institution, including their high school achievement level, family background, and the knowledge they have about the institution. In Maryland, students have the advantage of being able to aspire to a variety of four-year public institutions that are modestly selective and relatively affordable, at least in comparison to public institutions in other states. But students' aspirations, as we examine in the following sections, vary in terms of how realistic they are. When students aspire to institutions that fit their understanding and levels of academic achievement, it suggests that high schools and postsecondary institutions have done a good job of communicating their expectations. Conversely, unrealistic aspirations can indicate a breakdown in communication.

Conspicuously, the majority of surveyed Maryland students aspired to a four-year school outside Maryland. Most students who were taking more than one honors course (dual-honors students) aspired to attend college outside the state (80 percent), compared to 67 percent of single-honors and 53 percent of the nonhonors students. Few students expressed interest in attending community colleges. Community colleges received little interest. As these figures reveal (see Table 7.3), academic achievement levels in high school made a difference in students' aspirations. By contrast, there were no significant differences in students' aspirations based on their parents' educational and economic background.

Race, unsurprisingly, played a role in students' choice of historically black colleges and universities (HBCUs). HBCUs were considered options by one-third of black students.

The reality of college selection in Maryland, however, contrasts quite remarkably with the sampled students' desires. In 2000, approximately three-fourths of Maryland's college-going high school graduates attended college in Maryland. Community college enrollment constituted 40 percent, and public four-year campuses comprised 43 percent of all Maryland

---

Table 7.3. Schools Considered by Students After High School.

Postsecondary Options	Ninth Grade	Eleventh Grade	Dual-Honors Eleventh Grade	Nonhonors Eleventh Grade
Four-year college or university outside Maryland	61%	7%	8%	5%
University of Maryland, College Park	37	59	58	38
Four-year private college or university within Maryland	21	38	26	20
Historically black college or university	9	13	11	14
Towson University	17	34	20	25

Note: *Multiple responses accepted.*

undergraduate enrollments (Maryland Higher Education Commission, 2000).

UMCP is the primary four-year college in the state, and as the flagship campus of the University System of Maryland, the most selective of the public universities. Traditionally a comprehensive university for all Maryland high school students who fulfill the minimum admission requirements, the university has strenuously worked at becoming more selective in recent years. Generally, as Figure 7.1 shows, a larger number of higher-performing students than lower-performing students were attracted to UMCP, but many nonhonors students considered UMCP as well (almost 70 percent of C average students).

Students showed very little interest in less selective institutions such as Towson. One-quarter of the nonhonors students in the study selected Towson compared to one-fifth of the dual-honors students. Students with A averages shunned it. The university was not particularly popular among whites or blacks. Of the white students surveyed, 28 percent selected Towson as a postsecondary option; 18 percent of the black students selected it. Community colleges were even less desirable for students. They were chosen by 20 percent of the nonhonors students and by only 3 percent of dual-honors students.

When students were asked about community colleges in the focus groups, they replied, "Usually we're making fun of somebody [who goes to community college]." Students described community colleges as "last resort—you don't want to go there." Even so, some students pointed to the financial benefits of attending community college prior to transferring to a four-year school: "It's cheaper. If you want to go to community

Figure 7.1. Student High School GPA, by Postsecondary Aspirations.

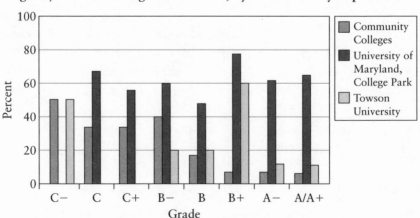

college for your first two years, you can get your credits transferred, and then, I mean, it will still be just as good, but then you can go to a university for the next two years." The literature on college choice has found that parental expectations have a strong influence on students' aspirations (McDonough, 1997). Surveyed parents' rank order of choices was very similar to that of students (not displayed). A four-year out-of-state college was the parents' top choice, followed by the in-state flagship campus and four-year private colleges. The less selective Towson garnered even less favor among parents than it did among students.

Overall, in the eyes of students and parents from these four schools, the state of Maryland had deficits in attracting particularly talented students whose sights were set on out-of-state options. Maryland postsecondary institutions did not meet the aspirations of highly ambitious students and parents. Data on aspirations also put in doubt notions of system alignment. In-state alignment is of lesser concern for large proportions of students and parents who envision attendance at schools outside the state.

As to choosing UMCP or Towson, it is not clear to what degree students and parents were aware of selectivity differentials between the two schools. While Towson is relatively unselective, UMCP has been able to improve the academic credentials among its admission pool. From fall 1988 to fall 1999, the mean high school GPA of entering freshmen rose from 2.98 to 3.61, and the percentage of entrants with SATs of 1400 or over increased from less than 4 percent to 15 percent.

We inquired about students' perceptions of the two schools in the focus groups and in the survey. While some thought that UMCP was "really big" and a "nice party school," others mentioned that it was becoming more competitive and thus more difficult to gain admission:

> It's hard to get in there . . . high SAT scores, high grade point average and all other stuff. They try to make it some kind of national university now.

> It's a lot harder than it used to be, I know. It used to be like anyone who wanted to go to Maryland could go to Maryland.

> Well, I heard the SAT [at Maryland] is going up and up each year.

Survey data confirm this sentiment. Over three-quarters of the surveyed students (77 percent) answered that it had become more difficult to gain admission to UMCP. Parents responded similarly to the same question. However, almost two-thirds of the students and more than half of the parents also agreed that Towson had become more selective (63 percent and 54 percent, respectively). Moreover, contrary to these fears of increased selectivity, students with low and high GPAs alike (see Figure 7.1) considered UMCP an option, continuing to view it as a comprehensive university open to students of all achievement levels.

In summary, students' and parents' expressed concerns about UMCP selectivity that may be more indicative of their general anxiety about college than of solid knowledge about admission criteria. The lack of distinction that students and parents made between UMCP and Towson undergirds the vagueness of their knowledge and suggests perhaps a failure on the part of academic institutions to convey their admissions standards adequately.

Knowledge of Standards, Admission Requirements, and Placement Tests

Students and parents were not only fuzzy about college in general; they also lacked clarity about institutions' selection criteria, high school course requirements, and placement procedures. Students were given a list of possible selection criteria on the student survey and asked to rate their degree of importance for admission to UMCP and Towson. (For the purpose of gaining clarity about admissions policies, the researchers could not rely on written policies alone, but had to interview admissions officers from the two schools about actual practices.)

Students estimated correctly that high school grades and SAT scores were the most salient criteria for both institutions. But unclear knowledge of the selection criteria was evidenced by several patterns:

- Generally students perceived more criteria as important than are actually used by the two institutions. For instance, the majority of students rated academic reputation of high school, extracurricular involvement, and numbers of college preparatory courses as "most important" or "very important" at Towson when they are actually considered only for borderline cases.
- A large percentage of students thought that social criteria were not considered by universities (such as racial/ethnic background, first generation in college, and first generation to speak English), when in fact they are.
- Students tended to overestimate the importance of essays, personal statements, and letters of recommendation for admission to both schools.

- Students showed little awareness of UMCP's consideration of factors other than test scores.
- Students were not aware of the differences in admissions standards between the more selective and the less selective campuses. Estimates were fairly similar for both schools.

Statements made in the focus groups revealed vague knowledge—for example: "Different schools say different things. Like at one it could be the essay you write, you know. One could be, like your grades, your GPA, your SAT. It depends on where you're applying."

Interestingly, approximately half of the students saw ability to pay tuition as a most or very important factor for admission. When examined by socioeconomic status, 60 percent of lower-income students overestimated the importance of ability to pay tuition as an admission criterion; only 37 percent of the higher-income students made this overestimation. Students' socioeconomic situation may strongly influence postsecondary aspirations when over half of middle- to low-income students incorrectly think that their ability to pay will be a decisive factor in the universities' decisions to admit them, and large numbers of students are unaware of the universities' consideration of social factors for admission.

Affirmative action, a red button issue in many states, was not particularly relevant for students in Maryland. Eighty-three percent of white students and 70 percent of black students either did not know whether race was considered or thought it to be an irrelevant criterion. Here again, the two universities themselves were either silent on the issue (Towson) or ambiguous in the language of their policy.

In summary, students in the sample tended to know about the centrality of GPA and SAT scores for college admission, but their understanding of the importance of other criteria, particularly social ones, was murky. Students' and parents' fuzzy knowledge was mirrored in the schools' less-than-clear admission policies.

As to course requirements for the two universities, students tended to estimate the English requirement (which is four years) correctly, but tended to overestimate mathematics and laboratory science requirements for both schools. In the eyes of students, college admission requirements loomed larger than they actually were, a fact that may temper their college aspirations. Student estimates of UMCP and Towson requirements were quite similar, but the actual high school courses required by the universities differed. Towson actually admitted students who had not completed the posted high school requirements if students completed them within the first college semester. Students were only dimly aware of the varying degrees of selectivity between the two institutions. Parents' estimates of high school requirements for college admission closely matched the estimates of their children.

Although most postsecondary remediation takes place at community colleges, four-year colleges and universities do require certain placement tests and remediation for those who do not pass entrance placement tests in specific subjects (typically mathematics and English). Knowledge of these placement criteria could give students an idea of what the universities expect students to know and be able to do when they enter college and begin taking college-level courses.

At the time of the study, there were no required placement tests in English at UMCP. They had been discontinued more than five years before. UMCP required only math placement testing. In the fall of 1998, 18 percent of new UMCP freshmen were placed in remedial math based on the math placement test scores. Towson University required all students not meeting specified exemption criteria to take placement tests in reading, English, and mathematics. Among 1997–1998 entering Towson students who had completed University System of Maryland requirements, 11 percent required remedial English, 6 percent remedial reading, and 19 percent remedial math. For new Towson freshmen who had not completed the minimum university system requirements, the percentages were higher: 18 percent English, 7 percent reading, and 31 percent math.

When students were asked to indicate what they thought were the required placement testing subjects at UMCP and Towson, they overwhelmingly (87 percent) gave correct answers as to Towson's English placement test, but they also indicated similarly (89 percent) that UMCP required an English placement test although only math was required. In addition, half of the students indicated that both UMCP and Towson required placement testing in laboratory science, when neither had such a requirement. Percentages for foreign language and technology were even higher. No placement testing existed in these fields. Thus, students lacked specific knowledge of placement test requirements.

Responses from the focus groups reflected students' confusion. When asked about UMCP or Towson placement tests, students mused:

> Um, I just thought there was some kind of test or something.

> I think that at Maryland [UMCP] they make you take a placement exam when you are trying to get in so that they put you in a certain math class.

[It depends on] your plans, like what you want to major in and what you did in high school.

You take the SAT, I think. There's some kind of test that you have to take.

On the whole, students were aware of the existence of placement tests, particularly in math, but they lacked detailed knowledge in this area. High school exit exams, a relatively new feature of the Maryland accountability system at the time, played no role whatsoever in students' assessments of college standards.

Student Knowledge of Costs

We already mentioned that large proportions of students, particularly middle- and low-income students, believed that ability to pay was an important criterion for admission. A realistic estimate of what higher education might actually cost is therefore paramount. Students and parents (see Table 7.4) were asked to estimate yearly tuition at UMCP, Towson University, and a community college.

In 1999, an average full-time Maryland community college student paid $2,171 per year for tuition and fees (Maryland Higher Education Commission, 2000). For Maryland residents, tuition and fees were $4,939 for UMCP and $4,520 for Towson University. It is evident that the sampled ninth and eleventh graders were not aware of actual tuition costs. Although they were less off-target for estimates of community college costs, the overwhelming majority grossly overestimated the expenses of both two-year and four-year tuition. Eleventh graders were slightly more realistic, but not by much.

Students' and parents' answers were similar on estimates of tuition costs. Overall, parents tended to grossly overestimate costs, although they were slightly more realistic. Both parent and student respondents tended to overestimate the more selective UMCP more so than either Towson or the community colleges. Socioeconomic status or race did not make a difference in parents' and students' estimates.

Summary of Student and Parent College Knowledge

Based on the analysis of data collected from 232 students in their ninth- and eleventh-grade English classes in two Maryland school districts during the spring 2000 school term, we find that many students and parents tend to aspire to four-year college attendance outside Maryland. UMCP

Table 7.4. Student Estimates of Yearly Tuition Costs.

Estimate Comparison with Actual Costs	Student Estimates of Yearly Tuition Costs	Community College		Student Estimates of Yearly Tuition Costs	University of Maryland, College Park		Towson University	
		Ninth Grade	Eleventh Grade		Ninth Grade	Eleventh Grade	Ninth Grade	Eleventh Grade
Below target	Less than $2,000	16	31	Less than $4,000	11	8	9	11
On target	$2,001—3,000[a]	6	13	$4,001—5,000[a]	3	11	2	11
Above target	$3,001—7,000	21	19	$5,001—9,000	7	18	11	22
Far above actual costs	Greater than $7,000	58	37	Greater than $9,000	79	63	77	56

[a]On target with actual yearly tuition costs.

presents an attractive choice as well. Although students have taken notice of more rigorous admissions criteria for the state's flagship university, it is still seen as an option for all achievement levels. The lack of distinction students and parents made between UMCP and Towson undergirds not only the vagueness of their knowledge of selectivity, but also the ambiguity with which the two universities convey their selectivity.

Second, students and their parents are generally unaware of the specifics of college admissions requirements, recommended high school courses, and selection processes of the feeder universities. An exception is knowledge about the importance of high school grades and the SAT. With regard to selection and admission criteria, neither students nor their parents could clearly distinguish between the more selective UMCP and the less selective Towson, although general knowledge about different levels of selectivity existed.

Although a sizable number of Maryland high school graduates will require postsecondary remediation in math or English prior to being admitted into college-level courses, respondents do not have knowledge of the specific placement test requirements at Towson or UMCP. Overall, their knowledge is fuzzy.

The Schools' Role in Helping Students Gain College Knowledge

In this section, we explore how educators' knowledge of college admissions, the type of information they share with their students, and the way they define their role in the college preparation process match with students' and parents' expectations. Our analyses are based on interviews with twelve teachers at four schools, four counselors and principals, as well as pertinent data from the surveys and student focus groups.

Student Communication with Teachers and Counselors

According to teachers, students showed great interest in talking with their teachers about college. When asked if students came to them with questions, teachers responded, "Yes, they always want to know where I went to school" and "All the time. I have both eleventh- and twelfth-grade classes, and of course both of them are intensely interested in anything they can learn about college." While students' articulated interest in communication seemed a fairly common occurrence, frequency of communication was low. Many teachers stated that very few or no conversations about college took place in their classes.

Table 7.5. Frequency of Student Conversations About Admission Requirements with Others, by English Class Level.

Significant Others	Many Times		Once or Twice		Never	
	Non-honors	Honors[a]	Non-honors	Honors	Non-honors	Honors
Your parents or guardians	57	71	34	26	9	4
Your brother or sister	26	25	33	30	42	45
Another relative	17	19	35	41	48	40
Friends and other students	41	52	38	40	20	8
Family friend	22	14	32	42	46	43
High school counselor	14	14	32	42	54	44
High school teacher	11	17	42	50	47	33
High school coach	6	11	20	22	74	67
College recruiter	6	8	17	24	77	68
Private college counselor	2	2	9	8	89	91

[a]*Includes single- and dual-honors students.*

For students, parents and friends, rather than teachers or counselors, were key sources for conversations. This is demonstrated in Table 7.5.

Almost half of the responding students had communicated about college with teachers "once or twice" and only 14 percent "many times." By contrast, 71 percent of honors students and 57 percent of nonhonors students had communicated with their parents about college many times. In the focus groups, students said that they had some conversations about college in their classrooms, but these conversations were not described as rich, sustained, or consistent. Some teachers were described as frank and informative, others as relishing in their own college experiences, and many as being silent on the issue. For students in the focus groups, English classes seemed the most important venue for college information. But overall, students clamored that conversations about college in their schools were few and did not provide them with the information they needed to make good decisions on college. Typical is the comment of this student: "They only give you 45 minutes worth, and that's not enough really. You don't get a chance to get into detail."

College counselors played an even smaller role than teachers in students' conversations about college. A lack of counseling time available to students was a recurring theme in the focus group conversations:

> Some of my friends' parents, like, made them go [for college counseling] their freshman year so they'd have, like, a relationship with their counselor. [But] there are just too many kids here, so a counselor can't just search after all their students. That's like 400 and some kids.

Even so, students were insistent on their need for individual assistance in their preparation for college, though they recognized that they were not receiving it.

Teachers' College Knowledge

When asked about their knowledge of admissions policies and procedures at the UMCP, Towson, and other colleges, teachers responded as follows:

> I guess I know what everyone else knows. The approximate SAT scores. The idea that they like to see an active, well-rounded student.

> I don't really know that much about College Park. Towson I attended a few years ago. I was a transfer student from another college, and I got a scholarship, so what else, I don't know.

> I know nothing. I'm from Pennsylvania, and I went to college in Pennsylvania, so I know nothing. I could probably guess there would be the same things [as in Pennsylvania] or that the expectations would be a little higher. But to be factual, I don't know anything.

> I know that College Park is working to become more competitive, so I've heard that their minimum SAT score is around 1200, and then that varies. I think that if you complete community college in Maryland, it's quite easy to transfer. I don't know about GPAs, what the requirements are, but I would say that probably at least a B, maybe higher. Towson I know, it's another school, they became a university. I know that they are looking to become more competitive. I don't know what their minimum scores are.

Most frequently, teachers knew about the importance of the SAT. A few teachers showed some familiarity with the SAT ranges for admissions into

UMCP. One teacher mentioned requirements such as letters of recommendation and an essay. Mostly, teachers admitted to being uninformed and were sometimes embarrassed about their lack of knowledge. Only two of the interviewed teachers felt comfortable with their knowledge of admissions requirements. But even they were unfamiliar with specifics. One of those teachers had previously served as a guidance counselor.

The interviews also touched on the subject of college placement tests. Considering that we inquired about the two largest public universities in the state for which the schools were primary feeders, information about these tests could have been quite useful to teachers in gauging adequate college preparation standards. We found that most teachers were completely uninformed about placement and unaware of the issue of remediation. When asked about freshman placement standards, some interviewees reflected back to their own experiences: "I simply remember what I took a thousand years ago." Another teacher commented: "I've never seen [a placement test], so all of my presumptions are based on my experience with the placement test ten years ago at a state college." One teacher expressed astonishment: "No kidding, every freshman has to take these tests?"

When asked if they received any feedback on whether their former students had had success in college, one teacher responded, "No, unfortunately, we only hear about that when students come back to say to you either 'I'm doing well when compared to everyone else' or 'I'm struggling.'" Another teacher described the lack of feedback this way: "I haven't ever received [information]; maybe our twelfth-grade teachers would. But I haven't received anything." Although some schools did receive data on students' college acceptance and scholarship awards, most teachers did not receive any formal and systematic feedback on their former students' success in college. One of our interviewees concluded this about the feedback schools received on former students:

> I think one of the problems in our educational system is there is no link once kids graduate from high school. It's as if they aren't our kids anymore, and that is not the case for K–12. There is a scope and a sequence, and there are learning activities that are supposed to go on throughout the twelve years. Then they drop off the face of the earth.

Schools are supposed to receive the so-called SOAR data, which track students' success at the college level by high school attended. These data have the potential to provide systematic feedback to schools, but were not mentioned in any of our interviews. Thus, teachers on the whole had no specific information on college admissions policies and procedures and lacked knowledge of how well their former students were performing at the college level. Their diffuse knowledge matched the fuzziness of parents' and students' knowledge.

Lacking specific knowledge, most commonly teachers would tell stories and anecdotes about their own college experiences:

> I tell them I was assigned *Moby Dick* on Friday and it was due Monday and that was my weekend. And I do the same with my kids, just two weeks ago, I said okay we finished *Huck Finn*, it's Wednesday, a paper is due Friday. And that's it for the instruction. That is what will happen.

> I have conversations about things I went through in high school, a lot. Things I went through in college. What difficulties I overcame. What bad habits I had and how they can avoid some of the things I did wrong.

Thus, absent current and detailed knowledge, students were left to strategize their transition from high school to college based on their teachers' college experiences.

The Roles of Teachers and Counselors in Helping with College

Teachers envisioned their role in students' college choice processes as limited; one eleventh-grade teacher said, "I don't sit down and have heart-to-heart conversations with them about what they need to do to be ready for college. That's more or less [what] the counselors drone into them." Teachers held students responsible for their own progress and motivation to succeed. Parental guidance was seen as essential: "I think we have got a middle group—and a lot of public schools are facing the same thing—they really don't have the direction; the parents haven't inspired that in them." Teachers deferred to the authorities when asked how they knew they were doing an adequate college preparatory job in their classrooms: "Well, I guess, I also see that as my county's responsibility. I am expected to teach my county's curriculum. My county's curriculum is designed to prepare them for college."

Whereas teachers assigned limited responsibility to themselves when it came to the provision of information (the counselors' task), the adequacy of standards (policymakers' task), and the motivation for college (students' and parents' task), they saw their college preparatory work primarily expressed in classroom instruction:

> I try to explain to them, in my class anyway, with the pace, the tone I set in my classroom, the level of responsibility. So I think I try to model ethics, study ethics and guidelines that they would have in a university situation.

> I teach an AP course which is taught at the college level. I always tell them it's because I think they need to be more prepared for college.

Thus, when teachers described their role in students' preparation for college, they were primarily classroom instructors. Their lack of detailed knowledge and the informal and sporadic nature of student-teacher interactions about college were not of great concern to them because the college choice process was seen as falling outside their responsibility.

Counselors at the four schools acted as the primary knowledge source for information on college admissions. Often they counseled students one-on-one, and sometimes they worked through teachers. Counselors had a better connection to colleges than teachers did. Higher education institutions tended to seek out the college counselors to share timely information. They visited the schools and invited counselors to visit their campuses. "We are well informed by all the Maryland state schools," summarized one counselor.

Counselors also believed it was their job to match student aspirations with actual course taking and preparation: "I say to students that you can't be a twelfth grader and decide that you want to go to Duke University and you haven't done the work in grades 9, 10, 11." Many students confirmed on the survey that they had received advice on course taking, and some of them said they had received counseling quite early in their careers.

Counselors, it seems, held almost a monopoly on college admission preparation in the four schools. Teachers looked to them to provide support to their students through individual counseling, college fairs, and hosting college representatives on campus. Principals as well lacked detailed knowledge of policies and procedures related to college admissions and preparation and referred to their counselors as the experts in this field.

But all counselors in this study had duties that went beyond college preparation or transition counseling. None of the interviewed counselors spent their entire working hours on college counseling because they were required to work with students on other personal issues as well. In the four schools we studied, counselors were assigned a portion of the student body as their caseload. One school had six counselors to serve eighteen hundred students, so each counselor was responsible for three hundred students. Another school had five counselors for seventeen hundred students. It is no wonder that about half of the surveyed students reported no communication with their counselors on college admission. Yet despite these heavy caseloads and multiple responsibilities, guidance counselors were the only ones at their schools to provide information to students, parents, and teachers and to serve as the primary contact for college representatives and recruiters.

In summary, teachers in the four studied schools tended to be sought out by students interested in information about college. Teachers lacked a solid knowledge base on admissions and placement. The information they shared was often anecdotal and based on teachers' own college experiences. Interviewed teachers did not see this state of affairs as a great problem as they envisioned for themselves a very limited role in preparing students for college. Counselors were the primary service providers, but their case overload made ongoing contact with students difficult. As a result, students' information on the college choice process was often based on unfounded information. During each of the focus group sessions, students frequently answered our knowledge questions with second-hand information or hearsay. Usually it was information or rumors they had heard from friends.

Parents viewed college preparation as a shared responsibility, with schools seen as more responsible for appropriate course taking and families more responsible for the actual application process. Parents stated on the survey that they talked with their children frequently about college plans, though they more frequently addressed general topics than the specifics of the process. The fact that many students' parents or teachers eschewed specifics might partially explain why children had such information deficits on college requirements.

College Programs

One way of facilitating the connection between high school and college is to involve students in organized activities. This is especially true for students who grow up in families whose members have not traditionally attended college. Few ninth-grade students in our sample had participated in specified college exposure activities since entering high school. About half of the eleventh-grade honors students reported visiting a college or university; about a third of the nonhonors students did. A group of about one-third of responding eleventh graders, however, was not reached with any of the listed activities by their schools. Level of parent education, income, or race made no difference in their participation rates. However, SAT preparation workshops were frequented more by white students (73 percent) than black students (50 percent).

All schools developed formal or informal bridge programs that help students get acquainted with college. A range of programs, such as Upward Bound, focused on low-income and minority youth; also common were college fairs. Occasionally teachers took the initiative for self-designed, informal bridge activities. As for sustained partnerships between schools and postsecondary institutions, community colleges were much more visible in schools than the four-year institutions. But the four-year institutions did provide services and programs to area high schools, although these were not described as intense or institutionalized.

Conclusion: Much Remains to Be Done

Our analysis of quantitative and qualitative data from students, parents, and educators suggests the following:

• A large proportion of sampled students in Maryland either wishes to attend a four-year college outside the state or the most selective University System of Maryland campus in College Park.

• Knowledge about costs, course requirements, selection criteria, and placement is very fuzzy with regard to college in general and the two focal institutions, UMCP and Towson University. Most students and parents overestimate admissions requirements and grossly overinflate the costs for a college education.

• Students have a general sense of differential selectivity with regard to Towson and UMCP, but they do not have a grasp of detailed knowledge. Ratings for both schools in terms of selectivity are rather similar. Students on the whole believe that it is becoming increasingly difficult to gain admission to either school. Informed decision making gives way to a diffuse sense of college scare.

• Affirmative action is not an issue for most students. Neither whites nor blacks attach much meaning to it. This peculiar attitude may find an explanation in the specific low-selectivity context of Maryland public higher education.

- Schools do not engage in frequent communications about college choice with students, though about half of the students report some contact. Students' interest in communicating with teachers about college choice is high according to interviewed teachers. About one-third of sampled students are seriously underserved by their schools with respect to college choice information.

- According to students' responses, schools seem to do a better job in counseling students about course taking than about college admissions. This is confirmed by teachers, who see course advising as an important domain of college preparation that falls within their duties.

- Not unlike the situation for students, teachers' knowledge is fuzzy. Teachers do not have accurate information on admissions criteria or know placement criteria and standards applied by institutions such as UMCP or Towson. They do not receive data on students' careers in higher education. Any feedback they receive depends on private and informal contact with former students and teachers.

- Communication between students and teachers about college is mainly informal and sporadic, though teachers report student interest in such communication.

- Lacking accurate knowledge themselves, teachers tend to share stories about their own college experiences. They also use their own college experience to construct today's college preparatory standards. Thus, much of what teachers dispense as knowledge about the college choice process is based on folk wisdom and life experiences.

- Teachers do not see for themselves a substantial role in students' college choice process. College choices are determined by circumstances out of teachers' control. They see students' previous performance record, their motivation, and parental influences as key. On the system side, they believe it is the duty of administrators to see to it that official curricula and materials reflect adequate standards. The teachers' role is to teach in the spirit of college preparation.

- Guidance counselors see themselves, and are seen by others, as key sources in students' college choice process. Teachers defer to them and expect information from them. Universities as well reach out to them. Principals too refer to them when asked about the school's role in the college choice process. While counselors are central in the process at their school, they express feeling overburdened by high caseloads and distracted by many other guidance duties.

- The new high school assessments, announced by the state to be graduation requirements in the not-so-distant future, are not mentioned as a concern for educators as far as college admissions are concerned. Neither teachers nor students see a connection between these looming graduation requirements and college admission.

These school-level findings suggest a rather loose connection between high school and college in Maryland. Our own analysis of conditions in Maryland supports this conclusion. To begin with, many students both leave and come into Maryland, making alignment problematic in terms of establishing closer connections. When fairly large numbers of students and their parents (certainly in the four schools, if not statewide) do not aspire to attend college in-state, concern for knowledge about admission to state colleges is not central for schools or their clients. Moreover, admission to the Maryland public colleges seems to be a somewhat less anxiety-ridden affair given that the state's institutions are rather comprehensive and open to a wide spectrum of achievement levels. Even C average students felt they had a shot at UMCP.

As to institutional linkages, the University of Maryland, College Park's admission criteria have been changing somewhat in recent years, making it difficult for students and teachers to keep abreast of the situation. At the high school level, systemic reform was stymied by the state's problems in institutionalizing high school assessments that could meaningfully connect to and communicate college admission standards. Initiatives under the auspices of the K–16 Partnership may have been helpful, but did not seem to have a systemwide effect that traveled all the way down to schools. Communication instead rests on the traditional bridges between particular institutions of higher learning and individual feeder schools. But guidance counselors at the school level seem to be the weak link in this chain. While they are seen by all actors as holding the keys to pertinent information, they themselves are overburdened with high caseloads and communicate with students and teachers infrequently. Our research documented the results: misinformation, fuzzy knowledge of standards and requirements, and perhaps a missed opportunity for the two state universities to present their profiles in a realistic light.

REFERENCES

Berdahl, R., and Schmidtlein, F. "Restructuring and Its Aftermath: Maryland."
    In T. J. MacTaggart and Associates (eds.), *Restructuring Higher Educa-
    tion*. San Francisco: Jossey-Bass, 1996.
Maryland Electronic Capital. "All About Maryland."
    [http://www.mec.state.md.us/]. June 2000.

Maryland Higher Education Commission. *Opening Fall Enrollment.* Annapolis: Maryland Higher Education Commission, 1999a.

Maryland Higher Education Commission. "Code of Maryland Regulations, 13B.02.02: Minimum Requirements for Degree-Granting Institutions." Annapolis: Maryland Higher Education Commission, 1999b.

Maryland Higher Education Commission. *College Performance of New Maryland High School Graduates: Student Outcome and Achievement Report.* Annapolis: Maryland Higher Education Commission, 1999c.

Maryland Higher Education Commission. *Data Book.* Annapolis: Maryland Higher Education Commission, 2000.

Maryland State Department of Education. *Maryland State Performance Report, State and School Systems.* Baltimore: Maryland State Department of Education, 1997.

Maryland State Department of Education. "The Maryland State Board of Education: The Voice of the Public. MSDE Website." [http://www.msde.state.md.us/stateboard /voiceofpub.html]. 2000a.

Maryland State Department of Education. "Maryland's High School Assessments . . . Building on Rigorous Requirements." [http:/msde.state.md.us/hsimprovement/creditrequirements.html]. 2000b.

Maryland State Department of Education. "MSDE Web Site." [http://www.msde.state.md.us]. 2001.

McDonough, P. *Choosing Colleges: How Social Class and Schools Structure Opportunity.* Albany: State University of New York Press, 1997.

Milton, T. H., and Schmidtlein, F. A. "The Bridge Project: Strengthening K–16 Transition Policies: Maryland Case Study Technical Report— Phase I." College Park: Department of Education Policy and Leadership, University of Maryland, 2000.

National Center for Education Statistics. *Residence and Migration of First-Time Freshmen Enrolled in Degree Granting Institutions.* Washington, D.C.: National Center for Education Statistics, Fall 1999.

State of Maryland. *Annotated Code of Maryland, Education Article, Section 11–701.* Annapolis: State of Maryland, 1999.

Timar, T., Krop, D., and Kirst, M. "Maryland Case Study, Role of State Agencies in Science/Math Reform." Draft report for West Ed., 1997.

University System of Maryland Board of Regents. "Policy on Undergraduate Enrollment (Revised and approved by the Board of Regents, October 4, 1996)." Adelphi, Md.: University System of Maryland Board of Regents, 1990.

8

THE MISSING LINK

THE ROLE OF COMMUNITY COLLEGES
IN THE TRANSITION BETWEEN
HIGH SCHOOL AND COLLEGE

Andrea Conklin Bueschel

COMMUNITY COLLEGES, often neglected in policy debates, are the point of entry for many higher education students. Over eleven hundred community colleges in the United States serve over half of the U.S. undergraduate enrollment, making them a potentially vital link in the transition from high school to college. They not only serve large numbers of students, but have a number of features that make them worthy of closer study. In many states, for instance, community colleges provide most of the costly postsecondary academic remediation that students need to complete a two- or four-year degree. Furthermore, in times of economic downturn, more people look to the community college for postsecondary education and training. An understanding of the role of these institutions in the preparation of young people for the job market can only benefit policy development. Finally, community colleges have an extensive history of collaboration with high schools, making them, in some cases, models for what other postsecondary institutions might attempt.

This chapter is based on research, analyses, and writing conducted by K. C. Boatsman in California, Ann Merck MacLellan in Maryland, and Andrea Conklin Bueschel and Andrea Venezia in Oregon.

(Although this chapter uses the term *community college* for all two-year institutions, some references may still use *junior college*. For the purposes of this chapter, the terms are interchangeable.)

In this chapter, we examine the role of the community college in serving the "silent majority" of postsecondary students—those often overlooked by a public focused on four-year institutions. Our research specifically looks at three issues:

○ The admission and placement policies and practices for recent high school graduates who are attending community college

○ The transition environment for these students and whether there are observed disjunctures between high school and community college curriculum, skills, assessments, and course placement

○ The types of transition services and programs (high school to community college, and community college to four-year institution) available to students

The chapter offers an overview of community colleges, describing some important trends, and explores the above issues in the context of six community colleges in three states. After providing a summary of our key findings, it offers some suggestions as to how the community college can be strengthened as a link between high school and four-year colleges and suggestions for further research.

Research Methods

This qualitative study consisted of interviews with key administrators, faculty, and staff; focus groups with students; and document review, including Web sites. All of the community colleges in the study were visited at different points in 2001, which is when interviews and the student focus groups occurred. Two campuses in each of three regions were studied. Table 8.1 lists the campuses studied and the number of staff and students interviewed.

The administrators, faculty, and staff who were interviewed were in key positions to offer information on counseling, assessment, admissions, orientation, instruction, curriculum, and outreach. The student focus groups included mostly students who matriculated soon after completing high school, as well as some older students. The students interviewed seemed to be representative of community college students in terms of gender and ethnic diversity; the focus group participants were deliberately younger when possible. In some cases, the focus groups were drawn from existing

_____

Table 8.1. Study Sites and Participants.

Region	Sites	Participants per Region
Sacramento, California	Sacramento City College, Cosumnes River College	27 staff interviewed, 48 students in focus groups
Baltimore, Maryland	Montgomery College, Rockville Community College of Baltimore, Catonsville	22 staff interviewed, 31 students in focus groups
Portland, Oregon	Mt. Hood Community College Portland Community College, Sylvania	28 staff interviewed, 36 students in focus groups

groups—for example, members of an activity board or students enrolled in a college success class (one that, for example, helps students develop skills like time management and course planning to help them succeed in a new educational setting. Although there may have been a bias toward more actively engaged students (not surprising when asking students to volunteer time for a study), students were nevertheless quite candid and critical, while also highlighting positive aspects of their experiences.

The documents reviewed included primarily institutional publications such as catalogues and schedules of classes, handouts and informational fliers given to students, documents required of students such as the application for admission, research reports where available, and campus Web sites.

An Overview of Community College in the United States

The first two-year institution in the United States was Joliet Junior College, opened in 1901 in Illinois. In the one hundred years since, the growth in community colleges has been dramatic—more rapid even than that of four-year institutions. Rosenbaum (1999) notes that between 1960 and 1990, four-year college enrollment doubled; for two-year institutions, enrollment increased fivefold. The dramatic growth in the 1960s was due in part to a newly created national network of two-year institutions. By the late 1990s, there were 1,166 public and private community colleges (about 1,600 counting separate multiple campus colleges). Over 100 million students have attended community college since 1901, for everything from workforce retraining to English language acquisition to advanced mathematics for university-level credit. Currently, over half of the undergraduates enrolled in the United States attend community colleges (Bailey, 2002).[1]

Community College Students

Community college students represent a wide diversity of backgrounds. Students in two-year institutions are likely to be older, more ethnically and racially diverse, and less affluent than their four-year counterparts. The American Association of Community Colleges (AACC), in conjunction with other surveys, provides this profile of community college students:

- Fifty-eight percent are women.
- Thirty percent are racial minorities (other surveys cite percentages as high as 60).
- Thirty-two percent are thirty years or older (36 percent are the traditional ages of eighteen to twenty-two).
- Sixty-four percent attend part time.
- Sixty-five percent depend on their parents financially (95 percent of four-year students do).
- Half are the first in their families to attend college.
- Depending on the survey, 12 to 28 percent already have a postsecondary degree.

Community colleges are the least expensive higher education option, which explains in part why such a wide range of students takes advantage of them. The average tuition for community colleges nationally is around $1,500, considerably less than that at four-year institutions (American Association of Community Colleges, 2002). The two-year institutions also have a different faculty profile. Doctorates are not required for faculty at most two-year colleges, and there is a higher percentage of part-time and adjunct faculty. Approximately two-thirds of public community college faculty are on part-time appointments; all faculty members are paid less than their four-year counterparts (American Association of Community Colleges, 2002). The two-year colleges also have a distinct mission in higher education, which helps account for the diverse population.

Community colleges serve as the point of entry for students who would not otherwise participate in postsecondary education. Low-income students, students of color, recent immigrants, and students who are the first in their families to attend college are often overrepresented in two-year institutions. Because many of these students do not feel as though they have access to four-year institutions, the community colleges are the only way for many of these students to improve their opportunities. According to the U.S. Census Bureau, about 85 percent of the growth in the population of those eighteen to twenty-four years old will come from minority and immigrant families over the next decade. Over 40 percent will come from low-income families (Kirst and Bracco, 2002). Given these trends, community colleges are likely to play a growing role in the higher education system.

The Community College Mission

Community colleges are defined by their commitment to being open access institutions. Generally if a student can benefit from education, that person is welcome. This philosophy has ensured that community colleges continue to attract students from all backgrounds. Community colleges have also become comprehensive institutions, providing a wide range of academic, training, and service functions. Because these institutions were created to serve public needs directly, they often change quickly to respond to these needs. As Bailey and Averianova (1999) note, "Starting primarily as junior colleges with an emphasis on academics, the [community] colleges are now complex institutions taking on a broad array of educational, social, and economic functions" (p. 1). Some critics contend that community colleges need to narrow their focus in order to provide better service in fewer areas. Proponents argue that the mission dictates the need to continue to offer a wide, and often growing, set of services and programs.

Research findings document the tension created on campuses in trying to maintain the commitment to open access with the need to uphold standards for both college-level work and industry-level expectations. Faculty and staff on community college campuses are often explicitly committed to the open access mission—and indeed believe that they are best positioned to respond to the needs of the community—but they struggle to uphold standards while meeting the ever expanding needs of the students and community. Grubb (1999) notes the particular struggle of those trying to balance the various standards in their departments and institutions. The mission of community colleges will likely ensure that they will continue to be necessary resources for all people in their communities. Bailey and Averianova (1999) observe, "Responding to educational needs often ignored by other institutions, community colleges have been profoundly transformed. . . . These functions of community colleges define its unprecedented social and economic significance. No other institution has demonstrated so much flexibility in adapting to the community's needs" (p. 5).

Remediation at Community Colleges

The need to remediate students who enter their institutions with limited basic skills has made remedial education (the terms *developmental* and *basic skills* are also used) an increasingly important function for community colleges. This is especially true in the light of a desire among politicians and policymakers to move all remediation from four-year to two-year colleges. Remedial courses address basic levels of reading, writing, and mathematics—skills that should have been taught before and during high school.[2] Although remedial courses are offered on college campuses, they are not considered college-level work, and students cannot receive college-level credit for passing them. It is quite difficult to track exactly how many students require remediation (for example, in some cases, students may be assessed as needing it but never enroll in the courses). Several estimates state that approximately one-third to four-tenths of first-time students are or were enrolled in at least one remedial course (Shults, 2002; Rosenbaum, 1999).

Remediation in postsecondary education highlights an important disjuncture between K–12 and higher education. The growth in remediation suggests that it is not just returning students who are "rusty" in algebra who need basic skills help. Rather, there seem to be more and more students leaving high school without having mastered these skills in the first place. It seems to be particularly difficult for community colleges to communicate their standards for college-level work given their mission to welcome all who want an education. Rosenbaum (1999) argues that "students' failures arise not from barriers inside colleges, but from a failure of colleges (and especially community colleges) to convey clear information about the preparation that high school students need in order to have a strong chance of finishing a degree" (p. 1).

Rosenbaum seems to be taking the position that if students are aware in advance of what it takes to succeed, they will adjust their behavior in high school and work to achieve at a higher level before matriculating.[3] He notes that a sizable minority of students he surveyed (46 percent) agreed with the statement, "Even if I do not work hard in high school, I can still make my future plans come true" (1999, p. 2). The "second-chance" message from community colleges (what he calls the "college-for-all norm") seems to be coming through clearly for these students.

The message that they may not be able to take the courses they want or get college-level credit does not.

Rosenbaum argues that the way to minimize remediation, which often leads to frustration and a failure to persist, is to communicate the importance of the "first chance" to be successful in high school. He believes that the "college-for-all" norm may harm more students than it helps (Rosenbaum, 2001). As he notes, "Second chances are a fundamental American tenet. However, open-admission policies and remedial programs inadvertently convey to students that high school is irrelevant and that there are no penalties for poor effort" (1999, p. 3).[4]

Mixed Signals, Missed Opportunities

High rates of remediation, caused by a lack of preparation of students coming out of high school, call attention to the lack of alignment between the systems regarding the standard for college-level work.

Rosenbaum argues that not all of the blame lies with the colleges in their failure to communicate standards. He says, "Guidance counselors do not tell students what level of high school achievement is needed for them to succeed in community college, so students are lulled into a complacency that leaves them unprepared for getting a college degree" (2001, p. 80). He does not address the other signals or sources of information for students; he focuses on traditional gatekeepers such as counselors, who in his research play a very different role than they did a generation ago (when many would tell students they were not "college material").[5] Perhaps most important, implicit in his research is the notion that people and institutions from different educational sectors should work together to communicate appropriate signals to students. He is aware that this lack of coordination can have additional detrimental effects on students: "Poor information allows many students to have high hopes but to use their high school experiences poorly, and thus they seem to be personally responsible for their failures" (Rosenbaum, 2001, p. 58).

Transfer Rates

Many students who enter community colleges express an aspiration to complete their education at a four-year college or university. Reports of intent to transfer (a notoriously tricky measure to track) range from one-quarter to over one-half of community college students (Cooley, 2000; Community College Survey of Student Engagement, 2002). Almost as hard to track is the actual rate of transfer for community college students.

Part of what makes data collection difficult on these measures is that so many students attend more than one institution during their careers, often going back and forth in a process that some call "swirling." It is also important to note that institutional retention is not the same as student persistence. Just because a student does not persist at the same institution does not mean this person is not continuing his or her education somewhere else. As noted above, anywhere from 12 to 28 percent of college students attend more than one institution concurrently (Community College Survey of Student Engagement, 2002; Phillippe and Valiga, 2000). Reported rates of transfer from two-year to four-year institutions range from 14 or 15 percent to about 40 percent (Rosenbaum, 2001; Wellman, 2002; Young, 2002). Regardless of the actual percentage, consistently fewer students actually transfer than say they want to.

Degree Completion Rates

Data on completion of degrees are highly variable. Wellman (2002) writes that one-third of all first-time degree-seeking students transfer within four years of enrollment—one-fourth of four-year students and 43 percent of two-year students. Rosenbaum's research (2001) finds that around 60 percent of high school seniors who plan to get a postsecondary degree fail to get any degree in the next ten years and that the rates are worse for low performers. Young (2002) reports that 37 percent of students finish their bachelor's degree in four years; one-quarter finish their associate degree in two years. A recent American Council on Education report (Choy, 2002) cites that "among those [community college students] who intended to earn a bachelor's degree, only 39 percent actually transferred" (p. 20). Bailey (2002) finds that "less than one tenth of students who begin in two-year colleges ever complete a bachelor's degree" (p. 61). Starting at a community college is considered a risk factor for completion given much lower rates: "Starting at a two-year institution rather than a four-year institution with the intention of earning a bachelor's degree also was associated with a greater likelihood of leaving postsecondary education without having earned a degree (46 percent versus 23 percent)" (Choy, 2002, p. 20). Again, it is clear that there must be better coordination of signals and expectations in order to begin to improve the level of work for entering students, and therefore their chances of persistence and completion.

Persistence and completion data are related to the issue of preparation. Additional analyses suggest that students who are less prepared and take remedial courses are less likely to persist, transfer, and complete. Rosenbaum (2001) reports that "only 13.9 percent of seniors with low grades attained their college plans" (p. 66). Bailey (2002) also relates poor preparation to lowered transfer and persistence: "Developmental education is a central component of the colleges' mission to provide access; however, large numbers of poorly prepared students complicate college efforts to improve transfer and graduation rates" (p. 61).

The Bridge Project's Community College Research Study

The focus of this chapter now shifts to our research of community colleges in California, Maryland, and Oregon.

Community Colleges in California

The role California and function of community colleges in California gained clarity through the Master Plan for Higher Education in California, the first version of which was written in 1960. Differentiation of mission and function created a three-tiered system of postsecondary education:

o The University of California, a system of selective research universities for the top one-eighth of California's matriculating students

o The California State University, a larger system of moderately selective institutions for the top one-third of California's matriculating students

o The California Community College system, the most extensive system of open access institutions, available for any student who can benefit from continued education.

According to the Master Plan:

The California Community Colleges have as their primary mission providing academic and vocational instruction for older and younger students through the first two years of undergraduate education (lower division). In addition to this primary mission, the Community Colleges are authorized to provide remedial instruction, English as a Second Language courses, adult noncredit instruction, community service courses, and workforce training services [University of California Office of the President, 1999].

The Master Plan established the principle of universal access to postsecondary education in California at the community college level, where all students "capable of benefiting from instruction" are to be admitted.

There are 108 community colleges in the California System. A sixteen-member board of governors, appointed by the state's governor, oversees the 72-district, 108–community college campus system. The board of governors is granted authority by the state legislature to develop and implement policy for the colleges in the system. In 2001, the California Community College system served over 2.5 million students, making it the largest system of higher education in the world.

We conducted research in two California community colleges.

SACRAMENTO CITY COLLEGE. In the fall semester of 2000, Sacramento City College enrolled 21,186 students. The student body is 58 percent female, ethnically diverse (42 percent white, 21 percent Asian, 15 percent Hispanic, 12 percent black), and relatively young (55 percent of the students were twenty-four years of age or less, the same as is true for 48 percent of community college students statewide). International students come from approximately fifty-five nations. As one administrator put it, "Our campus is blessed with wonderful diversity."

COSUMNES RIVER COLLEGE. Cosumnes River College (CRC) was founded in 1970 as the third college in the Los Rios Community College District, to which Sacramento City College also belongs. Although Cosumnes River College enrolls over 16,000 students, it has the feel of a small campus. The student population is just over half of that of its sister colleges, American River and Sacramento City. There is a physical center to the campus and a populated student center, which allows for casual interaction between students. On average, there is less ethnic and racial diversity at CRC and, like other campuses, more women than men.

Community Colleges in Maryland

Maryland has sixteen community colleges. The Maryland Higher Education Commission (MHEC) is the regulatory agency, and the Maryland Association of Community Colleges (MACC) is the organization through which the colleges lobby for legislative action in the state.

Maryland's community colleges, not unlike community colleges nationally, are open admissions. This means that students are not denied access to college courses and programs on the basis of standardized test scores or high school grades. Students under age sixteen, as well as students without a high school credential, are eligible to enroll.

We conducted research in two Maryland community colleges.

MONTGOMERY COLLEGE. Montgomery College (MC) is Maryland's oldest community college. It was founded in 1946 and was originally the higher education division of Montgomery County Public Schools. Campuses are located in Takoma Park, Rockville, and Germantown. Research for this study was conducted at the Rockville campus.

Montgomery College, Rockville Campus, has the highest credit student enrollment of the three campuses. For the fall 2001 semester, 14,334 students were enrolled. In fall 2000 collegewide, the mean age was 28.7 and the median age was 23.6. Approximately 35 percent of the students attending MC were full time (carrying at least twelve credits). A higher percentage of Rockville students are full time (39 percent) than at the other two campuses. Half of the students (54 percent) attend classes only during the day, one-fourth attend only in the evening, and 20 percent attend both day and evening. Most students (90 percent) live in Montgomery County, and approximately 25 percent of Montgomery County high school graduates attended Montgomery College in the fall of 2000.

COMMUNITY COLLEGE OF BALTIMORE COUNTY. The Community College of Baltimore County (CCBC) is a tri-campus public college located in the suburbs of Baltimore. It was created in 1998 as a result of a state-legislated restructuring that combined three independent community colleges into one institution. CCBC is one of the largest community colleges in Maryland and the number one provider of undergraduate education and workforce training in the Baltimore metropolitan area. Research for this study was done at the Catonsville campus.

CCBC serves approximately 17,793 credit and 33,000 noncredit students annually by offering a broad array of transfer and career programs and services. The Catonsville Campus of CCBC has the highest credit student enrollment of its three campuses and the largest minority enrollment. Of the over 9,000 credit students enrolled during the fall 2001 semester, 33 percent were African American, 6 percent Asian, 2 percent Hispanic, 52 percent white, and 7 percent other or unknown.

Community Colleges in Oregon

The state of Oregon has a community college system that encompasses seventeen colleges, with over sixty campuses and centers. The Department of Community Colleges and Workforce Development (CCWD) has oversight for all public two-year education in the state. Most generally, according to the Oregon Department of Community Colleges and Workforce Development (2001), its mission "is to contribute leadership and resources to increase the skills, knowledge, and career opportunities of Oregonians" (p. 3). The CCWD is headed by a commissioner appointed by the State Board of Education, which has oversight of all K–14 education in Oregon and also serves as the State Board for Technical and Vocational Education.

The Oregon postsecondary education system, including the seven Oregon University System institutions, has capacity for qualified students who meet minimum standards, so the desire for better-prepared students is less about selection than about overall minimum competency for college-level work.

We conducted research at two Oregon community colleges.

PORTLAND COMMUNITY COLLEGE. Portland Community College (PCC) is the largest of the Oregon community colleges. With three campuses and six academic centers, it enrolls over 23 percent of the state's community college students (Oregon Department of Community Colleges and Workforce Development, 2001). Research for this study was done at the Sylvania campus, which enrolls 26,000 students, the most of the three PCC campuses. Historically, the average age of the students at the Sylvania campus is thirty years, lower than the PCC average of thirty-six. However, for PCC, the most frequently listed age is twenty. Twenty-six percent of students are between eighteen and twenty-four years old. There are approximately 55 percent women at all three campuses. Sylvania has more white students than the PCC average.

MT. HOOD COMMUNITY COLLEGE. Mt. Hood Community College (MHCC), which opened in 1966, is also located in the Portland metropolitan area. Approximately 27,000 students enroll at either the main campus in Gresham or one of the centers that make up MHCC. In 2000–2001, MHCC had over twenty-seven thousand individual students enroll in at least one class. Of those students, 40 percent were enrolled in professional-technical programs, 41 percent were in college transfer courses, and 19 percent were in other educational programs. Twenty-eight percent declared an intent to transfer. MHCC has a younger campus than others in the community college system; 60 percent are under thirty years old. There is also a majority of students who are women.

Key Case Study Findings

Although individual campuses vary in some ways, we found that the similarities far outweigh the differences, allowing us to make generalizations about community colleges and the students they serve.

A Shared Mission of Accessibility

Our case study community colleges, like community colleges nationally, share a strong commitment to providing educational opportunity for any student who can benefit from it. As one director of admission explained, "We have everything from the kid who barely reads to the kid who, you know, could be at Harvard." Twelve to 28 percent of community college attendees already have a bachelor's or other advanced degree; anywhere from 25 to 80 percent require some remediation. The commitment to serve students regardless of their academic backgrounds is the most defining characteristic of community colleges. It is often also the greatest challenge.

Student Reasons for Attending Community College

The reasons for attending community colleges are as varied as the students themselves. In the focus groups, researchers heard students cite location, cost, specific programs, lack of other options, and convenience. Students also talked about how community college gave them a second chance. Following are some of common reasons students gave for choosing a community college:

> I chose CRC because I live five minutes away, and I also went to high school across the street. (California student)

> I came here because I really didn't know what I wanted to do yet. And it's like the only school that's somewhat near me . . . and it's cheap. (California student)

> The reason why I came here. . . . I didn't have a high school diploma, and I really needed to do something, and I hadn't had a job, didn't have any job skills . . . so I came here. (California student)

> I'm here just because it's the most convenient option for me. It's closest to home and it's the easiest to get to and get in and out and just get these credits out of the way. (Maryland student)

> I had made lots of bad choices and stuff, and then one day I kind of woke up and said, 'What am I doing? I don't want to be a clerk at 7–11, you know, for the rest of my days.' (Oregon student)

As these comments indicate, students are attracted to the access, convenience, and second chance that community colleges provide. But as some of the following sections suggest, students do not always have a clear idea of what it takes to enroll, matriculate, and complete an educational program.

Admission and Enrollment Policies

Because all of the institutions in this study (and most community colleges in general) are open admission, the role of admission staff on these campuses is not the traditional gatekeeping one. There is some recruiting at area high schools, but because students can come from almost any background, the admission office serves primarily as the point of entry for enrollment and registration (and is often the first college entity to communicate placement requirements). As one researcher noted, it is primarily a data gathering point. Students can walk in the day before classes, talk to an admissions official, and, with certain basic requirements met, enroll for that term.[6] While this ease of enrollment provides students with opportunity, it also presents a challenge to those working with students who may have little sense of what they want. One Oregon adviser explained, "The one thing—it's both the good thing and the bad thing about community college, I would say—is that a student can come here with absolutely no forethought?"

At all of the community colleges studied, recent high school graduates made up a significant subset of enrolled students (at some colleges, it was the largest subgroup). In Oregon, several staff members and students noted the growth in the enrollment of recent graduates. Some suggested that there is less stigma than in the past about attending community college, which has encouraged some higher-achieving students to attend. However, in all three states, the growth in the enrollment of recent graduates has raised concern in that it highlights the level of preparation of the recent graduates. Many respondents in this study reported a greater lack of preparedness among this population.

Given the presence of these recent graduates, the community colleges in the study tend to have relationships with area or district high schools. Admission staff speak to high school students generally about community college. In many cases, existing programs and partnerships are the point of contact between high school students and the community colleges.

In Oregon, where funding is enrollment driven, staff members are eager in most cases to attract more students. In California, however, individual colleges and districts generally do not have aggressive outreach practices. There is even a funding disincentive in place for recruiting too many new students. When colleges go "over cap" by enrolling more students than projected by the Chancellor's Office, the apportionment, or amount the college gets paid per full-time-equivalent student, is decreased. Thus, unless a community college is experiencing declining enrollment, there is no economic incentive to increase enrollment by recruiting more students.

An interesting point to consider about the open admission philosophy at the community colleges is that they must still find a way to maintain standards for college-level work, particularly as relates to transferable courses. As our Maryland researcher notes, the open admission policy may convey the impression that any student may register for any course, when in fact there are mandatory placement tests and course placement policies that often require students to take non-college-level courses. In many community colleges, open admission is preserved by ensuring that the first course in a prerequisite sequence is open to students of all abilities. In general, staff are committed to the open admission policy and philosophy, and share stories of students placed on the path to success. An admission officer explains,

> I see students every day who don't believe they belong in college, and, you know, they kind of want to take a class and so, maybe, they'll take a typing class or they'll take a, you know, and all of a sudden it's a college class, even though it's not a transfer class. And they get some success and then they build, and the next thing you know, they're transferring with a degree, and you know, it's just awesome.

Tuition and Financial Aid

There is no tuition at California community colleges, but there is an enrollment fee of eleven dollars per unit. Maryland and Oregon community college fees are also the lowest-cost alternative for postsecondary education in the state. In Maryland, the tuition is seventy-two dollars per unit. The Oregon community colleges cost between forty and fifty dollars per unit for tuition and fees. There are often other fees in addition to class materials—parking, technology, and student activities, for example. All of the institutions in the study charge higher fees for out-of-state and international residents. In most cases, some of the applied programs, such as dental hygiene, have higher fees.

All of the institutions in the study have financial aid offices that coordinate federal, state, local, and institutional support for all students who qualify. All of the campuses have seen an increase in demand for aid. As an Oregon financial aid officer said, "We have a 30 percent increase in the number of financial aid applications this year." The downturn in the economy and the "echo boom" (children of the large baby boom generation who are now college aged) are offered as explanations. One of the most difficult aspects of the financial aid officer's job is the timing of aid requests. Unlike most four-year college students, many community college students do not know several months in advance that they need to apply for financial aid. Aside from a general lack of awareness about filing deadlines, lots of these students do not decide to attend community college until right before the academic term begins. They are often surprised that they will not be able to get the aid immediately upon enrolling.

Another point of concern is financial aid and developmental or remedial education. A student who requires several terms of financial aid for non-credit work must be careful not to use up eligibility for government support.

Placement Tests and Policies

Community college students were surprised that they were required to take placement tests. They were also frequently surprised by their low scores, which indicated that they were not yet able to meet standards for college-level work. A Maryland staff member said:

> [Remediation is] a big issue with a lot of incoming students, and that's why we have the developmental education faculty come and talk to them about those courses at the group orientation at the end of the summer. So many students come to this college with not a clue that they're underprepared. They get those test results, and they are sometimes very upset. . . . I've had people walk out. "You know, if I can't get credit, then I don't need to be here." So, yeah, that's always an issue. It really is, and it's, I think in many ways, a high school issue because [the students] got some very false expectations. I mean, we have people here who got B's in English and test into developmental English, and they think they know how to write and read, so it's a surprise. You know, basically, if they've graduated from high school, I think they have a reason to believe that they have passed the basic requirements.

As Table 8.2 highlights, some students face multiple assessments. Although ACCUPLACER and COMPASS, national assessment products, are becoming more widely used, some states, including California, use tests about which students are unaware. The lack of standardization and signaling can be overwhelming. Given that most recent high school graduates

Table 8.2. Assessments Used at Each Case Campus.

Campus	Assessments
California	
Sacramento City College	ACCUPLACER
Cosumnes River College	College Tests of English Placement and Mathematics Diagnostic Testing Project
Maryland[a]	
Montgomery College, Rockville	ACCUPLACER
Community College of Baltimore County, Catonsville	ACCUPLACER
Oregon	
Portland Community College, Sylvania	ASSET/COMPASS
Mt. Hood Community College	ACCUPLACER

[a]*ACCUPLACER is used at all community colleges in the state.*

have already faced several standardized tests in high school (given the extensive K–12 reform), it is not clear how students are made aware of and keep track of the many assessments they are expected to take.

Many of the community college staff members were asked by researchers about the possibility of using one of the existing statewide assessments used in K–12 for placement.[7] A few acknowledged that a K–12 test could perhaps be used, though they said it would likely be used in conjunction with, not in place of, their existing placement exams, thereby not reducing the number of assessments students face in the transition from high school to college.

Interestingly, student reaction to the placement process in the focus groups was varied. While most students talked about being surprised by the placement assessment, few reported being upset about the requirement.[8] Particularly for the recent high school graduates, testing and assessment are a very common part of their educational experience. As one said, "We just took so many of those tests in high school, I don't even . . . we just took them and, you know, didn't really even pay attention to what it was about." Others were definitely thrown by the requirement: "So I did my orientation, and they told me something about testing. I was like, what? You have to do a test? So, oh man, I wasn't ready to do this because usually, you know, everybody said if there's a test, you have to get ready, you have to study, but no one told me about them when I graduated from high school." Overall, however, the fact that the placement test could often be retaken lowered the stakes for most students.

There was also variation in the reactions to the outcomes of the assessment. Many staff reported students as being stunned by their poor performance on the placement tests. They are particularly upset when they realize that they can enroll only in courses that do not receive college-level credit. It is at this point that students become painfully aware of their lack of preparation (and in some cases the consequence of not working hard in high school). Moments like these reflect Rosenbaum's concern that students are ill served by the college-for-all norm. According to one counselor:

> Well, I think the biggest thing for them is, here, they've graduated from high school but they come and take our placement test and they're still in, you know, pre-college reading, writing and math, and they don't understand that if they stop taking math in their sophomore year that, you know, they don't get it . . . no one. And I think the sad thing is that they say, and I don't know what really happens, I suppose it's different at every school, "No one told me that I should be taking math all the way through." They just weren't warned or they don't remember being warned, so now they're having to pay for it and sit through, and that is extremely frustrating. I think it's embarrassing, especially with reading and writing. It's embarrassing to them. And they'll almost start crying because [they'll say], "I graduated [from high school]."

While all the cases in this study reported examples of students who were stunned by the results, there are notable exceptions. In California and Oregon, most students said they were not fazed by the placement tests. They understood the need for the assessments and generally accepted where they were placed. One faculty member in Oregon said, "I remember a complaint, many more complaints about [placement] in past years, but in the last few years many students that say that are just accepting." The community colleges are now communicating the test requirements quickly upon admission. One student described how he got the message loud and clear: "Oh, man, they wouldn't let me move forward without placing. I couldn't even get into the school without taking a test. I mean, they wouldn't even look at me twice with my money in hand. They'd say, 'Go take the test.'"

Placement tests play an important role in community colleges, particularly given the absence of entrance examinations. The large number of students starting in the community colleges warrants greater attention to the role of placement tests.

The Adviser's Role

Advisers, who focus on such matters as scheduling and academic planning, must deal with the practical application of the community college mission to admit anyone who can benefit from the educational opportunity. Advisers are prepared to work with anyone who comes through their door, but often have limited options for some of their less prepared students. This adviser highlighted the challenge of serving them:

> The bad thing is though, as it gets closer to registration, we tend to see the more poorly prepared students who have the lowest test scores come in at the end, and suddenly all the little hoops that we set up to, hopefully, make them start thinking about what they're doing, those all just disappear. So our policy is if you come in the day before classes start, as long as you can get that placement test done and your admission form filled out, we'll register you even though you probably haven't really had time to think about how you're going to pay for it, how it's going to impact you, so the least prepared students get the least level of service because they come in right at the end, so we do a disservice to them by letting them register, when we probably should be saying, "Why don't you wait a term? By then your financial aid will be in place, and you'll have time to get proper advising."

The issue of preparedness is central to how staff members are able to serve their students best. Every day, community college staffers struggle with the best way to preserve the mission of the institution while confronting the deficits students bring.

Although some students were upset that they did not know what they were supposed to be doing—what classes to take, what requirements to meet—others understood that help was available to those who sought it. Although almost all the respondents who were asked about advising believed that their campuses could use more staff for advising, they also acknowledged that it was hard to accomplish given limited resources. A couple of students responded:

> Because, I think, that so many people just, basically, just get screwed. They go, "Whoa! Why didn't I know this?" I mean, you're not required to see an adviser at all, and I really sense, like, only, maybe ten advisers and, like, you know, thousands of students, but I think at some point in your curriculum and your planning, you should be required to see an adviser because they know what they're talking about, and most people that come here don't exactly know what they're doing.

I think that's a big issue, too, that the amount of advising and help that you receive is dependent on how much initiative you take. I mean, if you want to find out what classes you need to take to be able to transfer, . . . nobody is going to come to you.

Remediation Rates

The level of academic preparation of community college students is of central importance. Not only is insufficient preparation the most obvious example of the lack of alignment between K–12 and postsecondary education in terms of their academic standards, it presents perhaps the greatest challenge for those charged with addressing the gap. All community colleges offer remedial or developmental courses.[9] This function has been part of the mission from their inception. In the past, the assumption was that returning students who were rusty in their skills would need opportunities for review of basic concepts. However, it became clear that in lots of cases, both for returning students and recent high school graduates, many students never learned the basic skills in the first place.

On all of the campuses in this study, staff described students who were coming to the community colleges without basic skills. This trend is primarily responsible for the changes and strengthening of placement policies. Although the reported remediation rates range from small minorities of students to sizable majorities on each of these campuses, all of the colleges consider remediation an important issue.[10] Below are some data on remediation at the case campuses.

- California. At SCC, one-quarter of the math sections offered are considered remedial, and approximately two-fifths of the English and English as a Second Language (ESL) sections are considered remedial. At CRC, one-third of the math sections are considered remedial, and nearly two-thirds of the English and ESL sections offered are considered remedial (39 percent of English; 77 percent of ESL).
- Maryland. During the fall of 2001, 2,649 students attended the Rockville Campus of Maryland College directly from high school. The following percentages of recent high school graduates needed remediation collegewide: 40 percent English, 63 percent math, and 30 percent reading. There was a consensus among the administrators interviewed that the campus had changed over the years to meet the growing numbers of academically unprepared students graduating from Montgomery County high schools. Over the past several years, CCBC has enrolled approximately 34 percent of the graduates from Baltimore County Public Schools. For fall 2001, 44 percent of BCPS graduates attending CCBC needed

developmental English, 44 percent were in need of some math review, and 40 percent needed at least one reading course.

• Oregon. Although the data were not available for all the regions, there was evidence in Oregon that students in remedial course work were less likely to persist in their education. This finding is supported by earlier research and literature. At MHCC, recent graduates were less likely to need remediation. Only 21 percent of recent graduates, as opposed to a more typical 40 percent, fail to meet standards for college-level work. This finding is in line with the reporting in Oregon that some higher-achieving recent graduates are enrolling in community college.

The students also talked about their lack of preparation. Some expressed frustration with their high schools, upset that they had been passed along or told that their performance was acceptable:

> In my high school they didn't prepare you for college at all. Well, I had college prep classes, but my school, they're so quick to pass you. . . . When I got here I was so used to bein' in a fly-by [easy] class, I was like, okay, these teachers they don't care if I come or not. I'm not gonna come. But when I got my transcript it was a totally different story. I was like, they're not playin' here.

> This is the thing. I've always done well in grammar, and I've always done well in English. I got A's throughout high school, and I was placed in the lowest English [here].

> I didn't get any preparation in high school either. Like I said, I came to college for a fresh start. . . . Now, you know, there's respect for the teachers, there's [more] respect for learning here than my high school, [where] there was no respect for learning. I mean, some people, yeah, but a lot of people, no.

Others took responsibility for their lack of preparation. One student said that he goofed off in high school and now appreciates the second chance:

> And when you come here, it's like, whoa! It's an eye opener, and you see all these different people, and you see people that are older than you as well. And that's one thing that really drives me here is you see these people that are older coming to school, you know, trying to do something. And you're saying, "Well, look at how young I am. Look

at how much time I have. Why am I wasting it?" You know? And you end up, you know, getting your stuff together. The whole atmosphere at community college I like.

The ones who did feel prepared were often the higher-achieving students who were expecting to go to a four-year institution but for whatever reason did not:

> I felt like I was really prepared from high school. But it was hard for me my first semester. I didn't want to be here. I really wanted to be at Berkeley. And my grades weren't as high as they were in high school. But I got the hang of it here and I said, "You know, I still want to go to Berkeley and so in order to do that I need to get out of here first." So it was really rough. Just because a community college, like, my friends claimed it had the reputation of being an extension to high school, and it really isn't. And I just, I was really grateful that I came here because of the environment. I mean the atmosphere is just, it's like, it really brings you down to earth. So I thought my transition was like, it took a while to get there, but it's good.

Remediation and the related issue of preparation will continue to be a central focus for community colleges. It will also provide the best opportunities for partnerships with K–12 and the four-year institutions.

Transfer, Persistence, and Completion Data

Although intent data are difficult to track in community college, more and more students in two-year colleges aspire to complete their degrees at four-year institutions. Many of the students in the focus groups described plans, often very specific, for getting their bachelor's degree (in some of the focus groups, every student planned to transfer). One challenge to tracking intent is that students do not need to complete the associate degree to transfer to a bachelor's program. There are various agreements between two-year and four-year institutions regarding the transfer of students. In some cases, the articulation agreements are quite formal, offering statewide standards for all public institutions. In others, the partnerships are local, between two institutions, including some private colleges.

In California, the Master Plan for Higher Education charges the University of California (UC) and California State University (CSU) systems with giving preferential admissions to qualified California community college students. Generally a student is considered qualified if he or she has completed fifty-six transferable units with a grade of C or better. There are no specific intersegmental transfer policies. Each community college or district must work out articulation agreements with individual UC and CSU campuses. Some individual community college campuses and districts have developed transfer articulation agreements and specific guaranteed admissions plans with public and private four-year colleges and universities. Both SCC and CRC have multiple articulation agreements with institutions throughout the state.

A major premise of the Maryland public higher education system is that a student should be able to progress from a community college to a four-year college. The University System of Maryland maintains a computerized information system that provides students and advisers information about the transferability of credit from one institution to another in the state. There are articulation agreements with both public and private institutions.

By completing the course work for the associate of arts Oregon transfer degree (AA-OT), students can meet the lower division requirements for an Oregon University System (OUS) institution; however the AA-OT is not required for transfer. Research finds that PCC students who transfer to an OUS institution do as well as "native" students. The dean of students at PCC describes a conversation with a colleague at a four-year institution:

> I got a call at one point from one of the folks from a university . . . . who called actually to complain that we weren't properly orienting our students to life in the senior institutions. I said, "Really? Tell me more about that." "Well, they won't take 'no' for an answer. They don't respect things like faculty office hours and they're haranguing our professors for more out of class contact and tutoring and support." And I said, "You may think we're not preparing students for your environment, but I like what you're telling me."

Persistence and completion data can also be difficult to track. Most community college institutional researchers try to track term-to-term persistence. Persistence rates are generally lower at two-year than four-year colleges. The explanations offered include the different populations (age and background), different financial and family commitments, different levels of preparation, and different intentions. It is clear that students who are required to take remedial or developmental course work are more likely not to persist or complete. Another explanation for low persistence has to do with the path students take through their education.

Community college students do not often follow a linear path through their postsecondary education. In an effort to understand better how students in the Portland metropolitan area were progressing, several postsecondary institutional researchers studied student paths. They found not only that many students' paths were a "swirl"—moving in and out of several institutions—but that the nature of that swirl affected the students' progress and attainment (Bach and others, 2000). Generally, those who followed the traditional linear path were most successful in attainment.

Outreach, Special Programs, and K–16 Links

All of the community colleges in this study have relationships with other educational institutions, from formal articulation agreements to informal relationships between individuals on the campuses. All of the institutions provide opportunities for high school students to get to know the community college. In most cases, high school students can enroll in community college classes on campus (with appropriate permission and skills assessment), take community college credit courses at their high school, and take one of the community college assessments in high school.

Despite these multiple points of connections between systems, there was a very clear message from all of the community college respondents that the K–12 reforms—the standards and assessments in the high schools— had very little or no bearing on what happened at the community colleges. The colleges make clear that they are still going to do their own assessments of students' skills and abilities; they want no part of the myriad reforms going on in K–12. What little was known about the reforms came from having children in the system or from local media. None of the respondents had considered using existing K–12 assessments to measure incoming students' skills in the placement process. In some cases, students also spoke disparagingly of the high school reforms. Several respondents echoed one staff member who said wryly, "We prefer to remain ignorant of that." Another administrator said, "I think it's fair to say that the community colleges are not horribly anxious to get involved in [the state reforms.]. . . . Our students, when they transfer, do as well as native students," implying that the college's system of assessment was suitable for their needs.

One issue that became clear in the course of this research is that although there are few, if any, formal K–16 efforts statewide or systemwide, there are many local partnerships between K–12 and the community colleges—for example:

- At Sacramento City College, the assessment center offers placement tests during the spring at local high schools through the Senior Assessment for College (SAC) program. High school seniors are invited to complete basic skills assessment in math and English on their high school campus, and then are invited to attend an orientation at Sacramento City College. Once they complete the process, which includes some counseling at orientation, they are granted priority registration. Approximately twelve hundred students were assessed at sixteen local high schools in spring 2001.
- Basic college-level English courses are taught regularly by Sacramento City College faculty at a neighboring high school. The college is limited to offering only course work that is above high school level on site at the high school, and at times it is difficult to get enough qualified interested students to enroll in these classes. Still, the English department plans to offer classes at other local high schools in the future.
- Sacramento City College has many innovative programs with four-year colleges and universities. California State University, Sacramento (CSUS) offers students at Sacramento City College the chance to take one free class through the crossover enrollment program. This program allows students who are enrolled in nine units at SCC to enroll in one class at CSUS for no fee other than the cost of books and materials. The University of California (UC), Davis allows students who have fall semester transfer admissions agreements (for guaranteed transfer) on file to take one free class the spring prior to their full-time enrollment at UC Davis.
- At CRC, various faculty members interact regularly with high school teachers, especially in math, English, and ESL. The math faculty met with high school math teachers around the issues of math high school graduation requirements and better articulation of high school math with college math. Math instructors at both levels have also discussed approaches to teaching math with the goal of coordinating services. The English faculty has a long-standing relationship with local high school English teachers. In the past, high school English teachers would suggest course placement for former students now enrolling in English courses at Cosumnes River College. When the college realized this practice was contrary to Title 5 regulations, it was discontinued, but the English instructors continued to meet. Currently, the high school instructors in one of our studied school districts are hired as readers to evaluate and norm the final essay examination for CRC students enrolled in certain English

courses. In addition, many of the CRC courses at the high schools are taught by high school instructors who meet the minimum qualifications to be community college instructors.

• The Montgomery College (MC)/Montgomery County Public Schools (MCPS) Partnership was started as a pilot in three MCPS high schools in 1998 and expanded to include eight high schools in 2000. Partnership activities currently include all MCPS high schools. This joint initiative is a response to the needs identified by the Maryland Higher Education Commission and Maryland Student Outcomes and Achievement Report. Data indicate that too many graduates of Maryland's public schools require developmental courses before they have the skills necessary to succeed in college-level courses.

• There are early entry, tech prep programs, and dual-enrollment programs available for high school students in Maryland.

• PCC and MHCC participate in a coadmission program with Portland State University (PSU). Students are conditionally admitted to PSU for up to eight credit hours per term. Students who take more than these eight credit hours must meet PSU admission requirements.

• Both Oregon colleges in this study have early entry and dual-enrollment programs for high school students, which allow them to earn postsecondary academic and vocational-technical credits. Like other places, the college courses taught in the high schools use high school faculty who have met college requirements for instruction. At MHCC, these programs have created opportunities for high school and college faculty to determine together what it means to be doing college credit–level work. As the coordinator of the program explained:

> And I host meetings at least once a year in each of the various programming areas, so I'll bring all my . . . I'll stick with the same example. [I bring] all my Hospitality, Tourism teachers from all of my high schools . . . and sit them down with my Mt. Hood faculty in Hospitality, Tourism and any program changes are shared and talked about. Any issues, any problems, if students are coming over here and they're not matriculating well, and they're not doing what they need to be doing, then we look at that school's program and, you know, what needs to go on.

• The Mt. Hood Educational Consortium is creating a charter school that will link area high schools to MHCC. The district has provided a grant for a new charter school for five hundred to seven hundred eleventh and twelfth graders. As a district official explained, "The college district and three separate high school districts [will work] as one collaboration to go to a neutral site and deliver instruction."

These various partnerships, formal and informal, are good examples of how K–16 work can occur in practice. It is clear that there are many people who are committed to finding ways to make students' educational experiences a series of successful transitions. While these efforts remain primarily local, they provide models for possible wider-ranging plans. One of the respondents summed up the sentiment that lots of people in this study share:

> Probably just like everybody else, [I believe it should be] a seamless flow for the students. The content, the knowledge they had in high school should be a foundation for them to be successful in college. That transition should be as smooth as possible. They should be able to walk into those [college] classes and feel confident.

Summary of Findings

Below are the key findings of our community college research:

- There is a growing population of younger students on community college campuses. Some are recent high school graduates; many others have not completed high school. The community colleges have responded to this younger student population by increasing linkages with high schools.
- The mission of community college seems to be realized in most of the institutions researched. They were low-cost, convenient alternatives with open access and high standards. The commitment of staff and faculty was clear.
- The growth in the population of younger students has highlighted the lack of preparedness of many high school graduates. Unlike older returning students who tend to be a bit "rusty," some recent high school students may never have learned the material. One California staff member says, "We're seeing students coming out of high school not ready for community college work, and community college students not ready at the CSUs." Additional remediation is necessary, but the lack of academic preparation highlights the need for better alignment of standards and expectations.
- Many students entering community college do not seem to appreciate that they will not be able to do college-level work if they did not achieve

at a certain level in high school. One instructor said, "The transition between high school and the community college is an odd one for many people. For some students, the first year of community college is grade 13; it seems that they are just continuing on—all of their friends are coming here; they are just moving along with the pack. There's not even necessarily for some of the first-year students an acknowledgment per se that this is even college."

• Despite lack of information about myriad placement assessments, students generally seem unfazed about having to take the tests. Although some talked about being unhappy with the results, fairly liberal retake policies allow for some negotiation with advisers and instructors to determine preparedness for specific courses.

• The connection to four-year institutions is becoming more formal in some places. While articulation agreements are common, only co-admit or dual-enrollment arrangements produce specific curricular discussions among members of the campuses.

• Many faculty members talk about the tension of being "in-between." Community colleges can be perceived as both an extension of high school and the start of a path toward a bachelor's degree; they accept anyone who enters but have advanced and restricted entry programs. Most believe strongly in the mission but acknowledge the difficulty of balancing it. One faculty member explained the dilemma: "So, what's the message that we want to send? That you can always come here and because, you know, it's never too late to change your life? Or do we want to say, well, if you want to get here, you need to . . . shape up right now."

• There is a general lack of awareness on the part of administrative staff and faculty of K–12 reform efforts (especially standards and assessments faced by high school students) or even of K–16 efforts in some cases. What is known tends to be a result of general perception (such as media coverage) or of personal connection (perhaps a child in the system). There is little sense of any formal efforts to work between the systems, by using, for example, one of the high school statewide assessments as a placement tool. However, individual partnerships between specific community colleges and high schools seem to be flourishing on many campuses.

• In Oregon, there seems to be less stigma for high school students to go to community colleges than even ten years ago, so there is a population of motivated younger students who are more proactive in their education, applying and registering several months in advance instead of the day before classes.

• In several of the colleges, and especially in Oregon, many students spoke positively about their choice to attend community college, usually highlighting convenience, cost, and smaller class size. They noted that there is no "hand-holding" but that resources are available to those who seek them. One Oregon student said, "I think what high school students need to know is community college isn't just . . . like the last resort. Community college is a good place to take classes and really seriously think about what you're going to do with your life, and even if you're taking classes and don't know what you want to be, it's a really good place to actually find out more about yourself and . . . every credit that you get generally goes towards your major so it's not a waste of time at all."

Areas for Additional Research

The research by Bridge Project researchers in the community colleges addressed only a limited number of the important issues surrounding K–16 reform and the role of the two-year institutions. Several areas should be addressed more deeply (or for the first time) in future research— for example:

- Data are notoriously difficult to collect on community college campuses. More and more colleges have formal institutional research operations and more states are developing or refining statewide data-sharing systems, but the transitory and swirling nature of student enrollment means that some of the data collection problems will continue to be difficult to address.
- Few community colleges have played an active role in state and national K–16 reform efforts. It would appear that the informal and local partnerships with K–12 would make community colleges prime candidates for intersegmental coordination. In addition, since community colleges are the point of entry for most first-generation college students, it is imperative that they be involved in reforms focused on improving access to college success.
- Community colleges are the place where a majority of first-generation students and students of color begin their college education. While research has documented this trend and pointed out some of the issues associated with this growth, there needs to be additional research on how students who are traditionally underrepresented in college fare at community colleges.
- Preparation for college is a growing and persistent issue, particularly for recent high school graduates. There is a need for community colleges to connect more deeply with K–12 education, though progress has been made in this direction.

• Despite a decrease in the skills and abilities of many entering students, aspiration to transfer remains high. Students need to understand not only what it takes to succeed in transfer, but that basic skills in literacy and numeracy are necessary for occupational and vocational programs too.

• Bridge Project research focused heavily on younger community college students—the recent high school graduates. Most community colleges have tried to find ways to support their returning students. It would be helpful to know more about how adults learn about community college opportunities and about what resources are necessary to help them succeed.

• There has been some research on community college faculty, particularly emphasizing the focus on teaching. However, the presence of "freeway fliers," that is, part-time instructors teaching at several institutions concurrently, suggests that many faculty have little time or opportunity to work together to address the growing problems of lack of student preparation and remediation (among other issues).

• There is little research on community college staff. Bridge Project research suggests that many of those who have chosen to work at two-year institutions have strong, personal commitments to community college students (and in many cases are alumni and alumnae of the community colleges).

• The issues surrounding placement are significant, but they are often addressed only in other research with relation to remediation. Our finding that students do not always like the results of their placement, but are not really fazed by it, suggests that we may be making more of the consequences than they are. However, it is worth looking more closely at how that information is communicated to them and how they respond.

• More needs to be known about the signals sent to students about the expectations and requirements for entering community college. While the message that two-year institutions welcome everyone seems to be coming through clearly, there is a far dimmer signal about college-level expectations.

• One of the clear findings in community college research is that a majority of students who enter the two-year program expect to transfer to a four-year program. While the higher aspiration can help influence attainment, a lack of good information about what it takes to transfer, particularly before entering, means that many students are not persisting or completing, despite their aspiration. Good data are needed on persistence and completion.

Community colleges play an important role in the U.S. systems of post-secondary education, yet there is minimal research on the various roles and impacts. Given the growing number of students participating in a community college education (particularly students of color, low-income students, and first-generation college-going students), it seems clear that this population and these institutions warrant greater attention. Bridge Project research has just tapped the rich data available on community colleges and their students. Community colleges' unique position as a gateway in higher education and a link between high schools and four-year institutions makes them not only valuable resources for their communities, but also important subjects of study.

NOTES

1. The Community College Survey of Student Engagement (2002) notes that only one in six undergraduates meets the stereotype of college student, that is, eighteen to twenty-four years old, living on campus, and attending school full time.

2. Most of the literature does not address how those skills are assessed. Bridge Project research focuses on the placement tests and their role in the high school to college transition.

3. Bridge Project researchers found that there are many possible influences and structures that could help address this signal. Rosenbaum (2001) does not seem to ignore this, but his emphasis is on student effort.

4. It is worth noting that for many community college staff, the idea of second chances is integral. Bailey (2002) writes, "Weak high school preparation will also continue to create a role for community colleges, essentially giving students a second chance to prepare for college-level work" (p. 64).

5. Although counselors in some schools can work with students on postsecondary plans, Bridge Project research found that many counselors cannot even begin to address college plans for most of their students, suggesting that counselors may not play the role Rosenbaum (2001) ascribes them.

6. The most common requirements for admission are a high school diploma or general equivalency diploma, or being eighteen years or older. For high school students (and in some cases international students), there are often different procedures.

7. There is some indication that the California State University System is considering using K–12 assessments for college course placement. If it does, perhaps more community colleges will consider that option.

8. The exceptions were students who had access to their local community college assessments while they were still in high school. Some institutions

have partnered to expose students to expectations from the community colleges. Some of these partnerships will be described later.

9. For further information and discussion of remedial or developmental education, see Grubb (1999) and Koski and Levin (1997).

10. One of the challenges of this research is getting accurate counts of remedial courses and enrollments. Given the growing importance, most community colleges now do regular institutional research not only on enrollment, but also on persistence and completion of students in this population.

REFERENCES

American Association of Community Colleges. [http://www.aacc.nche.edu]. 2002.

Bach, S. K., and others. "Student Attendance Patterns and Performance in an Urban Post-Secondary Environment." *Research in Higher Education,* 2000, *41*(3), 315–330.

Bailey, T. "Community Colleges in the 21st Century: Challenges and Opportunities." In *The Knowledge Economy and Postsecondary Education: Report of a Workshop.* Washington, D.C.: National Academies Press, 2002.

Bailey, T., and Averianova, I. "Multiple Missions of Community Colleges: Conflicting or Complementary?" New York: Community College Research Center, 1999.

Choy, S. *Access and Persistence: Findings from 10 Years of Longitudinal Research on Students.* Washington, D.C.: American Council on Education, 2002.

Community College Survey of Student Engagement. *Engaging Community Colleges: A First Look.* Austin, Tex.: Community College Survey of Student Engagement, 2002.

Cooley, R. J. *The American Community College Turns 100: A Look at Its Students, Programs and Prospects.* Princeton, N. J.: Educational Testing Service, 2000.

Grubb, W. N. *Honored But Invisible.* New York: Routledge, 1999.

Kirst, M. W., and Bracco, K. "Bridging the Great Divide." Stanford, Calif.: Bridge Project, 2002.

Koski, W. S., and Levin, H. M. "Accelerating the Education of Remedial Students in Postsecondary Education." Stanford, Calif.: National Center for Postsecondary Improvement, 1997.

Oregon Department of Community Colleges and Workforce Development. "Oregon Community College 2000–2001 Profile." Salem, Ore.: Oregon Department of Community Colleges and Workforce Development, 2001.

Phillippe, K. A., and Michael J. Valiga, M. J. *Faces of the Future: A Portrait of America's Community College Students*. Washington, D.C.: American Association of Community Colleges, 2000.

Rosenbaum, J. "Unrealistic Plans and Misdirected Efforts: Are Community Colleges Getting the Right Message to Students?" New York: Community College Research Center, 1999.

Rosenbaum, J. *Beyond College for All*. New York: Russell Sage Foundation, 2001.

Shults, C. *Remedial Education: Practices and Policies in Community Colleges*. Washington, D.C.: American Association of Community Colleges, 2002.

University of California Office of the President. *Major Features of the California Master Plan for Higher Education*. [http://www.ucop.edu/acadinit/mastplan]. 1999.

Wellman, J. V. *State Policy and Community College-Baccalaureate Transfer*. San Jose, Calif., and Washington, D.C.: National Center for Public Policy and Higher Education and The Institute for Higher Education Policy, 2002.

Young, J. R. "Third of Students Transfer Before Gaining Degrees, Education Dept. Study Finds." *The Chronicle of Higher Education,* Dec. 19, 2002. [http://chronicle.com/daily/2002/12/2002121902n.htm].

9

WHAT HAVE WE LEARNED, AND WHERE DO WE GO NEXT?

Michael W. Kirst
Andrea Venezia
Anthony Lising Antonio

THE PRIOR CHAPTERS presented the major findings from our research in six states. This chapter discusses some major cross-cutting themes, integrates these findings with our conceptual framework from Chapter Two, and proposes some avenues for policy change. While this work is focused on using research to create reforms targeted at improving access to high-quality college preparation for all students, we recognize that change will not come easily. Indeed, one of the major obstacles to change is the public's high approval rating for the current performance of postsecondary education and satisfaction with status quo arrangements (National Center for Postsecondary Improvement, 2001). Colleges and universities earned a respectable B in a 2001 nationwide random sample, while secondary schools were a full grade or more lower. The public's collective sense is that colleges and universities are doing a good job and have little reason to reconsider their policies. Success in college, the public believes, is up to students; as young adults, they are responsible for meeting the academic performance standards set by universities. Only 12 percent of the public would raise entrance standards to postsecondary education (National Center for Postsecondary Improvement, 2001).

Although the public believes that college students are less prepared in 2001 than they were a decade ago, only 11 percent holds postsecondary institutions responsible for the fact that many students who attend college soon after high school, desiring a four-year degree, do not complete that degree. Half of a national sample thinks students are to blame, and another 40 percent think it is a failure of high schools to prepare students for college-level study that causes them to drop out. In short, postsecondary institutions are largely admired, while high schools are often identified as the weak link. Furthermore, very few people see high school and postsecondary education as a continuum in which both institutions play a shared role in preparing students. Hence, few respondents think the presence of K–16 services, such as better counseling or higher education working with public schools, can contribute much to increased student success. Moreover, a majority of the public thinks students of color have about the same opportunities as white, non-Latino students. This public opinion poll concluded, "There is no mandate for change—or even a suggestion of what kind [of higher] change would prove necessary" (National Center for Postsecondary Improvement, 2001, p. 36). The public message seems to be to stay the course.

In the light of this general resistance to change, what can we do to create the changes we think are necessary, as documented by our research? Public opinion surveys indicate that leadership for necessary improvement will not come soon from a bottom-up public opinion push. Rather, we believe that leaders in K–12 higher education and public policy must influence public opinion. In the last section of this chapter, we propose policy alternatives for those leaders to consider. But first we outline the major findings that are common across the six states.

Current Policies Perpetuate the Disjuncture Between K–12 and Postsecondary Education

As this research demonstrates, many K–12 students do not have a good sense of what is expected of them in college, and often K–12 educators do not know how to help students gain an understanding of those expectations. Across the six states, we found a number of state-level policy disjunctures that unwittingly promote and sustain the harmful separation between K–12 and postsecondary education.

Multiple and Confusing Assessments

State K–12 standards have swept across the country with scant participation by postsecondary education institutions or systems. Postsecondary admissions and placement officials overwhelmingly reported that they were unaware of K–12 standards and assessments, and K–12 educators were usually unaware of specific postsecondary admission and placement policies. Postsecondary education officials stressed that K–12 policies are politically volatile and may change quickly; therefore, they were wary about using data from K–12 assessments because they did not want to become tethered to tumultuous, politicized exams. Both K–12 and postsecondary education interviewees consistently stated that no one asked them to participate in devising the others' standards or assessments.

In addition, many K–12 respondents indicated that new testing burdens keep them too busy to attend to other needs, such as helping students prepare for college. Counselors have less time than ever before to be college counselors. Instead, they are often the testing coordinators for their schools, in addition to being in charge of course scheduling, academic advising, career planning, and mental health counseling.

From a student perspective, the resulting testing burden is very high; between high school and college, all students—particularly college-bound students—face a confusing set of exams. In high school, most students take state-mandated assessments, district tests, and exams in individual courses. Students preparing for college often take a number of other tests. These include multiple Advanced Placement (AP) tests, the multiple SAT II Subject Tests, the ACT, and the "pre" SAT and ACT tests, the PSAT and PLAN. Once students are admitted to a college or university, they typically have to take one or more placement exams to determine whether they are ready for college-level work. Departmental faculty members often develop their own placement exams as well. While many colleges use the same tests for admission, each may have its own placement test (or series of tests), and there is little uniformity among these tests. Community colleges do not require entrance examinations, but in most cases, degree-seeking students cannot enroll and register at a community college without taking a placement exam. For example, in 1998 in the southeastern United States, colleges and universities administered nearly 125 combinations of 75 different placement tests (Abraham, 1992). Departmental faculty members often develop their own placement exams as well. Compounding these issues is the finding that many postsecondary institutions were not confident that their placement processes met students' needs, and few conducted research regarding the efficacy of placement processes.

In California, college-bound students can end up taking over twenty tests between high school and the beginning of college, and that does not count district- and classroom-level exams. The former superintendent of Long Beach Unified Schools estimated that throughout their K–12 years, students in that district would take approximately fourteen district tests (Cohn, 2001). Texas has a required statewide postsecondary placement test, the Texas Academic Skills Program (TASP), but many Texas universities also use their own additional placement exams. Also, meeting exit-level standards on tests such as California's High School Exit Exam or for Oregon's Certificate of Initial Mastery does not signify that students are prepared for college-level work. Nor does it signify that students are prepared to score highly on the SAT or ACT, the dominant entrance examinations for college admission.

All of this testing creates a difficult situation for students. On each exam, many of which have different formats, students are tested on different content and on a range of standards. New K–12 standards and assessments increasingly require students to construct meaning, solve problems, and learn cooperatively, in addition to memorizing facts. At the same time, postsecondary education admission and placement policies are mostly based on multiple-choice tests, grades, and other "objective" measures of students' secondary-level performance. College placement exams often measure students' knowledge of a subject according to a standard set by large-scale assessment developers or by professors in university departments.

Differences in the content and format between assessments used at the K–12 exit and college entrance levels point to great variance in expectations regarding what students need to know and be able to do to graduate from high school and enter college. Many of those differences evolved in an era when only a small fraction of the student-age population attended college. But the differences in expectations are outdated, and the current situation can damage student preparation for a large number of students. Different standards can create confusion and can hinder students' abilities to prepare well for tests and college-level work. Many of the community college students studied reported not knowing of the existence of placement tests, and most high school and college students reported feeling overwhelmed by the testing burden. One college student highlighted the proliferation of tests noting, "We just took so many of those tests in high school. . . . We just took them and, you know, didn't really even pay attention to what it was about."

This study found several disjunctures between K–12 and postsecondary assessments. For example, approximately 33 percent of the items on any state high school–level assessment were framed within realistic situations, and as many as 92 percent of the items were contextualized. In contrast, the placement tests and college entrance exams assessed examinees primarily with abstract questions. Also, many states are using writing samples in their

K–12 assessments. In contrast, the ACT and SAT I use multiple-choice formats to test writing attainment, although the College Board is planning to add a writing component to the SAT I (Le, 2002)). Other studies have come to similar conclusions. For example, the Education Trust has shown that placement standards in mathematics often include algebra II, while admission tests rarely exceed algebra I (Education Trust, 1999).

Disconnected Curricula

Most states require that teachers teach, and students learn, a certain set of knowledge and skills by the time students graduate from high school. Usually, state- and school-level graduation plans vary, depending on whether a student intends to attend college. Consequently, many high school graduation standards do not meet the demands required by college entrance or placement requirements, but that is not usually well publicized. Compounding this issue are inequalities regarding who completes an honors program as compared to who completes a general education program. Students of color are overrepresented in nonhonors and general education graduation plans (Oakes, 1985, 1992). After this research was conducted, Texas legislated curricular alignment across the systems; the legislature has specified that the college preparation graduation plan will be the default curriculum for all public high schools by 2005.

Most states have large gaps between the two sets of standards. Table 9.1 illustrates California's curricular disconnects.

A particularly difficult issue arises with regard to community college standards. Community colleges admit any adult who can benefit from the college's courses; this policy seems to suggest to students that there are no curricular standards. That, however, is not the case. One set of community college standards is embodied in placement tests, which are usually set at a higher level than high school graduation requirements. If students are not prepared for college-level work when they enter a community college, they spend more than two years trying to earn a transfer degree. Another set of standards is attached to transfer degrees. In most public systems, in order to transfer to a four-year institution, community college students must complete two years of college-level work. In addition, many technical and medical programs in community colleges are selective and require students to go through an admission process. Because over 80 percent of high school students aspire to attend college and approximately 70 percent do attend some form of postsecondary education program, it makes sense to close the curricular gap between the two levels and provide opportunities for all students to prepare well for college.

Table 9.1. California's High School Graduation and University
Entrance Course Requirements.

	Requirements at Four-Year Public Universities in California	California's Minimum High School Requirements
English	Four years college preparatory classes; regular writing, and reading of classic and modern literature	Three years
Mathematics	Three years college preparatory classes required, four years recommended; elementary and advanced algebra and two- and three-dimensional geometry	Two years
Laboratory science	Two years required, three years recommended; fundamental knowledge in biology, chemistry and physics	Two years (including biological and physical sciences)
History and social science	Two years; U.S. history, American government, world history, cultures, and geography	Three years
Language other than English	Two years required, three years recommended; speaking, understanding, grammar, vocabulary, reading, and composition.	None
Visual and performing arts	One year; dance, drama/theater, music and/or visual art	One year of visual or performing arts or second language (other than English)
Electives	One year; visual and performing arts, history, social science, English, advanced mathematics, laboratory science, and languages other than English	Two years of physical education and other course work as the governing board of the school district may by rule specify

Lack of Longitudinal K–16 Data

Almost no state can answer these questions: What percentage of students who enrolled in an early childhood education program entered college? What percentage graduated from college? Few states can accurately determine their high school dropout rates. Most states are not able to identify students' needs as they move from one education system to another or assess outcomes from K–16 reforms because they do not have K–16 data systems. A state that has made progress in this arena is Texas. It is working to develop a K–16 data system and recently passed legislation to create one common identifying student number that would follow each student from K–12 into postsecondary education. Major hurdles to overcome in creating such a system include student privacy rights and student mobility.

If states are to determine students' needs across the K–16 continuum, they must collect and use longitudinal data from across the K–16 levels— for example, the percentage of the students of color in a state who graduate from high school, attend college, and graduate from college. In Illinois, Texas, Oregon, and Maryland, data from postsecondary institutions were shared with high schools. Of the K–12 educators who knew about those data, none reported using them for any purpose.

Few K–16 Accountability Mechanisms

A related issue is the development of K–16 accountability systems. No state has implemented a comprehensive K–16 accountability system that includes incentives and sanctions for postsecondary institutions and mechanisms that connect the levels. K–12 entities across the country face a variety of accountability measures, but postsecondary education has remained untouched. For example, under No Child Left Behind, schools will be accountable for closing the achievement gap between white, non-Latino students and students of color. Colleges and universities are not similarly held accountable, and their achievement gaps (as measured by college persistence and graduation rates) are rather large and equally problematic (Education Trust, 1999). It is important to note, however, that an accountability requirement that focuses on student persistence in, and graduation from, postsecondary education is difficult because it is hard to determine if students intended to graduate from college, and many students end up attending several colleges (sometimes in several states) before they earn an undergraduate degree.

Insufficient K–16 Governance Mechanisms

In traditional state education systems, no one is held responsible for K–16 reform, and the education sectors often act independently, without regard to each other's reforms or needs. Also, when states do consider policy options to connect K–12 and postsecondary education, community colleges are sometimes not included in the policy discussions. This is problematic considering the large proportion of students, especially students of color, who begin their postsecondary experiences in community colleges.

Few states have K–16 governing boards or councils, and when they do, they often have no legislated authority to develop and implement policies. Maryland and Georgia stand out as states that created P–16 or K–16 councils, comprising representatives from early childhood education through college. Maryland's councils focus more on connecting teacher preparation with the current K–12 standards movement, while Georgia's council has student- and teacher-centered activities. Oregon's Joint Boards Committee focuses primarily on the transfer function between community colleges and universities. In California, K–16 policymaking is divided among approximately a dozen groups, creating a rather fragmented approach (Kirst, 2001). In order to create coherent and aligned policies that span the K–16 continuum, states and regions need to have mechanisms in place to develop and oversee appropriate policies (Venezia, 2002). But these groups must have authority and a mandate to create change; often these groups are only symbolic in nature.

It is important to note, however, that most K–16 reforms are in their infancy. This is a critical time in their development, and well-implemented, systemic, and comprehensive models must still be developed.

With so many confusing expectations—multiple assessments, unaligned curricula—it is little wonder that students are confused about college entrance standards.

Student, Parent, and Educator Understandings— and Misunderstandings—About College

With the disconnections come confusion, poor knowledge about specific policies and practices, and the stratified possession of knowledge—an inequitable distribution of who knows what about college preparation.

Students, their parents, and K–12 educators expressed confusion and frustration when they discussed their understandings of college entrance and placement requirements and related state-level policies. A significant cause of their frustration has to do with recent policy turmoil in K–12 education. The current reforms, especially state assessments, are adding to already hectic environments in which college counseling and related activities too often fall by the wayside. The findings presented here highlight both the similarities and differences between states and regions in terms of individuals' college knowledge—what people knew about how to prepare for college and about college admission and placement policies. For example, some of the states had greater differences by race, and others by socioeconomic status (SES). Where significant, findings have been disaggregated.

The parent surveys did point to some good news. The majority of the parents surveyed had received college preparation information from their high schools, with proportions ranging from 61 percent in California to 68 percent in Georgia. When disaggregated by SES level, disparities emerged, however: fewer than half of economically disadvantaged parents in Illinois, Maryland, and Oregon stated that they had received college information, as compared with two-thirds to three-quarters of their more economically well-off counterparts.

Approximately half of the students wanted to go to the more selective institution in their region, and slightly less than one-quarter aspired to attend the less selective institution or local community college. As would be expected, a greater proportion of the students in honors English classes wanted to attend the more selective institutions than did the nonhonors English students, but nonhonors students did show a substantial interest in the more selective institutions.

Although the majority of students wanted to attend college after high school, they confessed that they have a certain level of apathy about the college preparation process. Many did engage in college preparation activities, however, such as visiting college campuses. Predictably, high-SES and honors students tended to participate more, and eleventh graders were more active in and informed about college preparation activities than were the ninth graders.

Student aspirations differed by type of high school. Students in higher-performing schools in Oregon, Texas, California, and Maryland tended to have higher aspirations in both honors and nonhonors classes. Also, many students across the six states, particularly honors students, looked down on community colleges. In Maryland, when asked about community colleges in the area, students in one focus group replied, "Usually we're making fun of somebody [who goes to community college]." Many high school students described community college as a "last resort" and said, "You don't want to go there." Even so, some students pointed to the financial benefits of attending community college prior to transferring to a four-year school.

Although students intended to attend college, the majority had not been involved in many college preparation activities. For example, only about one-quarter of the students sampled in California, Illinois, Maryland, and Oregon had attended a college night, and one-quarter of the students sampled in California, Georgia, Maryland, and Oregon had taken the ACT or SAT.

The high school students were, however, talking with others about college. The majority of students talked about college with their parents, counselors, and teachers. Our data reflect that almost across the board, a greater proportion of students have spoken with a teacher about college admission policies than with a counselor. Also, honors English students tended to talk with counselors and teachers more than did their nonhonors peers.

The vast majority of the K–12 educators we interviewed expressed a deep concern about students' preparation for college. They cited a number of problems facing them and their students, including inadequate college resources and materials, inequitable college advising by counselors and teachers, inequitable college preparatory curricula, and a general lack of teacher knowledge of college preparation issues. Community college educators reported similar concerns. One community college adviser explained the disjuncture between high school graduation and preparedness for college in this way:

> Well, I think the biggest thing for them is, here, they've graduated from high school but they come and take our placement test and they're still in precollege reading, writing and math and they don't understand that if they stop taking math in their sophomore year that, you know, they don't get it . . . no one. And I think the sad thing is that they say, and I don't know what really happens, I suppose it's different at every school, "No one told me that I should be taking math all the way through." They just weren't warned or they don't remember being warned, so now they're having to pay for it, and that is extremely frustrating. I think it's embarrassing, especially with reading and writing. It's embarrassing to them. And they'll almost start crying because [they'll say], "I graduated [from high school]."

Students' College Knowledge

Throughout the discussions with students, it became apparent that they had many misconceptions about college preparation and attending college. Table 9.2 presents ten myths that students believe about college.

Table 9.2. Ten Myths That Students Believe About College.

Common Student Beliefs	The Truth
I can't afford college.	Students and parents regularly overestimate the cost of college.
I have to be a stellar athlete or student to get financial aid.	Most students receive some form of financial aid.
Meeting high school graduation requirements will prepare me for college.	Adequate preparation for college usually requires a more demanding curriculum than is reflected in minimum requirements for high school graduation, sometimes even if that curriculum is termed "college prep."
Getting into college is the hardest part.	For the majority of students, the hardest part is completing a degree.
Community colleges don't have academic standards.	Students must take placement tests at community colleges in order to qualify for college-level work.
It's better to take easier classes in high school and get better grades.	One of the best predictors of college success is taking rigorous high school classes. Getting good grades in lower-level classes will not prepare students for college-level work.
My senior year in high school doesn't matter.	The classes students take in senior year will often determine the classes they are able to take in college and how well prepared they are for those classes.
I don't have to worry about my grades, or the kind of classes I take, until my sophomore year.	Many colleges look at sophomore year grades, and in order to enroll in college-level courses, students need to prepare well for college. This means taking a well-thought-out series of courses starting no later than the ninth grade.
I can't start thinking about financial aid until I know where I'm going to college.	Students need to file a federal form for aid prior to when most colleges send out their acceptance letters. This applies to students who attend community colleges, too, even though they can apply and enroll in the fall of the year they wish to attend.
I can take whatever classes I want when I get to college.	Most colleges and universities require entering students to take placement exams in core subject areas. Those tests will determine the classes students can take.

KNOWLEDGE OF CURRICULAR REQUIREMENTS. While the majority of students aspired to attend college after high school, their knowledge of specific college preparation issues was sporadic and vague. One measure of student understanding of postsecondary education admission policies is whether they know the course requirements for admission at the two targeted institutions in their region. Both institutions in California required a specific number of completed courses in six subject areas. Institutions in all other states required courses in five subject areas.

Knowledge of this aspect of admission policy was poor in all states. Less than 12 percent of the students knew all the course requirements for the institutions studied. This ranged from 2 percent of ninth graders in California to 14 percent of eleventh graders in Maryland. This is surprising in California, since the state has developed well-publicized public university eligibility requirements (the "a to g" requirements). Students do appear to have considerable partial knowledge of curricular requirements. Slightly more than half of the students knew three or more course requirements.

Students in California showed a more sophisticated knowledge of assessment processes than students in the other states, noting that the English placement exams are essays, while college entrance exams are multiple-choice and vocabulary tests. As part of a collaborative agreement between a studied district and California State University at Sacramento, some students had taken a practice placement exam for the University of California or the California State University System over the Internet. Those students received clearer signals about postsecondary standards than did students in other districts.

Many students believed that nonselective four-year institutions and community colleges do not have academic standards. This is not the case, as is evidenced by the widespread use of placement tests for access to credit-level courses. Across all the states, fewer than half of the sampled students knew the specific placement testing policy for the institutions in the study. This ranged from approximately 16 percent who knew the policies for the University of California at Davis and California State University at Sacramento, to 43 percent who knew the policies for the State University of West Georgia. Logically, a greater proportion of eleventh graders knew the policies than did ninth graders, but fewer than half of both groups knew the policies. Across five of the states, a greater proportion of students knew the required university placement exams of the less selective university than those of the more selective university, although knowledge about specific tests and subject areas was vague and incomplete. Texas was the only state with a statewide postsecondary education placement test; only 11 out of 110 students knew about the TASP and what it tests. Students tended to guess which subject tests were required and assumed there were test requirements when there were none. This overestimation could create additional barriers if students believe there are more hurdles to overcome.

Students in the community college focus groups reported being unaware that on enrollment they were required to take placement tests. Although they were not necessarily concerned or even fazed by these tests, it was clear that these standards conflicted with the perception of community college having low standards. As one community college student said, "So I did my orientation, and they told me something about testing. I was like, what? You have to do a test? So, oh man, I wasn't ready to do this because usually, you know, everybody said, if there's a test, you have to get ready, you have to study, but no one told me about them when I graduated from high school." Part of the reason students seemed relatively unperturbed by the tests, even though they were unaware of them prior to entering college, seems to be a result of the proliferation of tests they took in high school.

Nevertheless, many community college students were very concerned about their preparedness coming out of high school. One student explained, "In my high school, they didn't prepare you for college at all. Well, I had college prep classes, but my school, they're so quick to pass you. . . . When I got here I was so used to bein' in a fly-by [easy] class, I was like, okay, these teachers, they don't care if I come or not. I'm not gonna come. But when I got my transcript, it was a totally different story. I was like, they're not playin' here."

KNOWLEDGE OF TUITION. Across the board, students overestimated the cost of tuition at the sampled institutions.[1] This is consistent with other studies that examined students' tuition estimates (U.S. Department of Education, 2001).

In Texas, while most respondents guessed relatively close to the actual amount, 22 percent estimated the costs as between two to five times more than the actual costs. Across the states, students overestimated the cost of community colleges and the less selective university. Although they still overestimated the cost of the more selective university, in general, students were closer in estimates to the actual costs of these institutions. This pattern makes sense, since the costs of attending a community college or less selective institution are generally lower than the cost of attending a more selective institution. High-SES and honors English students tended to be slightly more accurate in their cost predictions. Overestimating costs can lead students and their parents to believe that they cannot afford college.

KNOWLEDGE OF STATE-LEVEL REFORMS. Student surveys in California, Georgia, Illinois, and Texas—states that had made recent education policy changes, such as the development of K–16 reforms—included questions regarding student knowledge of those policies. In California, since affirmative action practices had just been eliminated in public postsecondary institutions across the state, students were asked if they knew that race was not a factor in undergraduate admissions. In Georgia, the surveys collected data on whether students knew the HOPE Scholarship's program requirements.[2] In Oregon, the surveys gathered data on students' knowledge of the Proficiency-Based Admission Standards System. And in Texas, the surveys asked students to describe the statewide postsecondary education placement exam, the TASP. Across the states, less than 35 percent of students knew the policies, and there were knowledge gaps based on SES and honors status. One nonhonors focus group in Texas stated that the teacher talked about TASP during class; that explains why a greater percentage of nonhonors students knew about the TASP than did the honors students. Without that one class, no nonhonors students would have demonstrated knowledge of the TASP.

Teachers' College Knowledge and Their Role in Helping Students Prepare for College

Counselors often lack the time to provide adequate support for all students, and so teachers, especially honors teachers, often try to fill in where counselors leave off. Yet teachers, by and large, are not nearly as connected to colleges as are counselors. Several teachers stated that students talk with them more frequently about college planning than with counselors; this may be because teachers are more accessible. But teachers usually do not have the training or materials they need to provide students with accurate, up-to-date information. One teacher in Georgia stated, "I wish the counselors did it [college advising] instead of us. It terrifies me, and I think most teachers feel the same way—that we just do not know enough to be doing all this advising with our little hour or hour and a half session and our notebooks and the way they [college requirements] change. I'm always really worried I'll miss something." Other teachers wanted to be more involved but did not have up-to-date admissions and placement information. Sometimes they faced issues regarding territorialism when they trod on counselors' turf. Researchers in Maryland found that "counselors held almost a monopoly on college admission preparation in the four schools." Teachers in Oregon, Illinois, Texas, and Georgia reported that they get college information from graduates who are now in college, student teachers, newspapers, their own college experiences, and their children rather than from institutional sources.

Teachers in every state but California (a state with well-defined and well-publicized eligibility criteria) believed that admission and placement policies in the state and region are too complex. They often thought that the complexity of the policies, coupled with frequent K–12 policy shifts, made it difficult for them to stay abreast of the policies, especially in states where institutions were moving toward becoming more selective.

Most teachers throughout the states were completely uninformed about specific placement policies. A Maryland teacher commented, "I've never seen [a placement test], so all of my presumptions are based on my experience with the placement tests ten years ago at a state college." Another Maryland teacher asked in astonishment, "No kidding—every freshman has to take these tests?"

Inadequate College Resources, Connections with Postsecondary Institutions, and College Admissions Information

Students and educators from every state voiced some level of frustration about the resources, K–16 connections, and college information provided by the studied postsecondary institutions. For example, students in less advantaged schools and classes in Illinois, Oregon, and Texas in particular knew that students in wealthier schools had many more advantages.

Students, teachers, and counselors in Georgia, Illinois, Oregon, and Texas often stated that the information they receive from postsecondary institutions is not helpful; it is usually glossy and superficial. They want information about course-taking patterns students should follow in high school and the types of courses and majors offered at the institutions. One student in Illinois said, "Get rid of the nice, beautiful pictures and give us the actual details—what specific departments have to offer, the curriculum, what classes you'd be taking, what exactly you might be able to test out of . . . the job opportunities available after you graduate from college." Also, students are not always receiving current information. An Illinois high school student stated that her school counselor had recently given her a state university's application form from 1993.

In Texas and Illinois, states that sampled more rural high schools, there was strong networking between rural lower-performing schools and the less selective university in the study. Often teachers at those high schools had attended the less selective institution and encouraged their students to do the same. Many of the educators often believed that their schools were neglected by their local flagship university. In Oregon, the lower-performing high schools had more of a vocational connection with community colleges; the higher-performing high school had more of an academic connection with community colleges and with the four-year institution in the area. In all of the school districts in Illinois, staff members believed that articulation is smoother between high schools and community colleges than between high schools and four-year institutions.

Inequitable College Preparatory Opportunities for All Students

Students' high school course-taking patterns are the main predictor of college success. Taking a high level of mathematics in high school, for example, is crucial. Completing a course beyond algebra II more than doubles the odds that a student who enters a postsecondary education institution will complete a bachelor's degree. Research shows that a high-quality, rigorous high school curriculum is especially important for African American and Latino students in terms of their completing a college degree (Adelman, 1999).

Also, many students in middle- and lower-level high school courses are not reached by higher education outreach efforts or college counseling staff in their high schools. Furthermore, many economically disadvantaged parents often lack experience and information concerning college preparation for their children. While most students need better information about college preparation, students who are in accelerated curricular tracks in high school receive clearer signals about college preparation than do their peers in other tracks.

All the studied schools had curricular tracking processes in place, though many educators did not refer to their systems as being tracked. In Illinois and Texas, nonhonors English students were more likely to go along with the status quo (with their noncollege preparation path). Honors English students challenged the system more and started planning their curricular paths earlier. Some honors English students in Texas reported that starting the college preparation planning process when the schools give them information (often in the junior year) is too late for them, but might be sufficient for nonhonors students.

Many honors students believed that students need to start preparing for college in ninth grade or later but stated that they had started much earlier, often in elementary school. In the Texas sample, although both honors and nonhonors students seemed to believe that they did not have enough information regarding how to prepare well for college, they planned their paths in different ways. On average, the honors students said they enrolled in the most difficult classes in the hopes that they would be able to gain admission to a selective institution. The nonhonors students stated that they assumed that they could gain admission to some postsecondary institution if they graduated from high school, even if they had not taken rigorous courses. Although students perceived correctly that there would be postsecondary opportunities at the community college level, they did not receive the important message that they would still be expected to perform at a level beyond the general education graduation requirements.

Lack of College Counseling for All Students

Counselors face a range of responsibilities that compete for their time, including test administration, course scheduling, providing mental health or other counseling services, addressing disciplinary issues, and supporting students with special needs. This leaves many students with few available people at the school site who are familiar with college transition issues. Many high schools do not have counselors who specialize only on high school to college transitions (McDonough, 2004).

An inequitable distribution of academic counseling and curricular opportunities in high schools can close off opportunities to college for some students and lead to inadequate preparation for others. Many students in all of the states were dissatisfied with the college counseling in their high schools. For example, in Illinois, students reported their guidance counselors had been of little help in providing them with college admissions and placement information. One honors student said, "They just look at what you're required to take to graduate [from] high school. The counselors don't look at what you have to have to get into college."

In Georgia, Illinois, Oregon, and Texas, the general belief among counselors and students was that only the most motivated students talk with their counselors about college and that the conversations are initiated by students. For example, an Illinois student said, "You have to take the initiative. I think that a lot of times, a lot of students just don't talk to their counselors about it, and that's why a lot of us feel like we're not getting all that we need." Many students were concerned that college counseling is only for honors students.

Overall, our study found that many students, their parents, and educators are very confused or misinformed about how students should prepare for college. Students had vague understandings of specific admission and placement policies, and there were many inequalities between students in honors and nonhonors classes in terms of the amount and quality of the college counseling they received. Teachers in honors classes were more involved in college counseling than were teachers of nonhonors courses, and counselors had many responsibilities and could not focus on college preparation issues. Consequently, there was often no one at some of the schools who worked to level the playing field for all students.

The Senior Year Problem

Our Bridge Project data were supplemented by a literature review of senior year data. Students who slack off during their senior year of high school, a condition so common in the United States that it has become known as "senior slump" or "senioritis," are merely playing the hand that has been dealt them. High school seniors who take a break from tough academic courses are reacting rationally to a K–12 system and a college admissions process that provide few incentives for students to work hard during their senior year. However, these seniors fail to realize that slacking off often leaves them less than well prepared for challenging college classes.

In effect, the education standards reform movement has written off the senior year, and so have our colleges and universities. For instance:

○ The K–12 accountability movement has no strategy for assessment in the senior year. Only New York's statewide K–12 assessment includes subject matter from the senior year; most other state assessments extend only to the tenth-grade level. Grade 11 state tests are most useful for postsecondary purposes.

○ The college admissions calendar encourages students to excel in their sophomore and junior years but provides few incentives for them to study hard during their senior year.

○ Since the content of K–12 state tests differs significantly from the content of college placement tests, many students learn only after enrolling in college that their senior year in high school did not prepare them adequately for college-level work.

A Road Map for K–16 Reform

In this section, we offer recommendations for creating a more seamless K–16 system that provides students with clear signals regarding what they need to know and be able to do not only to get into college, but to succeed in college. First, however, we present a conceptual framework that has driven our thinking about better aligning systems and preparing students, especially traditionally underserved students, for postsecondary education.

Connecting Our Data with Our Conceptual Framework

For students who do not have an in-school or outside-of-school resource for college knowledge, aligned policies and programs can send clear signals regarding the knowledge and skills required for successful college preparation. Many other factors affect student preparation for college and college enrollment and completion; however, there are many state policy-level disjunctures that help promote and sustain the separation between K–12 and postsecondary education. These numerous policies and their conflicting natures often cause confusion among students, parents, and K–12 educators. Inadequate policy communication and lack of signals to students and parents are crucial parts of the preparation problem.

A central assumption underlying our conceptual framework is that if these aspects of the education systems were reformed, students, their parents, and K–12 educators would receive more consistent signals about college readiness. While such policymaking would not take away the need to have informed purveyors of college knowledge in high schools, state-level policy alignment and reform would certainly reduce, simplify, and more effectively communicate the amount and kinds of college knowledge students need to make successful postsecondary transitions. Improved data and accountability systems would help highlight problems and needs throughout systems and schools.

The conceptual framework developed for the Bridge Project captures the dynamics of the alignment of the K–12 and postsecondary education systems. The model first assumes that signals and incentives are crucial drivers of students' college knowledge and the actions they take to become prepared for postsecondary academic success. Moreover, clear, consistent, and appropriate signals and incentives create higher student motivation to meet college-level freshman standards (Henry, 2002; Bishop, 2003; Costrell, 1994; Powell, 1996). Given the widespread problem of academic preparation, the focus of the framework is on the 80 percent of high school graduates who aspire to postsecondary education institutions that are minimally selective or nonselective in their admissions. Many of these prospective students attend community colleges. The framework relies on several different concepts and partial theories that are integrated into a flow model (see Figure 9.1, reprinted from Chapter One).

Most secondary students encounter situations A or C in the framework. That is, they enter an education system within a high-stakes accountability environment and a state education policy that is primarily driven by either the K–12 or higher education system. Unilateral signals and incentives are sent out without regard to the other sector, resulting in misinformation

Figure 9.1. Bridge Project Conceptual Framework.

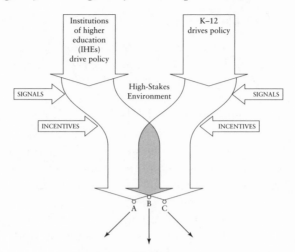

+ positive influence
− negative influence

	A Policy driven by IHEs in isolation from K–12	B Policy driven by combined efforts between IHEs and K–12	C Policy driven by K–12 in isolation from IHEs
K–12 stakeholders' understandings of K–16 policies and college knowledge	+ For elite pool of students − For more students − For postsecondary education since it has less information on K–12 students	+ For more students + For mutual reinforcement of understandings and expectations	− For more students enrolling in post-secondary − For K–12 since less information on postsecondary education policies
K–12 stakeholders' aspirations and actions	− Sends confusing signals that might have a negative impact on students' aspirations	+ For mutually reinforced signals that could have a positive impact on students' post-secondary aspirations	− Sends confusing signals that might have a negative impact on high school students' aspirations
Student mastery of college preparatory content and skills	+ For elite pool of students, who do not rely on high school information	+ For more students completing postsecondary education	− For more students not aspiring and completing post-secondary education

College Preparation and Qualification	+ For elite pool of students	+ For all students	− For most students
Postsecondary Success • Freshman placement and remediation • Dropout rate • Graduation rate	− Those not in elite pool face increased remediation and dropout rates and decreased graduation rates	+ Decreased remediation and dropout rate and increased graduation rate for more students	− Increased post-secondary remedia-tion and dropout rate and decreased graduation rate for more students

among students and K–12 teachers and administrators, such as gross overestimation of tuition costs and a lack of knowledge of placement and admissions policies at local colleges and universities. These unclear and mixed signals fail to develop adequate college knowledge concerning access and sufficient preparation to succeed in postsecondary education. "Elite" students—those already familiar with higher education through their family—are minimally affected by policy environments driven by either sector because of their familiarity with higher education and because they are less reliant on high schools for guidance and information. The majority of students, however, are likely to have little access to college knowledge, misunderstand higher education policies, and be unaware of their needs for academic preparation. The result is poor preparation, lowered aspirations, increased remediation, and lower college graduation rates.

It is not difficult to believe that the reality for most students resides in paths A or C. This country's diverse postsecondary institutions, ranging from community colleges to huge universities, have different standards, functions, and goals, so they see no collective need to send coherent messages to students. For example, community colleges focus their public messages on access rather than standards for readiness to complete credit-level work. Some state flagship universities are very selective and assume their selection processes will result in students who are adequately prepared. Private institutions are as varied as the public ones in their missions and admissions selectivity. Some private four-year postsecondary institutions have open enrollment to any high school graduate. This diversity results in many different placement exams that students should ideally be familiar with as they prepare themselves for college-level work.

Once students gain entry to a postsecondary institution (and most do), the lack of adequate preparation becomes a major roadblock to finishing their degree (Adelman, 1999). They gain entry by meeting certain criteria like high school graduation, being over age eighteen, or taking some specific academic courses beyond minimum graduation requirements. These criteria, however, are often inadequate for academic success beyond high school.[3] Moreover, the most disadvantaged students suffer the most from inadequate signals about preparation, because many disadvantaged students attend high schools that do not have an adequate college-going culture or the resources to provide strong postsecondary academic preparation. For example, if students want to place into college-level mathematics, it is not sufficient for high schools to offer only two or three years of college preparatory mathematics.

Early, persistent, and coherent signals from postsecondary education and K–12 in combination can improve students' academic preparation and success, as posited in column B. Here the systems coordinate, align, and connect their policies affecting postsecondary transitions. Many students use teachers as one of their primary information sources about postsecondary education, but colleges and universities do little to help teachers learn about admission and placement standards. In a coordinated K–16 education system, admission and placement standards would be related to high school standards, teacher education programs would include general information about college admission and placement, and teachers would be knowledgeable of the relationship between admission requirements and their school's graduation requirements. High school students, as they prepare themselves for high school exit exams, would also be aware of the content and format of admission and placement tests, aiding in their preparation for them. Admission and placement tests would be offered in high schools as diagnostic measures.

If state-level postsecondary and K–12 standards and assessments were on a continuum—if students knew what was expected of them when they make the transition from one system to another and they received the proper academic preparation—we propose that problems such as remediation and poor graduation rates would decrease.

How States, Regions, and the Federal Government Can Create a More Coherent K–16 System

Educators and policymakers should begin by asking themselves some fundamental questions:

- Are the K–12 academic content standards similar or dissimilar to the academic content in first-year courses at the college and university level?
- Does your state K–12 assessment ask students to know and do the same things that are required by your state's public colleges and universities for admission and placement?
- Does your state have a statewide postsecondary education placement examination? If not, how do individual colleges' tests relate to each other or the content of the state's K–12 assessment? How can your state consistently assess its needs regarding student remediation?
- Do your schools have a sufficient number of counselors whose main role is to advise students about college options?
- Do all students have early, repeated access to college preparation information?

○ Do your colleges and universities have outreach programs that connect them with local schools and districts? Are these outreach programs coordinated with national, state, and nonprofit outreach programs? Are these outreach programs evaluated using comparison groups of students who did not participate in outreach?

○ Are there course articulation agreements between your state's public universities, community colleges, and high schools?

○ Can your state agencies (K–12 and postsecondary) link their databases in order to assess needs throughout the K–16 continuum?

> Can policymakers and researchers tell whether there are inequalities in terms of who enters and graduates from college?

> Can they address issues of college preparation by tracking student success in higher education by district or by school?

> Can your state measure persistence rates among different types of students and determine which students drop out of college and when they do so?

○ Does your statewide accountability system hold high schools accountable for offering college preparatory work, including AP courses? Does it hold postsecondary education institutions accountable for graduating its students?[4]

○ Is there a stable or even permanent entity or mechanism that will allow K–12 and postsecondary education stakeholders to work together and overcome fragmentation concerning policy alignment, faculty interaction, and K–12 information systems?

The answers to these questions will determine the extent to which there are transitional breakdowns in the current system. These questions are congruent with our conceptual framework, suggesting that better student results are achieved when higher education and K–12 are sending similar reinforcing signals as early as middle school. Moreover, educators and policymakers should conduct a K–16 policy audit in order to understand the scope and alignment of their current policies.

These questions should be deliberated through a long-term state and regional institutional structure that overcomes the traditional separation of education governance into a K–12 governing board and one or more higher education boards. State funds are needed to allow activities, deliberation, and projects that cut across K–16 boundaries. K–16 education policymakers and practitioners from formerly separate higher and K–12 departments can use the questions and issues raised above to work together for policies and common goals. This K–16 process must involve educators as well as administrators and policymakers, so that the divide between high school teachers and postsecondary faculty can be broken down. In large states, implementation could be enhanced if a regional basis is used, as in Georgia. But these K–16 deliberative bodies usually must go back to their respective institutions for approval of any major policy change, so they are only a partial solution.

Recommendations for State-Level Policy Changes

We suggest that states develop a new accountability report card that spans secondary and postsecondary education to better inform the public about needed changes in K–16 policy. Postsecondary education needs incentives to increase student access and completion rates. Financial formulas should be devised to penalize low performance. Moreover, K–12 responsibility and accountability ends after a student is accepted to postsecondary education. There is no K–16 accountability framework that provides adequate incentives. More specifically, our research found that the following three areas are the most promising for immediate reform:

• Provide all students, their parents, and educators with accurate, high-quality information about, and access to, courses that will help prepare students for college-level standards.

• Shift media, policy, and research attention to include broad access colleges and universities attended by the vast majority of students (approximately 80 percent). Unfortunately, media and much public policy attention is focused on those highly selective colleges and universities where persistence and completion rates are not problematic (Adelman, 2001). Broad access colleges need the financial and policy attention of federal, state, and other leaders. Increasing the rates of student success at these colleges is a sound public investment because it can have a tremendous impact on the civic and economic well-being of each state by improving people's economic security, increasing their civic participation, and increasing college completion rates for economically disadvantaged students and students of color.

• Expand the focus of local, state, and federal programs from access to college to include access to success in college. For the past fifty years, it has made sense for the United States to concentrate its postsecondary education policies on opening the doors to college, and by and large these policies have had a major positive impact. For instance, the percentage of the young population enrolling in college increased from 50 percent in 1980 to approximately 70 percent in 2000. Nevertheless, there remain significant gaps in enrollment and completion among ethnic groups and between low- and high-income families. Also, college access varies greatly depending on where students live and the level of their parents' education. These gaps suggest that the nation's work, as effective as it has been, is not complete. Access to entrance to college, however, is only half the picture. The real issue is, Access to what? True college opportunity includes having a real chance to succeed, which clearly is not happening often, as indicated by the fact that the percentage of four-year graduates among the U.S. adult population has barely increased since 1980, despite increasing attendance rates (Barton, 2002). We found large differences in college knowledge and in understanding of what it takes to succeed in college among students within schools by academic tracks and between schools by SES. It is time to expand policy attention to emphasize not just access to college but also access to success in college. High school course content, academic counseling, college outreach, and other programming needs to reflect this so that students are clear about what it takes to succeed in college, including community college.

How can we achieve these ends? For a start, college-level stakeholders must be brought to the table when K–12 standards are developed. Also, K–12 educators must be engaged as postsecondary education admission and placement policies are under review. Reforms across the two education systems will be difficult, if not impossible, to implement without meaningful communication and policymaking between the levels.

There are several other important steps that states, K–12 schools and districts, postsecondary institutions and systems, and the federal government can take to improve the transition from high school to college for all students:

• Ensure that college and universities state and publicize their academic standards so that students, their parents, and educators have accurate college preparation information. Since almost all students are planning to attend college, all students should receive college preparation information and resources. Policy communication and signaling is key; not enough attention is paid to communicating clearly up and down the systems. This effort must go beyond targeted outreach and fragmented categorical programs to universal programs for all students. In addition, states should disseminate materials in languages other than English, depending on the language groups in their states.

• Examine the relationship between the content of postsecondary education placement exams and K–12 exit-level standards and assessments to determine if more compatibility is necessary and possible.

K–12 standards and assessments that are aligned with postsecondary education standards and assessments can provide clear signals and incentives if they are high-quality standards and assessments. Assessments should be diagnostic in nature, and the results should include performance levels that indicate to students that their scores meet or exceed the level for college preparation and placement without remediation. Appropriate K–12 assessments could be used as an admission and placement factor by public postsecondary education institutions, although caution must be taken to ensure that more than one measure of student preparation is used and that the stakes attached to K–12 assessments are not too high for students.

• Review postsecondary education placement exams for reliability, validity, efficacy, and the extent to which they promote teaching for understanding. This includes scrutiny of assessments developed by individual campuses, departments, and faculty. Data need to be maintained regarding the efficacy of placement procedures. Consider using K–12 assessment data for postsecondary course placement purposes.

• Allow students to take placement exams in high school so that they can prepare academically for college and understand college-level expectations. These assessments should be diagnostic so that students, their parents, and teachers know how to improve students' preparation for college.

• Reconceptualize the senior year to better prepare the 70 percent of high school students who will be moving directly into postsecondary education. This means improving academic preparation for college placement exams and college-level course work, with emphasis on the skills and knowledge that are components of a general or liberal arts education. Students should understand that access to higher education—college admission—is only one aspect of their senior year, not the sole goal. The U.S. Department of Education found that 42 percent of entering freshmen at public two-year colleges and 20 percent of entering freshmen at four-year public institutions enrolled in at least one remedial course in Fall 2000. Students are spending more time in remedial courses (U.S. Department of Education, 2003). The senior year is the last chance to become academically prepared for college. Moreover, high schools should link their senior year curriculum to the general education requirements for the first year of college or university, or the technical requirements of a community college vocational certificate. The federal government's Twelfth Grade National Assessment of Educational Progress (NAEP) test should include the skills and knowledge to succeed in postsecondary education. A NAEP performance level for senior year should be set at a level above remediation.

- Sequence undergraduate general education requirements so that appropriate high school senior year courses are linked to postsecondary general education courses (Venezia, Kirst, and Antonio, 2003).
- Expand successful blended institutions. This includes dual-enrollment opportunities, early college high school, and middle college high school. These programs and schools should include all students, not just traditionally college-bound students. Many students are not comfortable socially or emotionally in high school environments, while others complete their schools' highest-level courses as sophomores and juniors and have trouble finding appropriate courses as seniors.
- Collect and connect data from all education sectors. This means that states and regions should create common identifier numbers for students and track teachers during preparation and professional development programs. These systems can include data on the relationship between student course-taking patterns in high school and the need for remedial work, and longitudinal trends on what happens to students after they complete remedial-level course work. They also should be tied to a K–16 accountability system. Postsecondary institutions and K–12 schools need assistance in learning how to use data to inform curricular and instruction policies and practices.

Recommendations for Change in College Admissions and Placement Policies

Colleges and universities should make sure that recommended courses for high school students provide adequate preparation. The Trends in International Mathematics and Science Study (TIMSS) of course-taking patterns for math, physics, chemistry, and biology found that college preparatory students had seventy patterns, and no pattern was taken by more than 15 percent of the students.

The most common course pattern for general education students includes no chemistry or physics. Only a fourth of the general education students took biology and algebra II. TIMSS found a "bewildering array" of course titles for eighth-grade mathematics (Schmidt, 2002). This may be a special problem for community colleges.

Colleges and high schools should cooperate in setting formulas for how the high schools are to calculate GPAs and class rankings. (Currently, high schools in some states can elect to include or exclude grades from nonacademic courses in their computations.) Colleges should accord appropriate weight for honors and AP courses, and performance in senior-year academic courses should be an important component in computing class rank. Colleges should set explicit standards for senior year performance in all courses and withdraw admissions offers if those standards are not met. Students should be required to take a specific number of academic credits during each semester of their senior year. Since students often forget math taken during their high school junior year, colleges that require math proficiency for graduation should include a senior year math course in their admissions requirements. (Many states require only two years of math for high school graduation.)

The best way to assess writing is to review students' written work. Colleges should require all applicants to take a test that requires a writing sample. Until 2005, the SAT I and ACT will be multiple-choice tests with no writing sample; even the SAT II provides only twenty minutes for writing (the other forty minutes test grammar and mechanics). Some statewide K–12 assessments have a writing sample that could be incorporated into the college admissions or placement process. The California State University System will do this for its placement process starting in 2004.

Postsecondary placement exams need to be rethought in many states. We recommend that:

• If K–12 assessments are designed with high enough standards, colleges and universities should review their freshman placement exams to ensure congruence with state K–12 assessments and standards. This will help secondary school students get a clear idea from state K–12 tests about their possible postsecondary academic deficiencies that should be addressed in high school. Universities and colleges could set a specific performance level on high-level state K–12 tests such that if students met the proficiency level, they would not need to take remedial-level course work. However, colleges and universities first need to define their standards in the first year to see how they match with secondary school standards, assessments, and expectations.

• Colleges should include information about freshman placement exams in the admissions information packet sent to applicants, so students can plan their secondary programs in order to meet placement standards.

• Colleges should widely publicize reports about remediation and the freshman performance of students from specific high schools. Such reports are routinely sent to high schools and central district offices in some states, but they should also be publicized by the mass media and the results publicly reviewed by local school boards.

• Placement exams should be reviewed for their validity and reliability. Many placement exams are devised by departmental committees with no psychometric review.

- Postsecondary institutions need to inform secondary school teachers about standards and content for placement tests.

Rethinking Secondary and Postsecondary Curriculum

More fundamental curricular reform could be stimulated by reconceptualizing general education as a curriculum that spans the last two years of high school and the first two years of college. A common problem facing those involved in initiatives to align standards of college admission and placement with performance-based K–12 standards is that the crucial years of school-to-college transition, grades 11 through 14, are devoid of clear and sequential standards for student learning (Wellman and Erlich, 2003). Most state standards for high school graduation are anchored in tenth-grade-level (or lower) content. Some students spend the first two years of college fulfilling a smorgasbord of general education requirements and may not confront real standards until they begin work in their majors. In order for secondary schools to improve student preparation, postsecondary institutions must help them by rethinking their standards, curriculum, incentives, communication strategies, and K–16 faculty relations, and focus in the first year. Retention should be the overwhelming focus of first-year college assessments and go beyond quantitative data to include diagnosis of learning problems. Some four-year universities invest fewer resources in their first year than in the junior and senior years.

States could extend their K–12 standards into years 13 and 14 and also look downward from "grades" 14 to 10. This alignment of grades 10 through 14 standards would engender stiff resistance from higher education, but at least discussing it might help reconceptualize the connection between general education and the last two years of high school. Vocational education has used technical preparation curriculum designs to provide integrated grades 11 through 14 sequences with community colleges (Hershey and others, 1998). This promising development, however, has lost some of its federal earmarked funds and seems to be losing some of its momentum. Few postsecondary institutions collect data at the end of the student's first year, and the data that are collected rarely influence campus policy decisions.[5] Another idea is to design accountability systems for both K–12 and higher education to include outcomes that each system cannot possible deliver on it own. Postsecondary education could be held accountable for decreasing the number of freshmen requiring remediation. Haycock (2001) points out that if postsecondary mathematics departments taught only the mathematics not also taught in high school, 80 percent of the credit hours of postsecondary mathematics departments would be lost. There are powerful disincentives in terms of budgets and students for postsecondary mathematics departments to reduce remediation.

Accreditation for higher education institutions could stress course completion and overall student persistence more than it does now. Another option is an incentive to get postsecondary institutions to work hard to ensure that students persist: states could investigate the feasibility and efficacy of paying institutions more per student as students progress successfully through their college education (for example, $10,000 for first-year students, $12,000 for sophomores, and so forth).

One promising way to enhance K–16 alignment is through more dual-enrollment programs. Postsecondary education has been working with high schools to jointly develop programs to allow students who are ready for college-level work to undertake it. But these programs are often only for "high-achieving" students or focus on physical education and nonacademic courses. Dual enrollment needs to be open to all students who can profit from it and be better linked to general education in grades 11 through 14. Dual enrollment has particular promise for overcoming the high school senior slump, because many high school students are ready to explore academic courses at the next level. In a comprehensive study of college-level learning in high school, Johnstone and Del Genio (2000) found that a high school curriculum substantially laced with college-level courses is more rigorous and geared for postsecondary education. It can also lower the credits and costs required for a college degree. But they also caution:

> The enormous *variability* in the missions, governance, and perceived quality of institutions of higher education America, coupled with the precious principles of academic freedom and institutional autonomy, mean that college-level learning from high school will continue to be treated very differently by different institutions. . . . Some institutions . . . will resist these courses substituting for *their* courses, whether in a common general education core or the introductory courses to certain disciplinary majors . . . [or] on self-interested grounds of preserving enrollments, net tuition revenue, and jobs [p. 44].

A New Federal Role

The federal role emphasizes access through financial aid (Pell grants), outreach, and support for particular types of postsecondary institutions (historically black colleges and universities and Native American colleges and universities). Few federal resources are devoted to preparation and degree or program completion. For example, No Child Left Behind is a

K–8 program with no high school reform strategy. The only mandate is for local education agencies to give a test for grades 10 through 12, but none of the federal accountability requirements based on test score increases apply to high school. GEAR UP is the only federal program that extends students' preparation into the eighth grade, but it affects a small proportion of students. In sum, the federal approach to postsecondary equity has been need-based financial aid, without a concomitant strategy for improving student preparation, retention, and completion.

We recommend that renewal of the higher education and vocational education acts include added federal roles for K–16. The research in this book suggests a need for a fundamental overhaul in the relationship of and policy between K–12 and postsecondary education. The federal government can play a crucial catalytic role through stimulating grants to states that are willing to move forward. For example, David Conley of the University of Oregon has suggested (personal communication, 1996) that federal grants could be made on a competitive basis to public higher education systems, private postsecondary institutions, and public K–12 state systems for activities at the secondary and postsecondary levels. These activities could include collaborative discussions and mandatory examination of alignment across the education segments and joint development activities that enable students to make a successful transition from secondary to postsecondary education.

Each project would require formal participation from the department of education, the state higher education system, campuses from each tier in the state higher education system, and presidents or chancellors of participating public and private institutions. The project would be focused on increasing student completion rates, articulation of standards and assessments for the purpose of enabling improved matriculation, improved student retention rates, better placement procedures, and improved high school programs of college preparation and college entry-level courses.

Participating states would be required to develop a plan demonstrating how higher education would communicate its expectations more directly to high schools with large concentrations of students from underrepresented groups. State education departments would be required to develop training programs for staff at such schools to enable them to teach to these expectations. Higher education institutions would be required to have programs that supported students from underrepresented groups during the freshman year.

The federal government (possibly in conjunction with foundation support) could fund pilot projects that provide "college navigators" in underserved communities. Navigators would provide services that expensive college counselors provide for more financially affluent families. Policy signals and related information are not enough; people need individualized help. Underrepresented students need to know how to make a successful transition from high school to college, and they often do not have college counselors at their high schools. Navigators would be employed by community organizations that serve youth. This could help create pathways, information, and support for students who are not in AP, International Baccalaureate, or other related programs, who are not likely to get help at school, whose parents might not have attended college, and who might have problems persisting in college.

We also suggest that the federal government provide technical support to states by establishing voluntary data collection standards. The inability to obtain complete and current data on issues that span the education sectors (such as remediation, student success in college after the completion of a precollege outreach program, degree or certificate completion rates, the efficacy of placement procedures, and student persistence in postsecondary education) was evident throughout our study. Statewide data are spotty, and publicly available institutional data are rare. As a condition for receiving financial aid, the federal government could require institutions to report those data annually. Finally, we recommend that the federal government set a college readiness performance standard for its grade 12 NAEP test.

Concluding Thoughts

Some governors are already in the forefront, but the fear of state-level control of higher education limits their capacity for change and increased K–16 accountability. A broad coalition is needed that includes university and college staff, trustees, civil rights groups, teachers' unions, and higher education faculty unions. Crucial K–16 linkage groups like College Board must refine their message to encompass the changes we recommend here. A national policy issue network similar to the one developed in the 1970s by the Ford Foundation for school finance could be part of the solution (Kirst, Meister, and Rowley, 1984). Such a network needs to include many components such as students, faculty, administrators, advocacy groups, policy analysts, and politicians. It can use the accountability information system we recommend.

K–16 reform and students' successful completion of postsecondary education needs to be part of the social charter of the American people that emphasizes the public purposes of postsecondary education rather than just the private benefits from higher education. In return for financial support of postsecondary education, the public has expected postsecondary institutions to provide widespread and affordable access and academic results that enhance an educated citizenry, assist the disadvantaged, and contribute to economic development. But the social charter is a two-way street where postsecondary education expects societal support for academic values such as freedom of inquiry (Gumport, 2001). The public, however, has every right to expect a drastic improvement in postsecondary education completion rates. We believe that the recommendations we have outlined will help improve student opportunities and postsecondary outcomes and will buttress the social charter. We believe these are crucial steps to support all students in their efforts to fulfill their post–high school aspirations.

NOTES

1. The Texas surveys asked students to estimate the cost of tuition, fees, room, board, and books per year at the studied institutions. The other state surveys asked students to estimate the cost of tuition only per year at the studied institutions.

2. At public colleges, the HOPE Scholarship provides full tuition, approved mandatory fees, and a $150 per semester book allowance. For more information, see www.gsfc.org/HOPE/. High school students must maintain a 3.0 or better GPA to get aid. A recent statewide survey in Georgia found that the HOPE Scholarship is an effective signal for the majority of parents and students. See Henry and Rubenstein (2002).

3. We do not include analysis of inadequate finances as an issue in noncompletion, but it has a significant impact.

4. One promising practice is for all students to be enrolled in a college preparation curriculum, allowing them to be removed only by a parental request.

5. See the research of the Policy Center on the First Year of College, Brevard College, North Carolina, www.brevard.edu (go to FYI Survey).

REFERENCES

Abraham, A. A., Jr. *College Remedial Studies: Institutional Practices in the SREB States.* Atlanta, Ga.: Southern Regional Education Board, 1992.

Adelman, C. *Answers in the Tool Box: Academic Intensity, Attendance Patterns and Bachelor's Degree Attainment.* Washington D.C.: U.S. Department of Education, Office of Educational Research and Improvement, 1999.

Adelman, C. "Putting on the Glitz: How Tales from a Few Elite Institutions Form America's Impressions About Higher Education." *Connection: New England's Journal of Higher Education and Economic Development,* 2001, *15*(3), 24–30.

Barton, P. *The Closing of the Education Frontier.* Princeton, N.J.: Educational Testing Service, 2002.

Bishop, J. H. "Incentives for Learning: Why American High School Students Compare So Poorly to Their Counterparts Overseas." *Research in Labor Economics,* 1990, *11*, 17–51.

Bishop, J. H., and others. "Nerds and Freaks: A Theory of Student Culture and Norms." In D. Ravitch (ed.), *Brookings Papers in Education Policy.* Washington, D.C.: Brookings Institute, 2003.

Cohn, C. "Tests and More Tests: The Road Ahead for Student Assessment." Paper presented at EdSource's Annual Forum on California Schools, San Ramon, Calif., Apr. 6, 2001.

Conley, D. T. "Where's Waldo: The Conspicuous Absence of Higher Education from School Reform and One State's Response." *Phi Delta Kappan,* 1996, *78*(4), 309–315.

Education Trust. "Ticket to Nowhere. The Gap Between Leaving High School and Entering College and High Performance Jobs." *Thinking K–16,* 1999, *3*(2). [http://www2.edtrust.org/EdTrust/Product+Catalog/Reports+and+Publications.htm#ticket].

Costrell, R. M. "A Simple Model of Educational Standards." American Economic Review, 1994, 956–971.

Gumport, P. "Built to Serve: The Enduring Legacy of Public Higher Education." In P. Altbach and others (eds.), *In Defense of American Higher Education.* Baltimore: Johns Hopkins University Press, 2001.

Haycock, K. *Why Is K–16 Collaboration Essential to Education Equity?* Washington, D.C.: EdTrust, 2001.

Henry, C. T., and Rubenstein, R. "Paying for Grades." *Journal of Policy Analysis and Management,* 2002, *21*(1).

Hershey A., and others. *Focus for the Future: The Final Report of the National Technical Preparation Education.* Princeton, N.J.: Mathematica Policy Research, 1998.

Johnstone, D. B., and Del Genio, B. *College-Level Learning in High School: Purposes, Policies, and Practical Implications.* New York: Graduate School of Education, University of Buffalo, 2000.

Kirst, M. *Overcoming the High School Senior Slump: New Education Policies.* San Jose, Calif.: Institute for Educational Leadership and the National

Center for Public Policy and Higher Education, 2001. [http://bridgeproject. stanford.edu].

Kirst, M. W., Meister, G., and Rowley, S. "Policy Issue Networks." *Policy Studies Journal,* 1984, *13*(2), 247–264.

Le, V. "Alignment Among Secondary and Post-Secondary Assessments in Five Case Study States." Santa Monica, Calif.: RAND, Feb. 2002.

McDonough, P. "Counseling Matters: Knowledge, Assistance, and Organizational Commitment in College Preparation." In W. J. Tierney (ed.), *Nine Propositions Relating to the Effectiveness of College Preparation Programs.* New York: State University of New York Press, 2004.

National Center for Postsecondary Improvement. "The Public," *Change,* Sept. 2001, *33*(5), 23–38.

Oakes, J. *Keeping Track: How Schools Structure Inequality.* New Haven, Conn.: Yale University Press, 1985.

Oakes, J. "Can Tracking Research Inform Practice? Technical, Normative and Political Considerations." *Educational Researcher,* May 1992, pp. 12–21.

Powell, A. G. "Motivating Students to Learn: An American Dilemma." In S. H. Fuhrman and J. A. O'Day (eds.), Rewards and Reform: Creating Educational Incentives That Work. San Francisco: Jossey-Bass, 1996.

Schmidt, W. H. "Too Little, Too Late: American High Schools in an International Context." In D. Ravitch (ed.), *Education Policy: 2002.* Washington, D.C.: Brookings, 2002.

U.S. Department of Education. *The Condition of Education.* Washington, D.C.: National Center for Education Statistics, 2001.

U.S. Department of Education. *Remedial Education at Degree-Granting Postsecondary Institutions in Fall 2000.* Washington, D.C.: National Center for Education Statistics, 2003.

Venezia, A. "A Student-Centered P–16 Accountability Model." Briefing paper for the National Forum on Accountability sponsored by the Education Commission of the States and the Aspen Institute's Program on Education, Denver, Colo., May 2002.

Venezia, A., Kirst, M., and Anthony, A. *Betraying the College Dream: How Disconnected K–12 and Postsecondary Education Systems Undermine Student Aspirations.* Stanford, Calif.: Stanford Institute for Higher Education Research, 2003.

Wellman, J., and Erlich, T. *How the Student Credit Hour Shapes Higher Education.* New Directions for Higher Education, No. 122. San Francisco: Jossey-Bass, 2003.

APPENDIX A: RESEARCH DESIGN AND METHODOLOGY

THIS BOOK IS the result of six years of field research, literature review, and data analysis. The Bridge Project examined (1) the relationships between K–12 and postsecondary education as they relate to student transitions from secondary to postsecondary education and (2) high school student, parent, and educator understandings of policies at the high school graduation and college entrance levels.

The project looked at one region per state; the study states were California, Georgia, Illinois, Maryland, Oregon, and Texas. There are strong regional issues at play here. For example, the greater Sacramento, California, metropolitan region, a site where this research was conducted, is very different from an urban area like Los Angeles or a rural area such as the Central Valley. Likewise, Northern Illinois is very different from downstate Illinois. This is an issue in every state in this project. Also, since this project encompassed more schools that are categorized as middle to higher achieving than it did very low achieving, chances are that these problems are worse elsewhere.

The field research was divided into two phases. In the first phase of the project, researchers sought to answer the following research questions: (1) What are the postsecondary education admission and placement policies within the six states? and (2) To what extent are policies, procedures, practices, and expectations compatible across state education institutions? By compatibility, researchers sought to understand whether, for example, state K–12 high school graduation standards ask students to have the same knowledge and skills as do the postsecondary admission and placement standards of the studied institutions in that state.

Project researchers interviewed approximately 165 people in state education agencies, state-level K–16 committees or councils, twelve universities, and six community colleges. One region per state and two universities per region were in the project. One "more selective" and one "less selective" institution were included per region. Since funding was more limited for the community college part of the study, three states were examined (California, Oregon, and Maryland) and a comprehensive literature review conducted. Researchers selected two community colleges (per region, in three of the states) in the same feeder areas as the studied universities and high schools. Along with interviews with approximately fifteen administrators and faculty per institution, two student focus groups were conducted on each of the six community college campuses. When possible, recent high school graduates were included in the focus groups to examine the link between their high school and community college experiences. Their responses are provided here when appropriate.

In addition, RAND researchers conducted content analyses of high school exit-level and college entrance-level assessments in each Bridge state.[1]

For the second phase of the project, the main research questions were: How are postsecondary education admissions standards and placement policies and relevant state-level reforms communicated to, and interpreted by, K–12 stakeholders? Are there differences in how student groups receive and interpret those policies? Researchers conducted field research in twenty-four high schools across the six states; the high schools were all in the feeder area for the universities included in the study.[2] They interviewed K–12 educators and staff (usually the principal, a vice principal, a counselor in charge of seniors or of college counseling, and four teachers per school), surveyed two ninth-grade and two eleventh-grade classes (one honors and one nonhonors per grade level), surveyed those students' parents, and included subsamples of eleventh graders in focus groups.

The names of the schools and districts are being kept anonymous at the request of the K–12 participants, but they are all in feeder districts for the postsecondary institutions studied.

The project looked at a range of school types. Schools were selected on several criteria, including test scores on statewide exams, percentage of students enrolled in college preparation courses, Scholastic Aptitude Test and American College Test scores, racial/ethnic diversity, percentage free and reduced-price lunch, college-going rate, and involvement in K–16 reform. Researchers interviewed six to ten educators per school, conducted focus groups with groups of honors and "nonhonors" eleventh graders, and surveyed 2,013 students and their parents. Ninth- and eleventh-grade honors and nonhonors English classes were included, though a few classes were in other disciplines, such as social studies or history. Honors classes were defined as high-level courses that school staff believe prepare students well for college. Nonhonors classes were defined as mid- to lower-level courses that are academic in nature but not as rigorous as the honors classes.

Each state followed very similar data sampling and collection procedures to allow for cross-case analyses. In general, there are more young women than young men represented in our study, probably because there are more young women in honors classes, and honors classes composed half of the sample.

There were slight methodological differences across the states due to logistical issues (for example, gaining approval from schools to conduct research in certain schools and classrooms), which resulted in slightly differing student and parent samples in each state. Differences among the state samples should be kept in mind when examining cross-case data. The primary differences to note are, first, with respect to socioeconomic status (SES). In Georgia, Illinois, and Oregon, the majority of students in the samples fall into the middle-SES category. The samples in California and, especially, Maryland have a majority of high-SES students. Racially, the California sample is quite diverse; Maryland's is primarily African American and white, non-Latino; Texas's is primarily Latino and white, non-Latino; and the remaining cases are predominantly white, non-Latino (though there is some diversity within that category; for example, in Oregon, there are a lot of Eastern European immigrant and first-generation students). Texas was the pilot state, and consequently, the field research in the schools was substantially different from the other case studies. It was smaller in scope and more qualitative and included middle schools and high schools. Finally, the Illinois case is unique because data collection was spread out over two school years in which ninth and eleventh graders were surveyed in May of one year and tenth and twelfth graders were surveyed in September of the next (to keep the cohorts together).

Researchers conducted research at twelve public universities, six community colleges, twenty-four public high schools, three public middle schools, and approximately ten state-level agencies and organizations.[3]

Interviews were conducted with educators and administrators in the state agencies, postsecondary institutions, districts, and schools. Researchers, educators, and administrators at the postsecondary institutions in the study and the state education agencies were interviewed to provide contextual information for the field research in the schools and districts. After the completion of those interviews, school site administrators, teachers, and counselors were interviewed. The interviews were structured so that there were common questions asked of each person in a given role. In addition, the same protocols were used at universities and at the community colleges, and similar protocols were used at each school site (they changed slightly given the particular context of the school or district). Since the protocols were quite long for the postsecondary institutions, questions were divided by category (remediation, admissions policies, and data collection), and the interviewees were asked the questions that related to their respective areas of expertise.

In each K–12 school, an honors and a nonhonors class in ninth- and eleventh-grade English classes were sampled.[4] Students and their parents were surveyed, ten eleventh graders per class were included in focus groups, and the teachers were interviewed. English was chosen because it usually contains students from a single grade level, as opposed to mathematics or science classes. Eleventh graders were chosen because they are close enough to the K–16 transition time to expect that they would have some knowledge of the relevant policies and practices. Ninth graders were chosen because by that grade, students have usually chosen, or been placed in, a particular curriculum track that affects their academic preparation for college, and they can speak retrospectively about what is often called a "gatekeeping year"—eighth grade. Most of the literature suggests that students need to begin planning academically by eighth grade if they wish to attend a selective institution of higher education.

At least one counselor (the counselor who had the primary responsibility for seniors or college preparation activities) and one administrator were interviewed per school. For this study, "honors" is defined as a broad category including honors classes, Advanced Placement (AP) classes, college preparatory classes, and pre-AP classes. There is an inequitable distribution of higher-level courses throughout schools in most states, and by defining the honors category broadly, the results are applicable to a wider range of schools. Honors, AP, college preparatory, and pre-AP courses generally comprise the top curriculum track.

NOTES

1. Illinois was not included in the RAND analyses because its assessments were not fully developed when Bridge Project analyses were conducted.

2. The Texas sample, the pilot state, also included three middle schools.

3. The Texas pilot study included three middle schools; the other states did not. In all states, researchers conducted interviews with approximately fifteen to twenty postsecondary education representatives per institution, five to ten educators per K–12 school, and one to five public employees at state agencies and related organizations (such as state-level education committees).

4. Researchers chose English classes when possible because they usually include students who are all at the same grade level (as compared to mathematics classes, for example, which often have students from several grades in the same class). Sometimes scheduling difficulties or other problems made it impossible to sample from an English class; in those cases, other classes were used. Those instances are discussed in the state chapters.

APPENDIX B: RAND DATA

The disjunctures among the standards, assessments, and policies of K–12 education and postsecondary education are viewed by some policymakers as one of the contributing factors that hinder student achievement and access to higher education. Specifically, the lack of coherence in content and assessment standards between the higher education systems and the K–12 systems is believed to send students a confusing array of signals regarding the kinds of skills and knowledge that are needed to succeed at the postsecondary level.

The Bridge Project provided funds to RAND for the purpose of studying the extent to which the K–12, college admissions, and college course placement tests differ with respect to structural and procedural features, content, and cognitive demands. The study also examines the implications of the misalignments, focusing on the kinds of signals students may receive.

This appendix presents RAND's tables that highlight its findings for the five case study sites (all the Bridge states except Illinois, since the high school–level assessment was not available). The results should be of interest to educational policymakers who are interested in the transitions from secondary to postsecondary education.

Research Design

For both the mathematics and English language arts (ELA) assessments, raters examined discrepancies with respect to structural and procedural features, content, and cognitive demands. In math, the structural and procedural aspects of the tests were determined by simply examining several features of the test and items. These features include the number of items, time limit, format (for example, multiple choice, open ended), provisions for the use of tools such as calculators or protractors, the use of diagrams

The editors thank Vi-Nhuan Le and Laura Hamilton of RAND for their thoughtful analyses and report.

or other graphics, the use of formulas, and whether each item was embedded in a context (as in a word problem). Raters also coded for the content of the test, with topics ranging from prealgebra to trigonometry. In addition, the raters characterized the cognitive requirements of each test item using three categories: conceptual understanding, procedural knowledge, and problem solving.

The ELA framework covered three types of items: reading, objective writing (mainly multiple-choice items), and essay writing. In addition to features such as the number of items and time limits, the structural dimension of the ELA assessments had three categories: topic, type, and stimulus. Raters used all three categories when coding the reading and objective writing items, but used only the topic category when coding the essay writing questions. The cognitive framework for both the reading and objective writing measures consisted of three categories as well. Raters coded questions as assessing students' abilities to recall information, make inferences, or evaluate an item's style. For the essay writing tests, raters examined the scoring criteria, particularly the emphasis given to mechanics, word choice, organization, style, and insight.

Results

Although there were some notable exceptions, the majority of the math tests were low-level, abstract items that did not require students to explain or justify their responses. State K–12 tests rarely sampled from material beyond geometry, whereas the college admissions and college course placement tests drew on advanced content, such as intermediate algebra or trigonometry. In English, there was much consistency in the scoring criteria of the essay writing assessments, as virtually all of the tests emphasized skills such as grammar and word choice. However, only the K–12 tests tended to require an essay. Some of the college course placement exams and the majority of the college entrance tests assessed writing ability primarily with multiple-choice items. Both within and across the assessments, reading passages varied with respect to writing style and subject matter. Finally, the objective writing assessments showed many differences with respect to cognitive demands. Some exams focused on inference skills (for example, the SAT I), whereas other exams emphasized recall skills (such as Test of Standard Written English), and still other exams included a significant number of evaluate style items (such as the American College Test).

California

Table 1. Structural Characteristics of the Tests: California Mathematics.

Test	Materials Examined	Time Limit	Number of Items	Tools	Purpose	Framework	Content as Specified in Testing Materials
ACT	Full sample form	60 minutes	60 MC	Calculator	Selection of students for higher education	High school mathematics curriculum	Prealgebra (23%), elementary algebra (17%), intermediate algebra (15%), coordinate geometry (15%), plane geometry (23%) and trigonometry (7%)
Algebra Readiness Test	Full sample form	50 minutes	60 MC	Calculator	Assess preparation for first-year algebra	High school mathematics curriculum	Arithmetic, prealgebra
AP Calculus AB	Full form, 1997 released exam	Two 90-minute sections	40 MC, 6 free response	Graphing calculator on last 15 MC items	Provide opportunities for high school students to receive college credit and advanced course placement	AP Calculus Course Description	Calculus
California State University Entry Level Mathematics	Sample items	75 minutes	65 MC	Calculator	Assess whether admitted students possess entry-level math skills	*Statement on Competencies in Mathematics Expected of Entering College Students*	Algebra I and II (60%), geometry (20%), data interpretation, counting, probability, and statistics (20%)

(Continued)

Table 1. Structural Characteristics of the Tests: California Mathematics (Continued).

Test	Materials Examined	Time Limit	Number of Items	Tools	Purpose	Framework	Content as Specified in Testing Materials
Placement Exam						Reviewed by faculty from state community colleges, CSU, and UC systems	First-year algebra
Golden State Exam (Algebra)	Sample items	Two separate 45-minute sessions	30 MC, 2 OE	Calculator Ruler	Monitor student achievement toward state-approved content standards, provide special diploma	*Mathematics Content Standards for California Public Schools, Kindergarten Through Grade 12* adopted by the State Board of Education	
Golden State Exam (Geometry)	Sample items	Two separate 45-minute sessions	30 MC, 2 OE	Calculator Ruler	Monitor student achievement toward state-approved content standards, provide special diploma	*Mathematics Content Standards for California Public Schools, Kindergarten Through Grade 12* adopted by the State Board of Education	Geometry
Golden State Exam (High School Mathematics)	Sample items	Two separate 45-minute sessions	30 MC, 2 OE	Calculator, ruler	Monitor student achievement toward state-approved content standards, provide special diploma	*Mathematics Content Standards for California Public Schools, Kindergarten Through Grade 12* adopted by the State Board of Education	Algebra I and II, geometry, probability and statistics

Test	Form	Time	Questions		Purpose	Curriculum	Content
Mathematical Analysis Readiness Test	Full sample form	45 minutes	45 MC	Calculator	Assess preparation for precalculus	High school mathematics curriculum	Prealgebra, algebra, and geometry
SAT I	Full sample form	Two 30-minute sessions, one 15-minute session	35 MC, 15 QC, 10 GR	Calculator	Selection of students for higher education	General mathematics curriculum	Arithmetic (13%), algebra (35%), geometry (26%), and other (26%)
SAT II-Level IC	Full sample form	60 minutes	50 MC	Calculator	Selection of students for higher education	Three-year college preparatory mathematics curriculum	Algebra (30%), geometry (38%, specifically plane Euclidean (20%), coordinate (12%), and three-dimensional (6%), trigonometry (8%), functions (12%), statistics and probability (6%), and miscellaneous (6%)
SAT II-Level IIC	Full sample form	60 minutes	50 MC	Calculator	Selection of students for higher education	More than three years of college preparatory mathematics curriculum	Algebra (18%), geometry (20%, specifically coordinate (12%) and three-dimensional (8%), trigonometry (20%), functions (24%), statistics and probability (6%), and miscellaneous (12%)

(Continued)

Table 1. Structural Characteristics of the Tests: California Mathematics (Continued).

Test	Materials Examined	Time Limit	Number of Items	Tools	Purpose	Framework	Content as Specified in Testing Materials
Second Year Algebra Readiness Test	Full sample form	45 minutes	45 MC	Calculator	Assess preparation for intermediate algebra	High school mathematics curriculum	Prealgebra, algebra, geometry
Stanford 9	Full form	60 minutes	48 MC	Calculator, ruler	Monitor student achievement	National Council of Teachers of Mathematics Standards	Two subtests: mathematical problem-solving and mathematical procedures
Stanford 9 augmentation items	Test blueprints			Calculator, ruler	Monitor student achievement toward state standards	State standards	23% algebra I, 31% geometry, 31% algebra II, 14% statistics

Key: MC = multiple choice; OE = open-ended; GR = grid-in; QC = quantitative comparison.

Table 2. Structural Characteristics of the Tests: California English/Language Arts.

Test	Materials Examined	Time Limit	Number of Items	Purpose	Framework	Reading Section?	Objective Writing Section?	Essay Section?
ACT	Full sample form	80 minutes (35-minute reading section, 45-minute objective writing section)	40 MC reading, 75 MC objective writing	Selection of students for higher education	High school Reading and English/Language Arts curriculum	Y	Y	N
AP Language and Composition	Sample questions	60-minute MC section, 120-minute essay section	52 MC, 3 essays	Provide opportunities for high school students to receive college credit and advanced course placement	AP English Language and Composition Course Description	Y	N	Y
California State University Entry-Level English Placement Exam	Sample items	Two 30-minute sections (one section each for reading and objective writing), 45-minute essay section	45 MC reading, 45 MC objective writing, 1 essay	Assess whether admitted students possess entry-level English skills	CSU English curriculum	Y	Y	Y

(Continued)

Table 2. Structural Characteristics of the Tests: California English/Language Arts (Continued).

Test	Materials Examined	Time Limit	Number of Items	Purpose	Framework	Reading Section?	Objective Writing Section?	Essay Section?
Golden State Exam (Reading/ Literature)	Sample items	Two separate 45-minute sessions	30 MC, 2 essays	Monitor student achievement toward state-approved content standards, provide special diploma	*English-Language Arts Content Standards for California Public Schools, Kindergarten Through Grade Twelve*, adopted by the State Board of Education Standards	Y	N	Y
Golden State Exam (Written Composition)	Sample Items	Two separate 45-minute sessions	30 MC, 2 essays	Monitor student achievement toward state-approved content standards, provide special diploma	*English-Language Arts Content Standards for California Public Schools, Kindergarten Through Grade Twelve*, adopted by the State Board of Education Standards	N	Y	Y
Santa Barbara College Tests for English Placement	Full sample form	85 minutes (30-minute reading section, 35-minute objective writing section, 20-minute essay)	35 MC reading, 70 MC objective writing, 1 essay	Assess whether students possess entry-level English skills	High school Reading and Language Arts curriculum	Y	Y	Y

SAT I	Full sample form	Two 30-minute sessions, one 15-minute session	78 MC	Selection of students for higher education	High school Reading and English/Language Arts curriculum	Y	Y	N
SAT II-Literature	Full sample form	60 minutes	60 MC	Selection of students for higher education	High school English and American Literature curriculum	Y	N	N
SAT II-Writing	Full sample form	One 40-minute MC session, one 20-minute essay session	60 MC, 1 essay	Selection of students for higher education	High school Reading and Language Arts curriculum	N	Y	Y
Stanford-9	Full form	60 minutes	84 MC (54 reading comprehension items, 30 vocabulary items)	Monitor student achievement toward state standards	NAEP framework	Y	N	N
University of California Subject A Examination	Sample questions	2 hours	1 essay	Assess admitted students' writing skills	UC English curriculum	N	N	Y

Key: *MC = multiple choice.*

Table 3. Structural, Content, and Cognitive Features of the California Mathematics Tests.

Test	Format				Context	Graphs			Diagrams			Formulas		Content								Cognitive Requirements		
	MC	QC	GR	OE	C	S	RO	P	S	RO	P	M	G	PA	EA	IA	CG	PG	TR	SP	MISC	CU	PK	PS
ACT	100	0	0	0	22	5	2	0	13	0	0	15	0	17	22	5	15	25	8	3	5	40	53	7
Algebra Readiness	100	0	0	0	26	12	0	0	12	0	0	8	2	42	20	0	2	12	0	8	0	16	84	0
CSU	100	0	0	0	24	0	0	0	16	0	0	18	0	6	32	8	16	14	2	22	0	28	70	2
GSE (Algebra)	95	0	0	5	15	0	5	0	10	0	0	10	0	0	52	0	19	14	0	10	5	19	76	5
GSE (Geometry)	95	0	0	5	10	0	0	5	75	0	0	25	0	0	0	0	5	86	10	0	0	52	38	10
GSE (High School Math)	92	0	0	8	33	0	5	0	23	0	5	15	0	23	15	0	23	23	0	15	0	62	23	15
Math Analysis	100	0	0	0	7	0	2	0	18	0	0	18	0	2	31	31	7	29	0	0	0	13	82	4
SAT I	58	25	17	0	25	7	0	0	18	0	0	1	8	13	37	2	6	19	0	13	11	32	53	15
SAT II-Level IC	100	0	0	0	18	8	0	0	26	0	0	12	0	2	30	10	12	28	4	8	6	34	58	8

	MC	QC	GR	OE	M	G	S	RO	P	C	PA	EA	IA	CG	PG	TR	SP	MISC	CU	PK	PS
SAT II-Level IIC	100	0	0	0	2	0	0	10	0	2	14	22	0	12	14	18	6	12	26	54	20
Second-year Algebra	100	0	0	0	0	22	0	0	16	0	2	60	0	4	33	0	0	0	16	82	2
Stanford 9	100	0	0	0	42	0	0	6	0	6	0	13	2	19	19	40	4	4	63	31	6

Key:

Format:
MC = multiple-choice items;
QC = quantitative comparison items;
GR = fill-in-the-grid items;
OE = open-ended items.

Formulas:
M = formula needs to be memorized;
G = formula is provided.

Context:
C = contextualized items.

Content:
PA = prealgebra;
EA = elementary algebra;
IA = intermediate algebra;
CG = coordinate geometry;
PG = plane geometry;
TR = trigonometry;
SP = statistics and probability;
MISC = miscellaneous topics.

Graphs, Diagrams:
S = graph/diagram within item stem;
RO = graph/diagram within response options;
P = graph/diagram needs to be produced.

Cognitive Requirements:
CU = conceptual understanding;
PK = procedural knowledge;
PS = problem solving.

Table 4. Percentage of California Reading Passages Falling into Each Category.

Test	Type				Topic					Stimulus			
	Narrative	Descriptive	Persuasive	Informative	Fiction	Humanities	Natural Science	Social Science	Personal	Letter	Essay	Poem	Story
ACT	50	0	0	50	25	25	25	25	0	0	75	0	25
AP	75	0	0	25	0	25	25	0	50	0	100	0	0
CSU	100	0	0	0	0	100	0	0	0	0	100	0	0
GSE Reading/Literature	100	0	0	0	0	0	0	0	100	0	100	0	0
Santa Barbara City College	0	0	0	100	0	43	43	14	0	0	100	0	0
SAT I	40	0	0	60	20	40	20	20	0	0	80	0	20
SAT II Literature	100	0	0	0	63	0	0	13	25	13	25	50	13
Stanford 9	50	0	17	33	17	33	33	0	17	17	33	0	50

Table 5. Percentage of California Objective Writing Passages Falling into Each Category.

Stimulus	Type								Topic				
Test	Narrative	Descriptive	Persuasive	Informative	Fiction	Humanities	Natural Science	Social Science	Personal	Letter	Essay	Poem	Story
ACT	40	0	0	60	0	60	20	0	20	0	100	0	0
CSU	0	0	0	100	0	0	0	100	0	0	100	0	0
GSE Written Composition	100	0	0	0	0	0	0	0	100	0	100	0	0
Santa Barbara City College	50	0	0	50	0	100	0	0	0	0	50	0	50
SAT I	0	0	0	0	0	0	0	0	0	0	0	0	0
SAT II Writing	50	0	0	50	0	100	0	0	0	0	100	0	0

Table 6. Topic Contents of Essay Writing Prompts—California.

			Topic		
Test	Fiction	Humanities	Natural Science	Social Science	Personal Essay
AP		X			X
CSU				X	
GSE Reading/Literature		X			X
GSE Written Composition		X		X	X
SAT II Writing		X			
Santa Barbara City College					X
UC Subject A		X	X		X

Table 7. Percentage of Reading Items Falling into Each Category—California.

Test	Recall	Infer	Evaluate Style
ACT	58	42	3
AP	23	77	0
CSU	33	66	0
GSE Reading/Literature	86	14	0
Santa Barbara City College	54	46	0
SAT I	18	83	0
SAT II Literature	13	80	7
Stanford 9	71	29	0

Table 8. Percentage of Objective Writing Items Falling into
Each Category—California.

Test	Recall	Infer	Evaluate Style
ACT	48	4	48
CSU	14	21	64
GSE Written Composition	67	0	33
Santa Barbara City College	16	57	27
SAT I	0	100	0
SAT II Writing	50	3	47

Table 9. Factors Identified in the Scoring Criteria of Each Test—California.

Test	Scoring Criteria Factors				
	Mechanics	Word Choice	Organization	Style	Insight
AP	X	X	X	X	X
CSU	X	X	X	X	X
GSE Reading/Literature			X		X
GSE Written Composition	X	X	X	X	X
SAT II Writing	X	X	X	X	
UC Subject A	X	X	X	X	X

Georgia

Table 10. Structural Characteristics of the Tests: Georgia Mathematics.

Test	Materials Examined	Time Limit	Number of Items	Tools	Purpose	Framework	Content as Specified in Testing Materials
ACT	Full sample form	60 minutes	60 MC	Calculator	Selection of students for higher education	High school mathematics curriculum	Prealgebra (23%), elementary algebra (17%), intermediate algebra (15%), coordinate geometry (15%), plane geometry (23%) and trigonometry (7%)
AP Calculus AB	Full form, 1997 released exam	Two 90-minute sections	40 MC, 6 free response	Graphing calculator on last 15 MC items	Provide opportunities for high school students to receive college credit and advanced course placement	AP Calculus course description	Calculus
COMPASS (Algebra)	Full sample form	No time limit	Number of MC items given depends on ability	None	Assess whether admitted students possess entry-level math skills	High school algebra curriculum	Algebra
COMPASS (Numerical Skills)	Full sample form	No time limit	Number of MC items given depends on ability	None	Assess whether admitted students possess entry-level math skills	High school mathematics curriculum	Prealgebra

Test	Form	Time	Items		Purpose	Standard	Content
Early Math Placement Test (GEMPT)	Full sample form	45 minutes	32 MC	Calculator	Assess current mathematics proficiency level in relation to college-level mathematics courses	*Mathematical Association of America* guidelines	Prealgebra, elementary algebra, geometry, intermediate algebra
Georgia High School Graduation Test (GHSGT)	Sample items	3 hours	60 MC	Calculator	Monitor student achievement toward state standards	*Quality Core Curriculum* for grades 9–12, as established by the State Board of Education	Number and computation (17–19%), data analysis (19–21%), measurement and geometry (32–34%), algebra (28–30%)
SAT I	Full sample form	Two 30-minute sessions, one 15-minute session	35 MC, 15 QC, 10 GR	Calculator	Selection of students for higher education	General mathematics curriculum	Arithmetic (13%), algebra (35%), geometry (26%), and other (26%)
SAT II-Level IC	Full sample form	60 minutes	50 MC	Calculator	Selection of students for higher education	Three-year college preparatory mathematics curriculum	Algebra (30%), geometry (38%, specifically plane Euclidean (20%), coordinate (12%), and three-dimensional (6%)), trigonometry (8%), functions (12%), statistics and probability (6%), and miscellaneous (6%)

(Continued)

Table 10. Structural Characteristics of the Tests: Georgia Mathematics (Continued).

Test	Materials Examined	Time Limit	Number of Items	Tools	Purpose	Framework	Content as Specified in Testing Materials
SAT II-Level IIC	Full sample form	60 minutes	50 MC	Calculator	Selection of students for higher education	More than three years of college preparatory mathematics curriculum	Algebra (18%), geometry (20%, specifically coordinate (12%) and three-dimensional (8%)), trigonometry (20%), functions (24%), statistics and probability (6%), and miscellaneous (12%)
University of Georgia Placement Test (DMAT)	Full sample form	45 minutes	26 MC	Calculator	Placement of students into appropriate math course	High school mathematics curriculum	Arithmetic, algebra, geometry, trigonometry (see http://www.math.uga.edu/~curr/PlacementTopics.html for a complete list of topics)

Key: MC = multiple choice; OE = open-ended; GR = grid-in; QC = quantitative comparison.

Table 11. Structural Characteristics of the Tests: Georgia English/Language Arts.

Test	Materials Examined	Time Limit	Number of Items	Purpose	Framework	Reading Section?	Objective Writing Section?	Essay Section?
ACT	Full sample form	80 minutes (35-minute reading section, 45-minute objective writing section)	40 MC reading, 75 MC objective writing	Selection of students for higher education	High school Reading and Language Arts curriculum	Y	Y	N
AP Language and Composition	Sample questions	60-minute MC section, 120-minute essay section	52 MC, 3 essays	Provide opportunities for high school students to receive college credit and advanced course placement	AP English Language and Composition Course Description	Y	N	Y
COMPASS	Full sample form	No time limit	Number of MC questions given depends on ability	Assess whether admitted students possess entry-level English skills	High school Reading and Language Arts Curriculum	Y	Y	N
Georgia High School Graduation Test English/Language Arts	Sample items	3 hours, but additional time is allowed if the student is making progress	50 MC	Monitor student achievement toward state standards	*Quality Core Curriculum* for grades 9–12, as established by the State Board of Education	Y	Y	N

(*Continued*)

Table 11. Structural Characteristics of the Tests: Georgia English/Language Arts (Continued).

Test	Materials Examined	Time Limit	Number of Items	Purpose	Framework	Reading Section?	Objective Writing Section?	Essay Section?
Graduation High School Writing Test	Sample items	90 minutes, but additional time is allowed if the student is making progress	1 essay	Monitor student achievement toward state standards	Quality Core Curriculum for grades 9–12, as established by the State Board of Education	N	N	Y
SAT I	Full sample form	Two 30-minute sessions, one 15-minute session,	78 MC	Selection of students for higher education	High school Reading and English/Language Arts curriculum	Y	Y	N
SAT II-Literature	Full sample form	60 minutes	60 MC	Selection of students for higher education	High school English and American Literature curriculum	Y	N	N
SAT II-Writing	Full sample form	One 40-minute MC session, one 20-minute essay session	60 MC, 1 essay	Selection of students for higher education	High school Reading and Language Arts curriculum	N	Y	Y
University of Georgia English Placement Test	Full sample form	One 55-minute MC session, one 60-minute essay session	60 MC, 1 essay	Assess whether admitted students possess entry-level English skills	High school Reading and Language Arts curriculum	Y	Y	Y

Table 12. Structural, Content, and Cognitive Features of the Mathematics Tests—Georgia.

Test	Format				Context	Graphs			Diagrams			Formulas					Content					Cognitive Requirements		
	MC	QC	GR	OE	C	S	RO	P	S	RO	P	M	G	PA	EA	IA	CG	PG	TR	SP	MISC	CU	PK	PS
ACT	100	0	0	0	22	5	2	0	13	0	0	15	0	17	22	5	15	25	8	3	5	40	53	7
COMPASS (Algebra)	100	0	0	0	5	16	0	0	0	0	0	16	5	11	37	21	26	0	0	0	5	5	90	5
COMPASS (Numerical Skills)	100	0	0	0	41	0	0	0	0	0	0	0	0	88	0	0	0	0	0	12	0	12	82	6
DMAT	100	0	0	0	8	0	8	0	19	0	0	27	0	0	27	27	15	12	19	0	0	23	77	0
GHSGT	100	0	0	0	62	9	0	0	21	0	0	11	6	25	18	2	9	29	0	18	0	29	69	2
GEMPT	100	0	0	0	6	0	3	0	6	0	0	13	3	3	44	31	9	13	0	0	0	0	100	0

(Continued)

Table 12. Structural, Content, and Cognitive Features of the Mathematics Tests—Georgia (Continued).

Test	Format				Context	Graphs			Diagrams			Formulas		Content								Cognitive Requirements		
	MC	QC	GR	OE	C	S	RO	P	S	RO	P	M	G	PA	EA	IA	CG	PG	TR	SP	MISC	CU	PK	PS
SAT I	58	25	17	0	25	7	0	0	18	0	0	1	8	13	37	2	6	19	0	13	11	32	53	15
SAT II-Level IC	100	0	0	0	18	8	0	0	26	0	0	12	0	2	30	10	12	28	4	8	6	34	58	8
SAT II-Level IIC	100	0	0	0	12	12	2	0	2	0	0	10	0	2	14	22	12	14	18	6	12	26	54	20

Format:
MC = multiple-choice items;
QC = quantitative comparison items;
GR = fill-in-the-grid items;
OE = open-ended items.

Formulas:
M = formula needs to be memorized;
G = formula is provided.

Context:
C = contextualized items.

Content:
PA = prealgebra;
EA = elementary algebra;
IA = intermediate algebra;
CG = coordinate geometry;
PG = plane geometry;
TR = trigonometry;
SP = statistics and probability;
MISC = miscellaneous topics.

Graphs, Diagrams:
S = graph/diagram within item stem;
RO = graph/diagram within response options;
P = graph/diagram needs to be produced.

Cognitive Requirements:
CU = conceptual understanding;
PK = procedural knowledge;
PS = problem solving.

Table 13. Percentage of Reading Passages Falling into Each Category—Georgia.

Test	Type				Topic						Stimulus		
	Narrative	Descriptive	Persuasive	Informative	Fiction	Humanities	Natural Science	Social Science	Personal	Letter	Essay	Poem	Story
ACT	50	0	0	50	25	25	25	25	0	0	75	0	25
AP	75	0	0	25	0	25	25	0	50	0	100	0	0
COMPASS	38	0	0	63	13	25	25	25	13	0	88	0	13
GHSGT	73	0	2	25	45	9	9	14	23	2	55[a]	16[a]	30
SAT I	40	0	0	60	20	40	20	20	0	0	80	0	20
SAT II Literature	100	0	0	0	63	0	0	13	25	13	25	50	13
UGA Placement Test	50	0	0	50	0	50	0	0	50	0	100	0	0

[a]One passage contained both an essay and a poem.

Table 14. Percentage of Objective Writing Passages Falling into Each Category—Georgia.

Test	Type				Topic					Stimulus			
	Narrative	Descriptive	Persuasive	Informative	Fiction	Humanities	Natural Science	Social Science	Personal	Letter	Essay	Poem	Story
ACT	40	0	0	60	0	60	20	0	20	0	100	0	0
COMPASS	0	0	0	100	0	0	50	50	0	0	100	0	0
GHSGT	80	0	0	20	60	20	20	0	0	0	40	0	60
UGA Placement Test	0	0	0	0	0	0	0	0	0	0	0	0	0
SAT I	0	0	0	0	0	0	0	0	0	0	0	0	0
SAT II Writing	50	0	0	50	0	100	0	0	0	0	100	0	0

Table 15. Topic Contents of Essay Writing Prompts—Georgia.

Test	Topic				
	Fiction	Humanities	Natural Science	Social Science	Personal Essay
AP		X			X
GHSWT		X			X
SAT II Writing		X			
UGA Placement Test		X	X	X	X

Table 16. Percentage of Reading Items Falling into Each Category—Georgia.

Test	Recall	Infer	Evaluate Style
ACT	58	42	3
AP	23	77	0
COMPASS	75	25	0
GHSGT	30	70	0
UGA Placement Test	46	54	0
SAT I	18	83	0
SAT II Literature	13	80	7

Table 17. Percentage of Objective Writing Items Falling into Each Category—Georgia.

Test	Recall	Infer	Evaluate Style
ACT	48	4	48
COMPASS	80	3	17
GHSWT	30	44	26
UGA Placement Test	100	0	0
SAT I	0	100	0
SAT II Writing	50	3	47

Table 18. Factors Identified in the Scoring Criteria of Each Test—Georgia.

Test	Scoring Criteria Factors				
	Mechanics	Word Choice	Organization	Style	Insight
AP	X	X	X	X	X
GHSWT	X	X	X	X	X
SAT II Writing	X	X	X	X	
UGA Placement Test	X	X	X	X	

Maryland

Table 19. Structural Characteristics of the Tests: Maryland Mathematics.

Test	Materials Examined	Time Limit	Number of Items	Tools	Purpose	Framework	Content as Specified in Testing Materials
ACT	Full sample form	60 minutes	60 MC	Calculator	Selection of students for higher education	High school mathematics curriculum	Prealgebra (23%), elementary algebra (17%), intermediate algebra (15%), coordinate geometry (15%), plane geometry (23%) and trigonometry (7%)
AP Calculus AB	Full form, 1997 released exam	Two 90-minute sections	40 MC, 6 free response	Graphing calculator on last 15 MC items	Provide opportunities for high school students to receive college credit and advanced course placement	AP calculus course description	Calculus
ACCUPLACER (Elementary Algebra)	Full sample form, test specifications	Untimed	12 MC	None	Placement of students into appropriate math course	High school algebra curriculum	Signed numbers and rational numbers, algebraic expressions, equations, inequalities, and word problems

(*Continued*)

Table 19. Structural Characteristics of the Tests: Maryland Mathematics (Continued).

Test	Materials Examined	Time Limit	Number of Items	Tools	Purpose	Framework	Content as Specified in Testing Materials
Maryland High School Assessment (Algebra)	Prototype items	1 minute for each MC item, 2 minutes for each student-produced response item, 5 minutes for each brief-constructed response item, 10 minutes for each extended constructed-response item	To be determined	Calculator	Monitor student achievement toward state-approved content standards	*Core Learning Goals*, adopted by the State Board of Education	Algebra
Maryland High School Assessment (Geometry)	Prototype items	1 minute for each MC item, 2 minutes for each student-produced response item, 5 minutes for each brief-constructed response item,	To be determined	Calculator	Monitor student achievement toward state-approved content standards	*Core Learning Goals*, adopted by the State Board of Education	Geometry

Test	Form		Time	Items	Calculator	Purpose	Curriculum	Content
SAT I	Full sample form	10 minutes for each extended constructed-response item	Two 30-minute sessions, one 15-minute session	35 MC, 15 QC, 10 GR	Calculator	Selection of students for higher education	General mathematics curriculum	Arithmetic (13%), algebra (35%), geometry, (26%), and other (26%)
SAT II-Level IC	Full sample form		60 minutes	50 MC	Calculator	Selection of students for higher education	Three-year college preparatory mathematics curriculum	Algebra (30%), geometry, (38%, specifically plane Euclidean (20%), coordinate (12%), and three-dimensional (6%)), trigonometry (8%), functions (12%), statistics and probability (6%), and miscellaneous (6%)
SAT II-Level IIC	Full sample form		60 minutes	50 MC	Calculator	Selection of students for higher education	More than three years of college preparatory mathematics curriculum	Algebra (18%), geometry (20%, specifically coordinate (12%) and three-dimensional (8%)), trigonometry (20%), functions (24%), statistics and probability (6%), and miscellaneous (12%)

(Continued)

Table 19. Structural Characteristics of the Tests: Maryland Mathematics (Continued).

Test	Materials Examined	Time Limit	Number of Items	Tools	Purpose	Framework	Content as Specified in Testing Materials
Towson Mathematics Placement Test	Sample items	60 minutes	Number of MC items given depends on ability	Calculator	Placement of students into appropriate mathematics course	*Mathematics Association of America* standards	Arithmetic, elementary algebra, advanced algebra, and trigonometry
University of Maryland Placement Test	Sample items	70 minutes	63 MC	Calculator	Placement of students into appropriate mathematics course	*Mathematics Association of America* standards	Arithmetic, elementary algebra, advanced algebra, and trigonometry

Key: *MC = multiple choice; OE = open-ended; GR = grid-in; QC = quantitative comparison.*

Table 20. Structural Characteristics of the Tests: Maryland English/Language Arts.

Test	Materials Examined	Time Limit	Number of Items	Purpose	Framework	Reading Section?	Objective Writing Section?	Essay Section?
ACT	Full sample form	80 minutes (35-minute reading section, 45-minute objective writing section)	40 MC reading 75 MC objective writing	Selection of students for higher education	High school Reading and Language Arts curriculum	Y	Y	N
ACCUPLACER (Reading Comprehension)	Full sample form, test specifications	Untimed	20 MC	Placement of students into appropriate English course	High school Reading and Language Arts curriculum	Y	N	N
ACCUPLACER (Sentence Skills)	Full sample form, test specifications	Untimed	20 MC	Placement of students into appropriate English course	High school Reading and Language Arts curriculum	N	Y	N
AP Language and Composition	Sample questions	60-minute MC section, 120-minute essay section	52 MC, 3 essays	Provide opportunities for high school students to receive college credit and advanced course placement	AP English Language and Composition Course Description	Y	N	Y

(Continued)

Table 20. Structural Characteristics of the Tests: Maryland English/Language Arts (Continued).

Test	Materials Examined	Time Limit	Number of Items	Purpose	Framework	Reading Section?	Writing Section?	Essay Section?
ASSET Writing Skills	Full sample form	25 minutes	32 MC	Placement of students into appropriate English course	High School Reading and Language Arts curriculum	N	Y	N
Maryland High School Assessment (English)	Prototype items	To be determined	To be determined	Monitor student achievement toward state-approved content standards	*Core Learning Goals*, adopted by the State Board of Education	Y	Y	Y
Nelson-Denney Reading Test	Full sample form	Two sessions (24-minute vocabulary session, 32-minute comprehension test)	80 MC vocabulary items, 38 MC comprehension items	Assess student ability in vocabulary development and reading comprehension	High school Reading and Language Arts curriculum	Y	N	N
SAT I	Full sample form	Two 30-minute sessions, one 15-minute session	78 MC	Selection of students for higher education	High school Reading and English/Language Arts curriculum	Y	Y	N
SAT II-Literature	Full sample form	60 minutes	60 MC	Selection of students for higher education	High school English and American Literature curriculum	Y	N	N
SAT II-Writing	Full sample form	One 40-minute MC session, one 20-minute essay session	60 MC, 1 essay	Selection of students for higher education	High school Reading and Language Arts curriculum	N	Y	Y

Table 21. Structural, Content, and Cognitive Features of the Mathematics Tests—Maryland.

Test	Format				Context	Graphs			Diagrams			Formulas		Content								Cognitive Requirements		
	MC	QC	GR	OE	C	S	RO	P	S	RO	P	M	G	PA	EA	IA	CG	PG	TR	SP	MISC	CU	PK	PS
ACCUPLACER (Elementary Algebra)	100	0	0	0	25	0	0	0	13	0	0	13	0	0	88	0	0	13	0	0	0	0	100	0
ACT	100	0	0	0	22	5	2	0	13	0	0	15	0	17	22	5	15	25	8	3	5	40	53	7
HSA Algebra	32	0	11	58	89	37	0	16	11	0	5	0	0	5	53	0	16	0	0	16	11	0	68	32
HSA Geometry	53	0	12	35	65	24	0	6	65	6	0	0	41	0	0	0	24	71	6	0	0	6	71	24
Math Placement Test	100	0	0	0	0	6	0	0	13	0	0	25	0	19	13	31	13	6	19	0	0	25	75	0
SAT I	58	25	17	0	25	7	0	0	18	0	0	1	8	13	37	2	6	19	0	13	11	32	53	15
SAT II-Level IC	100	0	0	0	18	8	0	0	26	0	0	12	0	2	30	10	12	28	4	8	6	34	58	8
SAT II-Level IIC	100	0	0	0	12	12	2	0	2	0	0	10	0	2	14	22	12	14	18	6	12	26	54	20

Format:
MC = multiple-choice items;
QC = quantitative comparison items;
GR = fill-in-the-grid items;
OE = open-ended items.

Formulas:
M = formula needs to be memorized;
G = formula is provided.

Context:
C = contextualized items.

Content:
PA = prealgebra;
EA = elementary algebra;
IA = intermediate algebra;
CG = coordinate geometry;
PG = plane geometry;
TR = trigonometry;
SP = statistics and probability;
MISC = miscellaneous topics.

Graphs, Diagrams:
S = graph/diagram within item stem;
RO = graph/diagram within response options;
P = graph/diagram needs to be produced.

Cognitive Requirements:
CU = conceptual understanding;
PK = procedural knowledge;
PS = problem solving.

Table 22. Percentage of Reading Passages Falling into Each Category—Maryland.

Test	Type				Topic					Stimulus			
	Narrative	Descriptive	Persuasive	Informative	Fiction	Humanities	Natural Science	Social Science	Personal	Letter	Essay	Poem	Story
ACT	50	0	0	50	25	25	25	25	0	0	75	0	25
AP	75	0	0	25	0	25	25	0	50	0	100	0	0
ACCUPLACER Reading Comprehension	50	0	5	45	0	60	35	0	5	0	100	0	0
HSA English	100	0	0	0	0	67	0	0	33	33	0	33	33
Nelson-Denney	0	0	0	100	0	43	29	29	0	0	100	0	0
SAT I	40	0	0	60	20	40	20	20	0	0	80	0	20
SAT II Literature	100	0	0	0	63	0	0	13	25	13	25	50	13

Table 23. Percentage of Objective Writing Passages Falling into Each Category—Maryland.

Test	Type				Topic					Stimulus			
	Narrative	Descriptive	Persuasive	Informative	Fiction	Humanities	Natural Science	Social Science	Personal	Letter	Essay	Poem	Story
ACT	40	0	0	60	0	60	20	0	20	0	100	0	0
ASSET	67	0	0	33	0	100	0	0	0	0	100	0	0
ACCUPLACER Sentence Skills	0	0	0	0	0	0	0	0	0	0	0	0	0
HSA English	0	0	0	100	0	0	0	100	0	0	100	0	0
SAT I	0	0	0	0	0	0	0	0	0	0	0	0	0
SAT II Writing	50	0	0	50	0	100	0	0	0	0	100	0	0

Table 24. Topic Contents of Essay Writing Prompts—Maryland.

Test	Fiction	Humanities	Natural Science	Social Science	Personal Essay
					Topic
AP		X			X
HSA English	X				
SAT II Writing		X			X

Table 25. Percentage of Reading Items Falling into Each Category—Maryland.

Test	Recall	Infer	Evaluate Style
ACT	58	42	3
AP	23	77	0
ACCUPLACER Reading Comprehension	11	89	0
HSA English	25	75	0
Nelson-Denney	86	15	0
SAT I	18	83	0
SAT II Literature	13	80	7

Table 26. Percentage of Objective Writing Items Falling into Each Category—Maryland.

Test	Recall	Infer	Evaluate Style
ACT	48	4	48
ASSET	89	11	0
ACCUPLACER Sentence Skills	91	0	9
HSA English	13	13	73
SAT I	0	100	0
SAT II Writing	50	3	47

Table 27. Factors Identified in the Scoring Criteria of Each Test.

Test	Scoring Criteria Factors				
	Mechanics	Word Choice	Organization	Style	Insight
AP	X	X	X	X	X
HSA English	X	X	X	X	X
SAT II Writing	X	X	X	X	

Oregon

Table 28. Structural Characteristics of the Tests: Oregon Mathematics.

Test	Materials Examined	Time Limit	Number of Items	Tools	Purpose	Framework	Content as Specified in Testing Materials
ACT	Full sample form	60 minutes	60 MC	Calculator	Selection of students for higher education	High school mathematics curriculum	Prealgebra (23%), elementary algebra (17%), intermediate algebra (15%), coordinate geometry (15%), plane geometry (23%) and trigonometry (7%)
AP Calculus AB	Full form, 1997 released exam	Two 90-minute sections	40 MC, 6 free response	Graphing calculator on last 15 MC items	Provide opportunities for high school students to receive college credit and advanced course placement	AP Calculus, Course, Description	Calculus
Certificate of Initial Mastery Mathematics Assessment (CIM)	Sample items	Two untimed testing sessions	55 MC, 1 OE	Calculator	Monitor student achievement toward specified benchmarks	*Common Curriculum Goals* adopted by the State Board of Education	Calculations and estimations, measurement, statistics and probability, algebraic relationships, and geometry
Locator Test	Full sample form	40 minutes	24 MC	Calculator	Identify the appropriate form of CIM to be administered	*Common Curriculum Goals* adopted by the State Board of Education	Calculations and estimations, measurement, statistics and probability, algebraic relationships, and geometry

Test	Form	Time	Items		Purpose	Curriculum	Content
SAT I	Full sample form	Two 30-minute sessions, one 15-minute session	35 MC, 15 QC, 10 GR	Calculator	Selection of students for higher education	General mathematics curriculum	Arithmetic (13%), algebra (35%), geometry, (26%), and other (26%)
SAT II-Level IC	Full sample form	60 minutes	50 MC	Calculator	Selection of students for higher education	Three-year college preparatory mathematics curriculum	Algebra (30%), geometry (38%, specifically plane Euclidean (20%), coordinate (12%), and three-dimensional (6%)), trigonometry (8%), functions (12%), statistics and probability (6%), and miscellaneous (6%)
SAT II-Level IIC	Full sample form	60 minutes	50 MC	Calculator	Selection of students for higher education	More than three years of college preparatory mathematics curriculum	Algebra (18%), geometry (20%, specifically coordinate (12%) and three-dimensional (8%)), trigonometry (20%), functions (24%), statistics and probability (6%), and miscellaneous (12%)
University of Oregon Math Placement Test	Full sample form	50 minutes	40 MC	Calculator	Placement of students into appropriate math course	University of Oregon, Mathematics Departmental Standards and Mathematics Association of America Standards	Elementary algebra, intermediate algebra, geometry, precalculus

Key: MC = multiple-choice; OE = open-ended; GR = grid-in; QC = quantitative comparison.

Table 29. Structural Characteristics of the Tests: Oregon English/Language Arts.

Test	Materials Examined	Time Limit	Number of Items	Purpose	Framework	Reading Section?	Objective Writing Section?	Essay Section?
ACT	Full sample form	80 minutes (35-minute reading section, 45-minute objective writing section)	40 MC reading, 75 MC objective writing	Selection of students for higher education	High school Reading and English/Language Arts curriculum	Y	Y	N
AP Language and Composition	Sample questions	60-minute MC section, 120-minute essay section	52 MC, 3 essays	Provide opportunities for high school students to receive college credit and advanced course placement	AP English Language and Composition Course Description	Y	N	Y
Certificate of Initial Mastery Reading Assessment	Sample form	No time limit	65 MC	Measure student achievement toward specified benchmarks	*Common Curriculum Goals* adopted by the State Board of Education	Y	N	N
Certificate of Initial Mastery Writing Assessment	Sample essays	No time limit	1 essay	Measure student achievement toward specified benchmarks	*Common Curriculum Goals* adopted by the State Board of Education	N	N	Y

Locator Test	Full sample form	30–45 minutes	54 MC	Identify the appropriate form of CIM to be administered	*Common Curriculum Goals* adopted by the State Board of Education	Y	N	N
SAT I	Full sample form	Two 30-minute sessions, one 15-minute session	78 MC	Selection of students for higher education	High school Reading and English/Language Arts curriculum	Y	Y	N
SAT II-Literature	Full sample form	60 minutes	60 MC	Selection of students for higher education	High school English and American Literature curriculum	Y	N	N
SAT II-Writing	Full sample form	One 40-minute MC session, one 20-minute essay session	60 MC, 1 essay	Selection of students for higher education	High school Reading and Language Arts curriculum	N	Y	Y
Test of Standard Written English (TSWE)	Full sample form	30 minutes	49 MC	Evaluate student ability in recognizing standard written English	High school Reading and Language Arts curriculum	N	Y	N

Table 30. Structural, Content, and Cognitive Features of the Mathematics Tests—Oregon.

Test	Format				Content	Graphs			Diagrams			Formulas		Content								Cognitive Requirements		
	MC	QC	GR	OE	C	S	RO	P	S	RO	P	M	G	PA	EA	IA	CG	PG	TR	SP	MISC	CU	PK	PS
ACT	100	0	0	0	22	5	2	0	13	0	0	15	0	17	22	5	15	25	8	3	5	40	53	7
CIM	90	0	0	10	67	18	0	0	26	0	0	16	3	15	15	3	5	31	0	30	2	18	61	21
Locator test	100	0	0	0	60	20	0	0	20	0	0	15	0	25	5	0	15	20	0	30	5	20	75	5
SAT I	58	25	17	0	25	7	0	0	18	0	0	1	8	13	37	2	6	19	0	13	11	32	53	15
SAT II-Level IC	100	0	0	0	18	8	0	0	26	0	0	12	0	2	30	10	12	28	4	8	6	34	58	8
SAT II-Level IIC	100	0	0	0	12	12	2	0	2	0	0	10	0	2	14	22	12	14	18	6	12	26	54	20
University of Oregon Placement Test	100	0	0	0	8	0	0	0	0	0	0	5	0	0	65	15	5	3	13	0	0	10	90	0

Format:
MC = multiple-choice items;
QC = quantitative comparison items;
GR = fill-in-the-grid items;
OE = open-ended items.

Formulas:
M = formula needs to be memorized;
G = formula is provided.

Context:
C = contextualized items.

Content:
PA = prealgebra;
EA = elementary algebra;
IA = intermediate algebra;
CG = coordinate geometry;
PG = plane geometry;
TR = trigonometry;
SP = statistics and probability;
MISC = miscellaneous topics.

Graphs, Diagrams:
S = graph/diagram within item stem;
RO = graph/diagram within response options;
P = graph/diagram needs to be produced.

Cognitive Requirements:
CU = conceptual understanding;
PK = procedural knowledge;
PS = problem solving.

Table 31. Percentage of Reading Passages Falling into Each Category—Oregon.

Test	Type					Topic					Stimulus			
	Narrative	Descriptive	Persuasive	Informative	Fiction	Humanities	Natural Science	Social Science	Personal	Letter	Essay	Poem	Story	Chart
ACT	50	0	0	50	25	25	25	25	0	0	75	0	25	0
AP	75	0	0	25	0	25	25	0	50	0	100	0	0	0
CIM Reading	75	0	0	25	63	13	0	0	25	0	13	13	50	25
Locator Test	75	0	0	25	25	0	25	25	25	0	75	25	0	0
SAT I	40	0	0	60	20	40	20	20	0	0	80	0	20	0
SAT II Literature	100	0	0	0	63	0	0	13	25	13	25	50	13	0

Table 32. Percentage of Objective Writing Passages Falling into Each Category—Oregon.

Test	Type					Topic					Stimulus		
	Narrative	Descriptive	Persuasive	Informative	Fiction	Humanities	Natural Science	Social Science	Personal	Letter	Essay	Poem	Story
ACT	40	0	0	60	0	60	20	0	20	0	100	0	0
SAT I	0	0	0	0	0	0	0	0	0	0	0	0	0
SAT II Writing	50	0	0	50	0	100	0	0	0	0	100	0	0
TSWE	0	0	0	0	0	0	0	0	0	0	0	0	0

Table 33. Topic Contents of Essay Writing Prompts—Oregon.

			Topic		
Test	Fiction	Humanities	Natural Science	Social Science	Personal Essay
AP		X			X
SAT II Writing		X			
CIM Writing	X				X

Table 34. Percentage of Reading Items Falling into Each Category—Oregon.

Test	Recall	Infer	Evaluate Style
ACT	58	42	3
AP	23	77	0
CIM Reading	54	46	0
Locator Test	45	55	0
SAT I	18	83	0
SAT II Literature	13	80	7

Table 35. Percentage of Objective Writing Items Falling into Each Category—Oregon.

Test	Recall	Infer	Evaluate Style
ACT	48	4	48
SAT I	0	100	0
SAT II Writing	50	3	47
TSWE	90	0	10

Table 36. Factors Identified in the Scoring Criteria of Each Test—Oregon.

Test	Scoring Criteria Factors				
	Mechanics	Word Choice	Organization	Style	Insight
AP	X	X	X	X	X
CIM Writing	X	X	X	X	X
SAT II Writing	X	X	X	X	

Texas

Table 37. Structural Characteristics of the Tests: Texas Mathematics.

Test	Materials Examined	Time Limit	Number of Items	Tools	Purpose	Framework	Content as Specified in Testing Materials
ACT	Full sample form	60 minutes	60 MC	Calculator	Selection of students for higher education	High school mathematics curriculum	Prealgebra (23%), elementary algebra (17%), intermediate algebra (15%), coordinate geometry (15%), plane geometry (23%) and trigonometry (7%)
AP Calculus AB	Full form, 1997 released exam	Two 90-minute sections	40 MC, 6 free response	Graphing calculator on last 15 MC items	Provide opportunities for high school students to receive college credit and advanced course placement	AP Calculus Course Description	Calculus
Descriptive Tests of Mathematical Skills (Elementary Algebra)	Full sample form	30 minutes	35 MC	None	Assess student readiness for advanced mathematics courses	High school mathematics curriculum	Real numbers, algebraic expressions, equations, and inequalities, algebraic operations, data interpretation
End-of-Course Exam (Algebra I)	Full form, 1998 released exam	2 hours	39 MC, 1 GR	Calculator	Monitor student achievement of state-based standards	Texas Essential Knowledge and Skills	Elementary algebra

SAT I	Full sample form	Two 30-minute sessions, one 15-minute session	35 MC, 15 QC, 10 GR	Calculator	Selection of students for higher education	General mathematics curriculum	Arithmetic (13%), algebra (35%), geometry, (26%), and other (26%)
SAT II-Level IC	Full sample form	60 minutes	50 MC	Calculator	Selection of students for higher education	Three-year college preparatory mathematics curriculum	Algebra (30%), geometry (38%, specifically plane Euclidean (20%), coordinate (12%), and three-dimensional (6%)), trigonometry (8%), functions (12%), statistics and probability (6%), and miscellaneous (6%)
SAT II-Level IIC	Full sample form	60 minutes	50 MC	Calculator	Selection of students for higher education	More than three years of college preparatory mathematics curriculum	Algebra (18%), geometry (20%, specifically coordinate (12%) and three-dimensional (8%)), trigonometry (20%), functions (24%), statistics and probability (6%), and miscellaneous (12%)
Texas Assessment of Academic Skills (TAAS)	Full form, 1998 released exam	No time limit	60 MC	None	Monitor student achievement toward state standards	Texas Essential Knowledge and Skills	Fundamental math, algebra, geometric properties, and problem solving
Texas Academic Skills Program (TASP)	Full sample form	5 hours total testing time	48 MC	None	Assess whether students entering Texas public institutions of higher education possess entry-level math skills	Texas Essential Knowledge and Skills	Fundamental math, algebra, geometry, and problem solving

Key: MC = multiple-choice; OE = open-ended; GR = grid-in; QC = quantitative comparison.

Table 38. Characteristics of the Tests: Texas English/Language Arts.

Test	Materials Examined	Time Limit	Number of Items	Purpose	Framework	Reading Section?	Objective Writing Section?	Essay Section?
ACT	Full sample form	80 minutes (35-minute reading section, 45-minute objective writing section)	40 MC reading, 75 MC objective writing	Selection of students for higher education	High school Reading and English/Language Arts curriculum	Y	Y	N
AP Language and Composition	Sample questions	60-minute MC section, 120-minute essay section	52 MC, 3 essays	Provide opportunities for high school students to receive college credit and advanced course placement	AP English Language and Composition Course Description	Y	N	Y
End of Course Exam (English II)	Full sample form	2 hours	36 MC, 2 short-answers, 1 essay	Monitor student achievement of state-based standards	Texas Essential Knowledge and Skills	Y	Y	Y
SAT I	Full sample form	Two 30-minute sessions, one 15-minute session	78 MC	Selection of students for higher education	High school Reading and English/Language Arts curriculum	Y	Y	N

Test	Form	Time	Number of items	Purpose	Content basis			
SAT II-Literature	Full sample form	60 minutes	60 MC	Selection of students for higher education	High school English and American Literature curriculum	Y	N	N
SAT II-Writing	Full sample form	One 40-minute MC session, one 20-minute essay session	60 MC, 1 essay	Selection of students for higher education	High school Reading and Language Arts curriculum	N	Y	Y
Texas Assessment of Academic Skills (TAAS)	Full form, 1998 released exam	No time limit	89 MC, 1 essay	Monitor student achievement toward TX standards	*Texas Essential Knowledge and Skills*	Y	Y	Y
Texas Academic Skills Program (TASP)	Full sample form	5 hours	82 MC, 1 essay	Assess whether students entering Texas public institutions of higher education possess entry-level English skills	*Texas Essential Knowledge and Skills*	Y	Y	Y

Table 39. Structural, Content, and Cognitive Features of the Mathematics Tests—Texas.

Test	Format				Context	Graphs			Diagrams			Formulas		Content								Cognitive Requirements		
	MC	QC	GR	OE	C	S	RO	P	S	RO	P	M	G	PA	EA	IA	CG	PG	TR	SP	MISC	CU	PK	PS
ACT	100	0	0	0	22	5	2	0	13	0	0	15	0	17	22	5	15	25	8	3	5	40	53	7
DTMS	100	0	0	0	20	14	0	0	3	0	0	11	0	17	65	3	6	0	0	9	0	3	97	0
End of Course	97	0	3	0	38	15	3	0	15	0	0	0	25	5	43	5	25	15	0	8	0	8	92	0
SAT I	58	25	17	0	25	7	0	0	18	0	0	1	8	13	37	2	6	19	0	13	11	32	53	15
SAT II-Level IC	100	0	0	0	18	8	0	0	26	0	0	12	0	2	30	10	12	28	4	8	6	34	58	8
SAT II-Level IIC	100	0	0	0	12	12	2	0	2	0	0	10	0	2	14	22	12	14	18	6	12	26	54	20
TAAS	100	0	0	0	92	3	0	0	22	0	0	0	12	55	12	0	2	10	0	22	0	10	90	0
TASP	100	0	0	0	38	15	2	0	15	4	0	0	21	17	25	10	8	21	0	10	8	10	81	8

Format:
MC = multiple-choice items;
QC = quantitative comparison items;
GR = fill-in-the-grid items;
OE = open-ended items.

Formulas:
M = formula needs to be memorized;
G = formula is provided.

Context:
C = contextualized items.

Content:
PA = prealgebra;
EA = elementary algebra;
IA = intermediate algebra;
CG = coordinate geometry;
PG = plane geometry;
TR = trigonometry;
SP = statistics and probability;
MISC = miscellaneous topics.

Graphs, Diagrams:
S = graph/diagram within item stem;
RO = graph/diagram within response options;
P = graph/diagram needs to be produced.

Cognitive Requirements:
CU = conceptual understanding;
PK = procedural knowledge;
PS = problem solving.

Table 40. Percentage of Reading Passages Falling into Each Category—Texas.

Test	Type					Topic					Stimulus		
	Narrative	Descriptive	Persuasive	Informative	Fiction	Humanities	Natural Science	Social Science	Personal	Letter	Essay	Poem	Story
ACT	50	0	0	50	25	25	25	25	0	0	75	0	25
AP	75	0	0	25	0	25	25	0	50	0	100	0	0
End-of-Course	100	0	0	0	0	0	0	0	100	0	100	0	0
SAT I	40	0	0	60	20	40	20	20	0	0	80	0	20
SAT II Literature	100	0	0	0	63	0	0	13	25	13	25	50	13
TAAS	71	0	0	29	43	43	14	0	0	0	57	0	43
TASP	43	0	0	57	14	29	29	14	14	0	86	0	14

Table 41. Percentage of Objective Writing Passages Falling into Each Category—Texas.

Test	Type					Topic					Stimulus		
	Narrative	Descriptive	Persuasive	Informative	Fiction	Humanities	Natural Science	Social Science	Personal	Letter	Essay	Poem	Story
ACT	40	0	0	60	0	60	20	0	20	0	100	0	0
End-of-Course	50	0	0	50	0	0	50	0	50	0	100	0	0
SAT I	0	0	0	0	0	0	0	0	0	0	0	0	0
SAT II Writing	50	0	0	50	0	100	0	0	0	0	100	0	0
TAAS	56	0	0	44	11	22	44	0	22	11	67	0	22
TASP	50	0	6	44	0	69	19	6	6	6	94	0	0

Table 42. Topic Contents of Essay Writing Prompts—Texas.

			Topic		
Test	Fiction	Humanities	Natural Science	Social Science	Personal Essay
AP		X			X
End-of-Course					X
SAT II Writing		X			
TAAS		X			
TASP		X			

Table 43. Percentage of Reading Items Falling into Each Category—Texas.

Test	Recall	Infer	Evaluate Style
ACT	58	42	0
AP	23	77	0
End-of-Course	31	69	0
SAT I	18	83	0
SAT II Literature	13	80	7
TAAS	40	60	0
TASP	21	79	0

Table 44. Percentage of Objective Writing Items Falling into Each Category—Texas.

Test	Recall	Infer	Evaluate Style
ACT	48	4	48
End-of-Course	70	5	25
SAT I	0	100	0
SAT II Writing	50	3	47
TAAS	100	0	0
TASP	33	43	25

Table 45. Factors Identified in the Scoring Criteria of Each Test—Texas.

Test	Scoring Criteria Factors				
	Mechanics	Word Choice	Organization	Style	Insight
AP	X	X	X	X	X
End-of-Course	X	X	X	X	X
SAT II Writing	X	X	X	X	
TAAS	X	X	X	X	X
TASP	X		X	X	X

Cross-State Analysis

Table 46. Mathematics Assessments Used for Cross-State Analysis.

Test Name	State Used	Purpose	Framework	Student Population
State tests				
Certificate of Initial Mastery (CIM)	Oregon	Monitor student achievement toward specified benchmarks	*Common Curriculum Goals* adopted by the state Board of Education	Oregon public high school students
End-of-Course Algebra	Texas	Monitor student achievement of state-based standards	*Texas Essential Knowledge and Skills*	Texas public high school students
Georgia High School Graduation Test (GHSGT)	Georgia	Monitor student achievement toward state-approved content standards	*Quality Core Curriculum* for grades 9–12, as established by the State Board of Education	Georgia public high school students
Golden State Exam Algebra (GSE Algebra)	California	Monitor student achievement toward state-approved content standards, provide special diploma	*Mathematics Content Standards for California Public Schools, Kindergarten Through Grade 12* adopted by the State Board of Education	Students wishing to receive recognition on their diploma
Golden State Exam Geometry (GSE Geometry)	California	Monitor student achievement toward state-approved content standards, provide special diploma	*Mathematics Content Standards for California Public Schools, Kindergarten Through Grade 12* adopted by the State Board of Education	Students wishing to receive recognition on their diploma
Golden State Exam High School Mathematics (GSE HS Math)	California	Monitor student achievement toward state-approved content standards, provide special diploma	*Mathematics Content Standards for California Public Schools, Kindergarten Through Grade 12* adopted by the State Board of Education	Students wishing to receive recognition on their diploma
High School Assessment Algebra (HSA Algebra)	Maryland	Monitor student achievement toward state-approved content standards	*Core Learning Goals*, adopted by the State Board of Education	All students within Maryland public high schools

Name	State	Purpose	Standards	Population
High School Assessment Geometry (HSA Geometry)	Maryland	Monitor student achievement toward state-approved content standards	*Core Learning Goals*, adopted by the State Board of Education	Maryland public high school students
Locator test	Oregon	Identify the appropriate form of CIM to be administered	*Common Curriculum Goals* adopted by the State Board of Education	Oregon public high school students
Stanford 9	California	Monitor student achievement	National Council of Teachers of Mathematics Standards	California public high school students
Texas Assessment of Academic Skills (TAAS)	Texas	Monitor student achievement toward Texas standards	*Texas Essential Knowledge and Skills*	Texas public high school students
Texas Academic Skills Program (TASP)	Texas	Assess whether students entering Texas public institutions of higher education possess entry-level math skills	*Texas Essential Knowledge and Skills*	Texas public high school students
College course placement tests				
COMPASS (Algebra)	Georgia	Assess whether admitted students possess entry-level algebra skills	High school algebra curriculum	Students entering two- or less selective four-year institutions
COMPASS (Numerical Skills)	Georgia	Assess whether admitted students possess entry-level math skills	High school mathematics curriculum	Students entering two- or less selective four-year institutions
ACCUPLACER Elementary Algebra	Maryland	Placement of students into appropriate math course	High school algebra curriculum	Students entering two- or less selective four-year institutions

(*Continued*)

Table 46. Mathematics Assessments Used for Cross-State Analysis (Continued).

Test Name	State Used	Purpose	Framework	Student Population
Descriptive Math Placement Test Elementary Algebra (DMPT)	Texas	Assess student readiness for advanced mathematics courses	High school mathematics curriculum	Students entering two- or less selective four-year institutions
College admissions tests				
ACT	All states	Selection of students for higher education	High school mathematics curriculum	Students entering four-year institutions
SAT I	All states	Selection of students for higher education	General mathematics curriculum	Students entering four-year institutions
SAT II-Level IC	All states	Selection of students for higher education	Three-year college preparatory mathematics curriculum	Students entering four-year institutions
SAT II-Level IIC	All states	Selection of students for higher education	More than three years of college preparatory mathematics curriculum	Students entering four-year institutions

Table 47. English/Language Arts Assessments Used for Cross-State Analysis.

Test Name	State(s) Used	Purpose	Framework	Student Population
State tests				
Certificate of Initial Mastery (CIM)	Oregon	Monitor student achievement toward specified benchmarks	*Common Curriculum Goals* adopted by the State Board of Education	Oregon public high school students
End-of-Course English II	Texas	Monitor student achievement of state-based standards	*Texas Essential Knowledge and Skills*	Texas public high school students
Georgia High School Graduation Test (GHSGT)	Georgia	Monitor student achievement toward state standards	*Quality Core Curriculum* for grades 9–12, as established by the State Board of Education	Georgia public high school students
Golden State Exam (GSE) Reading/ Literature	California	Monitor student achievement toward state-approved content standards, provide special diploma	*Mathematics Content Standards for California Public Schools, Kindergarten Through Grade 12* adopted by the State Board of Education	Students wishing to receive recognition on their diploma
Golden State Exam (GSE) Written Composition	California	Monitor student achievement toward state-approved content standards, provide special diploma	*Mathematics Content Standards for California Public Schools, Kindergarten Through Grade 12* adopted by the State Board of Education	Students wishing to receive recognition on their diploma
High School Assessment (HSA) English	Maryland	Monitor student achievement toward state-approved content standards	*Core Learning Goals* adopted by the State Board of Education	Maryland public high school students
Locator Test	Oregon	Identify the appropriate form of CIM to be administered	*Common Curriculum Goals* adopted by the State Board of Education	Oregon public high school students

(Continued)

Table 47. English/Language Arts Assessments Used for Cross-State Analysis (Continued).

Test Name	State(s) Used	Purpose	Framework	Student Population
Stanford 9	California	Monitor student achievement	*Mathematics Content Standards for California Public Schools, Kindergarten Through Grade 12* adopted by the State Board of Education	Identify the appropriate form of CIM to be administered
Texas Assessment of Academic Skills (TAAS)	Texas	Monitor student achievement toward Texas standards	*Texas Essential Knowledge and Skills*	Texas public high school students
Texas Academic Skills Program (TASP)	Texas	Assess whether students entering Texas public institutions of higher education possess entry-level English skills	*Texas Essential Knowledge and Skills*	Texas public high school students
College course placement Tests				
ASSET	Maryland	Placement of students into appropriate English course	High school Reading and Language Arts curriculum	Students entering two- or less selective four-year institutions
COMPASS	Georgia	Assess whether admitted students possess entry-level English skills	High school Reading and Language Arts curriculum	Students entering two- or less selective four-year institutions
ACCUPLACER Reading Comprehension	Maryland	Placement of students into appropriate English course	High school Reading and Language Arts curriculum	Students entering two- or less selective four-year institutions

ACCUPLACER Sentence Skills	Maryland	Placement of students into appropriate English course	High school Reading and Language Arts curriculum	Students entering two- or less selective four-year institutions
Nelson-Denney	Maryland	Assess student ability in vocabulary development and reading comprehension	High school Reading and Language Arts curriculum	Students entering two- or four-year institutions
Test of Standard Written English (TSWE)	Oregon	Evaluate student ability in recognizing standard written English	High school Reading and Language Arts curriculum	Students entering two- or four-year institutions
College admissions tests				
ACT	All states	Selection of students for higher education	High school Reading and English/Language Arts curriculum	Students entering four-year institutions
SAT I	All states	Selection of students for higher education	High school Reading and English/Language Arts curriculum	Students entering four-year institutions
SAT II Literature	All states	Selection of students for higher education	High school English and American Literature curriculum	Students entering four-year institutions
SAT II Writing	All states	Selection of students for higher education	High school Reading and Language Arts curriculum	Students entering four-year institutions

Table 48. Structural, Content, and Cognitive Features of the Mathematics Tests.

Test	Format				Context	Graphs			Diagrams			Formulas		Content								Cognitive Requirements		
	MC	QC	GR	OE	C	S	RO	P	S	RO	P	M	G	PA	EA	IA	CG	PG	TR	SP	MISC	CU	PK	PS
State tests																								
CIM	90	0	0	10	67	18	0	0	26	0	0	16	3	15	15	3	5	31	0	30	2	18	61	21
End of Course	97	0	3	0	38	15	3	0	15	0	0	0	25	5	43	5	25	15	0	8	0	8	92	0
GHSGT	100	0	0	0	62	9	0	0	21	0	0	11	6	25	18	2	9	29	0	18	0	29	69	2
GSE (Algebra)	95	0	0	5	15	0	5	0	10	0	0	10	0	0	52	0	19	14	0	10	5	19	76	5
GSE (Geometry)	95	0	0	5	10	0	5	0	75	0	0	25	0	0	0	0	5	86	10	0	0	52	38	10
GSE (High School Math)	92	0	0	8	33	0	5	0	23	0	5	15	0	23	15	0	23	23	0	15	0	62	23	15
HSA Algebra	32	0	11	58	89	37	0	16	11	0	5	0	0	5	53	0	16	0	0	16	11	0	68	32
HSA Geometry	53	0	12	35	65	24	0	6	65	6	0	0	41	0	0	0	24	71	6	0	0	6	71	24
Locator test	100	0	0	0	60	20	0	0	20	0	0	15	0	25	5	0	15	20	0	30	5	20	75	5
Stanford 9	100	0	0	0	58	21	4	0	42	0	0	6	6	0	13	2	19	19	4	40	4	63	31	6
TAAS	100	0	0	0	92	3	0	0	22	0	0	0	12	55	12	0	2	10	0	22	0	10	90	0
TASP	100	0	0	0	38	15	2	0	15	4	0	0	21	17	25	10	8	21	0	10	8	10	81	8
College course placement tests																								
COMPASS (Algebra)	100	0	0	0	5	16	0	0	0	0	0	16	5	11	37	21	26	0	0	0	5	5	90	5
COMPASS (Numerical Skills)	100	0	0	0	41	0	0	0	0	0	0	0	0	88	0	0	0	0	0	12	0	12	82	6

	MC	QC	GR	OE	C	PA	EA	IA	CG	PG	TR	SP	MISC	S	RO	P	M	G	CU	PK	PS
ACCUPLACER (Elementary Algebra)	100	0	0	0	6	6	0	0	0	0	0	14	77	3	6	0	0	0	11	86	3
DMPT (Elementary Algebra)	100	0	0	0	20	14	0	3	0	11	0	17	65	3	6	0	9	0	3	97	0
College admissions tests																					
ACT	100	0	0	0	22	5	2	0	13	15	17	22	5	15	25	8	3	5	40	53	7
SAT I	58	25	17	0	25	7	0	0	18	1	13	37	2	6	19	0	13	11	32	53	15
SAT II-Level IC	100	0	0	0	18	8	0	0	26	12	2	30	10	12	28	4	8	6	34	58	8
SAT II-Level IIC	100	0	0	0	12	12	2	0	2	10	2	14	22	12	14	18	6	12	26	54	20

Format:
MC = multiple-choice items;
QC = quantitative comparison items;
GR = fill-in-the-grid items;
OE = open-ended items.

Formulas:
M = formula needs to be memorized;
G = formula is provided.

Context:
C = contextualized items.

Content:
PA = prealgebra;
EA = elementary algebra;
IA = intermediate algebra;
CG = coordinate geometry;
PG = plane geometry;
TR = trigonometry;
SP = statistics and probability;
MISC = miscellaneous topics.

Graphs, Diagrams:
S = graph/diagram within item stem;
RO = graph/diagram within response options;
P = graph/diagram needs to be produced.

Cognitive Requirements:
CU = conceptual understanding;
PK = procedural knowledge;
PS = problem solving.

Table 49. Percentage of Reading Passages Falling into Each Category.

Test	Type				Topic					Stimulus				
	Narrative	Descriptive	Persuasive	Informative	Fiction	Humanities	Natural Science	Social Science	Personal	Letter	Essay	Poem	Story	Chart
State tests														
CIM Reading	75	0	0	25	63	13	0	0	25	0	13	13	50	25
End-of-Course	100	0	0	0	0	0	0	0	100	0	100	0	0	0
GHSGT	73	0	2	25	45	9	9	14	23	2	55[a]	16[a]	30	0
GSE Reading/ Literature	100	0	0	0	0	0	0	0	100	0	100	0	0	0
HSA English	100	0	0	0	0	67	0	0	33	33	0	33	33	0
Locator Test	75	0	0	25	25	0	25	25	25	0	75	25	0	0
Stanford 9	50	0	17	33	17	33	33	0	17	17	33	0	50	0
TAAS	71	0	0	29	43	43	14	0	0	0	57	0	43	0
TASP	43	0	0	57	14	29	29	14	14	0	86	0	14	0
College course placement tests														
COMPASS	38	0	0	63	13	25	25	25	13	0	88	0	13	0
ACCUPLACER Reading Comprehension	50	0	5	45	0	60	35	0	5	0	100	0	0	0
Nelson–Denney	0	0	0	100	0	43	29	29	0	0	100	0	0	0
College admissions tests														
ACT	50	0	0	50	25	25	25	25	0	0	75	0	25	0
SAT I	40	0	0	60	20	40	20	20	0	0	80	0	20	0
SAT II Literature	100	0	0	0	63	0	0	13	25	13	25	50	13	0

[a] *One passage contained both an essay and a poem.*

Table 50. Percentage of Objective Writing Passages Falling into Each Category.

Test	Type					Topic				Stimulus			
	Narrative	Descriptive	Persuasive	Informative	Fiction	Humanities	Natural Science	Social Science	Personal	Letter	Essay	Poem	Story
State tests													
End-of-Course	50	0	0	50	0	0	50	0	50	0	100	0	0
HSA English	0	0	0	100	0	0	0	100	0	0	100	0	0
GHSGT	80	0	0	20	60	20	20	0	0	0	40	0	60
GSE Written Composition	100	0	0	0	0	0	0	0	100	0	100	0	0
TAAS	56	0	0	44	11	22	44	0	22	11	67	0	22
TASP	50	0	6	44	0	69	19	6	6	6	94	0	0
TSWE	0	0	0	0	0	0	0	0	0	0	0	0	0
College course placement tests													
ASSET	67	0	0	33	0	100	0	0	0	0	100	0	0
COMPASS	0	0	0	100	0	0	50	50	0	0	100	0	0
ACCUPLACER Sentence Skills	0	0	0	0	0	0	0	0	0	0	0	0	0
College admissions tests													
ACT	40	0	0	60	0	60	20	0	20	0	100	0	0
SAT I	0	0	0	0	0	0	0	0	0	0	0	0	0
SAT II Writing	50	0	0	50	0	100	0	0	0	0	100	0	0

Table 51. Topic Contents of Essay Writing Prompts.

			Topic		
Test	Fiction	Humanities	Natural Science	Social Science	Personal Essay
State tests					
CIM Writing	X				X
End-of-Course					X
GHSWT		X			X
GSE Reading/ Literature		X			X
GSE Written Composition		X		X	X
HSA English	X				X
TAAS		X			
TASP		X			
College admissions tests					
SAT II Writing		X			

Table 52. Factors Identified in the Scoring Criteria of Each Test.

Test	Mechanics	Word Choice	Organization	Style	Insight
State tests					
CIM Writing	X	X	X	X	X
End-of-Course	X	X	X	X	X
GHSWT	X	X		X	X
GSE Reading/ Literature			X		X
GSE Written Composition	X	X	X	X	X
HSA English	X	X	X	X	X
TAAS	X	X	X	X	X
TASP	X	X	X	X	X
College course placement tests					
SAT II Writing	X	X	X	X	

Scoring Criteria Factors

Table 53. Percentage of Reading Items Falling into Each Category.

Test	Recall	Infer	Evaluate Style
State tests			
CIM Reading	54	46	0
End-of-Course	31	69	0
GHSGT	30	70	0
GSE Reading/Literature	86	14	0
HSA English	25	75	0
Locator test	45	55	0
Stanford 9	71	29	0
TAAS	40	60	0
TASP	21	79	0
College course placement tests			
COMPASS	75	25	0
ACCUPLACER Reading Comprehension	11	89	0
Nelson-Denney	86	15	0
College admissions tests			
ACT	58	42	3
SAT I	18	83	0
SAT II Literature	13	80	7

Table 54. Percentage of Objective Writing Items Falling into Each Category.

Test	Recall	Infer	Evaluate Style
State tests			
End-of-Course	70	5	25
GHSWT	30	44	26
GSE Written Composition	67	0	33
HSA English	13	13	73
Stanford 9	79	6	15
TAAS	100	0	0
TASP	33	43	25
College course placement tests			
ASSET	89	11	0
COMPASS	80	3	17
ACCUPLACER Sentence Skills	91	0	9
TSWE	90	0	10
College admissions tests			
ACT	48	4	48
SAT I	0	100	0
SAT II Writing	50	3	47

THE AUTHORS

Michael W. Kirst has been professor of education and business administration at Stanford University since 1969. He is a faculty affiliate with the Department of Political Science and has a courtesy appointment with the Graduate School of Business. Kirst received his B.A. in economics from Dartmouth College, his M.P.A. in government and economics from Harvard University, and his Ph.D. in political economy and government from Harvard. He is a member of Phi Beta Kappa. Before joining the Stanford University faculty, he held several positions with the federal government, including staff director of the U.S. Senate Subcommittee on Manpower, Employment and Poverty and director of program planning and evaluation for the Bureau of Elementary and Secondary Education in the U.S. Office of Education (now the U.S. Department of Education). He was a budget examiner in the federal office of Budget and Management and associate director of the White House Fellows. He was a program analyst for the Title I ESEA Program at its inception in 1965. Kirst is active in several professional organizations. He was a fellow at the Center for Advanced Study in Behavioral Sciences. He has been a member of the National Academy of Education since 1979. He was vice president of the American Educational Research Association, a commissioner of the Education Commission of the States, and associate editor of the *Journal of Educational Evaluation and Policy*. He was the president of the California State Board of Education from 1977 to 1981. He has authored ten books, including *The Political Dynamics of American Education* (2001), and has published articles on school finance politics, curriculum politics, intergovernmental relations, and education reform policies. In 2000, Kirst led a team that produced *Crucial Issues in California Education 2000: Are the Reform Pieces Fitting Together?* Kirst is codirector of policy analysis for California Education (a consortium of Stanford, University of California, Berkeley, and University of Southern California), a California state education policy research group funded by the Hewlett Foundation. He is a member of the management and research staff of the Consortium for Policy Research in Education, a federally funded center.

Andrea Venezia is senior policy consultant and project director for the National Center for Public Policy and Higher Education. During the course of the Bridge Project, she was Director, K–16 Projects in the Stanford Institute for Higher Education Research (SIHER), including the Bridge Project. Venezia earned a Ph.D. in public policy from the Lyndon B. Johnson School of Public Affairs at the University of Texas at Austin, a master's degree in administration and policy analysis in higher education from Stanford University, and a bachelor's degree in English from Pomona College. She focuses much of her research and policy work on connections between high school and colleges, with a particular interest on students who are historically underrepresented in postsecondary education. Venezia has worked in a variety of state, federal, and nonprofit organizations, including the Texas Higher Education Coordinating Board, the Charles A. Dana Center at the University of Texas at Austin, the U.S. Department of Education, the National Education Goals Panel, and the American Institutes for Research. She has done consulting for a range of organizations, including SRI International, Policy Analysis for California Education, the Texas Education Agency, the Education Commission of the States, and the State Higher Education Executive Officers. She has authored and coauthored several publications on education reform, including "Betraying the College Dream: How Disconnected Systems Undermine Student Aspirations," the final policy report and brief of the Bridge Project (2003, with Michael Kirst and Anthony L. Antonio), "A Proposed Model for P–16 Accountability," for the Education Commission of the States (2003), "Early Outreach," (with Terese Rainwater) in *Student Success: Statewide P–16 Systems* published by the State Higher Education Executive Officers (2003), and "Bridging the Great Divide Between Secondary Schools and Postsecondary Education" (with Michael Kirst) in *Phi Delta Kappan* (2001).

David Ruenzel, the developmental editor of this book, has been a writer and contributing editor for *Teacher Magazine* and *Education Week* since 1990. In 1995, he was a finalist for the National Magazine Award for public affairs reporting. In addition to authoring dozens of articles on education, he has written and edited education policy materials for many institutions and organizations, including WestEd, Policy Analysis for California Education, EdSource, and Stanford University.

Anthony Lising Antonio is assistant professor of education and assistant director of the Stanford Institute for Higher Education Research at

Stanford University. He holds master's and bachelor's degrees in mechanical engineering from Stanford and the University of California, Berkeley, and master's and doctoral degrees in education from the University of California, Los Angeles. His research addresses many of the major issues facing American higher education, including equity in access to college, the status and progress of faculty of color in higher education, and student socialization in multicultural campus environments. His work has been published in the *Review of Higher Education, Research in Higher Education, Academe, Anthropology and Education Quarterly,* the *Journal of Higher Education,* and *Psychological Science.*

Samuel H. Bersola is interim vice president of student services and former dean of student support services at Mission College, a community college in Santa Clara, California. He earned a bachelor's degree in civil engineering from UC Berkeley; an Ed.M. in educational administration, planning, and social policy from Harvard University; and a Ph.D. in educational administration and policy analysis from Stanford University. While at Stanford, he was a research assistant with the Bridge Project and a research consultant to the University of California Office of the President (UCOP) and the Intersegmental Coordinating Committee (ICC) of the California Round Table. His research for the UCOP and ICC focused on the effects of high-stakes accountability testing on high school teachers. Prior to beginning his doctoral studies at Stanford, he worked as an assistant director of undergraduate admissions at the University of Southern California, director of the MESA/Minority Engineering Program at California State University Maritime Academy, and assistant dean of admissions at Amherst College in Massachusetts. He was a teaching fellow at Northfield Mount Hermon School in Massachusetts, as well as TASIS England Summer School. He also served as director of college counseling and taught mathematics at Marin Academy, a private secondary school in San Rafael, California.

Kathy Reeves Bracco is an independent education consultant. She previously served as senior policy analyst at the National Center for Public Policy and Higher Education and at the California Higher Education Policy Center, where she was project manager for the center's studies on higher education governance. She has also worked for the National Center for Research in Vocational Education and the American Association of State Colleges and Universities. She received her bachelor's degree in American studies from Stanford University and her master's and doctorate in education from the University of California, Berkeley.

Andrea Conklin Bueschel has spent her professional career working on high-school-to-college-transition issues. A former member of the admission staffs at Bates College and Stanford University, Bueschel has a specific interest in finding ways to improve postsecondary opportunities for historically underrepresented students. In addition, she has worked on college campuses in student affairs and alumni relations capacities and as a counselor for high school students. Bueschel has also served as a researcher and managing director for an educational consulting group, with a focus on the alignment of high school and college policies in California. She is currently a doctoral candidate in the School of Education at Stanford University. Bueschel holds master's degrees in education and in sociology from Stanford University. Her doctoral research is on students from families in which no one has previously attended college.

James C. Hearn is professor of public policy and higher education, Vanderbilt University. He received his Ph.D. from Stanford University. Prior to his academic career, he worked in policy research on student aid issues for the American College Testing program and for a consulting firm in Washington, D.C. His research and teaching focus on higher education policy and organization. Hearn's research has been published in sociology, economics, and education journals as well as in several books.

Lisa M. Jones is a research associate with the Joint Degree Program in Law, Health and the Life Sciences and the Consortium on Law and Values in Health, Environment and the Life Sciences at the University of Minnesota Law School. Her research interests include academic-industry research relationships, Pre-K–16 linkages, and research ethics. She is a member of the Association for the Study of Higher Education, the American Association for the Advancement of Science, and Public Responsibility in Medicine and Research and the Applied Research Ethics National Association.

Ann Merck MacLellan is an associate professor of sociology at the Community College of Baltimore County and was a research assistant for the K–12 field research component of the Bridge Project. She was also the principal investigator for the Bridge Project's community college study in Maryland. Her research interests include the effects of high-stakes accountability on school reform, learning outcomes, K–16 transitions, and community college student persistence. In addition to authoring and coauthoring reports for the Bridge Project, she has recently published

"School Improvement Plans in Schools on Probation: A Comparative Content Analysis Across Three Accountability Systems" in *Educational Administration Quarterly* (with H. Mintrop and M. Quintero, 2001). MacLellan earned a Ph.D. in education policy and leadership from the University of Maryland at College Park.

Betty Merchant is associate professor and chair of the Department of Educational Leadership and Policy Studies at the University of Texas, San Antonio. Prior to that appointment, she was a faculty member in the College of Education at the University of Illinois, Urbana-Champaign. Her research interests focus on educational policy, equity, student diversity, and school leadership. She has taught in public schools, preschool through high school, and in tribally controlled Native American schools in the Southwest. She received a Ph.D. in education from Stanford University.

The late *Toby H. Milton* worked in Maryland's community colleges for decades as a professor and an administrator. She edited *Adapting Strategic Planning to Campus Realities* (Jossey-Bass, 1990) with Frank A. Schmidtlein.

Heinrich Mintrop is an associate professor at the University of California, Los Angeles. He was a teacher in both the United States and Germany before he began an academic career. He received an M.A. in political science and German literature at the Freie University in Berlin and a Ph.D. in education from Stanford University. As a researcher, he explores how educational policies form institutional structures that shape teaching and learning in schools. His writings include *Educational Change and Social Transformation* (1996), written with Hans Weiler and Elisabeth Fuhrmann; "The Teaching of Civic Education" (with Bruno Losit); and a chapter in the *IEA Report on Civic Education* (2001). In recent years, Mintrop has turned to the issue of school accountability with an emphasis on policies that support school improvement in low-performing schools.

Frank A. Schmidtlein is associate professor emeritus in the College of Education at the University of Maryland at College Park. His research interests include postsecondary education governance, planning and decision making, and finance. He has authored or coauthored numerous articles and books, including *State Budgeting for Higher Education: The Political Economy of the Process* (1977) and *State Budgeting for Higher Education: Data Digest* (1975).

Caroline Sotello Viernes Turner is professor of educational leadership and policy studies at Arizona State University. She is an American Council on Education Fellow in the President's Office at California State University, Stanislaus. Her research and teaching interests include access and equity in higher education, faculty development, and organizational change. Her book publications include *Faculty of Color in Academe: Bittersweet Success and Racial and Ethnic Diversity in Higher Education*. Her latest book, published by the Association of American Colleges and Universities, is *Diversifying the Faculty: A Guidebook for Search Committees*. Her research includes a Spencer Foundation–funded study of the faculty search committee process and the hiring of faculty of color. She serves on the board of directors of the Association for the Study of Higher Education and the American Educational Research Association Committee on Scholars of Color. Turner received her doctorate in administration and policy analysis from the Stanford University School of Education.

INDEX

Selingo, J., 219
Senior Assessment for College (SAC) program, 276
Senior year performance: admissions policies about, 40, 42; disincentives for, 302; misperceptions of importance of, 17, 70, 295, 302; reform of senior year and, 310, 311–312; setting standards for, 312; student slacking in, 17, 302
Shults, C., 257, 283
Signal delivery paths, 21, 22–24, 303–306
Signaling theory, 19–20, 303
Signals: application of, to research findings, 303–306; to community college students, 258, 281; impact of, on student success, 4, 5; K–16 disconnect and, 303–306; mixed, 4–5, 16, 19, 38–39, 151, 258; theoretical framework of, 19–24, 303–306
Siporin, R. L., 37, 76
Sloan Foundation, 7, 8
Social charter, 316–317
Social criteria for admissions, 236, 237
Socioeconomic status (SES): achievement gap and, 14; as admissions criterion, 237; admissions requirements knowledge and, 135, 139; aspirations and, 50, 127, 128, 129–131, 166, 202–203, 237; in California study, 45, 50, 56, 57; college activity participation and, 140, 141, 145, 173, 174, 293; college knowledge and, 3, 15, 22, 237, 293; high school preparation and, 8; in Illinois study, 126–131, 127, 128, 133–137, 144; information sources and, 136, 137, 144, 172–173, 207, 209; in Oregon study, 166, 172–174, 180–181;

test-taking patterns and, 169; in Texas study, 94; tuition knowledge and, 56, 57, 107–108, 133–134, 177–178, 207, 208. See also Economically disadvantaged students
Southern Illinois University, 120
Southern Regional Education Board, 23
Southwest Texas State University (SWT), 78, 84; admissions policies of, 89–92, 106; assessment in, 85; communication and outreach of, 92, 102–104; enrollments in, 89–90; K–12 connections with, 102–104; overview of, 89; placement policies of, 91; policy evolution at, 91–92; remediation in, 85, 91; student demographics of, 90
Spanish Assessment of Basic Education, second edition (SABE/2), 36
Special admissions, 122–123, 185
Special review high schools, 118, 123
Standardized Testing and Reporting (STAR) Program, 35, 36, 43, 44
Standards, K–12: in California, 31, 33, 34–35, 43–44; class ranking and, 118; curriculum reform and, 313–314; in Georgia, 186–188; in Illinois, 117–118; postsecondary disconnect from, 286–289; reform context for, 5–7, 44, 188, 223–224, 275; senior slacking and, 302; in Texas, 82–83
Standards, postsecondary: communication of, and student success, 4–5, 233; community college, 289; disconnection of secondary standards with, 286–289
Standards for California High School Graduates, 33

Other Books of Interest

Finders and Keepers:
Helping New Teachers Survive and Thrive in Our Schools
by Susan Moore Johnson and The Project on the
Next Generation of Teachers
ISBN: 0-7879-6925-7 • Cloth • 336 pages • 2004

This book follows the experiences of ten new teachers as they find their professional footing in today's public school classrooms. Their stories provide rich examples of the challenges, successes, and failures the teachers encounter. While tracking these teachers' eventual career decisions, the book offers insights into what is most important to new teachers and what schools and principals must do, in order for these teachers to do good work, be supported, and remain in teaching.

Handbook of Research on Multicultural Education, Second Edition
by James A. Banks and Cherry A. McGee Banks
ISBN: 0-7879-5915-4 • Cloth • 1120 pages • 2003

This comprehensive new edition of the landmark original assembles leading scholars in multicultural education to discuss the history, philosophy, practice, politics, and future of this area of study. Collectively, they report and reflect on the major research that has developed since the field emerged in the 1960s and 1970s. From second language teaching to diversity in higher education, 20 new chapters and 29 completely revised ones represent the changes and scholarship of today.

The Jossey-Bass Reader on Teaching
ISBN: 0-7879-6240-6 • Paper • 288 pages • 2003

This anthology offers an accessible and engaging look at the challenges of becoming a teacher, inspiring teaching techniques, and the philosophies and passions that are the foundation of teaching. Among its many well-known contributors are Parker Palmer, Sylvia Ashton-Warner, William Ayers, Lisa Delpit, Robert L. Fried, Herbert Kohl, and Vivian Gussin Paley.

The Wisdom of Practice:
Essays on Teaching, Learning, and Learning to Teach
by Lee S. Shulman
ISBN: 0-7879-7200-2 • Cloth • 592 pages • 2004

Lee Shulman has been President of the Carnegie Foundation for the Advancement of Teaching since 1997. This is the first volume of a seminal two-book set, collecting his most important writings for the first time, Shulman addresses such compelling questions in K–12 education as, What are the most effective approaches to teaching? How important is subject matter knowledge to a teacher's success? And, how do we measure success in teaching and learning?

Teaching as Community Property: Essays on Higher Education
by Lee S. Schulman
ISBN: 0-7879-7201-0 • Cloth • 256 pages • 2004

This second book in the two-volume set contains the best writings of Lee Shulman on the topic of higher education. Shulman's scholarship has focused on the improvement of teaching (both K–12 and higher education), on new approaches to assessment of teaching, and on the methods and quality of educational research. This inspiring resource for faculty, staff developers, and researchers is also appropriate as a graduate text for courses in leadership or teaching and learning.